SAYING PEACE

SUNY series in Theology and Continental Thought
———————
Douglas L. Donkel, editor

SAYING PEACE

Levinas | Eurocentrism | Solidarity

JACK MARSH

Published by State University of New York Press, Albany

© 2021 State University of New York

All rights reserved

Printed in the United States of America

No part of this book may be used or reproduced in any manner whatsoever without written permission. No part of this book may be stored in a retrieval system or transmitted in any form or by any means including electronic, electrostatic, magnetic tape, mechanical, photocopying, recording, or otherwise without the prior permission in writing of the publisher.

For information, contact State University of New York Press, Albany, NY
www.sunypress.edu

Library of Congress Cataloging-in-Publication Data

Name: Marsh, Jack, author.
Title: Saying peace : Levinas | Eurocentrism | Solidarity / Jack Marsh, author.
Description: Albany : State University of New York Press, [2021] | Series: SUNY series in Theology and Continental Thought | Includes bibliographical references and index.
Identifiers: ISBN 9781438482651 (hardcover : alk. paper) | ISBN 9781438482644 (pbk. : alk. paper) | ISBN 9781438482668 (ebook)
Further information is available at the Library of Congress.

10 9 8 7 6 5 4 3 2 1

In memory of Jack E. Marsh Sr., an eternal friend to Israel
For Denise Miller McPherson, in Infinite gratitude
For Jenny Franco-Marsh, in Infinite promise

זכר לעולם בריתו דבר צוה לאלף דור

—Psalm 105:8

Contents

Acknowledgments		ix
Preface		xiii
Key to Abbreviations of Works by Levinas		xv
Introduction		1
Chapter 1	Empty Hands: The Tragic Irony of *Totality and Infinity*	9
Chapter 2	Of Form and Face in *Totality and Infinity*	43
Chapter 3	"Flipping the Deck," On *Totality and Infinity*'s Transcendental/Empirical Puzzle	69
Chapter 4	Ontology and Ethics in *Otherwise than Being*	99
Chapter 5	Levinas, Eurocentrism, Justice	129
Chapter 6	Levinas: A Life	151
Chapter 7	Levinas Today	175
Chapter 8	Conclusions and Beginnings	273
Notes		287
Bibliography		347
Name Index		365

Acknowledgments

A small group of persons has, in a quite singular sense, made this work possible. I owe a special debt of gratitude to my first philosophical mentor, Laura Duhan Kaplan. She identified and nurtured my intellectual potential and introduced me to phenomenology. Beyond her titanic influence on my philosophical trajectory, she was also a big sister, a rabbi, and a pastoral-philosophical guide at a time of great personal upheaval. Thanks, Laura. I owe an infinite debt to Richard A. Cohen. His kindness, friendship, generosity, and intellectual vivacity over the years were as decisive in my journey with Levinas as the power of Levinas's texts. Whatever force the critical turn I perform herein has, it is rooted in my having sought to live and think Levinas's truth radically. Without Richard A. Cohen, I might not have taken this journey. Thank you, Richard. I'd especially like to thank my advisor, Randy Friedman. His superlative patience, collegial warmth, and critical eye not only made this book better, but also wrought a decisive change in my style. Thanks, Randy.

Three individuals remain whose formative influence is pervasive herein: my father, Jack Marsh, who taught me to love with all my heart; my pastor, John Groblewski, who taught me to love with all my mind; and my mentor, Craig Osborne, who taught me to love with all my strength.

Near and far, so many other teachers, colleagues, friends, and cohorts mark this project professionally or personally, and often both at once. Of teachers, I express my deepest gratitude to Randy Friedman, Max Pensky, Bat-Ami Bar On, Anna Gotlib, and Lisa Tessman; David Rasmussen, Richard Kearney, David Hollenbach, John Sallis, and Axel Honneth; Laura Duhan Kaplan, Richard A. Cohen, William Gay, Reginald Raymer, Kari Coleman, Marvin Croy, Steven Fishman, Michael Eldridge, and Selman Halabi. Of senior colleagues, I'm deeply grateful to Michael Morgan for serving on my committee, to Kevin Houser, James McLachlan, John Drabinski, Richard Kearney, and Roger Burggraeve for their generosity in corresponding with me, and to Judith Wolfe, Bruce Ellis Benson, and N. T. Wright for their advice and support. I must single out Steven Crowell, Martin Kavka, and J. Aaron Simmons for special thanks. They went above and beyond the call of duty in reading, commenting on, and discussing my work. This book would not be what it is without them. Thanks also to my editors, anonymous reviewers, and technical workers at SUNY Press for their patience, good will, and professionalism. And to the many other colleagues and cohorts who so graciously participated in educating me over the years: thank you very much.

I thank Gareth Mathews-John for his generosity and keen eye in proofreading this text. Of friends, I express my deepest gratitude to Marlisa Moschella, Regan Rule, Alejandro Arango, Jess Kyle, Colin Brown, Matthew Klauber, Shoni Rancher, Jessie Payson, Sean Johnston, and Aaron Bell; Rowan Tepper, Yale Specht, Jason Phillips, Travis Holloway, Joshua Mousie, and Erin Tarver; Christopher Raymond Stapor, Robert Littlejohn, Michael Grady, Beth Blalock, Amanda Connolly, Greg Canning, Jason Matherly, Samuel Pinero, Caleb Stroup, Latoya Gardner, and Chris Vernarsky. Of cohorts, I thank Joice Bucceray, Audrey Morgan-Donnell, Nicholas Westgate, Christian Westgate, Victor Dodson, Waheed Abdulrahman, Mohammed Olaiq, Kimberly Al-Suffi, Hala Al-Najjar, Nicholas Scull, Moamoa Wu, Spencer Dunn, Amanda Young, Brian and Ruthie Gomez, Ron Pearson, Zach Adams, everyone at ICB, Leslie and Marco Napoletano, Zach and Megan Quinter, Renee and Bob Keiderling, Renee Draszkiewics, Dan Poppel, Michael and Lori Boll, James Richmond, David Allen, Gareth and Karen Mathews-John, Amanda Abel, Madi Boll, Fran and Cheri Molinari, William Easterday, William Henry, Michael Stauffer, John Moser, Marie and Lowell Hoffman, John and Diane Lexo, Kevin and Lisa Lexo, John and Tassia Schreiner, Hampton Morgan, Trese Strauss, Malcolm Stewart, Brett Young, Samantha Heaney, Jamie Easterday, Michael and Kelly Easterday, Kevin Hebdon, Filipe Johnson, Kathy and Fred Salcedo, Martha and Edgar Hernandez, Deborah Putri, Gina Franco, Jose Ayala Morales, Melissa Franco, Andrea Franco, Phillip and Patience Osborne, Roberto and Carmen Franco, Dan and Lou Ann Smoker, Amy Osborne, Leah Chichester, Kendra Dunstan, and everyone at NC4. Of Daniel Chichester, Michael Dunstan, Matthew Heaney, Robert Hoffman, Timothy Erickson, John Nester, and Will Salcedo, I can only say: truly friends closer than brothers. Thanks, guys.

I would commit an injustice if I failed to recognize the labor and kindness of strangers who have supported my philosophical endeavors.

Acknowledgments

From before I entered university to the words I currently scrawl, my intellectual labor has been largely performed in cafés, diners, and assorted pubs and eateries. I owe a special debt of gratitude to the many servers and bartenders who brought me sustenance, emptied ashtrays, and warmly tolerated my strange presence during literally marathon research sessions in their establishments. I thank the staff and management of Tic Toc Family Restaurant in Easton, PA; Ripper's Pub, Bethlehem, PA; Bob Evans Farms Restaurant of S. Tryon, Charlotte, NC; Shoney's of north Charlotte, whose staff—for a one-month period in November 2002—risked inviting me to eat when I could not pay; and to Denny's of Nashua, NH. I'm especially grateful to both Gertrude Gomez and my brother, Waheed Abdulraham, for respectively providing spaces to work when I first arrived in Kuwait; to the staff and management of the Holiday Inn, Salmiya, especially Salah Bakry at Sakura and Rajesh Padannakandy at L'Aroma Café; the staff and management of Circles Café, Ramada Hotel, Pudong, China, especially Zhang Zi Feng, Wen Long Wang, Luo Dan, and Guo Man Si. I owe an especially big thanks to the staff and management of Big Bamboo, Pudong, for inviting me into the family—and the occasional free whisky!—during a crucial period of writing, especially Li Jiao Jiao, Shen Fang, Ke Hai Feng, Li Song Jian, Su Lei Lei, Wu Li Hui, and Li Zhen Ni. I finally express my deepest gratitude to Airbnb and Myriam Marescq, for her superlative hospitality and charming home. I can imagine a no more enchanting accompaniment to the completion of this manuscript than the songs of the Firth of Forth, in vortal dance with the misty North.

Finally, I thank my family for their enduring love and support, especially Denise and Robert McPherson, Elizabeth and Jason Ackerman, Sarah and Scott McBride, Cody Bower, Deborah Graham, Janet Heller, Logie Heller, Jennifer Knecht, Devon Graham, Martin Graham, Elaine Marsh, Laura Lobo, Blanca Franco, Edgardo Ortiz, Leonardo Ortiz, Levy, Naphty, and Reuby, and the loving circle of rabbits, Francos, Millers, Marshs, and Hellers that have nurtured me on my way. Above all, I thank my partner in this adventure of a lifetime, Jenny Lorena Franco-Marsh. Her sacrificial love, patience, understanding, and support saw this project to completion.

Jack Marsh
St. Monans, Fife
November 2018

Preface

This book was born of crisis. In my own philosophical coming of age, three terms have come to inexorably matter to me: religion, democracy, and socialism. My first encounter with Levinas's philosophy was formative precisely because it seemed to provide a critical and constructive framework that empowered me to integrate these concerns, and in such a way that might inform my other disparate interests in art and activism. While quite early on I of course noted points of tension, or moments in Levinas's work that elicited my dissent, I largely set them aside on the assumption that they were of merely peripheral import. My academic career has largely proceeded as exploring other philosophical perspectives collaboratively with my Levinasian framework in an attempt to construct a relatively holistic and integrative position for justifying my own critical and constructive practices. After a long period of creative exploration, the bottom fell out of this project. This book is the result. As it turns out, what I youthfully set aside as of merely peripheral importance became the block on which the entire edifice crumbled.

For nearly a decade, I was *the* Levinasian among the sisters, brothers, and comrades I have sojourned with. This book reflects my more than seven years of positive engagement with and unqualified commitment to Levinas's philosophy, and a subsequent year of sincerely trying to work out an internal critique in a way that preserves his central insight. My style herein is reflective of that era, when distinctions between philosophical and political performances were more widely observed and more provocative modes of engagement more widely admired. This text also reflects my more than a decade of experience of utilizing Levinas's work in the public debates and discursive contests of the time. Whatever justified insights and standing problems this book contains cannot be fully understood outside of these contexts. Writing my dissertation was a difficult and strenuous process, freighted with various external life pressures. Early drafts of this work, and even my edited dissertation, were too saturated with the manifold emotions that gripped me while finding my conclusions. I want to publicly apologize to friends and colleagues for being too ungracious and rhetorically staunch in previous iterations of this text. I'm sorry. The new chapters I've added fill in the background questions and contexts I've been wrestling with and engaging throughout my entire journey as a phenomenologist, critical theorist, and theologian. I'm deeply grateful to all of my colleagues for giving me the chance to fill out and clarify the stakes at issue in my reading of Levinas since my initially tentative critical turn in November 2010. You have made this book better. Thank you. Solidarity!

Key to Abbreviations of Works by Levinas

BV *Beyond the Verse*, trans. G. Mole (London: Continuum, 1994).

DEH *Discovering Existence With Husserl*, trans. Cohen and Smith (Evanston: Northwestern University Press, 1998).

DF *Difficult Freedom*, trans. S. Hand (Baltimore: Johns Hopkins University Press, 1990).

EE *Existence and Existents*, trans. A. Lingis (Dordrecht: Kluwer, 1988).

HO *Humanism of the Other*, trans. N. Pollar (Chicago: University of Illinois Press, 2006).

IHP *Theory of Intuition in Husserl's Phenomenology*, trans. A. Orianne (Evanston: Northwestern University Press, 1973).

IRB *Is It Righteous to Be*, ed. J. Robbins (Stanford: Stanford University Press, 2001).

ITN *In the Time of Nations*, trans. M. B. Smith (London: Continuum, 2007).

OE *On Escape*, trans. B. Bergo (Stanford: Stanford University Press, 2003).

OGM *Of God Who Comes to Mind*, trans. B. Bergo (Stanford: Stanford University Press, 1998).

OB *Otherwise than Being or Beyond Essence*, trans. A. Lingis (Pittsburg: Duquesne University Press, 1998).

TI *Totality and Infinity*, trans. A. Lingis (Pittsburg: Duquesne University Press, 1961).

TO *Time and the Other*, trans. R. A. Cohen (Pittsburgh: Duquesne University Press, 1987).

UH *Unforeseen History*, trans. N. Pollar (Chicago: University of Illinois Press, 2004).

Introduction

Levinas's work has achieved near canonical status in European philosophy today. The best evidence for this claim perhaps lies in the sheer quantity of extent scholarly treatments of his texts. His ethics of alterity has inspired constructive and critical work in nearly every craggy nook of the humanities and social sciences. The literature is vast, spanning from familiar treatments in philosophy and religious studies, to more specialized applied fields, such as nursing and organizational management.[1] His popularity moreover bursts the bounds of the academy. As Atterton and Calarco have noted, Levinas's work has "inspired religious leaders, writers, dissidents, statesmen, and artists the world over."[2] When the breadth of influence encompasses such disparate regions of culture glossed by Pope John Paul II, Vaclav Havel, and Jean-Luc Godard, we certainly do seem to be approaching a wide signature. Yet with this expanding influence, a cluster of relatively *stable* philosophical questions and problems has also attended his work; "stable" because they recur across widely diverse thematic and disciplinary treatments of his phenomenology. The problems can be roughly specified as (1) *methodological* (the transcendental/empirical question), (2) *political* (the ambiguity of Levinasian justice), (3) *theological* (the ambiguity of the religion/philosophy relation), and (4) *intercultural* (the problem of his alleged Eurocentrism). In this book I take up the last of these problems in a fresh, critical approach to evaluating his core philosophical position.[3] In the process of getting a critical grip on the problem of his intercultural judgments, I moreover propose a general explanation for these four long-standing problems in his work.

Levinas's big idea is that our lived sense of moral obligation occurs in an immediate experience of the otherness of the Other person. Moral meaning is grounded in alterity rather than identity. Yet he also held what seems an inconsiderate—or Eurocentric—view of *other* cultural traditions. For example,

> Europe, that's the Bible and the Greeks. It has come closer to the Bible and to its true fate. Everything else in the world must be included in this. I don't have any nostalgia for the exotic. For me Europe is central.[4]

> The yellow peril! It is not racial but spiritual. Not about inferior values but about a radical strangeness, strange to all the density of its past, where no voice with a familiar inflection comes through: a lunar, a Martian past.[5]

Can we fairly describe these statements as *chauvinist*? As Drabinski has noted, informal discussion of these statements among specialists often resembles a kind of gossip.[6] How can Levinas—the philosopher of the Other and of unconditioned giving—have failed so miserably? Worse than gossip, the question itself is perhaps loaded.[7] In conventional usage, the term chauvinist connotes unfair and often assumed privilege given to the *same*. Whether this unfair privilege is granted to *my* gender, *my* nation, *my* culture, or my *x*, in each case it involves what I most *identify* with by comparison to negatively judged *others*. As such, it seems we are justified in asking: what are we to make of Levinas's above statements in light of the explicit meaning his philosophy stakes out?

As far as I've been able to ascertain, Robert Bernasconi was the first to broach this problem in the scholarship. In "Who is My Neighbor? Who Is the Other? Questioning 'the Generosity of Western Thought,'" Bernasconi performs a nuanced analysis of the problems that emerge in relating Levinas's ethics to his dismissive references to other cultures. Bernasconi ultimately concludes that "[i]f there is an answer in Levinas to the question of what judges cultures, it remains the classical Enlightenment answer, the idea of the West."[8] Critchley concurs and hints that Eurocentrism "looms large" in the overall problems of Levinas's politics.[9] Sikka, too, insists that Levinas "privileges a particular culture in an insufficiently critical, and therefore irresponsible, manner."[10] Finally, Ma, following McGettigan, asserts: ". . . Levinas's ethics cannot be accepted as a neutral philosophical construction."[11] But is there such a thing as a *neutral* philosophical construction? And what is responsibility such that Levinas fails at it here? Can we propose answers to these questions without straightaway performing prejudice? If we are irreducibly "cultural" beings, and if one persistent problem with European philosophy is *its very claims* to cultural-transcending truth, it is not clear that *"neutral philosophical constructions"* exist. One cannot, of course, retreat to some willy-nilly relativism or abstractly reject all context-transcendence to avoid the problem at hand. Indeed, will-to-power, the *Seinsfrage, différance*, "care of the self," and so forth *all* make specific claims for what it means *to mean* (and not mean), claims that are potentially universal in scope (Is Hinduism a species of the "metaphysics of presence"? Buddhism a life-denying nihilism? Islam a biopolitical terror? etc.). Or take more self-consciously particularist traditions: if Confucianism "is a rather typical non-universalism, even though it does believe that its own doctrines are indeed the ultimate truth," then how do we interpret these truths in relation to the *Yi* (夷), or "barbarian"?[12] What does it mean to be a *typical* "non-universalism"? Such questions suggest that the problem of prejudice in intercultural relations is more difficult than we normally assume. If we are to evaluate Levinas fairly, we must have some sense of what it means to be *unprejudiced* in an irreducibly intercultural world. Levinas in fact mounts an account of how this is possible, and this makes the question of his apparent chauvinism all the more pressing.

Levinas scholarship has presented three strategies for interpreting his apparently chauvinist statements. The first strategy holds that such statements present a failure of *the man*, not his philosophy. Here, Levinas fails to live up to his own best insights, as we all, philosophers especially, sometimes do. This position emphasizes the obvious fact that failing to live up to a norm does not "disprove" the norm itself, and hence we can correct Levinas the man with Levinas's philosophy. Richard Cohen and Oona Eisenstadt are good representatives of this position.[13] The second strategy holds that such statements are a failure of *both* the man *and* the philosophy. This position holds that Levinas's take on other cultures thwarts the overall integrity of his philosophical position, and we should look elsewhere for a better account. Sonia Sikka and Rudi Visker are good representatives of this position.[14] Finally, the third strategy holds that such statements are a failure of the man and a *problem* for the philosophy, a problem that does not undermine the overall integrity of Levinas's position, but does require its augmentation. Robert Bernasconi and Enrique Dussel are good representatives of this position.[15] All the positions I've sampled on this question seem to agree that statements of the above sort constitute a failure of Levinas the man, and this I do not dispute. My aim in this book is to explore the overall integrity of Levinas's position in light of his alleged Eurocentrism.

In what follows, I analyze Levinas's major philosophical works and seek to evaluate them from the perspective of his own account of what it means to be *disinterested*. This strategy seems promising for three reasons. First, to evaluate Levinas's philosophy on Levinas's own terms is to do him the justice of not performing external criticism. I seek to avoid at all costs importing another normative perspective in order to dismiss Levinas's through contrast. Next, Levinas's account of disinterest constitutes the absolute core of his ethics. As such, if it can be shown that his account is defective in some irremediable way, we will have to fundamentally rethink his approach. Finally, Levinas's take on disinterest is in part a response to Husserl and Heidegger's respective accounts of the phenomenological reduction.[16] Given the problem of chauvinism and disinterest, this is perhaps the most interesting aspect of my approach. For phenomenology, the reduction is the methodological technique—or existential/ethical event—said to yield a non-distortive perspective *on the world as it is*. In other words, it's held to yield a *true*, *authentic*, or *just*—and as such, *self-justifying*—form of context-transcending universality. My method, therefore, can be most aptly characterized as what I call *immanent critique*.

As a critical methodology, what I have chosen to call "immanent critique" must be distinguished from other various and useful methodologies popular in contemporary criticism. For example, I do not do immanent critique in the form of a materialist expressivism, or by reading Levinas's work to express some allegedly more basic logic or economy of desire, whether thought in terms of will-to-power, libidinal drives, the "play of the trace," or class struggle.[17] Moreover, I have chosen not to treat Levinas's work as merely a particular species of phenomenology, to be assessed in light of more generic questions that allegedly unite and differentiate Levinas, Heidegger, and Husserl. This has been fruitfully done elsewhere. Insofar as Levinas utilizes his own methodological innovations *against* Husserl and Heidegger, and wields them *against* the entire tradition, his method must be evaluated on its own terms. The immanent critique I propose to practice most closely resembles what Derrida has termed "deconstruction." Yet I have chosen to call my method "immanent critique" rather than "deconstruction" for a variety of reasons.

First, I am methodologically setting aside or "suspending" nearly *all* presuppositions, including particular claims for the conditions for meaning in general. In other words, I am not assuming the accuracy, validity, or usefulness of a critical concept or norm external to Levinas's own work, including what Derrida calls "the metaphysics of presence." This is not a criticism of Derrida's approach, but rather a choice premised on my own considered judgment that methodologically presuppositionless criticism might better assess a philosophical proposal through probing its internal coherence, on the basis of the proposal's own terms. Whether Levinas succumbs to the "metaphysics of presence" is of little interest to me. That his view is relatively consistent on its own terms is what I propose to ascertain. This allows, therefore, Levinas's proposal to potentially withstand immanent critique, if it can be shown to pass the very minimal test of internal consistency. This approach clearly does *not* require Levinas to satisfy a more specific set of epistemic or ethical tests imported from alien philosophical assumptions. Nor does it mandate total or absolutely systematic transparency from his texts. As I'm proposing, an alleged instance of structural inconsistency or substantive contradiction is fatal if and only if (a) it imperils the entire analytic structure of the proposal in question, or the overall web of concepts, categories, or relations a proposal utilizes to achieve its specific results; (b) it violates a proposal's own posited norms, on its own stipulated terms; and (c) the consequences of (a) and (b) undermine the proposal's general conclusions on the proposal's own methodological terms. The first (a) is a logical test that probes the overall descriptive integrity of the proposal on offer. The second (b) is a logical test that probes the congruence between a proposal's stipulated norms and its actual practice at a methodologically basic level. Does a text do what it claims to do, in the way it claims to get this doing done? If inconsistencies are to be found in ways unanticipated by the proposal, and if those inconsistencies can be shown to render the position self-undermining, the proposal succumbs to immanent critique. As should be clear, my approach does not impose alien norms or an alien account of meaning on a proposal under consideration. My *only* assumption here is that a specific proposal must, at the very minimum, be relatively self-consistent.

Performing immanent critique in the way I've proposed subjects me to some constraints, and also entitles me to certain disciplined liberties. First, the proper practice of critique requires a thorough and charitable reconstruction of Levinas's actual descriptions. Ideally, my reconstruction should attempt to read Levinas according to his own intentions. Moreover, my reading should also reflect what appears to be the prevailing scholarly consensus on the interpretation of Levinas's texts. Insofar as Levinas's allegedly Eurocentric statements are motivating my inquiry, and insofar as these statements are puzzling in light of Levinas's self-interpretation and the prevailing scholarly treatments of his work, I must keep these interpretations in view in my own reconstruction. Once these charitable reconstructions are performed, I can then turn to critical analysis. The liberty critique affords me ultimately consists in no longer being solely guided by Levinas's apparent intentions, or by conventional scholarly opinions on what he may have wished to mean or to do, and instead performing an evaluation of what he actually does, solely guided by Levinas's own proposals and the norm of internal consistency. As should be clear, the liberty of my critical practice is not arbitrary for two reasons: Because (1) I am motivated by what seems the genuine moral problem of Levinas's allegedly chauvinist statements, and (2) subjecting Levinas to the very minimal discipline of internal consistency *in light* of his own performed method and proposed meaning, renders my critical liberty normatively oriented and practically constrained.

Because a rigorously performed immanent critique necessitates a close textual reading and analysis before larger conclusions can be drawn, my writing is constrained by both the protocols of my method and the particularities of Levinas's oeuvre. Levinas's core proposals and central arguments are performed in his major philosophical works: *Totality and Infinity* (*TI*) and *Otherwise than Being* (*OB*). As such, I first conduct immanent-critical readings of these works before explicitly turning to a diagnosis of his Eurocentric statements. Moreover, insofar as there are explicit differences between *TI* and *OB*, I have chosen to read each by turns, and as independent philosophical proposals. My philosophical aim is not to present a philological interpretation of the trajectory of Levinas's development, but rather to ascertain what he means by "the Other," "responsibility," "disinterest," and so forth; how he achieves these meanings; and then to evaluate his allegedly chauvinist statements in their light. To this end, chapters 1, 2, and 4 conduct immanent-critical readings of Levinas's major works, and chapters 3 and 5 perform a general diagnosis of his proposals based on the results of my immanent critique.

One final preparatory word is in order on the problem style. Because immanent critique requires me to thoroughly and charitably reconstruct a text's central proposals and to analyze the text on its own terms, I am presented with a difficult challenge. Levinas's texts are notoriously difficult, so much so that Bernasconi calls them among "the most difficult . . . in the history of philosophy."[18] On the one hand, if my reconstruction and critical analysis stray too far from Levinas's explicit descriptions, for example, by crisply translating them, say, into ordinary language or into the terms set by an alternate methodological program, I might be accused of "failing to read Levinas closely," or perhaps of "misunderstanding" him by distorting his meaning through alien linguistic or conceptual resources. On the other hand, if my reconstruction and critical analysis stick too close to Levinas's explicit descriptions, for example, by steadfast employment of his own rhetoric and descriptive terms, I might be accused of "reading too closely," or perhaps of "misunderstanding" him by distorting his meaning through failing to achieve a sufficiently holistic interpretation. I have tried to steer a middle course through this gauntlet. In chapters that conduct immanent critique, I stick as close to the text as possible, while interposing what I hope is clarifying commentary in my reconstructive phase, and while presenting what I hope are clear arguments during the critical phase. Though chapters 1, 2, and 4 proceed by textually privileged reconstruction and critique, I have still endeavored to write them as clearly as possible. If they remain stylistically dense, this is because Levinas's texts are stylistically dense. When I move from textually privileged immanent criticism to present a general diagnosis of its results, I cease to grant the text deference, and instead privilege my reader by giving deference to stylistic clarity. Because I am ultimately criticizing Levinas, I have chosen to stylistically err on the side of the text in chapters 1, 2, and 4. Because I owe my reader clear arguments, I have chosen to err on the side of my reader in the general diagnoses I perform. With these qualifications on the style and structure of my presentation in mind, my first two chapters perform an immanent critique of *TI*, focusing on Levinas's (i) ego-analysis (chapter 1) and (ii) other-analysis (chapter 2). Chapter 3 performs a comprehensive diagnosis of Levinas's method based on the results of chapters 1 and 2. In chapter 4, I perform an immanent critique of *OB*, performing a comprehensive assessment of Levinas mature approach. Chapter 5 verifies the results yielded in preceding chapters, by brief analysis of Levinas's political and religious writings. Chapters 6 and 7 conclude my procedure by locating my results in biographical and historical contexts, empowering a precise specification of the normative legacies and potentials that remain in Levinas's work for the problems and possibilities of our day.

Chapter 1

Empty Hands: The Tragic Irony of *Totality and Infinity*

> He who depends on a miracle will experience none.
>
> —Sefer Hachinukh

I. Introduction

In the voluminous secondary literature on Levinas's work, it must be noticed how little focused attention has been paid to the precise specificities of his ego analysis. Most treatments analyze his phenomenology of sensibility and economy—of the "Same"—as a kind of necessary propaedeutic to the face. Such an approach seems questionable, insofar as Levinas himself appears to insist on its central importance for grasping the overall sense of his ethics. Indeed, if ethical "alterity presupposes the tranquil identity of the same," and if this sense entails that "no . . . interhuman relationship can be enacted outside of economy: no face can be approached with empty hands," then meticulous attention to his ego analysis is necessary to both understand and assess Levinas's broader claims.[1] In this chapter, I endeavor to fill this lacuna in the scholarship by giving exclusive attention to his description of the genesis and meaning of the ego, in section II of *Totality and Infinity*.

Beyond the interest this holds for Levinas scholarship in its own right, a more thorough analysis of Levinas's account of the ego may also be illuminating for intra-phenomenological debates. As Lee has recently underlined, nearly the entire tradition of *TI* interpretation simply accepts Levinas's own claims for sensibility at face value.[2] The story goes something like this: Husserl's transcendental phenomenology (allegedly) gives "representation" or theory the most basic status in its overall account of meaning, and hence repeats the empty "theoreticism" of tradition he heroically sought to overcome. Heidegger's phenomenological ontology properly criticized Husserl's (alleged) theoreticism by describing *Dasein* as a more primitive transcendence disclosed in pre-theoretical *Zuhandenheit*, being-in-the-world, being-with, and ultimately care. Though Heidegger's description of the priority of practice over theory is a laudable contribution, he nevertheless repeats the alleged "violence" of tradition by construing self and other in primarily ontological terms. As such, Heidegger also (allegedly) fails to grasp a more primitive structure still, what Levinas puts forth as *sensibility*. With a few notable exceptions,[3] nearly the entire tradition of *TI* scholarship simply accepts Levinas's own narrative, or what Lee calls a "process of unidirectional development": theory/practice/sensibility, Transcendental Subject/Being/Other, phenomenology/ontology/ethics.[4] In this chapter, I pay special attention to whether this narrative is tenable on the basis of Levinas's *descriptions alone*.

In what follows, I begin by conducting a close review of Levinas's account of the ego. I have chosen to systematically ignore the numerous debates, differentiations, and polemical asides Levinas conducts with other philosophers, unless their treatment is deemed necessary to clarify his own position on a matter. These moments pepper *TI* from cover to cover, and I by and large seek to avoid them. I propose here to read *TI* as a phenomenology, or, in other words, as Levinas wanted it to be read.[5] To read in this way means to pay very close attention to the (alleged) "phenomenological deduction[s]" Levinas performs, and to the "expressions [he uses] such as 'that is,' or 'precisely,' or 'this accomplishes that,' or 'this is produced as that.'"[6] As is well known, Levinas's phenomenology is controversial.[7] I do not intend to take sides in this controversy or question Levinas from an external point of view. I perform strictly *immanent critique*, along the lines laid out in my introduction. As such, I pay special attention to whether and if Levinas's descriptions *actually show* what they purport to show, and whether and if these descriptions are internally consistent. To practice immanent critique fairly, I must perform a detailed and charitable reconstruction of his descriptions. Only then do I turn to critical analysis. In what follows, I show that, on Levinas's own methodological terms, his (1) analysis of the "Same" is viciously circular, that is, sensibility actually presupposes the various meanings held to be subsequent to it. (2) Levinas's account of "substance" is methodologically arbitrary. (3) The circularity of (1) and arbitrary of (2) is concealed by his own determination of theory as so-called "anterior a posteriorly." I argue that (a) the "anterior a posteriorly" is a question-begging confusion of *empirical* and *phenomenological* priority, (b) this confusion is rooted in a correlative problem with Levinas's description of the singularity of the ego, and (c) the consequence of his own descriptions suggests that the ego *must* tragically—and ironically—approach the other with *empty hands*.

II. Phenomenology of the "Same"

Levinas's account of the ego proceeds by way of a threefold movement of progressively enriched phenomenological description: enjoyment, dwelling, and labor. As Cohen notes, these moments present three distinct yet related "syntheses of identification," or distinct ontological modes of ecstatic existence.[8] As such, Levinas is careful to mark the difference between "relations analogous to transcendence and that of transcendence itself."[9] As we will see, qua "ecstatic," the ego originates or comes-to-itself in being-outside-itself—that is, in relation to "others" of various kinds—and hence resembles a movement of transcendence. But insofar as these movements consist in identification, they do not delineate transcendence proper. Transcendence proper, construed as a meaning presupposed by and determinative for intentionality as such, is reserved for the ethics of the face. We should also note that each form of identification is presented as remaining dependent on the one that precedes it (theoretical activity presupposes practical activity, practical activity presupposes dwelling, and dwelling presupposes enjoyment within the regime of sensibility), and all three, taken as whole, present a "phenomenological deduction" or something like a phenomenological constitution of subjectivity qua the Same.[10]

II.A. Enjoyment

> Subjectivity originates in the independence and sovereignty of enjoyment.[11]

Primordially, life is lived as enjoyment [*jouissance*]. We "live from 'good soup,' air, light, spectacles, work, ideas, sleep . . ."[12] In the first instance, all the contents that fill my life signify neither as the means for brute survival nor as objects of reflection. Prior to our practical relations with things and our theoretical relations with ideas, "things" and ideas are *lived from . . . [vivre de]*. The enjoyment of the *lived from . . .*, or what Levinas also calls *nourishment*, constitutes the I's independence, the independence of *happiness*:

> Nourishment is the transmutation of the other into the same, which is the essence of enjoyment: an energy that is other, recognized as other, recognized . . . as sustaining the very act directed upon it, becomes, in enjoyment, my own energy, my strength, me.[13]

The dependence involved in the *lived from* . . . is enveloped by happiness. When I am hungry, I anticipate the fulfillment of my need in eating, and even enjoy my hunger: hunger heightens the anticipation I feel while planning, shopping, and cooking the meal. I will not only savor the shwarma that awaits me at Ahmed's eatery down the street, but I also savor the hunger I now experience and the anticipation of that shwarma as I write these very lines. Need heightens and enhances enjoyment. In just this way, "The human being thrives on his needs, is happy for his needs."[14] Happiness is an outcome "where the memory of the aspiration confers upon the outcome the character of accomplishment. Enjoyment is made of the memory of its thirst; it is a quenching."[15] What of the suffering undergone in, for example, poverty or famine? Suffering, too, is one dimension of our affective pre-practical and pre-theoretical life in sensibility. In the first instance, suffering is of the "order" of sensibility, not theory or practice. As we will see below, suffering opens another dimension of our originary relation to the world. This dimension will involve the insecurity undergone when the happy ego becomes aware of the fragile character of its happiness, when it runs up against a situation or milieu not completely under its sway (think of famine). Egregious forms of suffering rooted in injustice—poverty, oppression, exploitation, and so forth—presuppose the affectivity of the I, and the ethics and justice proper to sociality (to which subsequent sections of *TI* are dedicated). At this level of description, Levinas insists that "Life is affectivity and sentiment; to live is to enjoy life. To despair of life makes sense only because originally life is happiness. Suffering is a failing of happiness; it is not correct to say that happiness is the absence of suffering."[16] Put another way, Levinas presents suffering as a deficient mode of happiness. Though suffering originarily belongs to sensibility, its "sense" is secondary within the order of sensibility.

At this point, let us underline the "alimentary" or consumptive character of enjoyment and broach the specific character of its "independence," "sovereignty," "self-sufficiency," or in a word: "separation."[17] "[B]ecause life is happiness," Levinas insists, "life is personal."[18] Happiness opens what Levinas calls the "unicity" or *ipseity* of the I; it constitutes the I as an ego:

The self-sufficiency of enjoying measures the egoism or the ipseity of the Ego and the same. Enjoyment is withdrawal into oneself, an involution. . . . The I is the very contraction of sentiment.[19]

As "contraction," the self emerges as "a being absolutely isolated."[20] What precisely can he mean, because he appeared to describe above a self that enjoys, at the very least, "others" as contents *lived from*? First, the ego not only enjoys its needs and the contents that sate them, but it also enjoys its own enjoyment of these contents. "In enjoyment we maintain ourselves always at the second power, which, however, is not yet the level of reflection."[21] Happiness produces a self and self-awareness, but not (as of yet) practical or theoretical self-consciousness. In this spontaneous self-sensing or affective reflexivity, "others"—all the contents I *live from* . . .—are both (a) "recognized as other" and (b) "transmuted into the same," and these two dimensions display the "ecstatic" character of enjoyment.[22] The happy ego comes to itself outside of itself, or put another way: "contracts"[23] or *originates* in both enjoying what it is *not* and in enjoying this enjoyment of what it is *not*. By enjoying the contents *lived from*, the ego *identifies* them (in a pre-theoretical way)—that is, precisely consumes and enjoys them— and as such absorbs their alterity. In enjoying its enjoyment of what it *lives from*, the ego comes to and becomes aware of itself. The ego is outside of itself in itself, that is: in contact with "others" it enjoys and consumes as it folds back and affects itself. The self produced in this moment has become aware that its sensibility is properly its *own*: no one else can feel my joys for me or inhabit my sentience from my own first-person perspective. In this sense, the self is "a being absolutely isolated."[24] This "contraction" occurs as a fundamentally temporal differentiation:

> Happiness is a condition for activity, if activity means a commencement in duration . . . Action implies being, to be sure, but it marks a beginning and end in an anonymous being—where end and beginning have no meaning. But within this continuity enjoyment realizes independence with regard to continuity: each happiness comes for the first time. Subjectivity originates in the independence and sovereignty of enjoyment.[25]

The moment of enjoyment opens an interval in which, as Peperzak notes, "I feel myself as independent and sovereign with regard to the anonymous continuity from which it emerges. Instead of being taken away by the river of Heraclitus, I feel that my life is being gathered, recollected for a while."[26] Enjoyment interrupts the endless continuity of anonymous being, it marks a time qualitatively different from that of its immediate surroundings and from the contents it enjoys, a discontinuous instant that the happy ego itself *is*. As we will see presently, "anonymous being" or being in general is characterized by Levinas as *nothingness*, and the "birth of . . . separated being"—enjoyment—is said to "proceed from nothingness" as an "absolute beginning."[27] It is in (i) the enjoyment of the contents *lived from* and (ii) enjoy*ing* the enjoyment of those contents—*enjoying itself*—that the ego "occurs," contracts, or is constituted as distinct from its immediate surroundings and as discontinuous from the contents it consumes: this is the basic structure of "separated being." We should emphasize that (i) and (ii) are internal moments of enjoyment itself: they are not presented as chronologically discrete. Moreover, as we hinted above: the "intentionality of enjoyment" is different from the intentionality of theory, in that it "holds on to," as Levinas says, "the exteriority" of its surroundings and of the contents it *lives from*.[28] The self-sensing or affective self already somehow "knows" or *feels* that the others it consumes are *not* itself ("exterior") as it absorbs their alterity in enjoyment. This affective awareness is somehow part and parcel of the corporeal character of enjoyment.

We are now in a position to fully specify in what sense the "self-sufficiency of enjoying measures the egoism or the ipseity of the Ego."[29] The ego is (1) *self-sufficient* in that it has the "en-ergy" or *power* to fulfill its needs and spontaneously acts to do so; is (2) *independent* in that it "proceeds from nothingness," marking an "instant" or "absolute beginning" with regard to its surroundings and that distinguishes it from the contents it enjoys; and (3) with self-sufficiency and independence, taken together, it can be called *sovereign*: the happy ego can freely initiate or act and becomes relatively autonomous with respect to its place, what Levinas will call its *extra-territoriality*. As we will see below, Levinas will further specify the character of this "contraction" of ipseity, further concretizing the meaning of its separation as the *inwardness* of *dwelling* within "anonymous being," and involving the "recollection" Peperzak hints at above. Thus far, we have a description of the concrete way "enjoyment is the ultimate consciousness of all the contents that fill my life" and an initial description of how the ego originates in enjoyment.[30] At this point Levinas will turn to describe the specific character of ego's environment—"anonymous being"—assumed in the constitution of the separated ego, and its analysis will deepen his description of the happy ego.

II.b. The (Pleasant) Elements

As I hinted above, the contents *lived from* arise from a specific background, or what Levinas will call a *medium* [*milieu*]:

> the medium from which [the contents enjoyed] come to me lies in escheat, a common fund or terrain, essentially non-possessable, "nobody's": earth, sea, light, city. Every relation or possession is situated within the non-possessable which envelops or contains without being able to be contained or enveloped. We shall call it the elemental.[31]

The elements are what we might call our *environing context*. They do not initially occur to the ego as "a system of operational references"[32] or as an object of theoretical contemplation. They are as yet too immediate and indeterminate, and this indeterminacy is essential to the sense of the element as a medium: "The relation adequate to its essence discovers it precisely as medium: one is steeped in it; I am always within the element."[33] Primordially, the sea is not a giant "thing" but a medium in which I live and move: where I enjoy a swim, where I moor a boat after an afternoon of fishing, where I gaze while overcome by the grandeur of the setting sun. In these three examples, I am not contemplating the nature of the sea, but enjoying and utilizing it. Unlike the boat that supports me, the sea is not a product of human labor. And when I stand entranced by its natural beauty, I am not in that moment measuring water molecules or pondering the idea of planetary accretion: I remain seized in the sea's grasp in its convergence with sky, in the brilliance of the colors it reflects, and so forth. When we approach the sea theoretically, say, as a chemist or oceanographer, "We can, to be sure, represent the liquid or the gaseous to ourselves . . . , but then we are abstracting from our presence in the midst of the element."[34] Unlike objects, Levinas claims, the elements have no forms that might contain them. They consist of a proliferation of profiles that do not yield a form but open upon an unfathomable depth: "The depth of the element prolongs until it is lost in the earth and the heavens. 'Nothing ends, nothing begins.'"[35] As a medium, Levinas insists, it is a region of pure "qualities without substances."[36] As such, the elements "remain entirely anonymous. It is wind, earth, sky, air. . . . Quality manifests itself in the element as determining nothing."[37] Given its anonymous, indeterminate character, the "intentionality" proper to the elements (if intentionality can be said here) is the "intentionality" of *bathing*:

> The interiority of immersion is not convertible into exteriority. The pure quality of the element does not cling to a substance that would support it. To bathe in the element is to be in an inside-out world, and here the inverse is not equivalent to the obverse.[38]

The happy ego is always already bathed and immersed in the elements. If we take the above description seriously, it apparently entails that that "which envelops or contains without being able to be contained or enveloped"[39]—the elements—is "not convertible into exteriority," that is: *completely enveloped by the happiness of the ego "immersed" in it.* As "not convertible into exteriority," would it not be more proper to say that *the elements are "immersed" in the ego*? Apparently the elements do not originally signify as "real." Levinas will say they are originally presented as "the reverse of reality, without origin in being, although presented to us in familiarity—of enjoyment—as though we were in the bowls of being."[40] This is difficult to understand. Perhaps we should interpret this as presenting a rather radical interpretation of the ecstatic character of enjoyment: the happy ego contains *more than it can possibly contain* in its immersion or bathing in the elements. It "comes to itself" or *originates* "outside of itself" in enjoying the very medium it inhabits. Though this may be what Levinas is getting at, even this seems wrong. Levinas deepens this problem even further, it appears, in his discussion of the ego's *stand*. After stressing once more that the happy ego is content in its happiness and undisturbed by "theoretical" questions, he discusses the self-relation that emerges in sensibility. In this context, I quote him at length:

> This relation of myself with myself is accomplished when I *stand* [*me tiens*] in the world which precedes me as an absolute and unrepresentable antiquity. . . . I cannot think the horizon in which I find myself as an absolute, but I stand in it as an absolute. Standing there is precisely different from "thinking." The bit of earth that supports me is not only my object; it supports my experience of objects. Well trampled places do not resist me but support me. The relation with my site in this "stance" precedes thought and labor. The body, position, the fact of standing—patterns of the primary relation with myself—nowise resemble idealist representation. . . .[41]

How, precisely, is it possible to speak of earth as an "absolute and unprecedented antiquity" if earth "manifests no exteriority" or remains the "reverse of reality"? Levinas appeals to a distinction between *thinking* the earth as absolute and *standing in* it *as* absolute, and elsewhere insists: "One does not know, one lives sensible qualities."[42] But what does this distinction do? He appears to mean that the *meaning* of my position on the earth is distinct from Husserl's account of transcendental self-constitution, that is, the kinaesthetic experience at issue is not "theoretical" and does not primarily function to constitute a relation to the world and other existents. My primordial relation with the elements is not a species of theoretical knowing or structurally accessible for it. He also appears to mean that the *meaning* of my position on the earth is distinct from Heidegger's analysis of the *Da* of *Dasein*: the ego is not originally *thrown*, does not originally orient itself as a "care for Being," does not achieve its self-relation in its ecstatic projects before death. My primordial relation with the elements does not presuppose an "understanding of Being." My self-relation or *ipseity* is (always) already accomplished in merely standing here, in this little patch of earth that I occupy. It is accomplished in the self-sensing of my *stance*: where all "others" in which I'm immersed and which I consume are originally there "for me" in the "accessibility of enjoyment."[43] The earth and all the contents the ego consumes are simply given, without problem and without provoking questions, in the immediacy and happiness of enjoyment. All of that said, it seems that his distinction between thought and immediacy does not really resolve the problem: how can that which lacks "exteriority" and "reality" be called "absolute" or an "unprecedented antiquity"? We will have to return to these questions later. For now, let us follow Levinas in his descriptions and continue with our reconstruction.

Thus far, Levinas's analysis of the elements has yielded the following structure: the elements originally signify as (i) a *medium*: as that in which the ego lives and moves, *bathes*, or is *immersed*; (ii) qua *medium*, it is a region of pure qualities without substances: the sunset is brilliantly "pink," the wind is refreshingly "cool," the grass is comfortably "soft," and so forth. The ego absorbs "pink," "cool," and "soft" as pure qualities in enjoying "brilliance," "refreshment," and "comfort." The ego does not *wonder*, here, *what* the sun, the wind, and the grass *are*. Finally, the elements signify as that which "supports me," as surroundings in which I am thoroughly and utterly "content," surroundings where I "relate myself to myself" in the happy self-sensing of enjoyment.[44] This is not all Levinas has to say about the elements. As we are about to see, they also have a dark side.

II.c. The (Horrific) Elements

As we have just seen, the elements signify as a medium and as a pure proliferation of qualities. They come from "nowhere" and do not provoke questions such as "what is . . . ?" or "from where . . . ?" in the thoroughly contented ego. The indeterminate dimension of the elements, as pure qualities without substance (without "reality"), takes on a different affective character when the ego becomes aware—at the level of sensation—that its happiness is fundamentally *fragile*. This occurs to the ego as "concern for the morrow."[45] The indeterminacy of the elements "overflow[s] . . . the instant . . . of enjoyment" and occurs as the *future* "of sensibility and enjoyment."[46] This "disquietude" and "insecurity" remain, like enjoyment, "already in the pure quality which lacks the category of substance."[47] Levinas strenuously and repeatedly insists that this "disquietude" is not sufficient to provoke questions in the ego: it is of the order of sensibility, and does not provoke a *theoretical identification* of the non-I that might initiate Hegel's dialectic. At most, the ego becomes aware of "the insufficiency of the lived from," or in other words, becomes aware that the contents it enjoys are not always constantly and immediately at its disposal.[48] This awareness occurs to the ego as a "menace" to its enjoyment, and allows us to consider other qualitative experiences with a different character than that of enjoyment.[49] It's important to underline the secondary character Levinas attributes to this "negative" or unpleasant dimension: he insists that suffering befalls an already happy ego that can always already act to fulfill its needs. This "disquietude," and the experiences that concretize it, properly belong to sensibility, but the sense it opens is dependent on a more original happiness. I quote Levinas at length:

> The nothingness of the future ensures separation: the element we enjoy issues in the nothingness which separates. The element I inhabit is at the frontier of a night. What the side of the element that is turned toward me conceals is not a "something" susceptible of being revealed, but an ever new depth of absence, an existence without existent, the impersonal par excellence. This way of existing without revealing itself must be called mythical. The nocturnal prolongation of the element is the reign of the mythical gods. Enjoyment is without security. But this future does not take on the character of *Geworfenheit*, for insecurity menaces an enjoyment already happy in the element, rendered sensitive to disquietude only by this happiness. We have described

this nocturnal dimension of the future under the title *there is* [*il y a*]. The elements extends into the there is. Enjoyment, as interiorization, runs up against the very strangeness of the earth. But it has recourse to labor and possession.[50]

This is an extremely loaded passage that I seek to explicate with care. First, "the nothingness of the future ensures separation." It is not immediately clear from this context why this needs to be said. Separation was presented as already *accomplished* in the auto-affection of happiness. Because the "sense" of suffering is dependent on the more primitive and already achieved happiness, why must this be reiterated here?[51] I come back to this question. Next, "The frontier I inhabit is at the edge of night." "On the edge of night" is explicated in the very next sentence: as we saw above, the profiles the elements offer do not open upon, manifest, or reveal "a substance." At this level of description—in sensibility—the question of substance does not and *cannot* emerge. The indeterminacy of "a night" broached here refers to a feeling or a mood that signifies as the "insecurity" of enjoyment, as a momentary lapse of enjoyment that will open upon (a) dwelling and labor, and (b) intimate a void-like or *apeironic* malaise periodically disturbing the happy ego. Next, "This way of existing without revealing itself must be called mythical. The nocturnal prolongation of the element is the reign of the mythical gods." This is an extremely strange contention. Myth, whatever else it might involve, is meaningful or not only at the level of being and thought. The question of whether myth is "illusion" or if it harbors some sort of truth cannot be adjudicated at the descriptive level Levinas is operating at, as he himself constantly insists.[52] Perhaps the pre-veridical sense of "myth" he is aiming at involves this: like the Greek gods or the Mayan Gaia, the elements remain fundamentally unknown, elusive, and arbitrary in their dispensing of good and bad *fortune*. By "mythic" he appears to mean a kind of painful arbitrariness we *feel*, as when a storm strands me at the airport or when lightening fries my hard drive. Myth signifies, here, the uncertainty the elements exhibit as (good or mis-) *fortune*. Next, "Enjoyment is without security. But this future does not take on the character of *Geworfenheit*. . . ." Here, Levinas is distinguishing what he means from Heidegger's account of "thrownness." Life does not originally consist in *dereliction* or a feeling of abandonment and suffering. The disquietude emerging here resembles *thrownness* to the extent that we affectively register the insecurity of enjoyment and the instability of the elements—the *groundlessness* involved in affective life—but elemental instability and the troublesome quality of this realization only signify in lieu of originary happiness. Finally, "We have described this nocturnal dimension of the future under the title *there is* [*il y a*]. The element extends into the there is. Enjoyment, as interiorization, runs up against the very strangeness of the earth. But it has recourse to labor and possession." Here, Levinas finally delineates the (quasi-) "exterior" character of the elements. The elements function as a limit to happiness, and the *il y a* delineates their "strangeness" or otherness. Levinas refers here to the analysis he performed in *Existents and Existence*, where being in general is cast as a suffocating and indeterminate generality experienced in, for example, nausea or insomnia. There, the "meaning" the *il y a* fundamentally yields for the subject is the *impossibility to escape itself*.[53] Here, the *il y a* functions differently. It appears to name the terrifying anonymity of being in general, a terror opened in the subject's suffering of "horror, trembling, and vertigo, [the] perturbation of the I that does not coincide with itself." Unlike *EE*, the subject does not come to birth in a recoil from and refusal of being in general, but rather originates in a primordial happiness and in the spontaneous appropriation of (elemental and lived from . . .) "others" that this involves. Horror still remains secondary within the regime of sensibility.

II.d. The Feminine and Dwelling

Thus far, Levinas has constantly insisted that the "otherness" of the elements and of the contents *lived from* were not sufficient to provoke questions; their "exteriority," though "held on to" by the ego, to this point has only registered affectively.[54] In the instant of enjoyment, the happy ego stands out from the anonymous continuity of its surroundings and *simultaneously envelops these surroundings as a pleasant enveloping medium*. In the instant of enjoyment, everything signifies as "for" the ego: the ego is "outside itself in itself" or ecstatic, both enveloped and enveloping. The "disquietude" of the future troubles the instant of enjoyment and appears to threaten it with dissolution into the horrific anonymity of the *there is*.

Levinas now turns to more fully specify the character of the "contraction" or ipseity of the ego. The threat of dissolution or horror the ego undergoes allows for the more precise description of ipseity as *inwardness*, habitation, and dwelling. As Levinas asserts repeatedly: "the I is at home with itself."[55] At the opening of this section, Levinas insists that dwelling constitutes an "originality" within sensibility. He also underlines that the menace the future presents to enjoyment is not sufficient to account for or describe the full sense dwelling exhibits. Happiness delineates a self-coincidence or describes the instant of self-sensing that constitutes egoity, but a new event is necessary to fully account for the sense that emerges in dwelling.

As Peperzak hints at above, a unique dimension of the ego's separation is its ability to "withdrawal from the elements . . . , from immediate enjoyment, already uneasy about the morrow," what Levinas describes as *recollection*.[56] Recollection is "a work of separation, is concretized as existence in a dwelling, economic existence."[57] The ego not only experiences its happiness as kind of event: for the ego *is* its happiness. But the ego can also work to sustain and recommence its enjoyings by retreating into itself, or in other words: *by having time*. Levinas writes:

> Recollection . . . designates a suspension of the immediate reactions the world solicits in view of greater attention to oneself, one's possibilities, and the situation. It is already a movement of attention freed from immediate enjoyment, for no longer deriving its freedom from the agreeableness of the elements.[58]

"From what then"? If recollection no longer "derives its freedom" or separation from its happiness in the elements, and if the "disquieted" of concern for the future cannot adequately explain its emergence, "From what then?" does recollection "derive its freedom" or separation? Or put slightly differently: "How . . . is a distance to be produced" that would allow for the transition from the immediacy of enjoyment to the "suspension" and "attention to oneself" dwelling involves?[59] Levinas writes:

> The familiarity of the world, which take from its roughness and measure the adaptation of the living being to a world it enjoys and from which it nourishes itself; familiarity and intimacy are produced as a gentleness that spreads over the face of things. This gentleness is not only a conformity of nature with the needs of separated being, . . . but is a gentleness coming from *an affection for the I*.[60]

This marks a very significant moment in the descriptions of *TI*. For it is the first introduction of a human "other."[61] "For the intimacy which familiarity already presupposes is an *intimacy with someone*."[62] Levinas calls this "someone" *the feminine*.[63] Though the feminine is specifically human, Levinas insists that its event still occurs at the pre-linguistic level of sensibility:

> For the intimacy of recollection to be able to be produced in the oecumenia of being the presence of the Other must not only be revealed in the face which breaks through its own plastic image, but must be revealed, simultaneous with this presence, in its withdrawal and with its absence.⁶⁴

The feminine signifies precisely in its "withdrawal and . . . absence," and signifies as a pre-linguistic affective intentionality *aimed at* the ego as a gentle welcome in the intimacy of the home. The "Woman" signifies here as an otherness that "produces the distance" necessary for dwelling to emerge, and hence is the "condition for recollection." As should be clear, this does indeed deepen and concretize the ego: the ego is no longer simply its happiness in the instant. With the Woman, it becomes inwardness and comes to have *time*. The feminine transforms the happy ego:

> Familiarity is an accomplishment, an *en-ergy* of separation. With it separation is constituted as dwelling and inhabitation. To exist henceforth means to dwell. To dwell . . . is recollection, a coming to oneself, a retreat home with oneself as in a land of refuge, which answers to a hospitality, an expectancy, a human welcome. . . . The separation that is concretized through the intimacy of dwelling outlines new relations with the elements.⁶⁵

Before broaching the new relations with the elements dwelling enables, let us specify, as clearly as possible, the structure of dwelling as it has thus far been presented. First, in enjoyment the ego "derives its freedom" or separation from happiness by enjoying its needs, while in dwelling the ego "derives its freedom" or separation from the *intimacy of a welcome*. The feminine is the condition for this transition and the new sense introduced. Because the otherness of the feminine and the otherness of the elements both involve indeterminacy, what distinguishes these two indeterminacies? The otherness of the elemental emerges in its never terminating in a substance, or "reality." It signifies as both a happy medium and as a horrific anonymity, and hence as ultimately unstable and arbitrary ("mythic") in character. The otherness of the feminine is never really specified by Levinas. He flatly asserts that the feminine signifies as "absence and withdrawal" in the gentle welcome and intimacy of the home. Apparently, there is no "dark side" or anything that marks the Woman as genuinely other ("exterior"), hence distinguishing it from the ego. The only possible clue we are given as to the otherness of the feminine is in its "affection *for* the I," that is, in its "*referring* to a welcome."⁶⁶

The otherness of the Woman announces itself as an affective intentionality *aimed at* the ego. The first intentionality the happy ego confronts (and not only exhibits) is an "intention" *aimed at it*: that of being welcomed in an original familiarity and gentleness.[67] Because the character of this intention is ultimately pleasant and "welcoming," Levinas calls it "modest." The ego affectively registers that it is being welcomed by something foreign, but not as yet foreign enough to provoke questions or *to put the ego into question*. Nevertheless, the character of *being intended* is apparently sufficient for the ego to mark the otherness of the Woman, and it precisely signifies in a different way than elements, because they—as happy medium and horrific anonymity—intend nothing, and signify as arbitrary or "mythic." Next, as a condition, the feminine enables the ego to re-collect itself from the instant of immediate enjoyment and from the menace of dissolution in the horrific anonymity of the elements. Finally, whereas enjoyment is (almost) pure immediacy, the feminine *gives time*, it is the *affective* opening of duration. "Affective" must be underlined, because Levinas insists that dwelling "is not yet the transcendence of language."[68]

Let us underline here that, in the context of his overall phenomenology, both enjoyment and dwelling delineate the overall structure of the "same." In enjoyment and dwelling, the ego is fundamentally and spontaneously *content* and has the power to sustain its contentment. At both moments within sensibility, this contentment is fundamentally delineated by *time*: the instant of enjoyment that stands out from the anonymous continuity of the elements, and the duration of dwelling that enables the continuity of elemental time to be punctuated with beginnings and ends. Moreover, both the instant of enjoyment and the duration of dwelling are fundamentally ecstatic in character: in enjoyment, the ego consumes and envelops the elements as a sating and enveloping medium, and as we are about to see in more detail, in dwelling the ego "familiarizes" the elements through labor. This is not a description of an empirical situation, but a description of the origin of the ego in its ecstases: of the ego as it *lives through* the various "others" it encounters. In enjoyment and dwelling, the ego "comes to itself outside itself," that is to say: is "independent," "self-sufficient," "sovereign," or in a word: "separate."

II.e. Dwelling and Labor

Dwelling "makes labor and property possible."[69] Labor presupposes dwelling as that familiar space from which I leave to work and to which I retreat when work is concluded. I always "head to the office" from my home, and this is the case even if my office is in my home. Exiting one's tent to attend to the herd, retreating to the cave after the hunt, opting to sleep under the clear night sky cloistered aside my bamboo shack: such is the meaning of dwelling. Labor is not always pleasant, but whenever we labor we do so from a dwelling in the phenomenological sense Levinas is opening. This is apparently the case even for those who suffer the injustice of homelessness. After the rummage the homeless man retreats to his favorite ally; after a day of panhandling the homeless woman takes shelter in a corner of the park. The injustice of these situations is identifiable only because in a primordial way, we all know what it means to dwell. As the prison volunteer or ethnographer can attest, even those who do not empirically own a dwelling indeed do dwell in the sense Levinas opens: adorning the walls of a cell, inhabiting this specific patch of jungle for the duration of the hunt. These examples disclose the character of dwelling as "set back from the anonymity of the earth, the air, the light, the forest, the road, the sea, the river. It has a 'street front,' but also its secrecy. With dwelling the separated being breaks with natural existence . . ."[70] Dwelling establishes a porous boundary—a "door" or "window," a log that marks a boundary between the camp I inhabit and the jungle where I hunt—between the "secrecy" or interiority of the separated ego and the elements that surround it, and as such deepens and renders concrete the personal and properly human dimension of life. As Levinas says: "separation does not isolate me, as though I were simply extracted from the elements."[71] We always work and think from a dwelling, and our working and thinking always function to transform the elements and to make the earth habitable, or in other words: *functions to constitute a world*. In its unpleasant dimensions, labor does not signify as unrelenting wretchedness. Even in the *absolute evil* of slavery the victims retreat to their "quarters." Perhaps this is why the *spirit* produced in such circumstance strikes us as so exceedingly poignant, fierce, and action-motivating: old Black spirituals, songs around the fire in the barrios, the poetry of resistance we call graffiti, the protestor's unified turn toward Mecca in present-day Cairo or Homs, and so forth.[72] They signify a meaning—*goodness*—that the evils of slavery, exploitation, and oppression cannot utterly or forever quench, a goodness irrupting in the very life of those called "human beings." We are not yet licensed to talk about this properly human dimension in its full sense. The identification of injustice presupposes the meaning of the Other, or the ethics and justice proper to sociality. With dwelling, we have the condition for labor, to which we now turn.

With dwelling, the meaning of the elements for the ego is transformed from that of unstable milieu to that of *standing reserve*:

> The elements remain at the disposal of the I—to take or leave. . . . Labor will henceforth draw things from the elements and thus discover the world. This primordial grasp, the emprise of labor, which *arouses* things and transforms nature into a world . . ."⁷³

Levinas will insist that the "postponement of enjoyment has no other concrete significance than this putting at one's disposal which accomplishes it, which is its en-ergy."⁷⁴ At this level of description, labor emerges as completely "for" dwelling and motivated by enjoyment: when the ego is not dwelling, that is, when it's working, it does so solely to nurture the home in its familiarity and for the sake of its own happiness. Levinas writes:

> [Labor is an] access to the world . . . produced as a movement that starts from the utopia of the dwelling and traverses a space to effect a primordial grasp, to seize and take away. The uncertain future of the element is [here] suspended.⁷⁵

Labor overcomes the insecurity of the elements, and in so doing, produces a *world*. It opens upon "a world to be possessed, to be acquired, to be rendered interior. The first movement of economy is in fact egoist—it is not transcendence."⁷⁶ Labor *humanizes* or renders the earth familiar, and as such "founds possession": its "possessive grasp, suspends the independence of the element: its being."⁷⁷ How is this so? Levinas writes:

> The labor that draws the things from the elements in which I am steeped discovers durable substances, but forthwith suspends the independence of their durable being by acquiring them as movable goods, transportable, put in reserve, deposited in the home.⁷⁸

Levinas calls these goods *furnishings*. Here, the ego takes possession of the earth by: (1) suspending "the independence" of the "substances" it "discovers," and (2) "Possession removes being from change."⁷⁹ In the first sense, labor transforms raw materials into *artifice*: the slab of wood becomes the frame encasing a Chagall print, becomes both the shelves that hold and the books that populate my office. They can be traded, bought, sold, or refashioned into something else and are, in this sense, "transportable," and "lack independence." In the second case, "possession removes being from change" in the relative sense of "depositing in the home." In other words, possession interrupts the natural cycle of growth and decay in rendering raw materials durable as things. The slab of wood in a Coptic church in Old Cairo has endured beyond the natural cycle of the Cyprus tree that composes it; think of the papyrus of the Dead Sea Scrolls or the charcoal of the Gabarnmung cave paintings. These examples illustrate how labor and possession involve a relative power over the future. Levinas also has in mind here the more obvious sense of the pantry: sand becomes the glass that encases brined red pepper; burlap becomes a bag that holds winter's portion of rice, and so forth. In these two senses—durability and transportability—the ego relatively overcomes the future, and in this sense "possesses the elements." Unlike the elements, everything that *identifiably* endures does so as marked by human labor. This durability is only relative, and this relativity is signaled in the perpetual "return" of the anonymity and arbitrarity of the elements: chairs break, buildings are destroyed, we do not know who built this hut or scratched these markings in the cave. As Levinas writes:

> The hand's rigorous economic movement of seizure and acquisition is dissimulated by the traces, "wastes," and "works" this movement of acquisition, returned to the interiority of the home, leaves in its wake. These works, as city, field, landscape, recommence their elemental existence.[80]

Elemental existence is "recommenced" at a higher level as the anonymity of past generations or unknown civilizations: a city not built by me, an old shack in an isolated landscape I discover but never inhabited, signal that in the end, the element swallows everything. We are all food for worms. The subject is both the "support of qualities" and imbues elemental life with substance, yet remains tragically destined to be swallowed by the elements.[81] The home is the very *postponement* of this tragic destiny as the *time of life*; and labor is the very power that "masters the future and stills the anonymous rustling of the there is, the uncontrollable stirring of the elemental."[82]

II.F. "Representation"

We now approach representation, or Levinas's account of the ego's theoretical life. Any attempt to reconstruct Levinas's account of theory in *TI* is immediately faced with a difficult challenge. Throughout the text as whole, Levinas everywhere seeks to distinguish his account from other philosophers (Heidegger, Husserl, Hegel, Kant, Aristotle, Plato, and so forth—almost every major philosopher in the tradition). As has been my practice thus far, I set aside these moments unless they are deemed important to clarify Levinas's own stance and try to present his core position as it takes shape through his analyses. In what follows, I beg the reader's pardon for my generous use of quotations. Levinas analysis of theory is difficult, as we will see.

According to Levinas, "The theoretical, being after the event, being essentially memory, is to be sure nowise creative; but its critical essence—its retrogressive movement—is no wise a possibility of enjoyment and labor."[83] Here he stresses once more that enjoyment and labor *are life*, that is to say: *lack memory*, they are not knowledge but precisely happiness and practical possession. As "not creative," Levinas's own account of theory and representation can immediately be distinguished from German Idealism and from Cartesian interpretations of Husserl. Theory in Levinas does not proceed as speculative *creation* or *pure* transcendental constitution. Theory rather "nourishes itself and lives from the very being it represents to itself" and "refers to an exceptional possibility of this separated existence."[84] It seems that Levinas is not rejecting phenomenological constitution outright; it in fact "refers to an exceptional possibility." He is insisting that the meaning produced in any constitutional analysis necessarily presupposes the meaning produced *as life*, and specifically to this point: the meaning yielded in his analyses of enjoyment, dwelling, and labor. Levinas writes:

> Representation is conditioned. It's transcendental pretensions are constantly belied by the life that it is already implanted in the being representation claims to constitute. But representation claims to constitute itself after the event for this life in reality, so as to constitute this very reality. Separation has to be able to account for this constitutive conditioning accomplished by representation—though representation is produced after the event.[85]

As this passage makes clear, Levinas has set himself the task of *accounting for*—or in other words: *conditioning*—the "constitutive conditioning" of which constitutional analysis or "representation" consist, and is not simply rejecting constitutional analysis outright.[86] On the one hand, without "accounting for" or determining the limits of the "constitutive conditioning" of theory, we would yield to the "eternal temptation of idealism" and imply that consciousness and thought completely swallow or determine life without "being determined by" it.[87] On the other hand, Levinas is doing phenomenology—not conducting empirical theory or doing metaphysics in the traditional sense—and hence wants to retain the "constitutive conditioning" of phenomenology within its proper limits. The problem with Husserl's account of theory, according to Levinas, is this:

> Every anteriority of the given is reducible to the instantaneity of thought and, simultaneous with it, arises in the present. It thereby takes on meaning. To represent is not only to render present "anew"; it is to reduce to the present an actual perception which flows on. To represent is not to reduce a past fact to an actual image but to reduce to the instantaneousness of thought everything that seems independent of it; it is in this that representation is constitutive.[88]

The problem with constitutive analysis or "representation" (these are always synonyms in his discussion of theory) is that they treat as full-fledged objects perceptions or "givens" that both precede and, as it were, "keep going passed" the thinking subject in constitution. If we are dealing with an apple or a bottle of Talisker, this is apparently not a problem. But when we are dealing with life as such—and especially with other human beings—this can become a problem. The fact that constitution yields as whole what only ever gives itself as a part or profile does indeed entail just what Levinas claims: the reduction to the instantaneous moment of thought everything that *in fact* both precedes and survives a theoretical intention or any specific meaning bestowal. Levinas writes:

> That representation is conditioned by life—that idealism is an eternal temptation—results from the very event of separation . . . The fact of the after-the-event does show that constitutive representation . . . [and] the production of separation is bound to time . . .[89]

Levinas's analysis of "separation"—of enjoyment, dwelling, and labor—precisely gives an account of the meaning that is prior to theory and representation. The meanings yielded in this analysis determine theoretical life. Before we ask, "what is?" "from where?," or "why?" we always already enjoy, dwell, and work. These meanings are determinative, that is to say: *condition* the "constitutive conditioning" involved in theory. This is just to say that Levinas *derives* the freedom or independence of theory—its "separation"—from these meanings (and ultimately from ethics proper), and does not derive the "separation" of the enjoying, dwelling, laboring ego from the theoretical subject forever implied in representation. This precisely designates the "after the event" character, or the fact that it is not creative or not idealist: *essentially memory*.

All this being said, Levinas also wants to do justice to the relative autonomy of theory. Theory signifies a "radical possibility" for separated being.[90] Levinas writes:

> The possibility of a representation that is constitutive but already rests on the enjoyment of a real completely constituted . . . indicates the radical character of the uprootedness of him who is recollected in a home, where the I . . . takes up its position before Nature. The elements in and from which I live are also that to which I am opposed.[91]

Theory does not simply reflect "Nature," but in some sense empowers us to overcome "Nature," for example, with technology. Though theory *derives* its "uprooted" character from the "separation" Levinas has analyzed as enjoyment, dwelling, and labor; theory can appear to be anterior to the world only in a being "proceed[ing] from nothingness"[92]:

> A marsh wave that returns to wash away the strand beneath the line it left, a spasm of time conditions remembrance. Thus only do I see without being seen, like Gyges, am no longer invaded by nature, no longer immersed in a tone or an atmosphere. Thus only does the equivocal essence of the home hollow out interstices in the continuity of the earth.[93]

The "ultimate essence" of theory is "critique . . . the recapturing of its own condition," and "to be in possession of its own origin."[94] Hence, as "possessing its own origin" in the *nothingness* of the elements, "separated" being can posit itself as *anterior to the world*, as a moment in the intersubjective origin of meaning. "Separated being" is presented here as both *anterior* to the world and as a concretization *through* the world—as both *anterior* and *after the event*—and both at once: "*Anterior posteriorly*: separation is not thus 'known,' it is thus produced."[95] Rather than choosing between idealism and realism, Levinas claims that theory is essentially *anterior posteriorly*, or in other words: theory is *not conditioned* by—radically "uprooted" from—Nature *and conditioned* by—in its constitutive conditioning—Nature, and both *simultaneously*. Such is the meaning of theory "produced" in these analyses.

Needless to say, we shall have occasion to question this "anterior posteriorly" and the "meaning" it is said to produce. Levinas ultimately derives the meaning of and justification for theory from ethics, and hence to his account of the veritable Other and the meaning it invests. Nevertheless, for the ego to approach this Other with *full hands*, Levinas must *succeed* in describing an ego *capable* of doing so. If I have done justice to his phenomenology of the ego in this reconstruction, then it is *not* clear that he has succeeded in this regard.

III. Critique

Levinas's particular analyses of sensibility—and of happiness and dwelling specifically here—constitute a fascinating and original contribution to phenomenology. Yet, as the attuned reader has no doubt intimated, it is necessary to distinguish between the meanings beautifully described and the *structural priority and function he attempts to attribute to them*. From the perspective of the ego, the fundamental categories Levinas posits, and the relations between them, it must be admitted that *TI* is caught in what can only be called *strained coherence*. As I hinted above, almost the entire history of *TI* interpretation is characterized by simply accepting Levinas's claims for sensibility at face value, as if the logic of his descriptions does not matter. Let's see if this assumption is justified.

III.a. Labor and the "Miracle" of Substance

First, let us note again that dwelling and labor display an ecstatic character. They are described together as rendering the elements familiar, or, as what we might call provisionally, *civilization*. We must qualify "civilization" as provisional because this level of description was said to be pre-theoretical and is still essentially ego analysis. The ego comes to itself outside itself in constituting a dwelling and possessing the elements. Levinas has insisted to this point that enjoyment and dwelling are regions of pure sensibility. Their meanings ultimately emerge as affections and signify as concretions of the *ipseity* of the ego. Labor presupposes enjoyment and dwelling; it does not "put into practice an antecedent 'knowledge,'" and is said to produce the "latent birth of the concept."[96] Theory and cognition in general presuppose enjoyment, dwelling, and labor. And yet, in the midst of describing labor, he entitles himself to talk of *substance*:

> The hand takes and comprehends; it recognizes the being of the existent, seizing upon the substance and not the shadow; and at the same time suspends that being, since being is its possession. . . . For a time it is posited as durable, as substance.[97]

Perhaps there is some kind of "affective awareness" inherent to labor that explains this? This seems to be the case when Levinas insists: "The primordial technique does not put into practice an antecedent 'knowledge,' but has immediately a hold on the matter."[98] Here, he seems to be positing a kind of intermediate region between sensibility and cognition, a region that faintly resembles Heidegger's account of *Zuhandenheit*. There is a spontaneous and pre-theoretical familiarity with things that signify as the "in-order-to" and "for-the-sake-of-which" of tools—that is, exhibit the instrumental character—of labor. That Levinas is nodding to Heidegger here seems to be confirmed in his discussion of the will and of death:

> Labor characterizes not a freedom that has detached itself from being, but a will: a being that is threatened, but has time at its disposal to ward off threat. . . . To will is to fore-stall danger. To conceive the future is to fore-stall. To labor is to delay its expiration.[99]

Levinas's discussion of dwelling and labor harbors both a nod to and a criticism of Heidegger. He follows Heidegger in holding that labor primordially signifies as a pre-theoretical, practical familiarity with the world, but strenuously insists that the "in-order-to" and the "for-the-sake-of-which" are oriented by happiness and *not ontological care*.[100] This criticism is hammered home when he says "the ontology that grasps the being of the existent is a spontaneous and pre-theoretical work of every inhabitant of the earth."[101] Heideggerian ontology is simply banal, whatever useful insights it might harbor. Though this comparison somewhat clarifies what Levinas is aiming at, it does not resolve the problem of *substance* mentioned above. As Levinas's critical remarks suggest, *Zuhandenheit* in Heidegger always already emerges in a primordial *understanding of being*, and its analysis involves the *disclosure* that issues in Heidegger's alternative account of *truth*. Heidegger can coherently talk about a pre-theoretical practical familiarity with things because he offers an alternative account of truth. There is nothing in Levinas's analyses that phenomenologically *justifies* or *presents* how the elements transformed by labor can signify—at a pre-theoretical level—as *substance*. We cannot assert that labor involves a pre-theoretical yet practical awareness, because Levinas himself insists that "Substantiality does not arise in the sensible nature of things."[102] The elements are said to only signify as happy medium and horrific anonymity: as "pure qualities with supports," as "without substance," or, in other words, as "*nothing*."[103] As such, labor appears to wrestles with ghosts. How do we deal with this problem?

III.b. Vicious Circularity

On close inspection, we can only concluded that Levinas's hand is indeed wrestling with ghosts. This becomes explicit in his own descriptions when he refers to labor as "the quasi-miraculous grasp of a thing in the night."[104] There is no need for the qualifier "quasi-" here. The *pre-theoretical* appearance of "substance" occurs as a *pure miracle* on the descriptive terms Levinas himself has set out; that is, its use is methodologically gratuitous. There is nothing in Levinas's analyses that phenomenologically *justifies* or *presents* how the elements grasped by labor can signify—at a pre-theoretical level—as *substance*. Moreover, his gratuitous use of substance illumines what can only be called a *vicious circularity* that troubles his analysis as a whole. To see why, let's look more closely.

(1) *Suffering* must *precede happiness for happiness to* "precede" *suffering*. For happiness to be "constitute[d]" by lived from . . . "others," the ego must have already undergone suffering. It was the abyssal, "mythic" quality of the elements (the *il y a*) that was said to confer upon them a (quasi-) "exterior" character. Without having *already* undergone this suffering, there would be no *others* "distinct from my substance but constituting it."[105] As such, for suffering to "take place within [the] horizon [of happiness] and refer to the joy of living"—for it to be *secondary*—it *must* necessarily be *first*.[106]

(2) *Dwelling* must *precede enjoyment for enjoyment to* "precede" *dwelling*. Happiness was said to be an "outcome . . . where the memory of the aspiration confers upon the outcome the character of accomplishment. Enjoyment is made of the memory of its thirst."[107] Without the *memory* and *anticipation* dwelling opens, happiness could *not* be what Levinas himself determines it to be. Happiness as instant *depends* on the *duration* of dwelling, or a "subjective" continuity (always) already distinct from nature. The "privileged role of the home does not consist of being the end of human

activity but in being its condition, and in this sense a commencement."[108] In other words, for "Happiness [to be] a condition for activity . . . ," dwelling *must have always already "commenced."*[109] As such, for enjoyment to apparently "proceed from nothingness" as an "absolute beginning"—for enjoyment to be *first*—it *must* necessarily be *second*.[110]

(3) *Labor* must *precede dwelling for dwelling to* "precede" *labor*. Labor miraculously introduces what we might call the *regime of the hand*: "the grasp operated on the elemental is labor."[111] Levinas writes:

> The hand takes and comprehends; it recognizes the being of the existent, seizing upon the substance and not the shadow; and at the same time suspends that being, since being is its possession. . . . For a time it is posited as durable, as substance.[112]

What being does the hand take and as such seize "upon the substance and not the shadow"? As we've already seen, because he has already described the elements as "pure qualities *without substance*," there is apparently *nothing* to grasp, *nothing* to comprehend, and as such *nothing* to "discover." Because labor "constitutes the latent birth of the concept," we can only conclude that the "being and not the shadow" the hand seizes upon is *nothing other* than the *laboring being itself*, or in other words: "the *existent, support* of qualities."[113] To show this more clearly, I quote the paragraph from which the last phrase I was excerpted:

> The hand delineates a world by drawing what it grasps from the element, delineating definite beings having forms, that is, solids; the informing of the formless is solidification, emergence of the graspable, the existent, support of qualities.[114]

With these contentions, we immediately know two things: Levinas's assertions that (i) labor is "antecedent" to theory, and (ii) that representation is "not creative" are simply false on his own terms.[115] The hand does not "discover solidity" because on Levinas's own terms it has no access to ready-made forms strewn about nature for it "to take or leave."[116] We cannot suddenly and gratuitously summon empirical realism, for example, to account for his use of substance, because "substantiality" apparently "does not arise from the sensible nature of things."[117] Nor can "solidity" be accounted for as a kind of new event that labor would specify, because it was already "felt," as it were, in the meaning of the elements as medium. Nor can we speculate, here, that labor involves something like Heidegger's account of *Zuhandenheit*, because Levinas everywhere insists that sensibility is pure of all disclosure potential.[118] He has made it abundantly clear that ego "grapples with" and "subjugates" *nothing*, or as he says explicitly: with "pure qualities without supports" or "the fallacious resistance of matter."[119] The only possible way Levinas can account for natural kinds is through the "creativity" of theory, or a *constituting consciousness*. Consciousness, not labor, "delineat[es] definite beings having forms," or in other words *bestows meaning* on the "fallacious matter" labor encounters.[120] If idealism consists of a "mastery exercised by the thinker upon what is thought in which the object's resistance as an exterior being vanishes," then Levinas has eminently succeeded in being idealist.[121] How does this analysis bear on labor's relation to dwelling?

The familiarity that characterizes dwelling remains, Levinas insists, "an *accomplishment*, an *en-ergy* of separation."[122] Dwelling, here, is presented as an already accomplished event such that it serves to "found possession," and hence functions as a condition for labor. Labor and possession "presuppose . . . the recollection of the I in its dwelling."[123] Labor, in turn, is said to be "an en-ergy of acquisition," and this delineates the essence of the hand as *grasp*, *mastery*, and *domination*.[124] The hand manifests these forceful descriptors in that it

> traverses the indetermination of the element, suspends its unforeseeable surprises, postpones the enjoyment in which they already threaten. The hand takes and comprehends; it recognizes the being of the existent . . . and at the same time suspends that being, since being is its possession.[125]

Though Levinas again insists that labor "does not belong to the order of sensibility," he has already described dwelling as "a *work* of separation."[126] Just as he sought to make the "meaning" of suffering depend on a more originary happiness, he now seeks to make the meaning of labor depend on a more original dwelling. However, dwelling and labor emerge together in his actual description, such that dwelling is not "first," and then labor happens to come along. Dwelling is presented as the "*perpetual* postponement of the expiration in which life risks foundering. . . . The domiciled being stands out from . . . things only because *it accords itself* a delay, . . . [only] because it labors."[127] Indeed, if "*to will* is forestall danger. To conceive the future is to forestall," and if, further, forestalling means *to act* to prevent or *delay* an *anticipated* event, then dwelling involves, in its own very structure, an *activity* of some kind.[128] Levinas's own descriptions suggest that the very being of dwelling, as "perpetual," enduring, or a temporally extending *postponement* of death, depends on this: "[the] primordial grasp, this emprise of labor, . . . transforms nature into a world."[129] Only through *grasping hands* can dwelling "*accord itself* a delay," *accord itself* a "perpetual postponement," or in other words: "*accord itself*," in general and *as such*.[130] This *must* be the case given Levinas's actual description of the feminine. In signifying as "discreet," Levinas's hand indeed

> traverses the indetermination of the [feminine], suspends its unforeseeable surprises . . . The hand takes and comprehends; it recognizes the being of the existent [as feminine] . . . and at the same time suspends that being, since being is its possession.[131]

The full transcendence of the feminine must, Levinas writes, "be reserved so as to open up the dimension of interiority."[132] Or in other words: must be *put in reserve*, must be "deposited in the home," must always already *be grasped* in the "work of separation."[133] He cannot posit dwelling and labor as two pure and distinct orders of meaning, one characterized by "passivity" and the other by "activity," because the ego only recollects itself through *grasping itself* in the face of the feminine. The ego *must* "perpetual[ly]" *grasp itself* in grasping elements and the feminine, that is, *must possess them in-order-to* "accomplish" *his* separation.[134] As such, for "the very project of acquisition [to] presuppose the recollection of dwelling"—for labor to be *secondary*—it must necessarily be *first*.[135]

(4) *Theory* must *precede labor for labor to* "precede" *theory*. The ambiguity of theory we witnessed above, and which we review more closely below, is premised on this stark circle: on the one hand, Levinas wants to avoid idealism by "holding on to . . . the exteriority" of the elements.[136] "[T]o assume exteriority is to enter a relation with it such that the same determines the other while being determined by it."[137] On the other hand, the elements or "anonymous being" is fundamentally *nothing*: "Quality manifests itself in the elements as determining nothing."[138] Hence, the only "substance" or *real determination* the hand can grasp in labor is the *hand's own essence as grasp*. Levinas's actual descriptions suggest nothing but this: in labor the *contented ego grasps itself*, grasps itself *as hand*, as a "mastery, domination, [and] disposition."[139] In the last analysis, Levinas can only

"hold on to . . . the exteriority" of *lived-from* contents, elements, and the feminine—can only avoid idealism—by *grasping* and "holding on to" them: by *bestowing* them with a *meaning* all his *own*.

III.c. "Theory"

Is this analysis fair? This is a difficult question, and we will see why. On the one hand, Levinas sincerely does believe that life involves the meaning and nonsense we concretely experience as happiness and suffering, a meaning and nonsense that befall or *happen* to the ego and are not merely a result of its own cognitive, meaning-bestowing activity. We are originally bodies exposed to both joys and pains of the world. At one point, Levinas insists, "the ambiguity of the body is consciousness."[140] The problem is not that life involves ambiguity or that we are bodies, but that Levinas appears to posit life's ambiguities to *mask* the problems with *his own* structural determinations.[141] Happiness simply *cannot* be first in the order of meaning *according to his own descriptions*, because the self-sensing ego already requires (i) *others* to be enjoyed, (ii) the *duration* involved in the "memory [and] aspiration"[142] that constitutes the structure of enjoyment, (iii) the *ability* to sate its own needs implied by the *anticipated* sating, and (iv) the theoretical activity necessary for sating contents to be anticipated *as* sating contents, for example, berries instead of gravel, Rosemary instead of Oleander, or fresh instead of spoiled flesh. Levinas writes:

> The suffering of the recollected being, which is patience in the primary sense, pure passivity, is at the same time openness upon duration, postponement within this suffering. In patience the imminence of defeat, but also a distance in its regard, coincide.[143]

According to this very description, the genesis of the ego occurs not as "pure passivity," but as activity and passivity together, because duration has an active dimension. The circularity in Levinas's account is ultimately rooted in his insistence that the ego emerges as a "pure passivity" that "at the same time" opens upon duration. This "at the same time" belies the "pure" in "pure passivity." They actually emerge simultaneously, but then Levinas *imposes* an order of priority: first happiness then suffering, first dwelling then labor, and so forth. This problem is repeated at every descriptive level in his ego-analysis. For example, "Consciousness does not fall into the body—is not incarnated, it is disincarnation."[144] But also: "To regard language as an attitude of the mind does not amount to disincarnating it, but is precisely to account for its incarnate essence."[145] The *essence* of consciousness is *in*carnation and *dis*incarnation *at once*. When Levinas wants to distinguish his own method from idealism, consciousness is incarnate. When he wants to distinguish his method from ontology, consciousness is disincarnate. And rather than "playing by the [methodological] rules,"[146] or, say, conduct a plausible description of originary co-constitution that would render his descriptions non-arbitrary, he imbues his own methodology with ontological significance. In other words, *Levinas* is not being inconsistent, but rather the inconsistency is in *life itself*: "*Anterior posteriorly*: separation is not thus 'known,' it is thus *produced*."[147] Levinas's appeal to the "miraculous grasp" on substance *prior* to the entrance of theory bears out the problem.

III.D. "ANTERIOR POSTERIORLY"

Levinas aptly characterizes his own description of the ego's theoretical life as "absurd."[148] This absurdity is consequential for his overall claims, however. Far from being an "ontological structure" in its own right, his use of "anterior posteriorly" renders his various overall results *arbitrary*. Lets see why.

With the "anterior posteriorly," Levinas is out to describe the "possibility of a representation that is constitutive but already rests on the enjoyment of a real completely constituted . . ."[149] We need not read another word to question the "possibility" he is after. If constitution means bestowing wholeness or reidentifiable meaning on life and its contents, then it cannot be the case on *TI*'s own descriptive terms that *both* life *and* consciousness confer meaning in this way, at least not without making explicit or describing a plausible interactionist account of constitution. Levinas presents no such alternate account; therefore, his account of the "anterior posteriorly" is viciously contradictory. One the one hand, when distinguishing his method from Husserl and Heidegger, he allows the "anterior posteriorly" to signify as *nothing other* than a sort of empiricism: the contents "lived through" are said to be fully constituted "reals" that of themselves "constitute" the ego.[150] On the other hand, Levinas insists, "before [sensible content] impose[s] itself as an empirical fact, [it] conditions every empiricism, and the very structure of fact imposed by contemplation."[151] In other words, to distinguish his account from his phenomenological predecessors, he appeals *to the priority of* "*facts*," and to distinguish his account from empiricism, he claims *priority of meaning*. Whether the relations described are sown into the fabric of the world, or conferred by our minded activity, we are never told. When we hold Levinas's feet to the fire on the question of *structural* priority—as I demonstrated above: on his own terms sensibility actually presupposes all the meanings asserted to be subsequent to it—Levinas can respond: "in concrete life sensibility *in fact* comes first." When we hold Levinas's feet to the fire on this very claim to *empirical* priority, and point out (a) this bars him from attributing "substantiality" to sensible contents in his own account, and (b) this move commits him to a sort of empiricism, then Levinas will respond: "of course not, sensibility is a 'condition' for every empiricism, it is phenomenologically originary or first in the *order of meaning*." As if by magic, *substance* leaps whole from Levinas's hat to *simultaneously* (i) provide him "real" others to "constitute" the sensible ego, and (ii) to separate the ego from its others so it can subsequently "constitute" these very "constituting" others.[152] The big question here is *why?* Why insist on radical "separation" that is everywhere asserted but nowhere actually described in his ego analysis?

III.e. "Conceptless Individual"

Answers to these questions become evident in a close review of the text, and involve a correlative equivocation to that which we just reviewed. Before examining this correlative equivocation, it's worth dwelling for a moment on Levinas's possible motivations. The first sentence opening Levinas's ego analysis reads: "In describing the metaphysical relation as disinterested, as disengaged from all participation . . ."[153] "Participation," it must be said, is the fundamental "enemy" that orients the logic of *TI as a whole*. Levinas endeavors to describe the ego in such a way that strips it of all traces of concepts or categories. His fervent desire to avoid "participation" is ultimately why he does *not* make use of dialectical, constitutive, or projective means to describe the co-originality of sensibility, labor, and theory, means that might enable a coherent account of both their distinctness and mutual dependence. By positing sensibility as *prior* to labor and theory, he claims to have slain tradition in one stroke, that is, he believes that sensibility empowers a description of the ego free of categorial or existential "participation." Has he succeeded?

Levinas is ultimately conducting a somewhat complex game, and in such a way that masks the contradictions I identify. In his opening descriptions of the sensible ego, he writes: "We are catching sight of the possibility of rendering the unicity of the I intelligible."[154] We need not read another word to realize he is *rendering intelligible* that which, by his own insistence, is absolutely and irreducibly *unintelligible*. The uniqueness of the ego is said to consist "in existing without having a genus, without being the individuation of a concept." He immediately stresses: "The refusal of the concept is not the resistance to generalization of the *tode ti*, which is on the same plane of the concept—and by which the concept is defined, as by an antithetical term."[155] He insists that the "unicity" he has is mind here is not a *formal* specification, not Aristotle's "this here" of a brute existent. He continues:

> Here the refusal of the concept is not only an aspect of its being, but its whole content; it is interiority. This refusal of the concept drives the being that refuses it into the dimension of interiority. It is at home with itself. The I is thus the mode in which the break-up of totality, which leads to the presence of the absolutely other, is concretely accomplished.[156]

Notice what is happening here: he is summoning phenomenological concreteness and the transcendental logic and generative categories it involves *against* formal logic, and the *tode ti* as a formal specification. Yet by claiming that the "refusal of the concept" composes the ego's "whole being," he in fact implies nothing other than the inscrutable "this here now" he disavows. Levinas believes he has twisted free from formal logic by *characterizing* the "this here now" *as* enjoyment: "it is not formal, it is lived concretely *as* enjoyment." He does this phenomenologically by positing an *order of priority*: enjoyment is "first" with respect to theory. Once this *priority* is asserted, Levinas then believes he has twisted free from classical phenomenology, and does so by appeal to the singularity of formal logic. Levinas's phenomenological method "defies" formal logic by way of transcendental logic, and then "defies" transcendental logic by way of formal logic. When the logician points out that singularity is a formal specification, Levinas responds as a phenomenologist with "it is lived concretely *as* enjoyment." When the phenomenologist points out that the meaning ascribed to the ego *as* enjoyment necessarily involves generality, Levinas will respond, "no, it's pre-theoretical, it exceeds ontology, or is, in a word, *singular*." But what does the priority of sensibility to theory really do here?

Levinas always insists, "The unicity of the I, its status as conceptless individual, would disappear in this *participation* in what exceeds it."[157] He incessantly seeks to "separate" the immediacy of lived individuality from the categories that make it legible. Does the immediacy he summons really function as he wants it to? For example, how are we to interpret the following?

> The need for food doesn't have existence as its goal, but food. . . . need is naïve. In enjoyment I am absolutely for myself. Egoist without reference to the Other, I am alone without solitude, innocently egoist and alone. Not against the Others, . . . but entirely deaf to the others, outside of all communication and refusal to communicate—without ears, like a hungry stomach.[158]

He here describes a particular sort of immediacy, namely, a hungry ego urgently seeking food. But if sensibility really consists of being "outside of all communication and refusal to communicate," outside of language and reflection, then its hunger and happiness cannot *mean anything for it*. Here the ego is simply incapable of experiencing meaning or non-meaning, or in other words: *is not an ego at all*. Who could object to this description? A Buddhist or a naive materialist might happily grant this immediacy before explaining the ego away as an epiphenomenon of chemical processes or as conventional illusion. The only sense "conceptless individual" can have is this: an entity that *lacks concepts* or the capacity for concept creation; an ameba, in other words, or any other entity that conducts itself solely for the satisfaction of immediate needs. If, on the other hand, we accept the meaning of enjoyment as Levinas presents it, then we already *know* that he is not simply describing *his own* enjoyment, or any particular person's enjoyment, but *enjoyment in general* as the very meaning of *egoity*. He is conducting an existential phenomenology that describes *the genesis of the ego (in general) and the categories that articulate its meaning*. Levinas refuses to call them categories, or even "existentials," but that's in fact what's happening. Levinas knows full well that is what he is doing, which is why he later explicitly states that "Happiness is a principle of individuation . . ." and "a universal category of the empirical."[159] As such, "the refusal of the concept" *is not* "the whole content" of the being of the ego: as a "universal category," happiness *identifies others* capable of this experience and establishes a class of entities who *share* in it.[160] On his own terms, sensibility is precisely one way the ego orients and individuates itself from its surroundings, and from others it will come to enjoy *with*. The singularity of the ego precisely consists in that no else can *immediately* enjoy or inhabit its sentience *for it*, in the first person. If I come to be happy *for* my neighbor when he receives a raise, I do so *as*, precisely, my self. He and I do not "disappear" in the happiness we *share*, as in some straw-leviathan called "participation." I can refuse to be happy for him; I can envy him, or simply ignore him. Without the categorial or "existential" status of enjoyment, I could do none of these things: only shudder and flinch like an ameba. Not only does the ego *always already know* the *difference* between her neighbor's happiness and her own, she also knows the difference between the experience of happiness and its communicability. Levinas writes: "When the I is identified with reason, taken as the power of thematization and objectification, it loses its very *ipseity*. To represent to oneself is to empty oneself of one's subjective substance and to insensibilize enjoyment."[161] Communication can, to be sure, "insensibilize" enjoyment; for example: I can attend an incredibly boring lecture at the "happiness studies" department; I can write a note to my wife, "I enjoyed our date last evening"; or I can read section II of Levinas's own *Totality and Infinity*. In all three cases, I am not immediately in a moment of enjoyment, and in that sense it is momentarily "insensibilized." But I also might enjoy the lecture on enjoyment, my wife might enjoy my *thoughtful* note, and I in fact enjoy Levinas's phenomenological descriptions of enjoyment (while not enjoying the gratuitous "logic" he interposes). When I consider the meaning of enjoyment, I am not alienated from myself because others around me happen to enjoy themselves too or because there happens to be others who *resemble me*.

In the last analysis, Levinas's whole account of enjoyment and dwelling belies the "radicality" he asserts for *ipseity*. That he has "insensibilized" enjoyment—written a book about it—that he has explicitly presented these analyses as a phenomenological description of meaning of the ego (*in general*) already suggests that the *secret is out*: "whatever transfigurations this egoism will receive from speech, it is for the happiness constitutive of its very egoism that the I who speaks pleads."[162] Happiness yields an enduring or repeatable meaning, a meaning that can be "insensibilized," which is just to say: communicated, shared, recalled when I am bored or in pain, written down in a book, and so forth. Levinas performs the categorial or existential "participation" he is out to escape by simply engaging in phenomenological description.[163]

IV. Conclusion

As I have shown, Levinas's analysis of the "Same" is viciously circular. His own descriptions disclose that sensibility actually presupposes the various meanings held to be subsequent to it. I located the root of this incoherence in his account of the so-called "anterior posteriorly" structure of theory, shown to be a question-begging confusion of *empirical* and *phenomenological* priority, such that against phenomenology he essentially claims an empirical realism, and against empirical realism he claims phenomenology. I further demonstrated a correlative equivocation in his account of the singularity of the ego in light of his own utilized method.

In conclusion, I underline the climactic tragedy—and irony—of Levinas's gratuitous descriptions. In his eagerness to distinguish his account from transcendental (Husserl) or ontological (Heidegger) phenomenology, the ego of Levinas's actual descriptions can only ever approach the other with *empty hands*. By reducing the elements and the feminine to *nothing*, the ego has *nothing to give*. Moreover, if the ego is "a hungry stomach," and if to "recognize the Other is to recognize a hunger," then both self and other, famished as they are, must *jointly* await a so-called "miraculous grasp" to sate them; a grasp that does not reduce non-human (and non-male) "others," and the practical and theoretical life they occur for, *to mere straw*.[164]

Chapter 2

Of Form and Face in *Totality and Infinity*

> Love your neighbor as yourself.
>
> —Leviticus 19:18

I. Introduction

The conclusions of my last chapter are clear: 1) Levinas's account of "pre-theoretical" labor depends on a gratuitous and phenomenologically unjustified positing of *substance*; 2) on Levinas's own descriptions, his ego analysis is caught in vicious circle. Happiness and sensibility in general actually presuppose the meanings asserted to be subsequent to them; and 3) the arbitrarity of (1) and circularity of (2) are rooted in the contradiction at play in the attempt to *phenomenologically describe* an asserted *radical "singularity."* The basic aim of this chapter is to thoroughly examine section III of *TI* and explore the question: does Levinas's account of the face *rectify* the problems in his ego analysis, or do the problems in his ego analysis *recur* in his analysis of the face? Because Levinas ultimately seeks to ground theory in the meaning that issues in the face, this might mean that his ethics in general will clarify the status of theory within the overall phenomenology performed in the text.

As has been my practice thus far, I systematically ignore the numerous debates, differentiations, and polemical asides Levinas conducts with other philosophers, unless their treatment is deemed necessary to clarify Levinas's own position on a matter. I continue to analyze what Levinas *actually* does, rather than what he might have *wished* to do. To practice immanent critique fairly, I first perform a charitable and detailed reconstruction of his analysis. In what follows, I show 1) Levinas's description of the face is viciously circular, that is, the face's "revelation" depends on already posited form, a positing the face is *subsequently* said to "ground"; 2) Levinas posits a "real" human biological genus in a methodologically arbitrary way. I argue (3) that the circularity of (1) and arbitrarity of (2) is concealed by what I call the "*a posteriori anteriorily*" structure of ethics, and that this "structure" is premised in a viciously indeterminate account of theory in general.

II. *Prima Facia*: Preliminary Considerations

As we have seen in chapter 1, enjoyment, dwelling, and labor each has an ecstatic character. With each layer of meaning, the ego encounters and absorbs "others": contents *lived from*, the feminine, and the elements. The ego "comes to itself outside of itself" or *originates* in the self-sensing that occurs *through* the enjoyment of need in happiness, the contentment of welcome in dwelling, the expansion of dwelling's familiarity through the power of labor and possession, and the enhancement of this power by theory, for example, technology. This is the structure of "separated being": that is the happy, sated, content, and powerful ego. Though the separated ego "holds on to" the "exteriority" of the "others" it consumes and possesses, the "otherness" of these "others" is only *relative* and, Levinas claims, ultimately "fallacious," because they are always already *affectively* identified by the ego in enjoyment and *actively grasped* in labor and theory.[1] The Same consists in the "satisfaction of needs," with the essential happiness and relative security this involves.[2] The otherness of what I consume and of what I work on can be affectively, practically, and theoretically overcome. With the face, something very different is held to emerge.

The face "puts the I in question."[3] The meaning erupting in and as the face occurs as an intentionality *aimed at* the ego, as a *putting into question* its fundamental *contentment*. The alterity heralded in the face of the other "resists" the ecstatic movement of ego-identification. Unlike lived-from contents, the otherness of the intersubjective Other is apparently *not* absorbed in enjoyment; unlike the feminine, the character of this intentionality is *not welcoming*, but *puts into question*; and unlike the elements, the otherness of the intersubjective Other does *not yield to* possession, but is said to "paralyze the very power of power."[4] Levinas insists that the negative character of "resistance"—the "nots" in my preceding sentences—*ought not* be construed ontologically as a negative term that relationally functions to establish the ego's identity, as in Hegel, for example. To so construe the "not" would allegedly "destroy transcendence" by putatively obliterating the "separation" of both the ego and the Other by either 1) reducing the Other to a moment in the ego's self-identification, or 2) reducing the ego to a mere moment of the Other, as in, for example, a naturalistic or pantheistic metaphysics. And in what would amount to the same thing, Levinas insists that we *ought not* take the above "nots" in a purely *theoretical* way, for example, as occasioning a progressively more thorough logico-descriptive specification of the Same or the Other, because any such movement necessarily terminates in either a theoretical Subject in the idealist sense or Being in the realist sense. The otherness of the Other is held to be *absolute*. As absolute, what meaning can the Other have for the ego, which is just to ask: how does an absolute Other precisely *relate* to the ego? How does this relation "obtain" or come to *affect* the ego?

First, the mode of relation operative here is what Levinas formally specifies as an "unrelating relation," as "in relation while separated."[5] Next, this relation occurs as "The presence of a being not entering into, but overflowing, the sphere of the same" and this "determines its 'status' as infinite."[6] The "content" of the idea of infinity necessarily "overflows" its concept for finite minds. The absolute Other is said to come to *affect* the ego precisely in this mode of *overflowing*, and as we will see, *affects* it as speech, discourse, or call. Finally, because the *meaning* of this "overflowing" *ought not* be construed as theoretical or ontological, and hence not remain determined by its negative character, Levinas insists that it occurs as an absolutely original and fundamental positivity: the meaning of this "overflowing" or *surplus* is irreducibly *ethical*.[7]

II.a. The Face

> *The idea of infinity is produced in the opposition of conversation, in sociality.*[8]

In the *speech* proper to conversation, or what Levinas names *discourse*, a "divergence . . . inevitably opens between the other as my theme and the other as my interlocutor . . ."[9] Here, the Other becomes

> emancipated from the theme that seemed a moment to hold him, [and] forthwith contests the meaning I ascribe to my interlocutor. The formal structure of language thereby announces the

ethical inviolability of the Other and, without an odor of the "numinous," his "holiness." The fact that the face maintains a relation with me by discourse does not range him in the same; he remains absolute within relation.[10]

The face emerges here as my interlocutor: *the face of the Other human being*. "The face resists possession, resists my powers," but does so positively in "the transcendence of expression."[11] The face does not oppose the ego on the same plane, for example, as a struggle for recognition: "The expression of the face" *defies* "my ability for power."[12] The Other "can oppose me . . . , not [as] a force of resistance, but the very *unforeseeableness* of his reaction."[13] Levinas writes:

> This infinity, stronger than murder, already resists us in his face, is his face, is the primordial expression, is the first word: "you shall not commit murder." The infinite paralyzes power by its infinite resistance to murder, which, firm and insurmountable, gleams in the face of the Other, in the total nudity of his defenseless eyes, in the nudity and absolute openness of the Transcendent. There is here a relation not with a very great resistance, but with something absolutely other: the resistance of what has no resistance—ethical resistance.[14]

"The epiphany of the face" irrupts here in a descriptively rich *double asymmetry*: the face appears as both (i) *elevation* or *height* and (ii) *destitution*, and both of these together delineate the (iii) *nudity* of the face.[15] Let's look at each moment by turns, while underlining that we cannot ultimately abstract them as discrete moments without losing the overall sense Levinas is describing.

(i) The Other's *height* manifests as "primordial expression," or "the first word: 'you shall not commit murder.'"[16] The face presents an absolute "resistance" to my powers: to being an object of enjoyment or a mere matter to be possessed, but does so positively as a *first meaning*, or *as the very possibility for meaning*. Levinas writes, "[speech] produces the commencement of intelligibility, initiality itself, principality, royal sovereignty, which commands unconditionally. The principle is possible only as command."[17] The "height" of the face is produced as an *unconditional command*, as an *absolute obligation* to "not murder." But this "royal sovereignty" only signifies thus in (ii) *destitution*. The Other is a "royal highness" only because she is also *destitute*, *vulnerable*, or "defenseless," *exposed* to hunger, suffering, and ultimately death.[18] The "royal sovereignty" that commands is none other than the *helpless*: "the Stranger, the widow, and the orphan."[19] With the height and destitution of the face so delineated, we can see what Levinas precisely means in calling it a *"total nudity."*[20]

(iii) The *nudity* of the face consists in its "straightforwardness."[21] The face *overflows* its empirical visage or "plastic image," and the obligation it invests *exceeds* and *precedes* the contest of truth that in fact characterizes discourse about the world (and the persuasion this inevitably involves).[22] The resistance of her "don't kill me!" and the *ethical* force of his "please help!" are *urgent, immediate,* "straightforward," or in a word: *sincere*. In precisely these senses is the face *nude*: "a resistance that has no resistance—ethical resistance."[23] The nudity of the face designates the manner in which a "divergence . . . inevitably opens between the other as my theme and the other as my interlocutor . . . ," or in other words: delineates the way the Other remains irreducible to his empirical traits, substantial form, or any other empirical or ontological determinant that would capture her identity.[24] The Other does not coincide with her empirical or ontological "image," but precisely, as face, presents an

> essential coinciding of the existent and the signifier. Signification is not added to the existent, . . . to signify is not equivalent to presenting oneself as a sign, but to present oneself, that is, to present oneself in person.[25]

The face's nudity consists in presenting itself to the ego properly *in person*, or in other words: as, precisely, *itself*. "The face of the Other at each moment destroys and overflows the plastic image it leaves me . . . It does not manifest itself by these qualities, but *kath-auto*, [the face] *expresses itself*."[26] The face signifies as my interlocutor, as the other who always already addresses me first, always *calls to me* in thematizing the world. The face with whom I speak is held to never be reducible to a moment of my own self-identity or to larger term we both might inhabit; which is just to say that the face is not reducible to the world or the contents we converse about. Levinas writes:

> Language thus conditions the functioning of rational thought: it gives a commencement in being, a primary identity of signification in the face of him who speaks, that is, who presents himself by ceaselessly undoing the equivocation of his own image, his verbal signs.[27]

The face *opens* the "space of meaning" as an irreducibly dialogical situation.[28] Whether we are giving and receiving reasons or giving and receiving gifts, we do so only because of the primordial ethical meaning—*the givenness* or *donation*—of the face. The identity of the other remains irreducible to discourse about the world, to the "plastic image" of either (a) her empirical face, (b) her purported membership of the species "homo sapient," or (c) her alleged identity presented as, say, "female sex," "Black," "transgendered," "Buddhist," "communist," "child of God," or any other descriptor whose meaning would involve theoretical or ontological mediations. Even when a face *tells me*, "My name is Jane, I am a transgendered, Muslim woman from Timbuktu," her *own* factual and ontological—or passive and active—self-determinations are "destroyed," or better: *exceeded*, in the meaning she presents in simply addressing me. Her face first signifies not *as* anything she might tell me *about* herself; it rather signifies as an inaugurating "me": Jane signifies as and from herself. Discourse about being and the possibility of true and false judgment—*the possibility of theory*—depends on the meaning issuing in the face. The face attends the necessary "masks" she *overflows* in her height and destitution, attends her equivocal "image" by, for example, clarifying what she means when we are talking about the Syrian Revolution, the relative quality of Turkish tobacco, or the injustices of a particular political platform. Such conversations can come to acquire a conflictual character, but as the debate ensues I am always already grasped by my interlocutor's vulnerable command, by the sincerity of his or her visage, and remain so even if he or she comes to argue unfairly, or manifests actual insincerity in the course of conversation, for example, by reasoning fallaciously, or even rejecting reasonableness altogether in an arbitrary affirmation of the superiority of his or her own position. The demand for or the *authority* of reasonableness in a conflictual situation is dependent on the primordial *a-reasonableness* of the face: even my enemy is a vulnerable-height enjoining me to not murder and to attend her suffering; even my enemy exhibits a face. In just this way, "War presupposes peace, . . . [war] does not present the first event of encounter."[29] Levinas writes:

> The relation with the face . . . is nonetheless my Idea, a commerce. But the relation is produced without violence, in peace with this absolute alterity. The "resistance" of the other does not do violence to me, does not act negatively; it has a positive structure: ethical.[30]

The formal structure of language already signifies as peace. Peace does not necessarily signify in yielding to the force of better reasons, or in total agreement about the character of the world. My "no" to our building's Muslim security guard, who invites me to convert to Islam, and the unfolding debates we conduct about the meanings of human life, are not an invitation to war. The conflictual character of the disagreement presupposes and exhibits peace: we are not killing each other; he still treats me with kindness and generosity across this conflict, I seek to respect his commitments even while not adopting all of them myself. We remain friends across this conflict. This example suggests how the face precedes and opens the space of reasons, and is not itself a reason.

Why "a-reasonable"? Because I cannot answer this question without performative contradiction—without transforming the face into a reason—I proceed by way of description. The face appears not *within* the space of meaning but "above" and "below" it as its condition: from "below" as the *irreducibly irrational* character of *mortal suffering*, and "from above" as the *exorbitant command* to not murder and to attend the other's sufferings. This first meaning on which all others depend *ought not* be derived, Levinas insists, from anything else because that would reduce the other to the same, evince the stability of an ontological identity, or at the very least exhibit a momentary coincidence of the other with her worldly "image," where she would no longer express only herself (*kath-auto*), but signify or express as a putative truth of some kind. For Levinas, if one must ask the question: why ought I not murder? or why feed the hungry?, one is already lost, or rather: *inhuman*. We always already "know why," and we apparently always already know that ethics is not a knowledge: that might does not make right, that the way things are isn't necessarily the way things ought to be. Only because the ego is originally *put into question* can theoretical questions be raised. Only because the face *gratuitously gives* (meaning), is any other meaning given at all.

The a-rational character is especially evident in the exorbitance of the responsibility the face invests. The infinite alterity of the other invests an infinite and absolute responsibility. Levinas writes:

> *The infinity of responsibility denotes not its actual immensity, but a responsibility increasing in the measure that it is assumed*; duties become greater in the measure they are accomplished. The better I accomplish my duty the fewer rights I have; the more I am

just the more guilty I am. The I . . . is confirmed in its singularity by purging itself [of its self-centeredness], purges itself interminably, and is confirmed precisely in this incessant effort to purge itself. This is termed goodness.[31]

The ego's responsibility is beyond its capacity to fulfill. Helping my neighbor does not *satisfy* the responsibility due her, but *increases* it. This exorbitance can appear to be mere hyperbole until we think about it concretely. Say my neighbor is a single mother with a disabled child teetering on the brink of poverty. I give as much as I can of my resources: money, food, job references, invitations to dinner, spending time at the park, baby-sitting, and so forth. When I run up against the limits of what I can give as delineated by, say, my own family's budget, participating in a political demonstration, or money earmarked to my mosque or to the Socialist Party, I still feel a *pull*, a *twinge*, a sense that this precious little girl is owed more than I can reasonably offer, owed even more than I *in fact unreasonably give*, or in other words: is owed *everything*. The *gratuity* of her disability is met by a *gratuitous obligation* to give, and the *injustice* of her family's poverty only comes to signify *as* injustice in light of the exorbitant responsibility she invests me with: as vulnerable, commanding, and sincere, as referring to herself *kath-auto* before she can signify as, say, physically unlucky or an instance of the injustice of the capitalist system, or the like.

Levinas insists that expression "precedes the coordinating effects visible to a third party."[32] It *opens*, and does not appears *in*, the space of meaning, is not a reason, but the meaning that opens and conditions the giving of reasons and whatever other meanings that might emerge in the world as an encompassing space of meaning. The face appears only from a first-person perspective: only as *one lived life encountering an Other does the face-to-face affect us*.

What of the contents talked about—*thematized*—in discourse, or in other words, what of theory and ontology? Theory proper only emerges with what Levinas calls the Third Party:

> The third party looks at me in the eyes of the Other—language is justice; the epiphany of the face opens humanity. . . . [The face's] equality . . . consists in referring to the third party, thus present at the encounter, whom in the midst of destitution the Other already serves. He comes to join me.[33]

Theory becomes possible when beyond the ego and the other, "other others" enter consideration. After referring only to itself, the face refers to all others, to "the whole of humanity which looks at us" through her eyes.[34] With the Third Party, a face can be attributed to every other human being, including, apparently, "one's self."[35] Levinas writes:

> Equality is produced where the other commands the same and reveals himself to the same in responsibility; otherwise it is but an abstract idea and word. It cannot detach from the welcome of the face, of which it is an abstract moment.[36]

The universal attribution of a face to all of humanity remains grounded in the properly original or *lived* face-to-face he's been describing. We can thus identify the injustice of her poverty, the gratuity of her physical disability, and so forth. But, as I underlined above, the equality introduced does not reduce the "asymmetries" of responsibility: my responsibility always and *forever* exceeds the formal distribution of duties and rights that ethics makes possible in justice, is always already a responsibility *in excess* of what can reasonably be expected.

All this being said, Levinas insists that the face does not destroy freedom or thought or "freedom of thought." The face properly founds thinking in yielding the *intersubjectivity*—or humanity—that thinks, and it renders freedom *meaningful* by calling it to responsibility. This responsibility does not necessarily constrain one to decide for this worldly or ontological regime over that, to prefer this style over that, or to conduct this project over that. Freedom remains but is constrained in that whatever ontology I decide for, whatever style I prefer or create, whatever project I take up, I do so in a world of which I am not the sole origin. I do so with and for others who are not only or merely expressions of my own preferred ontological meaning, not only or merely others who furnish me with books to read or paintings to contemplate, not only or merely others *simply there* as *my* audience, *my* readership, *my* "market," or *my* enemies, but as others who are *faced*, who exhibit a meaning all their own: *who signify kath-auto*, and do so *in excess of* the various ways they come to signify as something worldly, whether as "female sex," "child," "disabled," "victim of injustice," and so forth.

Given the gratuitous or a-rational character of the face and its surplus over the equality that issues in the third, its meaning *ought not* be explained by or grounded in any larger context. It signifies against the whole, and its meaning is solely anchored in itself. In one sense, such a meaning can only ever be asserted, because to explain it by or ground it in something else would obliterate its *kath-auto* character. Nevertheless, Levinas seeks to *show* how this meaning comes to bear on the ego. I have tried my best to faithfully repeat this showing, but it's important to underline the structural determination that renders this a-rationality *presentable*. The Same and the Other—as ego and the face—signify as *singularities* or "individualities," and for Levinas, singularity is fundamentally temporal in character. Recalling above: as happy, the ego *is* its instant of enjoyment; as intimately content, the ego *is* its duration as dwelling; as possessing, the ego *is* itself across the interface of home and elements, *is* itself through time or across the beginnings and endings inherent to action. With the advent of the face, the ego is held to encounter something it utterly and absolutely *is not*. The face signifies absolutely as a temporality apparently irreducible to *my own* temporality, which is just say: *my own experience*. Just as the elements signify as an "absolute . . . antiquity" and an "uncertain future"—just as the elements *precede* and "keep going passed" representation and theory—so the face also signifies as both "unforessableness" and "a past that [has] not traversed the present of representation."[37] The face delineates a "before" and "after" the ego encounters as irreducibly temporal limits. These limits are *limits to experience* in general: self and other cannot inhabit each other's experience from a first-person point of view or definitively represent, from a third-person perspective, their experience in descriptive categories always already provisionally "objective," that is: categories always *open to question*. Each one's experience is properly its *own*. We can only question as a being originarily *put into question*, we can only question thanks to ethics. When self and other come to "share" an experience, they do so precisely *as* self and other, and apparently not as two moments of a generality that precedes them. As singularities, the ego and the other are held to name two distinct *temporal "flows"* that cannot sustainably be reduced to one another or to the time of the world. Levinas is not arguing for the immortality of the soul: the ego and other are mortal. When the other dies, my responsibility to her or him does not cease, but comes to signify differently, for example, as honoring his memory as dead when he is no longer available to face me, or by doing justice to his philosophical position as I read and argue with the books that bear his name. Singularity names a *becoming* that theory inevitably and momentarily "cuts into," as it were, by proposing him as a "man," a "father," a "veteran of the Second World War," a "surviving victim of the Holocaust," a "French phenomenologist," and all the predicates we ascribe to the name "Emmanuel Levinas." But none of those predicates fully and finally captures what he was to the women and men who actually faced him; nor do they fully and finally render him the *unique one* he was for us who read *in his wake*.

III. Critique

Levinas's analysis of the face constitutes a fascinating contribution to phenomenology. But, just as we witnessed in his ego-analysis, we must ultimately distinguish between the meanings he beautifully describes and *the transcendental work and structural priority* he seeks to attribute to it. Levinas's ethics is also caught in a vicious circle. The circularity in his ego-analysis came into view by analyzing his (1) gratuitous positing of substance, (2) question-begging determinations of theory, and ultimately (3) the performative contradiction inherent in the attempt to phenomenologically describe an asserted "absolute singularity." The circularity in his ego-analysis recurs at the ethical level in very precise and homologous ways: in a (1a) late and gratuitous declaration of "the existence of a biological genus," (2a) a still indeterminate account of theory, (3a) the contradiction in play in his utilization of form. Let's look at each at each in more detail.[38]

III.A. The Miracle of a "Biological Genus"

Just as "substance" miraculously leapt from Levinas's hat in the ego-analysis he performs, a correlative miracle is performed in his analysis of the face and the sociality it is said to open:

> Like a shunt every social relation leads back to the presentation of the other to the same without the intermediary of any image or sign, solely by the expression of the face. When taken to be like a genus that unites like individuals the essence of society is lost sight of. There *does indeed exist a human race as a biological genus, and the common function men* [sic] *may exercise in the world* as a totality permits the applying to them a common concept. But the human community instituted by language, where interlocutors remain absolutely separated, does not constitute the unity of genus.[39]

In the preceding 200-plus pages, the entire discourse of *TI* seemed premised on an all-out assault on ontology, totality, and theory. We now learn that ethics appears to *validate* "a common function men [sic] exercise in the world." This totalization is just what the face is supposed to contest. Levinas declares the above to be the case in an apparent attempt to acknowledge biological "reality," while also distinguishing the *meaning* ethics invests in a contrast to this "reality." The face emerges in the divergence between interlocutor and "theme," or in the difference between *talking to* and *talking about* him or her. Does the meaning of the face "destroy" the identification with the empirical face that speaks to me, that is, is her biological "reality" *real*? Or is it merely "plastic"? There is nothing in Levinas's descriptions that gives a clue as to how such questions might even be *treated*, let alone potentially answered, and this is indicative of the larger problems in his descriptions. Before broaching these larger problems, let's look more closely at what this biological declaration means for his overall account.

As should be clear, on Levinas's own descriptive terms, the face-to-face encounter is *always already* structured by "theory" or "ontology." Before the other exhibits a sense that "exceeds" her biological form, she is necessarily *identified with* her biological form. This simply means that on the basis of his own description, the other must (always) already be "reduced to the same" for a putative "ethical" excess to appear. Without having *first* been so identified, no contrast would be possible between her "plastic [or *real*?] image," and no ethical "excess" could be detected in her face. Moreover, not only does this identity structure the face-to-face encounter, but this identity necessarily *survives* and functions *through* this encounter. This simply means that the other's brute and passive individuality does absolutely *nothing* to contest the fact that she and I are of the *same* biological genus, and this *co-belonging* is *assumed* in Levinas's own descriptions of the face (as "there exists a biological genus . . ." makes plain). The other very well *could* contest this identification by, for example, *telling me*: "true humanity is pure spirit free of all animality." She very well *could* contest a particular construction of this identity by *performing* a subversion of it, for example: growing a beard, undergoing gender-reassignment surgery, or conducting other culturally mediated subversions. In both cases, the contestation occurs at the level of *theme* or at the level of *practice*; the contestation does *not* occur by simply tilting one's ear while earnestly squinting at her face. If we momentarily grant that "there does indeed exist a biological genus" was a mere slip of the Levinas's pen, it would not alter the structural point I analyze here. Take his own phenomenological descriptions of the ego, for example. His beautiful description of the face's height and destitution precisely *depends* on an *initial* "reducing the other to the same." The imperative—"help!"—*depends* on the ego *having already undergone suffering* such that it *knows* what it means *to be* destitute and vulnerable. Levinas himself holds as much when he's forced to consider non-human alterity: "It is because we, as human, *know* what suffering is that we can have this obligation."[40] Likewise, the imperative "don't kill me!" would be completely incomprehensible to an ego that does not *know* what it means to *care for its own being*. The absoluteness we may want to attribute to these imperatives manifestly cannot be derived from or somehow co-extensive with an "absolute" alterity, because Levinas's actual descriptions nowhere reveal such alterity. His descriptions rather *show*: in face-to-face conversation, the ego *always already knows* that the other is *another ego*, an ego that, *like me*, thinks, works, and feels. The other ego might think, work, and feel *differently* than I do, but think, work, and feel *she does*. Even if we grant that the face retains an originary dimension, its *meaning is not purely self-standing*. On Levinas's own terms, the face's demand does not *only* refer to itself, but *also* refers to the ego's own suffering and to the ego's own *self-care*. On Levinas's own description, every face-to-face encounter is structured by the fundamentally *stable* and *unaltered* senses he described (i) in his ego-analysis, and (ii) as a "real" [or "plastic"?] biological genus. At most, Levinas's descriptions suggest that the other's identity *ought not* be reduced *merely* to her biological form or *solely* to her egoic being. They certainly do *not* entail or justify the brute assertion that her face totally "destroys" her "plastic [or *real*?] image," or that her brute individuality, all by itself, in any way contests Levinas's own *structurally determinative identifications*. For such a contestation to occur, a *different* (performative and thematic) *description* would be required.

Next, to stress this point in a different way: sincerity is not purely *ethical* expression, but *internally* depends on ontological mediations. For example, to return to our disabled child above: if her individuality really "destroyed" her plastic image, and if her expression were veritably *kath-auto*, then her physical disability, her victimization by the capitalist system, and so forth would be *wholly irrelevant* to the fundamental responsibility due her. In my attempt to give a sympathetic reconstruction of Levinas's meaning above, the excessive sense of responsibility I described actually *depends* on so-called "plastic" images: "physically unlucky" and "victim of capitalism," and so forth. If ontology, theory, or worldly determinations as such were "destroyed" or totally left behind in her pure ethical expression, there would be no *difference* between the responsibility due her and that due to, say, Vladimir Putin. If we face Putin instead of our disabled child, and supply a relevant description of the particularities of Putin's life situation, my above sympathetic description of *excessive* responsibility completely falls to the ground. That Putin is an individual, that he will one day die, and that he experiences bodily suffering does *not* suggest I am "infinitely responsible" to him. Granting that I also owe Putin some sort of moral regard, it is clear that certain factual determinants lend *force* to the suggestion that I owe the disabled girl *in excess* of what I can reasonably give, a *force* that *disappears* if I am instead faced by Mr. Putin.[41]

Finally, the other's expression does not only involve the passivity of suffering but also involves an *active* dimension. Let's return to Jane, our transgendered Muslim woman from Timbuktu. Jane *tells me* who she regards herself to be; she seeks to *perform* or live a life that creatively repeats religious meaning. In the face-to-face discourse we conduct, Jane might *regard me* as created by Allah, and might *tell me* I am valuable and due respect and aid for that reason. Even if I reject her religious account of humanity, and resist her appeal to commit myself to the meaning she claims for herself, I am nevertheless confronted with her own *active commitments,* her *will-to-be in a particular way.* The responsibility due her has not only to do with the passivity inherent to her suffering, but also with her *will to live* a *particular* life, and the will *to think the meaning* of her life in a particular way. Her *choice, commitment,* and *reflective grasp* of meaning are not a priori "destroyed" by her merely passive and brute individuality. Her choice and commitment—*her will*—are signaled in her expression. If we bracket the actual content of her own account, or the *particular* way she *creatively performs* and *thematizes* fundamental meaning, her *will-to-live* and her *will-to-name* meaning and its limits remain at play in expression.[42] When Levinas writes, "attestation of one's self is possible only as a face, that is, as speech," he not only implicitly attributes this active dimension to the face, but he also implicitly generalizes egoic ascriptions and ontological determinants to what is supposed to be purely ethical meaning.[43] On Levinas's own description, rather than signifying *kath-auto*, the face says something like this: "*I am* an ego who labors, dwells, and feels, I *belong* to a biological genus," and *simultaneously,* "I am *not only* an ego who labors, dwells, and feels; I do *not only* belong to a biological genus, I *also* refer to myself *as a distinct individual.*" On Levinas own descriptive terms, the *face does not refer to itself alone,* it *depends* on a *general egoic being* and *universal ontological determinants* to meaningfully manifest *as* face, and even if we grant that it does signal an individual dimension, and that this individuality must be reckoned in the theories of meaning or ontologies we construct, its clear that Levinas is asserting equivocal and mutually exclusive determinations in his account, and in such a way that renders his larger claims question begging.

III.b. Expression Kath-Heteron

Just as we saw in his account of "substance" above, Levinas entitles himself to a gratuitously posited "common function among men [sic]," which ethics apparently *validates*. Because the explicit meaning asserted to issue in the face is presented as a *total contestation* of just such a "common function," why, in spite of everything, does he declare a "real" [or "plastic"?] biological genus just now?[44] Why is ethics said to *chastise* and "destroy" such a function while *simultaneously* also *validating* it? Before proposing answers to such questions, we should underline that Levinas ultimately falls victim to the vicious circularity we saw above, and any possible defense of his position must ultimately take on a question-begging character. For example, to defend Levinas, we might say something like this: "a biological genus is a *pure* empirical determination, a determination that explicitly acknowledges and *depends on* transcendental ethical meaning. As such, acknowledging biological 'reality' does no violence to the other *as other*, because the other exceeds and does not (fully?) coincide with her biological form. Her biological 'reality' is contingent to what she truly is as an individual: *purely other*." Here, Levinas is an empiricist: the identification of biological *form* is implied to be a *pure perception* unmediated by the activity of idealist constitution, or by the "violent grasp" of Aristotle's "agent Intellect," or by the necessary physical processes modern science enumerates. Ethics, and the transcendental meaning it is alleged to inscribe, is held to signify in *pure* first-person sensibility. In response to this defense, one might point out: for the face to signify *as* face, the other *must have already been identified with* her form. Levinas essentially treats the face as a *mere addition* of ethical meaning to an already operative psychological empiricism. He may *wish* to attribute to the face a transcendental function, but his descriptions do not actually succeed at disclosing this transcendental status. To such an objection, then Levinas's defenders might leap to idealism: "no, sensibility is phenomenologically *prior* to theory. The truth and falsity of theory in general *depend on* the responsibility and call to justice that issues in the face. The other is not 'ontological,' but inscribes the *Idea* of Infinity in me, and does so in the pure sensibility of the face as a content that exceeds its concept, phenomenologically revealed in the excessive responsibility in the face." As is clear, empirical perception *depends on* the ethical meaning of the face, and the ethical meaning of the face *depends on* an empirical face to "exceed." In his ego analysis, this circle was rendered explicit in his question-begging "anterior posteriorly" determination of theory, and in his ethics, it is rendered explicit in a seemingly opposite direction: ethics has an *a posteriori anteriorily* "structure." The ego was said to be constituted by "real" others, others that then, *after the fact* and at temporal remove, are "constituted" by the ego. Whereas for his ethics, the other is said to be the *condition* for theory, but the other can only manifest as a *condition* in excess of *form*, or in other words, *after* form *has already been posited*. Hence, my above question, essentially unanswerable on *TI*'s own descriptive terms, captures the problem precisely: does the other "destroy," or merely gently "exceed," her biological form, that is, is her biological "reality" *real* or merely "plastic"? To the empirical realist skeptical of his claims for the face, Levinas will respond, "of course 'there is such a thing as a biological genus,'" and will proceed to talk of ethical meaning theory depends on, claiming title to the transcendental tradition in phenomenology. If we push Levinas from an idealist direction, he will say, "but biological form is merely 'plastic.' It is contingent to what the other truly is—*purely other*—and ethical sense 'destroys' the identification of the other with her biological form."

III.c. Ethics and "Theory"

Clearly, *TI* turns on the *question of form* and the involvement of ethics vis-a-vis form, a question on which Levinas's position remains *indeterminate*. For example, "Behind theory and practice is the enjoyment of theory and practice."[45] Yet behind naive enjoyment is the effective activity of theory and practice that yields all the "others" on which enjoyment itself depends. Or again, "Knowledge or theory designates first a relation with being such that the knowing being lets the known being manifest itself while respecting its alterity and *without marking it* in any way whatever by this cognitive relation."[46] And yet elements and lived-from contents are declared to be "nothing," and "there exists a biological genus" clearly does *mark* specifically human others. It is clear that mere factual priority does absolutely *nothing* to contest or belie the *activities*, whether idealistically or realistically construed, that function behind the naive ego's back. These problems become even more glaring when we take Levinas's own claims for the transcendental status of the ethical other *seriously*.

What I describe above as the *a posteriori anteriorily* structure of ethics is explicitly marked in Levinas's texts at two critical moments. The first occurs in Levinas's explicit account of revelation, or in the specific way the other's transcendental status is "revealed" to the ego, and the second moment occurs at the tail end of his analysis of the feminine. I treat each by turns.

(a) "Revelation," Levinas declares, is "absolute experience," a "coinciding of the expressed with him who expresses, . . . the manifestation of a face *over and beyond form*."[47] The revelation of the face is a "truth . . . more fundamental than theory"; its meaning "*precedes* [the] coordinating effects visible to a third party."[48] The precedence here is clearly intended in terms of phenomenological *meaning*: theory is derived from and oriented by the *first meaning* "revealed" in the face. Theory depends on ethics for its orientation and proper function. Form is a problem because "it incessantly betray[s] its own manifestation, congealing into a plastic form, for it is adequate to the same—[it] alienates the exteriority of the other."[49] As such, the face appears above and behind theory as a "truth . . . more fundamental than theory," or as theory's transcendental condition. Yet for the face to reveal itself *over and beyond* form, it already requires *a form* to contrast itself with. On Levinas's own terms, without form, no face could appear *as face*, no alleged "absolute experience" could reveal the other to be *prior* to the form it *exceeds*. As a "truth . . . more fundamental than theory," the face is also and *simultaneously* declared to be "not true, [because] the true refers to the non-true, its eternal contemporary."[50] Levinas *simultaneously* asserts that the face is "truth" *prior* to theory and is a *condition* for theory's own normative distinctions. Insofar as this alleged "experience" already *depends on* the positing of form, when Levinas asserts the "priority" of ethics, he is *also* and *simultaneously* asserting the "priority" of theory, while switching between *real* and *transcendental* conditionality, between the empirical and phenomenological, and between real and transcendental *genesis*. In empiricist mode, theoretical determination is taken as psychological phenomenon occurring between real entities, though dependent on transcendental ethical meaning. In phenomenology mode, empirical bodies are said to deliver transcendental meanings that determine the practice of theory. In the first mode, identifying determinations are cast as mere empirical facts ignorant of their enabling conditions; in the second, identifying determinations are cast as ontological occurrences, as original experiences of transcendental, not merely empirical, meaning.

The circle I've identified at every level of Levinas's descriptions becomes explicit in the text at the tail end of his analysis of the feminine. That the circularity shows up precisely here is not accidental. Levinas writes:

> Inhabitation and the intimacy of dwelling which make the separation of the human being possible *thus imply the first revelation*

> of the Other. *Thus the idea of infinity, revealed in the face, does not only* require *a separated being, the light of the face is necessary for separation.*[51]

After having asserted ad nauseam that the ego "accomplishes" its "separation" in happiness and dwelling, its separation is only actually produced in the face. As Bernasconi puts it: "'the alleged scandal of alterity presupposes the tranquil identity of the same,' while at the same time making it possible."[52] Precisely *in* its transcendental function, "separation" occurs both as a *result* of the Other's appearance and as the *ground* for its appearance. Describing the ego as already "separated" prior to the advent of the Other serves to conceal this circularity. If we take Levinas's transcendental claims seriously, then this amounts to saying that the Other *prescribes* separation, and that this command is *implicit in* or somehow functions *behind the sensible ego's back*. This seems to be the case when Levinas insists: "The forgetting of transcendence is not produced as an accident in a separated being; the possibility of forgetting is *necessary* for separation."[53] Forgetting the other is a "necessary possibility," and if this possibility is genuinely "necessary," it implies that the ego *unconsciously obeys* this "command" before the face manifests *as* face, or *obeys without knowing it*. In other words, if the other is genuinely transcendental, nothing remains to distinguish properly ethical from ontological *necessity*: the other functions to constitute the ego *as what it is* and does not merely call forth what *it should be*. Yet, given the priority he posits for sensibility, its not immediately clear how Levinas can legitimately speak of memory and forgetting here. On his own terms, sensibility *is life*, not memory. Its meanings are held to be *purely lived*, apparently unmediated by "representation" or thought. And, as if to keep us on our toes, he'll elsewhere insist on the apparent "*impossibility* of forgetting the intersubjective experience that leads to the social experience."[54] Forgetting the other is both "necessary" and "impossible." On the one hand, Levinas's entire critique of the ontological tradition seems premised on the charge that forgetting the other is a culpable totalitarian mistake. On the other hand, his own descriptions of the ego seem to prescribe forgetting as a "necessary possibility," and imply that the other is the "real" (not merely conceptual) condition for the very being of the ego. Is it "possible" to forget what is declared to be "impossible" to forget? Perhaps he means that ontology *actively* forgets the unforgettable, and is culpable and "totalitarian" for this reason. The other is not *really* forgotten, but rather is willfully repressed. On the other hand, his own descriptions present this irrepressible memory as absolutely *unmediated by memory*. The face is an immediate and *lived* reality, and he elsewhere chastises ontology for involving it in memory.[55] In one stroke, ontology is chastised for forgetting the other precisely when it remembers her, and when it remembers, it's simultaneously enjoined to forget: the face is an "experience of what is in no way a priori." We could perhaps address this problem by giving an account of remembering *rightly*, and by stressing that the forms memory necessarily employs do not and cannot fully capture her. As promising as this move might be, it's not authorized by Levinas's text. Such a move would mediate the relation between self and other, and Levinas insists that "a third term, a neutral term" is imperiously ontological, wherein "the shock of the encounter of the same with the other is deadened."[56] Remembrance, even one aware of its limits, would quell the shock of the other, who, we are also told, "precisely reveals himself not in a shock . . . but as a primordial phenomenon of gentleness."[57] Because the other is presented as the *ground* for separation to begin with, the command to *remember a life* presented as *absolutely refractory to memory* seems no less capricious than the arbitrariness that manifests with the elements.

I more closely examine both Levinas's account of theory and his own method in the next chapter. For now, it's enough to note that Levinas appears to switching between transcendental and real conditionality, here opposing "reals" to the conceptual meaning of transcendental ideas, there opposing "ideal" meanings as determinative for "reals," to ward off charges of empiricism. He appears to summon allegedly *real* conditions against idealism and allegedly *ideal* conditions against realism. This switch finally becomes explicit when he turns to an analysis of eros.

III.D. Eros and Divine "Effectuation"

If Levinas is unequivocal about anything in *TI*, it's on the notion that the face, and the idea of the Infinite, is the absolute font of all meaning. The "face [is the] source from which all meaning appears," is "the commencement of intelligibility, initiality itself, principality, royal sovereignty, which commands unconditionally."[58] That's pretty clear. Yet as we move "beyond the face" to eros, fecundity, and paternity, things change once again: "Hence truth requires as its ultimate condition an infinite time, the condition for both goodness and the transcendence of the face."[59] Because Levinas never specifies what truth is, we can set that question aside. What is remarkable in this sentence is that he posits a "condition" for what has been declared to be utterly and absolutely unconditioned. This places the face in a wider context and tells us it is *determined*—limited by—something deeper. The circularity is clear: "The face founds a more profound relation: . . . fecundity," but there nevertheless remains yet another "condition for both goodness and the transcendence of the face."[60] If even the face is "conditioned" by something deeper, whatever this deeper condition might be, it is what is doing the real determinative work throughout the entire text.

Levinas titles the final section of *TI* "Beyond the Face." In this section, he performs an analysis of fecundity, paternity, and fraternity under the heading of eros. As we've just seen, these relations are said to be "founded" in the face, hence the term "beyond," and yet are presented as an elaboration of relations that somehow "condition" the face. The central aim of his analysis is to propose what he calls "messianic" time. Eros is presented as a paradoxical "relation" between two egoisms, described as a "union" that nevertheless "presupposes the total, transcendent exteriority of the other, of the beloved."[61] Levinas casts sexuality "as the reverse of expression of what has lost expression, it thereby refers to the face."[62] Even ethical expression—necessarily implied to be conceptual here—can be "reversed" into pure immediacy in enjoyment: "An enjoyment of the transcendent almost contradictory in its terms."[63] Indeed. The key point of his poetics of eros consists of the claim that in it, we come to discover the "not-yet."[64] The "not-yet" is not merely the future, and Levinas everywhere seeks to distinguish it from possibility: "[a] *not yet* more remote than the future."[65] Eros opens upon what Levinas will call "infinite time," a time understood in contrast to both the possible and the perpetual, as what he terms the "eternal," in a quite fascinating theory of "pluralistic" time. Eros "discovers the child," or *fecundity*.[66] At bottom, fecundity is biological procreation where, through erotic love and the children it produces, we somehow come to grasp that "[i]nfinite being is produced as times."[67] Though eros and fecundity "condition the positing of a unique being," a deeper relation ties everything into a whole: *paternity*.[68] Levinas writes,

> It is necessary to go back to the primordial phenomenon of time in which the phenomenon of the not yet is rooted. . . . Paternity, as a primordial effectuation of time, can, among men, be borne by the biological life, but be lived beyond that life.[69]

It's important to underline the central importance Levinas ascribes to paternity. Not only does it constitute the center of eros and fecundity, but it also *grounds* Levinas's account of fraternity. Insofar as even the face is "conditioned" by infinite paternal time, Levinas's description of paternity literally constitutes the *core* of *TI as a whole*.[70]

The drama of father and son—paternity and filiality—is the central drama of *TI* on the text's own terms. Levinas casts the "relation" of father and son in terms of *election*, understood in terms of *created freedom*: "Paternity remains a self-identification, but also a distinction within identification—a structure unforeseeable in formal logic."[71] The basic idea here is that sons are created, not caused. That no matter how many sons a father might have, each one of them is a chosen one, or unique. All multi-child families, or even those with a multitude of very intimate friends, can readily grasp what Levinas is after.[72] For our purposes here, what's fascinating is the complex ontological identity Levinas posits between father and son.

> To be one's son means to be I in one's son, to be substantially in him, yet without being maintained there in identity. . . . The son resumes the unicity of the father and yet remains exterior to the father: the son is a unique one. . . . He is unique for himself because he is unique for his father.[73]

What can it mean to say that the father is "substantially" in the son? Throughout *TI* as a whole, Levinas uses "substance" to name the ego's affective ipseity, and the "real" bodies and qualities that produce it. It is achieved in a purely passive sensibility. Levinas cannot mean the father's *genes* are in the son. That is too "theoretical." If our egoity is purely experiential and issues in a pure sensibility, how, precisely, are we to understand "substantially" above? On *TI*'s own explicit descriptive terms, no understanding is possible. In any case, though the father *is* the son, nevertheless "possession . . . by the father doesn't exhaust the relationship."[74] The son is also *unique* unto himself. The son recommences life anew: his own revolts, experiences, enjoyments, labor, thoughts, and responsibilities. The son is his own being, yet "owes his unicity to the paternal election."[75]

At last, we have come to the final lap in Levinas's deepest circle. I quote Levinas at length:

> The human I is posited in fraternity: that all men are brothers is not added to man as moral conquest, but constitutes his ipseity. Because my position as an I is effectuated already in fraternity the face can present itself as a face. The relation of the face in fraternity, where in his turn the Other appears in solidarity with

all others, constitutes the social order, the *reference of every dialogue to the third party* . . . encompasses the face to face opposition."[76]

The purely ethical face that "founds" eros *beyond* the face precisely "effectuates" the biological fraternity that *also* "founds" the face. The face "founds" eros; eros "founds" the face. This lovely circle entails that whenever Levinas speaks of disinterested Desire, he is *simultaneously* talking about *erotic* Need. Levinas's reference to "third party"—to God—here, is *not*, as elsewhere, a secondary moment that distributes faces to all of humanity. The God Levinas refers to here "effectuates" fraternity. This deeper, more determinative God does not only command, and does not create by *only* a moral commanding, but simply and straightforwardly *creates*.[77] This creation is not only sheer moral summons, but also the "effectuation" across time, space, and generations of the entire "human race."[78] Levinas's Creator God utilizes biological reproduction to "enclose a [plurality] of the Identical."[79]

In light of his phenomenology of eros, it is clearly *not* the case that it is the face that does the primary "relating." Instead, eros assigns divine-Paternal "effectuation" this task. When the divine-Pater does his creative work, Levinas explicitly describes it as the creation of *a people*: "Monotheism signifies this human kinship, this idea of a human race that refers back to [a Creative Father]."[80] When Levinas moves from fecundity to fraternity, the Eros that "encloses a duality of the Identical" becomes an Eros that "encloses a [plurality] of the Identical."[81] Here, "existing an existence which still subsists in the father the I echoes the transcendence of the paternal I who is the child."[82] Every member of the human race contains a divine trace and *belongs* to an eternal people. Each person and each generation is released to their specific times and places, but nevertheless remain members of a community not definitively bound by time and space, and all related to the *same* "effectuating" Other, the *same* "effectuating" God. Levinas's account of the face was meant to constitute the ego as "separate" and singular. In that context, election is a fundamentally individual affair. Yet the "condition" for the face in this last realist "reversal" is ultimately the election of *a people*. Clearly, Levinas gratuitously deploys alterity and singularity to critically uproot individuals from the alleged "violence" of ontology and identity, only to obliquely reinstall the individual in an originary ontological community by way of a theistic ontology of creation. Clearly, this most basic level of *TI*'s story quite explicitly relies on concepts, differentiated identity, and a merely *relative* sense of human individuality.[83] Of course, Levinas is perfectly free to commit to an absolute divine alterity and to posit and defend his theistic ontological-moral metaphysics. He is *not* free to baldly declare that identification, and the concepts they involve, are "violent," when he positively performs conceptual identifications in his vision of *ideal* community, or to sketch his own account of a determinate *created order*.

III.e. Ontology and "Theory"

As should be clear, the "anterior posteriorly" of his ego analysis and the "a posteriori anteriorily" of his other-analysis are, in fact, *identical*. He is spinning in a circle. Against idealism, he deploys an essentially realist logic premised in divine "effectuation." To ward off charges of realism, he'll ceaselessly refer to the *transcendental* meaning of the face and a logic of conceptual determination (*ideas* of infinity, responsibility, obligation, etc.). He is not entitled, of course, to refer to an "unconditional" face at a moment he is describing the "condition for both goodness and the transcendence of the face."[84] On his own terms, he cannot ultimately *ground* fraternity on what was presented as the purely moral meaning of the face. Fraternity becomes grounded by something else in his last realist reversal, and he uses the term "effectuate." Despite this use, we perhaps should not insist that he commit to the notion of a *cause*. Something like *ground* seems a more useful term for capturing the ontological, as well as moral, dimensions in play, of creativity as well as solidarity. Levinas wants his God to be both Father and Law Giver, but he achieves these characterizations by essentially different and mutually exclusive routes. Consider:

(1) By positing egoic singularity as a *result*, as "produced" by the "light of the face," while simultaneously positing an "effectuated" fraternity as the *ground* for the face's appearance, he is inscribing egoic time and experience within a more basic and "real" account of human collectivity. In so doing, the radicality he asserts for singularity and alterity is specious on his own descriptions. Self and other are actually articulated through basic categories or "existentials," and become inevitably mediated by various predicative concepts. Here, faces do not resist predication, but are articulated by ontological categories, and *depend on* predication to express themselves. Any particular case of expression ultimately refers to both "the whole of [a *real*] humanity, [that] . . . look at me [in her eyes]" and the "primordial effectuation of time" performed by a real divine Father who always already labors behind their backs.[85] Though this is what Levinas's actual descriptions perform, to back away from this straightforward metaphysics, what might a Levinasian do? Circle back around to the face.

(2) By positing egoic singularity as the *ground* for the face's appearance, the *idea* of divine fatherhood could potentially be presented as *grounded* in the more basic idea of moral obligation given in the face-to-face. The meaning of the face considered in the dramatic context of human reproductive sexuality permits something like an analogical synthesis of moral sense and human fatherhood. The *idea* of God is a *product* of the purely human face-to-face, and the *idea* of divine fatherhood is the *product* of an analogy to human fatherhood. The *idea* of God only achieves its meaning and necessity through phenomenological constitution of these purely human phenomena, which is perhaps why Levinas claims that belief in God does not matter. Only Divine Law qua infinite responsibility and the limits inherent to our creaturehood matter. While this, too, seems to be what Levinas has in mind, it cannot be justified on a strict reading of the text. Levinas *simultaneously* and circularly performs *both* 1 and 2.

With 1, intersubjectivity is presented as an *originary* determination of a human people. A real "effectuating" Father God determines us in such a way that freedom and responsibility are built into original existential-categorial *creaturehood*. With 2, intersubjectivity is *also* presented as an *originary* determination of a human people. We are determined by a singularizing responsibility that constitutes our concepts of humanity and of meaning across time. The question becomes: is God (1) a *real* (creative) *condition* for human belonging and moral meaning? Or is God (2) a merely *conceptual* necessity that renders the *idea* of a plurality of moral faces *intelligible*? Clearly, both these accounts are potentially coherent on their own terms. Clearly, Levinas is leaping between them, between transcendental and real "originality," between transcendental and real *genesis*. Clearly, Levinas is performing *both accounts at once*, and this partly explains the circularity that troubles the entire text.

When Levinas is in phenomenological mode, 2 above, he necessarily performs something like analogy-perception, where the other is fundamentally an *alter ego*, such that the attribution of lived originality to the other *grounds* the intelligibility of the face's demand. This simply means that the ego "understands" the face's appeal because the self and other are the *same*, that is, sentient creatures who feel and suffer.[86] Whether or not the *relative* alterity of the alter ego is *also* involved in the genesis of egoic obligation, Levinas's own descriptions necessarily require what Rodemeyer calls a primordial "intersubjective temporality."[87]

In "realist" mode, 1 above, he necessarily performs something like existential-categorial determination, where the other is fundamentally a *being-with* or *co-creature*, such that intersubjectivity is fundamentally *original*, and the other's "singularity" proceeds as an individuation of an ontological category. Of course, the other's alterity is only relative in this case too, and her freedom and responsibility *are what and who she is*. On these terms, Levinas's own descriptions require something like Heidegger's historicity, or a relatively *open* theistic temporality of something like the *imago Dei*. In all cases, there is no such thing as "absolute alterity" and "absolute singularity" for human beings. Levinas can only claim that there is through methodological equivocation.

IV. Conclusion

As I have shown, Levinas's description of the face repeats, rather than rectifies, the vicious circularity I identified in chapter 1. In both his ego- and other-analysis, this took the form of simultaneously utilizing "reals" against purely transcendental meaning, and utilizing transcendental "ideals" to assert a determinative status for the ethical meaning he posits (and to ward off charges of empiricism). I unearthed this circularity through contrasting his mutually exclusive claims that "the alleged scandal of alterity presupposes the tranquil identity of the same," and "the *idea of infinity, revealed in the face, does not only* require *a separated being, the light of the face is* necessary *for separation*."[88] Separation is both the *ground* and *result* of other's appearance. When egoic-separation functions as the conditional *ground* for the appearance of the face, Levinas is deploying a phenomenologically idiosyncratic *progressive* logic of *discovery*, wherein a naive, "real" psychological ego progressively becomes aware of the *ideal* meaning its experience requires for its general intelligibility. When egoic separation functions as the necessary *result* of the "light of the face," Levinas is deploying non-phenomenological regressive logic of "real" conditions, wherein a minded ego becomes aware of the *real* origin of its own being in a divine "effectuating" Other.[89] In the first case, meaning determines fact; in the second, fact determines meaning. The entire text spins in this circle, such that the *idea* of God is secured in the first case, and a *real* God is secured in the second. I further demonstrated that the meaning of the face as Levinas actually describes it internally depends on 1) necessary reference to the ego's own experience of suffering and self-care, and 2) conceptual or categorial mediation ("real biological genus" vs. "conceptless individual," disabled child vs. Vladimir Putin, performative/thematic contestation vs. merely brute, passive individuality), and these impugn the *kath-auto* character he asserts for expression. If we commit to an absolute alterity, we must necessarily commit to disembodied meaning and, as Derrida was the first to notice, purchase peace at the price of absolute silence. If we retain an original intersubjective otherness—whether achieved through analogy-perception or existential-categorial determination—we still give up "absolute" alterity, but retain a means for the critique of *particular* concepts and *particular* concept applications. Finally, if we wish to coherently commit to an "absolute alterity," while also disavowing its purely conceptual status, we must commit to something like Levinas's ontological God as the creative ground for meaning *in general*, and not *only* moral meaning.[90] If even Levinas must admit that self and other are "at the same time unique and non-unique," then on his own terms concepts cannot be "violent" per se.[91]

Indeed, the methodological problems in *TI*, first diagnosed by Derrida, are probably why Levinas's later work simply abandons claims for ethics as "first philosophy." As the informed reader is already well aware, the relation of the transcendental and empirical is a long-standing puzzle for the interpretation of *TI*. If my analysis in this chapter is sound, I have gone a long way toward diagnosing the problems in Levinas's method. In chapter 3, I undertake a more thorough analysis of his stated method and propose a holistic explanation for the problems reviewed in chapters 1 and 2.

Chapter 3

"Flipping the Deck," On *Totality and Infinity*'s Transcendental/Empirical Puzzle

> How does one perceive a transcendental condition?
>
> —Martin Kavka

> . . . if it is legitimate to hold Levinas to the standards that he himself imposes on other philosophers.
>
> —Robert Bernasconi

> I do not believe that transparency is possible in method, or philosophy is possible as transparency.[1]
>
> —Emmanuel Levinas

I. Introduction

As my above analysis demonstrated, the question of the precise methodological status of the face has yet to be satisfactorily resolved. The best evidence for this claim perhaps lay in texts intended to introduce Levinas to a general philosophical audience. If even first-rate philosophers wrestle still with the puzzle *TI* bequeaths us, we seem to still await a full diagnosis. For example, Michael Morgan holds that the "face-to-face and the responsible self—they are one thing characterized from two perspectives—. . . is the transcendental condition for a meaningful human life," yet elsewhere concedes, "it seems utterly unavoidable that in some sense or other the face-to-face does occur as an actually lived experience." If Morgan's own nuanced treatment of this question still lands him in equivocation, the problem is certainly *not*

Morgan's own.² As Atterton notes, Morgan must finally hold that Levinas's method is a "transcendental enterprise *of a certain sort.*"³ But of what sort? Indeed, this question has been asked or analyzed in one way or another from the beginning of *TI*'s English-language reception.⁴ Of course, Derrida was the first to broach the question of *TI*'s general intelligibility, alleging that Levinas ultimately succumbs to a form of empiricism. Of course, de Boer was the first to mount a rigorous Cartesian reading of the text as an (apparently) "ethical transcendental philosophy." Of course, Bernasconi's response to de Boer, and his creative repetition of Derrida's critical point, were the first to give the problem a precise formulation.⁵ Derrida, de Boer, and Bernasconi hand us the now canonical problem of what I call the text's "transcendental/empirico-metaphysical puzzle."⁶ The issue boils down to Levinas's duel insistence that the face "cannot . . . be stated in terms of experience," yet is nevertheless "reflected *within* experience."⁷ How should we understand Levinas's references to various "formal structure[s]"—"of language," "of interpellation," "of the idea of infinity"—next to talk of "pure" or "concrete moral experience"?⁸ Does the Other occur in "pure experience," or is she "deduced" as a condition of possibility for experience in general? In this chapter, I propose an internal *explanation* for *TI*'s long-standing methodological puzzle. By proposing to "explain" this puzzle, I am making at least three distinct claims: to show (1) *that* the text suffers from genuine incoherence, thus confirming the general criticism of Derrida, Bernasconi, and others; (2) precisely *how* this incoherence follows from the details of Levinas's own explicit method; and (3) precisely *why*, philosophically, he may have constructed and performed his method as he did.⁹ By proposing to *explain* the text's incoherence, I can also make specific hermeneutic predictions. If *TI*'s transcendental/empirico-metaphysical puzzle is genuinely aporetic, it follows that no resolution to it is possible on the text's own terms.¹⁰ As such, any attempt to resolve the puzzle must either (a) augment the text's own descriptions, (b) utilize other philosophical resources to render its moves coherent, or (c) precisely attempt resolution in either a transcendental or empirico-metaphysical direction. As it turns out, extant scholarship reflects just these hermeneutic strategies.

Over the years, many philosophers have contributed to this long-standing debate, variously arguing for or against the general intelligibility of *TI*'s account of the face. On the one hand, scholarship that questions the text's intelligibility does so from a variety of methodological perspectives.¹¹ On the other hand, scholarship that mounts a defense of the text seems to proceed in one of three ways: by (i) apparently repeating *TI*'s methodological problems, (ii) anticipating Levinas's later work read to rectify these problems, or (iii) utilizing other philosophical resources in an attempt to render its arguments coherent. I set the first two aside, because the relevant scholarship is either subject to my impending criticism or rests on a reading of Levinas's late work. Scholarship that utilizes other resources precisely reflects the above predictions by either augmenting or going outside the text, and tends to resolve in either a transcendental or empirico-metaphysical way. As one might expect, empirico-metaphysical coherence strategies tend to downplay Levinas's appeals to purely formal structures, and invariably utilize one or another type of quasi-realist *logic*. Theodore de Boer and John Drabinski present spirited and rigorous coherence strategies in precisely this form.[12] And as one might expect, transcendental coherence strategies tend to take either Kantian or Husserlian form. In Kantian form, transcendental readings of the face tend to downplay or ignore Levinas's reference to "experience" by stressing the cognitive *meaning* of the face.[13] In Husserlian form, transcendental readings tend to re-outfit talk of "experience" to align with the affective/perceptual dimensions of phenomenological-constitutive processes.[14] Martin Kavka and Steven Crowell present spirited and rigorous coherence strategies in these general directions. Beyond extant scholarship, Levinas himself seems to circulate between transcendental and empirico-metaphysical readings of his own work. For example, in his interview with Hirsch, Levinas holds, "but I like to insist . . . on the primordial *intellectual* role of alterity" and "to *think* the other as other, to *think* him or her straightaway before affirming oneself, signifies concretely to have goodness."[15] By contrast, in an interview with Rötzer, he holds, "Responsibility for the other is *the experience* of the good, the very meaning of the good, goodness. Only goodness is good."[16] What is ultimately interesting in both Levinas's self-interpretation and the above coherence strategies comes down to this: transcendental strategies must ultimately sacrifice the text's plain empirico-metaphysical claims to either transcendental *Life* (Crowell) or transcendental *Ideas* (Kavka), and either way give up his explicit appeals to *pure bodies* allegedly "exterior" to theory. Likewise, empirico-metaphysical strategies must ultimately sacrifice the text's own transcendental claims to either a theistic (de Boer) or materialist (Drabinski) *logic*, and either way give up Levinas's appeals to *pure meanings* allegedly "exterior" to thought. The *only* way to keep both *pure* "exterior" *bodies* and *pure* "exterior" *meaning* is to "flip the deck."

By way of introduction, a good metaphor for grasping *TI*'s circularity is something like the "deck-flipping" of a poker dealer. As when a dealer spreads a deck of cards and uses one of the cards to flip the deck back and forth, face-down to face-up and back again: the "other" remains stable and outside the series of cards. On the one hand, when Levinas or Levinasians are faced with criticism for the text's explicit empirico-metaphysical language, they "flip the deck" to the language of transcendental "condition of possibility," "deduction," "not an experience," and so forth.[17] On the other hand, when Levinas or Levinasians are faced with anti-formalist, anti-transcendental criticism, they "flip the deck" back again, using quasi-realist language of "pure experience," "pure sensation," "pure qualit[ies]," and the critique of "pure thought."[18] Back and forth, either way, the Other remains outside the series, and either end of the flip always appears as the "first." As Levinas performs this deck-flipping, he is performing something like a gestalt switch: the Other, its structural status, and alleged determinative meaning remains stable (remains atop the deck and guides the flip either way), while the surrounding logical and justificatory infrastructure is transformed, here utilizing formal-transcendental claims to describe and justify his position, there using empirico-metaphysical claims to do so. On one pole, the Other is construed as *transcendent fact*; on the other pole, the Other is construed as *transcendental idea*. One reason *TI*'s transcendental/empirico-metaphysical question remains a puzzle, and hard to sort out, is that the respective methodological infrastructures he is switching between are each relatively coherent, and the deck-flipping in play is premised in a phenomenological vocabulary that lend his claims prima facia plausibility. With notable exceptions, the entire tradition of Levinas scholarship simply circulates within this circle and repeats its game, deploying one or the other descriptive/justificatory discourse depending on the type of criticism being addressed.[19] There is textual support for both transcendental and empirico-metaphysical readings, and this is the entire problem. There are no resources within Levinas's text to resolve the puzzle or adjudicate the question, because it is *built into* his explicit method. As I shortly show, *TI*'s own explicit account of theory is viciously indeterminate. This indeterminacy empowers his "flipping," making it hard to initially detect, and ultimately renders some of his central claims arbitrary.

Given the history of Levinas scholarship, and the prevailing interpretive consensus that seems to dominate the general presentation of Levinas's philosophy, it's not enough for me to simply point to the circularity through purely textual analysis. Indeed, if the general criticisms of Derrida, Bernasconi, and others have failed to provoke a thorough reckoning, my own focused diagnosis would likely fair no better. If I stop at textual analysis, I might be accused of "misunderstanding" what Levinas is up to, perhaps in a way that my critic simply repeats the problem I'm treating. I would therefore fail to clarify *TI*'s methodological puzzle, as is my aim. To avoid this, I must render the circularity more fully transparent at the precise level of its structural function, rather than *only* at important, though nevertheless particular, moments of its performance in Levinas's actual descriptions. My "flipping the deck" metaphor, and the logico-justificatory gestalt "switching" it tracks, nicely captures my proposal for how the puzzle might be properly understood, but to fill out this proposal requires at least two further tasks.

First, beyond only confirming *that* the text suffers incoherence, I must show—precisely and in detail—*how* this incoherence is *built into* its own methodological construction(s). Next, if my proposed "deck-flipping" description is accurate, and if this accuracy is fully established by detailed methodological analysis, I must finally propose a textually plausible reason for *why* Levinas constructed and performed his method as he did. Only by confirming *that*, showing *how*, and proposing *why* can my "deck-flipping" metaphor move beyond rough description to a more *precise explanation* of *TI*'s transcendental/empirico-metaphysical puzzle.

II. Fact or Idea?

Why fact or idea? As I show in more detail, Levinas himself forces this question on us. He everywhere claims that any "third term" or mediating structure does "violence" to the alterity of the other and the singularity of the self.[20] This assertion renders *all* discourse, in general and as such, guilty of "violence." This suggests to me that there is something wrong with the claim that concepts are "violent" per se. But given the serious consideration granted this assumption in extant scholarship, simply rejecting the claim outright is not enough. For this reason, and by the fact that Levinas himself explicitly rejects all mediation, his own logic forces this question on us: is the Other a *transcendent fact* or *transcendental idea*? This guiding question pushes the intrinsic equivocalness of Levinas's method into the open. Levinas is quite clearly using both Kantian and empirico-metaphysical vocabulary within his phenomenological debate with Husserl and Heidegger. This is the entire problem. If I were to tell a long and complicated story about Husserl's categorial intuition, his subsequent embrace of transcendental idealism to fully twist free from the psychologism controversy that haunts his "realist" phase,[21] Heidegger's rejection of this neo-Kantian debate through creative use of categorial intuition in his own transcendental-ontology, and

Levinas's attempt to outgun Heidegger, no clarification of the text's methodological puzzle will have taken place. Levinas's own explicit method is summoned *against* Husserl and Heidegger, and wielded *against* the entire tradition. His method proceeds as just the "deck-flipping" I'm proposing, and therefore no question-begging comparisons to Husserl or Heidegger's work can ameliorate the problem.[22] In other words, Levinas's method must be evaluated on its own terms.

II.a. Levinas Between Realism and Idealism

Levinas explicitly claims that "[my] analyses are guided by a formal structure: the idea of Infinity in us."[23] The idea of the infinite is unique, because it implies that "content overflow[s] the container" for finite minds.[24] Now, Levinas also insists that "the formal structure of language . . . announces the ethical inviolability of the Other."[25] How do the formal structure of "the idea of Infinity in us" and "the formal structure of language" relate? The answer to this question constitutes nearly the entire story *TI* has to tell. These two formal structures are related by what Levinas calls "the formal structure of interpellation," or what he'll come to call *discourse*.[26] As it turns out, interpellation is described as not *only* a formal structure. Levinas's account of discourse is just his description of the face, where the idea of the infinite is allegedly "put into me."[27] The face is presented as "pure experience," or as an event a passive and sensible ego *undergoes*.[28] How are we to interpret these references to "formal structure" and "pure experience"? Let's consider.

Now, if "discourse" is inherent to the "formal structure of language," then my interlocutor is a necessary and irreducible *element* of this structure. Here, *all* Levinas's descriptive rhetoric is precisely what he claims it is *not*: "empirical and contingent data, laid over [a] formal skeleton . . ."[29] Here, *all* empirical faces are *instantiations* of the interlocutor-pole of the formal structure of discourse, and this discourse-structure supplies *norms* that *universally* govern *all* language users. In the order of *fact* (for example, natural history), the discourse-structure comes late. In the order of *meaning*, the discourse-structure comes first (e.g., we cannot do biology without supposing discursive norms, scientific practice refers to them). Interlocutors remain, of course, "other," but only in a relative sense determined by the discourse-structure itself, apparently inherent to and constitutive of the "formal structure of language." Adding content to this structure, or any worldly instance of discourse, does not and *cannot* alter it, because this structure and its norms are necessarily presupposed in any conversation. At the absolute minimum, this is what it means to be a transcendental structure. Whenever Levinas or Levinasians talk of "ethical *transcendental* conditions," this is what they are actually summoning, protestations to the contrary not withstanding.[30] If, on the other hand, "the formal structure of language" is *dependent* on the idea of infinity, and if, further, the idea of infinity is "*put into me*," then, indeed: talk of the face, "pure experience," "breaking up of [merely] formal [thought] structures," and so forth, do not merely involve "empirical and contingent data, laid over [a] formal skeleton . . ." but describe or articulate a genuine metaphysical event occurring in remote (biographical or historical) yesteryear, and accessible via reconstructive abstraction through some form of "real," as opposed to purely conceptual, relation. In this case, discourse is not *only* a formal structure, but is derived from the "fact" of the Infinite, the "fact" of its idea "being put into" finite minds, and the affective "fact" of the Infinite's "manifestation" in actual faces and speech-contexts. On the one hand, if the "formal structure of language" is a counterfactual transcendental discourse-structure, then *thought determines being*, that is, discursive norms do not rely on any particular description of how the world stands for their validity. On the other hand, if the "formal structure of language" is *dependent* on specific metaphysical facts and experiences, then *being determines thought*, that is, discursive norms are grounded in a higher-order moral realism (say, natural law, objective virtues, religious ethics, etc.) embedded in higher-order accounts of our empirico-metaphysical nature. Some suitably mediating position, wherein norms are sensitive to their contexts of application, and "facts" are sensitive to competing interpretations, are just that: *mediating*, that is, inevitably involves either deliberative or hermeneutic infrastructures where the relation between fact and norm is explicitly rendered, and where others remain *relative* as either *co*-performers or *co*-determinants of the relevant infrastructure.[31] What must be noticed, here, is that in both cases, all selves and others are held subject to universally valid norms, and come to be descriptively-conceptually mediated in a variety of different ways (biologically, culturally, etc.). In both cases, some kind of normatively governed account of *freedom* is in play. Has Levinas given moral realists, Kantian constructivists, or hermeneutic phenomenologists good reasons to adopt his position? Probably not, and precisely because his method appears arbitrary and equivocates on questions central to meta-ethical and philosophical debate. As we are about to see in more detail, Levinas clearly "flips the deck," leaps back and forth between idealist and realist justificatory/descriptive vocabulary throughout the text, and by excluding any mediating structure, he leaves himself no means to render his circle virtuous. If we try to adjudicate *TI*'s puzzle in light of what transcendental and realist moral philosophy are, variations of what I roughly describe here are our fundamental choices.

III. Levinas's Method: "Overflowing" Concepts

The key to Levinas's whole method is packed into his notion of "the overflowing of concretization," of "the overflowing of finite thought by . . . content," of "content overflowing the container," or in short, "[content] overflows the concept."[32] This constitutes the core of his intrinsically equivocal method, and renders his "deck-flipping" possible. "Overflowing," "surplus," "exceed," and their cognates occur some sixty times throughout *TI*. As with nearly every other key term in the text, Levinas's use is not always consistent. But in general, Levinas uses these notions to specify moments where concepts do not or cannot do all the semantic work. The paradigmatic instance of "content overflowing concept" is, of course, the idea of the infinite. But he also uses this notion in his ego analysis. Here is a sample of typical uses:

> This sinking one's teeth into the things which the act of eating involves above all measures the surplus of reality of the ailment over all represented reality.

> The event of dwelling exceeds the knowing, the thought, and the idea in which, after the event, the subject will want to contain what is incommensurable with a knowing.

> Infinity is transcendence, the overflowing of an adequate idea.

> What counts is the idea of the overflowing of objectifying thought by a forgotten experience by which it lives.[33]

Whenever Levinas attacks idealism, he always and in some way refers to "overflowing," "surplus," or "exceeds." In each case, it seems intended to distinguish between the *lived immediacy of "real" experience* over-against mere reflection on or communication about this experience. If we subtract the "overflowing" from "contents 'overflowing' concepts," for example, by thinking of or talking about our experience, the immediacy is lost. His various talk of "overflowing" is at the basis of his claim that thought distorts, and that conceptuality is "violent." In its methodological function, "overflowing" fundamentally means *sensible force in the lived moment*, "an ultimate relation with the substantial plenitude of being," or "manifestation . . . over and beyond form."[34]

Unfortunately, this distinction can't do what Levinas wants it to do. No one doubts that thinking of or talking about having fun isn't necessarily *to be having fun*. Levinas's critique of idealism is premised in attributing what amounts to subjective metaphysical idealism to Kant and Husserl, and his critique of ontology is premised in attributing a naive conceptual determinism to Heidegger. Here, constitution means something like full-fledged *creation*, where an idealist Subject or impersonal Being fully "creates" the objects or entities it constitutes. In opposition to these straw men, Levinas must and does posit a naked empirical reality populated by all sorts of self-standing entities merely awaiting egoic notice. He uses a general distinction between thought and experience to *posit rules* held to determine logically distinct meaning-domains, such that he can assert on four separate occasions, in four separate contexts: x "does not belong to the order of" y.[35] Clearly, simply describing an uncontroversial difference between an event of thinking and an event of fun does not justify the controversial claim that enjoyment is "transcendentally" prior to thought. While I can certainly enjoy thinking, it is by no means clear that enjoyment structurally and necessarily orients thinking in general. Why do I still engage in thought when I am *not* enjoying it, or when it causes me suffering? If "enjoyment . . . [truly] does not belong to the order of thought," then Levinas himself could not have written *TI*.[36] Enjoyment would remain simply and wholly inaccessible to thought: *not thinkable, communicable, or utterable at all*. If "the order of enjoyment," as opposed to thought, only specifies a difference between actual moments of enjoyment and reflection on those moments, then Levinas has failed to constitute a truly distinct meaning-domain. He is doing something else, for example: classifying types of experience. Mere classification does not justify his claim that sensibility "is incommensurable with a knowing," nor does it institute a legitimate rule for what can or can't count as knowing.[37] Indeed, a relatively determinate account of knowledge is what *TI* fundamentally *lacks*. Sensibility must rely on either mind or world—or mind *and* world—to ultimately discriminate between types of experience or particular regions of meaning. Levinas wants moral sensibility to do the primary and orienting labor, but clearly: such meaning must fundamentally suppose either structures of mind or structures of world to do its semantic work. Some suitably interactionist position, where mind and world are co-constituting or reciprocally determinative, necessarily requires categorial or conceptual mediation, and therefore precludes access to putatively "absolute" singularities or alterities. While Kant distinguishes between theory and practice and grants the latter priority, *both* are *cognitive* in nature; that is, Kant discriminates between different kinds of meaning, but *finite mind* is what ultimately does the discriminating in its original relation to the world. While Heidegger grants priority to practice over theory, he *actually describes* how this priority functions, and lays out the ontic-transcendental structures that render this priority describable. Unlike Kant or Heidegger, Levinas's own construal of meaning in terms of "content overflowing concept" allows him to equivocate on what does the philosophically determinative work: here pointing to ideas, there pointing to sensible force, as what ultimately constitutes or validates meaning.[38] Levinas's own account of theory never *precisely* specifies *how* meaning is constituted, or *how* pre-theoretical meaning opens upon the theoretical.[39] "Content overflowing concepts" points to being/experience and thought/concept—structures of *world* and structures of *mind*—*at once*, couched in a *simultaneous* rejection of all mediation.[40] In the midst of Levinas's anti-concept polemic, his own "contents overflowing concepts" invariably utilizes concepts. Consider: "Infinity is transcendence, the overflowing of an adequate idea."[41] This implies that transcendence is *more*, not *less*, than adequate. If "overflowing" simply means "the sheer presence of *sensible force*," than adequation, here, is still the determinant of *truth*.[42] For example, tomorrow I intend to go to the pub and have a rollicking good time. I intend to do this because the last three times I went to the pub, I in fact had a rollicking good time. If tomorrow I *fail* to have a rollicking good time, my expectations will have been *unfulfilled*, and I'll judge the experience *inadequate*. Clearly, the presence, absence, or intensity of a particular "affective moment" does not *ruin* or contest adequation, but precisely supplies the *norm* by which I judge subsequent experiences as more or less adequate. On reflection, I might identify a reason for this failure; say, I was thinking too much about Levinas's description of enjoyment instead of letting myself loose in the moment. In this case, a particular episode of thinking has short-circuited my intention to enjoy, but this clearly and in no way challenges the accessibility of enjoyment to thought, or renders thought less necessary because it is not in each case pure enjoyment. The whole episode *supposes* the *memory* and *anticipation* without which I would be constitutively unable to *know* that I ever have, or ever will, enjoy. Levinas's attempt to define the ego as just its immediate enjoyment—as pure instant in the moment—fails to actually exhibit the *transcendental* "priority" of sensibility to thought.

The *same* goes for the "other." When I converse with another human face, I necessarily hold either culturally mediated assumptions or reflectively held commitments that *pre-structure* what and who my interlocutor *is*. What can it mean to claim that the "affective force" of my interlocutor's sheer presence *contests* these assumptions or commitments? How might this "overflowing" show my pre-conceptions to be *inadequate*? If my interlocutor insistently and earnestly *tells me*, "I am a god," he would straightaway fail to *fulfill* my expectation of, say, rationality. I would judge him to be insane and in need of psychiatric care. If my interlocutor proceeded to demonstrate his divinity-claim by, say, flying around the room, bodily de-materializing and re-materializing, recounting to me all my deep-dark secrets, or causing a stack of money to materialize out of thin air, I would initially assume that *I am insane*, either hallucinating or dreaming. But if my life continued on in its otherwise normal rhythm; if a bank validated the magic money he bequeathed me; if I introduced him to my wife, friends, and Daniel Dennett; and they, too, after repeated observation and due consideration, agreed he really is more than human, my pre-conceptions will have been veritably *contested*. They would be *altered*. I would continue on expecting merely human interlocutors to behave and speak in anticipated ways, while admitting a whole new class of potentially divine interlocutors, and revise my ontology accordingly. The purchase, here, is that "content overflowing concepts"—*all by itself*—does absolutely *nothing* to contest ontology, concept inclusion, or the mediations involved in any particular face-to-face encounter. An interlocutor might behave or talk in unexpected ways, but they nevertheless *act* and *speak*. She or he is a living body, born of a mother, becomes a relationally autonomous actor capable of intentional movement, a language-user capable of giving reasons, and so forth. Her or his experiences and choices are ultimately their own, but this ownness does not solely issue from an indeterminate vortex of pure qualities, nor do I become aware of their ownness by merely tilting my ear while earnestly squinting at their face. For a face to actually contest either my conventional assumptions or reflectively held commitments, she or he must either *perform* a subversion of them (like our potentially divine magician), or *argue for* and exemplify a better set of commitments. Without performatively or thematically *showing me* that my expectations are wrong, indifferent, unethical, or unreasonable, my expectations are in each case *fulfilled*. I fully endorse Levinas's desire to grant interlocutors their originality, but arbitrarily positing a purely immediate "absolute" alterity does not get the job done. Recognizing others' originality *supposes* the *memory* and *anticipation* without which I would be constitutively unable to *know* that I ever have been, or ever will be, contested. Levinas's attempt to present the other as just its immediate presence fails to actually exhibit the *real* "priority" of sensibility to thought.

Now, I expect, my Levinasian friends might chime in here and claim I simply "misunderstand" his claims. For example, they might say something like this: "The question is: what make your intention to go to the pub possible? What must be presupposed by intentionality as such? The face is an answer to this question. Levinas is ultimately claiming (1) Your enjoyment is who you are, and by this meaning you *utilize* thought to seek and repeat happiness as an end. You can't have fun by sheer will. In just this way, sensibility is prior to thought. In your above example, you intend to go to the pub in-order-to have fun, not, say, to sell popcorn or perform sociological observations. (2) Your divine-magician perfectly exemplifies Levinas's point. He burst the bounds of your expectations. Every interlocutor intimates just this sort of unpredictability, and its sense is primarily moral. Moreover, revising your ontological assumptions does *not* revise your moral presuppositions. If your divine-magician used his power to murder and enslave, you would rightly conclude he is evil. The face gives us an unalterable ethical transcendental principle, a necessary presupposition that structures all discourse, even discourse with a putative divinity. The unpredictability and moral sensibility of the face make this, and all intentionality, possible. We can choose to ignore this fact through indifference or exploitation, but it remains a fact. In just this way, ethics is prior to ontology."

To the first point: selling popcorn and performing sociological observation are available possibilities. Enjoyment *alone* doesn't motivate *all* my acts and is not the totality of what I am. I like enjoying. I like the rare moments of contentment that visit me. Enjoyment and contentment do partly motivate my various activities, but they cannot do all the motivating work. Why do I continue on in whatever activity when I am *not* enjoying, or when it causes me *dis*contentment? At the end of the day, because I strive to achieve creative and moral excellence, to live a good life. In this light, Levinas's ego-analysis is quite inadequate. My intentionality presupposes historically mediated and socially constituted contexts of motivation and the contestable self-conceptions they involve. Sensibility is one aspect, but not the entirety, of these contexts. Levinas's ego-analysis seems explicitly intended to set the stage in such a way that "absolute alterity" talk can appear plausible. However salient some of his particular analyses might be, they do not rectify the problems I diagnose here. If enjoyment doesn't constitute the totality of my motivation, then Levinas's claims remain unvindicated. Simply setting aside sociality as wholly irrelevant to our sense of identity, only to admit it late on the basis of "absolute alterity," seems artificial and strategic, rather than phenomenologically disinterested and justified.[43]

To the second point: but your rejoinder does not touch the central issue. Your own claims imply that the otherness of the other is *not* "absolute." I can judge our divine-magician's acts by what are taken to be *universally valid* norms. If our putatively divine entity can be *subject* to normative moral evaluation, then, unlike a cat, a rose, or the Grand Canyon, she is the sort of entity susceptible to such evaluation, that is, an *intentional being*. Levinas's talk of "asymmetry" is an exotic way of saying that the binding force of norms is not contingent on whether others treat me in kind, or according to the same normative light. I happily grant this point, without granting the arbitrary claim that norms spring whole from our affects, or that they are purely and unilaterally imposed. Your "unpredictability" claim brings my own point into relief: I *expect* others to act variously, and this expectation is not purely normative, but mediated by various natural, cultural, and ontological notions on *who* human beings are. The best descriptions grant relational, normatively governed autonomy to human beings and individual language users and the capacity for (relatively) creative self-determination this involves. But even this is always in some way embedded in larger assumptions or reflectively held commitments on how the world stands. Norms do not depend on these descriptions for their validity, but neither is it possible to simply abstain from description. Because Levinas himself cannot and does not avoid it, why suppose that conceptual mediation is violent? In *TI*, Levinas tries to *thematize* the difference between self and other as purely and sublimely moral, and this seems a transparent attempt to a priori exclude all competing ontologies. It works like this: concepts are violent, therefore ontology is violent, and therefore any descriptive attribution of *common* properties or capacities is violent. Levinas can label any interlocutor he might debate as "immoral" for merely speaking, and by reference to his or her own passive individuality, rather than listening to what they say, and arguing with them, or watching what they do, and revising his picture of the human in its light.[44] What is sold as "respect for the other" in fact gives a basis for simply ignoring others, or worse: accusing them before they even speak. Of course, Levinas himself must assume common properties or capacities, for example: language use. On his own terms, if it were not for the communicative dimension, all mammals would be faces. Of course, positing "absolute alterity" and using it to build a concept of humanity has the following, quite convenient, implications: he can charge all comers (everyone but skeptics and Levinasians) with "violence," while at the same time using "alterity" to *define* an identity ("humanity"). This is contradictory and arbitrary. He can always claim that what humans share is merely contingent to who we truly are as individuals: "absolutely other." Positing "absolute alterity" as both a critical and constructive notion places him in a bind: if we take his critical use seriously, he is not entitled to use alterity to positively construct concepts, even a concept of humanity. If he is entitled to mediate alterity in positive concept construction, then it cannot be the case that *pure* alterity is a useful critical concept. Levinas's "deck-flipping" is precisely an attempt to skirt this issue. It necessarily involves performative contradiction on his own terms. As Derrida noted, Levinas forces us to choose between respecting "absolute alterity" and performing "violence" by mere speech. I reject that choice. The very nature of the choice tells me the problem lies in Levinas's claims, not in concept use per se. Simply setting aside our conceptual capacities as wholly irrelevant to our sense of being-obligated, only to admit them late on the basis of "absolute alterity," seems artificial and strategic, rather than phenomenologically disinterested and justified.

III.a. Levinas's Method: "Reversing" Constitution

Levinas's "deck-flipping" comes to light in this question: is the face a transcendent *fact* or a transcendental *idea*? Because he principally excludes all mediation, he simply switches back and forth throughout the text, here suggesting moral-metaphysical realism, there suggesting transcendental formalism. The methodological hinge of this switch is that "the process of constitution . . . is reversed," or what he sometimes calls "deformalization."[45] In order to get the gist of what "reversing constitution" might mean, I must briefly say something about constitution. To brutally oversimplify, constitution is a complex act in which the objects I intend can be recognized and reidentified. As I look at the teacup beside me, I only see a profile. Were I to continually rotate it, I would only ever see profiles. What allows me to grasp the teacup as a *whole* and not merely a succession of profiles? What allows me to recognize any future teacup I might encounter *as* a teacup? What allows me to spontaneously *know* that my teacup and this glass of water "fit" together in a way my teacup and computer do not? Constitution, or the mind's activity of rounding out, organizing, and relating perceptual content. For our purposes here, it's sufficient to know that constitution empowers the reidentifiability of anything I might encounter in the world, that is, that the relations in play are ultimately *minded achievements, not necessarily sown into the fabric of the world*. When Levinas talks of "reversing" constitution or "deformalizing" various objects, he means something like this: *this* apple is "reversed" from "fuel-object" to something yummily enjoyed, "reversed" from an instance of a kind to "sweet nectar I devour," and so forth. Of course, such presents no fundamental challenge to Husserl or Kant. It rather creates intractable problems for Levinas's own position. His term for what we find at the other end of this "de-formalizing reversal" is *substance*. Presumably, he is making use (in phenomenological translation?) of Aristotle's "substance," that is, "real" individuals:

> [Affective contents are] distinct from my substance but constitut[e] it.

And

> The sensible quality already clings to a substance.[46]

On Levinas's view, all the things and elements I enjoy "constitute" my lived sense of wholeness and identity, that is, my "substance." And when I move from immediate enjoyment to dwelling and labor, the "*pure* qualities" I enjoy are attributed "substance," that is, that which makes them recognizable and reidentifiable as what they *are*.[47] The problem is clear. He is presenting what we might call a *seesaw* theory of constitution: "reversing constitution" and deformalizing concepts terminates in an "overflowing affective force" shot from "real" bodies through allegedly "pure" qualities. Are wholes sown into the fabric of the world, such that we grasp them by inference or by "discovery" of "real" relations? Or are wholes rather the constituted achievement of minded activity? Levinas asserts the former *and* the latter *simultaneously*, couched in a concurrent rejection of all mediation. On his own descriptions, de-formalization (i) *starts with* concepts, (ii) "reverses" to "real" bodies and qualities interposing a temporal gap between affection and thought, yet nevertheless (iii) retains "the possibility of a representation that is constitutive."[48] Clearly, he is dancing in a question-begging circle. On his own terms, faces *must* initially be posited as wholes in order for "overflowing containers" to work. In just this way, ethics *depends* on either mind or world—or mind *and* world—to supply a form to "exceed." Clearly, he is "flipping the deck": in "reversing the process of constitution," the constitut*ing* becomes the constitut*ed*. "Thinking constitutes objects" becomes "experienced objects constitute thinkers."

> [the ego's] needs . . . affirm "exteriority" as non-constituted, prior to all affirmation.

And

> the epiphany that is produced as a face is not constituted.[49]

In both of these cases, "overflowing" as "the real presence of sensible force" is at the basis of his claims for non-constitution. Whenever an *x* the ego experiences or encounters is "non-constituted," it becomes what does the constituting, and is given a different label ("enjoyment," "ethics"). Whenever Levinas summons "overflowing," "surplus," or "exceeds," he is summoning empirical bodies, fully accessible "real" individuals, and some unspecified "real" relation, while nevertheless couching his meaning-claims in phenomenological terms. When this point apparently occurs to him, Levinas then arbitrarily leaps to idealism: "[sensibility] conditions every empiricism and the very structure of the fact imposed on contemplation."[50] He must commit to either the realist, psychologistic account of the genesis of the ego he actually performs, and specify the relations involved, or simply accept that for sensibility to signify it must rely on and pass through either determining acts of consciousness or determinative ontological structures. What he can't do is what he does: simultaneously entitle himself to plainly realist claims utilized against phenomenological constitution, while also utilizing phenomenological constitution against the realism he actually performs. To sheerly assert the ego's indifference to questions of "theory," or merely summon the standpoint under description, is to beg the question.[51] Either transcendental constitution is working behind the naive ego's back, or there is some form of "real" determination going on (as his own descriptions imply).[52] Some of the most the nearly nonsensical passages of *TI* are precisely those that try to tackle this problem head-on. For example, "the possibility of a representation that is constitutive but already rests on the enjoyment of a real completely constituted . . ."[53] If constitution means one thing here (conferring reidentifiability), then this sentence is plainly nonsensical. If he intends constitution in different senses, he should tell us what they are.

Levinas's entire method is premised in a systematic failure to distinguish between *real* and *transcendental* conditionality, *real* and *transcendental* genesis. When attacking Husserl or Kant, real conditionality is summoned against the transcendental. When attacking Heidegger or Aristotle, transcendental conditionality is summoned against the real. When he is responding to critics, the face is presented either as a transcendent *fact* or transcendental *idea* depending on the question being posed.

III.b. Levinas's Method: "Theory"

Beyond "overflowing" and "reversal," Levinas's explicit account(s) of theory exhibit just the sort equivocity one would expect if my reading of *TI* were right:

> Knowledge or theory designates first a relation with being such that the knowing being lets the known being manifest itself while respecting its alterity and *without marking it* in any way whatever by this cognitive relation.

And

> to know is not simply to record, but always to comprehend . . .[54]

His first statement implies just the kind of innocent recording his second statement denies. This contradiction fits perfectly within my "deck-flipping" explanation of *TI*'s methodological puzzle. The highly polemical account of "comprehension" Levinas performs throughout the text is ultimately driven by his untreated assumption that concepts are inherently "violent." By positing unmediated empirical reality populated by "real" bodies and "pure" qualities, he hands himself apparently pure "others" the concept is alleged to oppress.[55] For his critique of the concept to hold water, he needs something like the innocent "recording" notion of theory above. Yet for his own phenomenology to do philosophical work, he cannot renounce comprehension altogether. For the empirico-metaphysical side of the flip, "sensible force," "substance," "[seesaw] constitution," real condition, and the *purely* accessible empirical bodies they involve, theory just passively and innocently jots them down on its tabula rasa. Once sensibility registers the human other's empirical body, the idea of the Infinite is apparently "put into me," and in a stroke, comprehension apparently becomes fair game. Indeed, "comprehension of this destitution and this hunger constitutes the very proximity of the other."[56]

Beyond Levinas's explicit methodological concepts, his "deck-flipping" is explicitly performed in transition-terms between different stages of description. His ego analysis is ultimately *progressive*. It tells a story of the birth of the ego in enjoyment, its transformation into dwelling, its vigorous laboring activity, to its climactic encounter with the Other. Throughout this story, Levinas deploys "surplus" and "deformalization" in the way I describe above. Each stage is described as an "a posteriori event," as "opening up new possibilities," as "discover[ing] a world," or in short: "add[ing]" something new.[57] He does not want the ego's journey to be purely explicative. Above all, the idea of the Infinite must be "put into me," and he therefore posits "real" others "exterior" to the blind ego in its progressive journey of becoming-aware. The ego is made to interact with a wide cast of characters: things consumed, environing elements, welcoming feminines, pagan gods destroyed, and materials exploited. After having apparently won its "separation," the ego finally happens to notice another human face, and the divine word arrives: *Pure Alterity*. Once a specific empirical face has performed its divine postal service, everything changes. What has been to this point a *progressive* story of discovery become *regressive* story origins. The idea of Infinity "put into me" becomes "the common source of activity and theory," that is, *always already there*.[58] *TI* perpetually circulates within the following fundamental claims:

> The alleged scandal of [ethical] alterity presupposes the tranquil identity of the same.

And

> . . . *the idea of infinity, revealed in the face, does not only require a separated being, the light of the face is* necessary for separation.[59]

"Separation" is presented as both the *ground* and the *result* of the Other's appearance. Moreover,

> Like a shunt every social relation leads back to the presentation of the other to the same without the intermediary of any image or sign, solely by the expression of the face.

And

> Because my position as an I is effectuated already in fraternity the face can present itself as a face. The relation of the face in fraternity, . . . the *reference of every dialogue to the third party* . . . encompasses the face to face opposition.[60]

The face is presented as both the *ground* and *result* of divinely "effectuated" fraternity. Paternity "encloses a [plurality] of the Identical," that is, envelops "the whole of humanity," where *all* selves and others are "at the same time unique and non-unique."[61] Finally, at the level of his explicit methodological statements:

> The method here does indeed consist in seeking the condition of empirical situations, but it leaves to developments called empirical, in which the conditioning possibility is accomplished—it leaves to the *concretization*—an ontological role that specifies the meaning of the fundamental possibility, a meaning invisible in that condition.[62]

Because "reversing constitution" *starts with* a purely formal idea, and "reverses" to its putatively empirical contexts of "accomplish[ment]," the "ontological role" of concretization remains fundamentally indeterminate. Do human bodies *incarnate* the formal idea? Or does the idea of the Infinite *originate in* these empirical contexts? Does the *Infinite itself* create these empirical contexts and "reveal itself" in them? Or is the *Infinite itself* "created" in them? What "accomplish[es]" what? And *how*?

> [T]he production of the infinite entity is inseparable from the idea of infinity, for it is precisely in the disproportion between the idea of infinity and the infinity of which it is the idea that this exceeding of limits is produced. The idea of infinity is the mode of being, the infinition, of infinity. Infinity does not first exist, and then reveal itself. Its infinitum is produced as revelation, as a positing of its idea in me.[63]

The "production of the infinite entity" implies that *we* "produce" the "reality" of God. Yet "positing its idea in me" implies that God "produc[es]" *its* "idea" in us. Because "content overflowing concept" is *nothing other* than the "disproportion between the idea of infinity and the infinity of which it is the idea," his account is viciously circular. The "infinite entity" *must first exist* to "posit its idea in me," yet we must *always already have this idea* to "[produce] . . . the infinite entity." Because the "*idea* of infinity" is cast as a "mode of *being*," Levinas's use of "production" remains indeterminate. Finally,

> [T]he break-up of the formal structure of thought (the noema of a noesis) into events which this structure dissimulates, but which sustain it and restore its concrete significance, constitutes a deduction—necessary and yet non-analytical. In our exposition it is indicated by expressions such as "that is," or "precisely," or "this accomplishes that," or "this is produced as that."[64]

Because the first sentence describes *nothing other* than "reversing constitution," the very meaning of "produced" and "accomplishes" remains indeterminate. God remains both an "infinite entity" and the "idea of infinity," and this so-called "deduction" never specifies what precisely is being deduced: the Reality of the Infinite, or its Idea? A "necessary and yet non-analytic" deduction implies *Real ontological* "*necessity*," yet "Infinity does not first exist" implies *Ideal transcendental* "*necessity*." As should be clear, Levinas really does "flip the deck" between *transcendent fact* and a *transcendental idea*. As "the common source of activity and theory," the Other is simultaneously cast as both a *real* metaphysico-Paternal origin and as a *transcendental* "origin of all signification," or put simply: a *pure idea* necessary for the *general intelligibility* of moral meaning, and a *pure reality* necessary for the *actual existence* of moral human relationships.[65]

IV. Conclusion: Why?

Constitution or "effectuation"? Ideal or real relation? Transcendental or psycho-metaphysical genesis? Positing the "relation" between self and other as a "relation without relation"—as between an "absolute" singularity and an "absolute" alterity—bars him from, with Husserl, utilizing the world to mediate the "relation"; bars him from, with Heidegger, Gadamer, or Ricoeur, utilizing hermeneutic infrastructures that could render his circle virtuous; bars him from utilizing the counter-factuality of purely formal transcendental discourse-structures, and keeps him from owning up to the quite conventional metaphysics he performs. All he can do is "flip the deck," or perpetually spin in a vicious and tragic circle. While I have amply indicated the text's circularity, in what sense is this circularity tragic? Levinas writes, "There does indeed exist a human race as a biological genus, and the common function men [sic] may exercise in the world."[66] On the text's own terms, if my interlocutor is genuinely "*absolutely* other" and pure of all mediation, then she is necessarily *also* "absolutely *other*" than her own *bodily form*. This would annul the self-reference of her demand (her "help *me*!"). The face that suffers and demands is *not* the face that suffers and demands. If we instead hold that her alterity manifests *just in* her singular *Leib*, then inclusion in "there does indeed exist . . ." is apparently *validated*, rather than *contested*, by ethics, and hence: her self-reference is never *pure*. Here, categorial mediation or concept inclusion does not constitute a "violence" per se. If we finally say that her body is not *all* that she is, we perform a *mediate* identification and have simply given up on all talk of her "absolute alterity." Levinas can keep a *pure body* or a *pure meaning*, but he cannot keep both *at once*. Because "revelation" was precisely cast as the face's *kath'auto* expression, and because his own descriptions include references to *both* (1) the ego's own experience of suffering *and* (2) existential-categorial "creaturehood," he has *failed* to present a purely self-referring entity.[67] By failing to present a self-standing entity or meaning, Levinas has failed to show that *ethics is "first philosophy.*"[68] The descriptions he actually performs rather *show* that the meaning ascribed to the face is *dependent* on (a) human sentience *in general* (empiricist Levinas), (b) human intentionality *in general* (idealist Levinas), or (c) human being-with or creaturehood *in general* (ontological Levinas). Whether the relevant meaning or entity is achieved through empirical generalizations (conventionalism), cognitive performances (Kant), phenomenological-constitutive processes (Husserl), or original and *relatively* open ontological categories (Heideggerian or theistic ontology), in all cases, there is no such thing as *pure* "separation" or *pure* alterity, and hence no "violence" per se by concepts or categories.

Finally, why? This is the big question. As valid and interesting as the question of Levinas's potential psychological motivations might be, I here restrict myself to the text alone. Why did Levinas construct and perform his method as he did? For my "deck-flipping" description to do *explanatory* work, I must finally propose an answer to this question. As the attuned reader will have already recognized, the reason is not hard to surmise. In the opening sentence of section II, Levinas writes: "In describing the metaphysical relation as disinterested, *as disengaged from all participation* . . ."[69]

"Participation," it must be said, is the fundamental "enemy" that orients the logic of the text *as a whole*. Participation names the alleged "violence" wrought on the hapless inhabitants of "totality."[70] Levinas's fervent desire to avoid "participation" is ultimately *why* he posits the ego as a "concept-less individual," *why* he asserts that sensibility is "the mode in which the break-up of totality . . . accomplished," *why* he posits an "absolute other" as a "void that breaks the totality," and finally *why* he casts "relation" as a "relation without relation."[71] "To break with participation," he assures us, "is to maintain contact," but of what can this contact consist?[72] On Levinas's own terms, the ego can only "breach totality" by *becoming a totality*: the element that "envelops or contains without being able to be contained or enveloped" is "not convertible into exteriority," that is, *completely enveloped by the ego* "immersed" in them;[73] all while *simultaneously* "maintain[ing] contact" with *real* bodies, "*pure* qualities," in "an ultimate relation with the *substantial* plenitude of being," held "[d]istinct from my substance but *constituting* it.[74] Likewise, the other can only "breach totality" by *creating a totality*: as "the common source of activity and theory," divine effectuation "encloses a [plurality] of the Identical"—"the whole of humanity"—where *all* selves and others are "at the same time unique and non-unique,"[75] all while *simultaneously* maintaining "absolute distance" between *real* bodies ("multiple singularities"), through a *pure* "call from the Other," revealed "over and beyond form" as "the ultimate relation in Being."[76] The sensible ego can only "breach" totalizing-concepts through *reference* to *real* "exterior" bodies by *real* external "effectuation." The sensible other can only "breach" totalizing-categories by having a *sense* always already "put into him." By enforcing a ban on all mediation, Levinas can only "breach totalities" by alternate and circular appeals to original *sense* and original *reference*, to originary *meaning* and originary *reality*, to transcendental *idea* and transcendent *fact*: "Discourse is thus . . . a *pure* 'knowledge' or [pure] 'experience,' a *traumatism of astonishment*."[77] Astonishing indeed. And why? *Because he arbitrarily declares concepts a sin.*

At the outset, I claimed that *TI*'s circularity is somewhat difficult to detect. But is it really so difficult? My detailed argumentation and excessive use of quotations were motivated by a desire to *show*, once and for all, *that* the text's incoherence is both plain and irresolvable. My analysis of his method endeavored to show *how* this incoherence issues from an intrinsically equivocal and indeterminate account of theory. My proposal for *why* he constructed his method as he did—to avoid the alleged "violence" of concepts or categories—quite plausibly explains the philosophical motive for his aporetic methodological construction and performances. If the more general criticisms of Derrida, Bernasconi, and others have yet to finally settle the question of the tenability of *TI*'s claims, I hope my focused demonstration might finally get the job done. By incoherently performing simultaneous realist and idealist accounts of necessary conditions ("content 'overflowing' concept," "[seesaw] constitution," simultaneous "pure recording" and "comprehension" accounts of theory, etc.), his general claims remain fundamentally *arbitrary*. When a skeptic questions whether the Other is really a transcendent "fact," Levinas will point to the *concept* in "content 'overflowing' concept," that is, to a *transcendental Idea*. When a realist questions the purely formal character of the idea, Levinas will point to the "content" in "content 'overflowing' concept," that is, to *a transcendent Fact*. And quite interestingly, if a post-structuralist questions the way I've framed this problem, what might he or she do? Point to the "contents" and the "overflowing" in "contents 'overflowing' concepts," that is, to individual bodies, affectivity, and performativity in asserting the allegedly contingent character of all concepts. *TI* has something for everyone. Its intrinsically equivocal logic and method, and the highly relevant nature of its subject matter, means we can find almost whatever we want in its pages, so long as we embrace the idea that ethics is primary. If the explanation I've proposed here is cogent, the *question* of the priority of ethics must be posed anew. Perhaps there *really* is such a thing as an "absolute other," or perhaps the idea of Infinity is a genuine condition for moral intelligibility in general. But if there is and if it is, some other form of description or argumentation will have to reveal it to us.

To conclude, Levinas declares: "I do not believe that transparency is possible in method, or philosophy is possible as transparency."[78] Are transparency in method and royal rationalism the same thing? One might insist that for a philosophy that embraces the limits of reason (and hence, of transparency), *methodological* transparency—of what counts as condition and consequent, what form of relation gets us from the former to the latter, what counts as evidence, and so forth—is even *more necessary*. Without telling readers the explicit methodological norms in play, they have no way to directly assess a claim. In my view, such is to *fail to take responsibility for one's claims*, that is, to "accept . . . the rules of the [methodological] game, [while] cheating."[79] There is no evidence that Levinas cheated on purpose. Indeed, insofar as he augmented his methodological approach in his own late work, he seems to have acceded to Derrida's judgment that *TI*'s problems are irresolvable. Later I provide a way to treat the living potentials and validity of Levinas's particular phenomenological analyses as distinct from the methodological problems I've diagnosed here.[80]

V. Appendix: Formal Restatement of the Argument

V.A. Formal Restatement of *TI*'s Internal Logic

Levinas positively asserts, "There does indeed exist a human race as a biological genus, and the common function men [sic] may exercise in the world."[81] He wants to say that fraternal sociality grounded in the face-to-face ethically constitutes humanity, and only subsequently "there does indeed exist. . . ." If (a) my interlocutor is "absolutely other" and pure of all conceptual/categorial mediation, then she is necessarily *also* "absolutely other" than her own *bodily form*. This would annul the bodily reference of her demand ("help *me*!"). The other that suffers and demands is *not* the other that suffers and demands. If (b) her "absolute alterity" manifests *just in* her singular *Leib*, then inclusion in "there does indeed exist . . ." is *validated*, rather than *contested*, by ethics, and hence her self-reference is never pure. In this case, categorial mediation or concept inclusion does not constitute a "violence" per se. If we finally say (c) the other's body isn't *all* that she is, we employ a *mediate* identification and have simply given on all talk of her "absolute alterity." On Levinas's own terms, (i) alterity is only ever *relative*, (ii) general concepts are being positively utilized, and (iii) the precise forms of relation in play are *never specified* in his wholly equivocal account of "theory."

V.A.1. In either realist or idealist mode, (i) alterity is only ever *relative*, (ii) general concepts/categories are *positively utilized*, and (iii) the precise forms of relation he utilizes are *never specified* in his wholly equivocal account of "theory."

(i) *Alterity is only ever relative.*

(i.a.) *Phenomenology mode*: The ego's "comprehension"[82] of the face's demand necessarily presupposes something like Husserl's analogy-perception: the perceptual identification of the other's *Leib* as "like" or analogous to my own, and the attribution of original consciousness to them based in this kinesthetic analogy. The other is an *alter ego* whose alterity is *original*, though nevertheless *relative*, that is, *mediated* by the ego and indicative reference to the *Lebenswelt*.

(i.b) *Realist mode*: Self and other are explicitly and originally "comprehended" in either (a) something like Heidegger's being-with, or (b) Levinas's own posited category of "creature."[83] Being-with or creaturehood renders intersubjectivity *original*, but also ontologically *determinative*, that is, alterity is *relative*, not absolute, because these categories constitute *who* individuals are *as* human beings.

(i.c.) Levinas switches back and forth between these two accounts, and on either front: the other retains an originality, while alterity remains relative, as i.a and i.b show.

(ii) *General concepts/categories are positively utilized.*

(ii.a) *Phenomenology mode*: the constitutive achievements of Husserl's transcendental subject are held to disclose original, necessary, a priori meanings. These meanings are attributed to *all* transcendental subjects, that is, *all* subjects capable of repeating phenomenological *Evidenz*, and so forth. General concepts are ultimately founded in original *Evidenz* and phenomenological-constitutive processes, but they of necessity apply to *all*, and can be repeated by *all*. Minded activity does the determining, but its meanings are *universal*. It's debatable whether Levinas's ego-analysis can be construed along these strict Husserlian lines, given his indeterminate account of theory. But the generality of the meaning of the ego is plain in Levinas (he is describing *all* ego's, egoity in general, not just his own ego).

(ii.b) *Realist mode*: being-with or creaturehoods occur as a necessary and determinative ontological structure, not merely a product of the mind. Our concepts are determined by "reality."

(ii.c) Levinas switches back and forth between these two accounts, utilizing world against mind (ego-analysis), then utilizing mind against world (other-analysis), spinning in a circle throughout the text. Whether as achievements of minded activity (Kant, Husserl), or as determinations of a fundamental reality (Heidegger, Aristotle), concepts are being positively deployed.

(iii) *The precise forms of relation he utilizes are never specified thanks to his equivocal account of theory.*

(iii.a) *Phenomenology mode*: On Levinas's own terms, in sensibility, the ego must necessarily and *in fact* rely on *memory*, that is, the mind psychologistically construed. Levinas relegates this "fact" secondary to the "original" phenomenological sense of enjoyment, dwelling, labor, face.

(iii.b) *Realist mode*: On Levinas's own terms, in sensibility, the ego must necessarily and *in fact* rely on consumed, environing, elemental, and human "others," that is, *bodies* and qualities realistically construed. Levinas relegates these "facts" secondary to the "original" phenomenological sense of enjoyment, dwelling, labor, face.

(iii.c) Causality or constitution? Real or ideal relation? Psycho-metaphysical or transcendental genesis? This is why the transcendental/empirical puzzle has taken so long to crack: the formal structure of his claims are nearly identical, but (meaning qua) "fact" and (meaning qua) "idea" are changing places. On the one hand, Levinas achieves affective meaning by assuming causality: "real" qualities from "real" exterior bodies impact the mind and imprint on its memory and generate the affective "sense" he describes. Here, *fact determines meaning*. On the other hand, Levinas asserts a determinative status of his descriptions by assuming formal constitution: enjoyment constitutes the *telos* to which suffering refers, "dwelling" qua meaning constitutes dwelling qua fact, the face *determines all*. Here, *meaning determines fact*. His posited "relation without relation" between self and other—"absolute" alterity of the other and "absolute" singularity of the ego—bars him from, with Husserl, utilizing the world to mediate the relation between self and other; bars him from, with Heidegger, Gadamer, or Ricoeur, utilizing hermeneutic infrastructures that could render his circle virtuous; bars him from utilizing counter-factual transcendental discourse structures and their purely formal character, and bars him from owning up to the conventional metaphysics he performs. All he can do is "flip the deck," and spin in a circle, in a vain attempt to escape concepts.

Given i, ii, and iii, *therefore*:
General Conclusion (GC). The face's expression is not *kath'auto*; therefore, *ethics is* not *first philosophy*.

GC1. Given i.a. and i.b., by virtue of Levinas's own descriptions, the face does *not* refer to itself alone. By way of i.a., the face *also* refers to my own knowledge or experience of suffering. By way of i.b., the face necessarily refers to the fact that I *care for my own being*, it *expresses not merely itself*, but a universal fact of human being. The face expresses its primordial Dasein or ontological-fraternal creaturehood.

GC2. Clearly, whether we opt for i.a. or i.b. (Levinas performs both), responsibility originates in a *relative* identity between self and other, whether as a co-performing subject or co-determined Dasein/creature, human "co-ness" or relative "likeness" is internally involved in the face's own signification.

GC3. Because the face's *kath'auto* expression was presented as defining and instituting "ethics as first philosophy," and because further Levinas has failed to actually present a purely self-standing meaning or self-referring entity, he therefore has failed to show that ethics is first philosophy. The descriptions he actually presents show that the meaning of the face is dependent on either (a) our sentience (empiricist Levinas), (b) our intentionality (idealist Levinas), or (c) our being-with or ontological-fraternal creaturehood (ontological Levinas).

V.B. FORMAL RESTATEMENT OF LEVINAS'S ARGUMENT

The other individual's *resistance* to generalization constitutes the *negativity* of the intuition of the face: the other is empirically given but *not* intellectually intuited.[84]

V.B.1.a. Negative intuition necessarily implies perceptual reference to an empirically *given* individual *body*.[85]

V.B.1.b. Negative intuition necessarily implies perceptual awareness of the empirically given individual's (i) bodily movement and (ii) capacity to psychologically suffer.[86]

V.B.2. Negative intuition is asserted to yield a "positive" *surplus* meaning: an "ought" (rather than an "is").

V.B.2.a. The "positivity" of the "ought" issues in the empirically given individual's (*empirical*) capacity for speech.

V.B.2.b. The "positivity" of the ought issues from an (alleged) phenomenologically "revealed" (*essential*) meaning of 2a, "expression *kath'auto*."[87]

Therefore,
V.B.2.b. = unification of 1.a, 1.b, and V.B.2.a.

V.B.3. "V.B.2.b" is presented as only generalized with the entrance of a third, simultaneously construed as (i) a numerically distinct empirically given individual body and (ii) a non-empirically given divine "other" presented as a logically necessary extension of V.B.2.b.

V.C. FORMAL RESTATEMENT OF MY OBJECTIONS

Objection 1. V.B.2.b. refers to 1a, 1b, and V.B.2.a, and therefore supposes empirical generalizations that necessarily refer to (i) the ego's own psychological experience and (ii) an empirically given "likeness" between a specific ego's and specific other's respective *bodies* and *psychological experiences*.

Therefore,

Conclusion 1: The "not" in "*not* intuited" is question begging. Negative categoriality supposes *positive epistemic* or *positive ontological* generalizations.

C1.a. Levinas's realism equivocates between *sensuous* (empirical) and *semantic* (metaphysical) *immediacy*. Between the other individual's *body* and an individual real *God*.

O2. Categorial relations, whether predicative, conjunctive, imperative, and so forth, are inherently *general*.

Therefore,

C2: By way of 1, 2b, and O1, Levinas necessarily depends on *general categories* that identify empirically given individual others, equivocating between (idealist) transcendental constitution or (realist) general classification.

C2.a. (Positive proof): *Resistance* to generalization performatively presupposes theoretical practice (or *attempted generalizations*), however construed.[88]

C2.b. (Negative proof): The empirically given individual other can only signify *as* an individual through contrast to other individuals *of her kind*.[89]

O3. Levinas's account of the third is premised in equivocal reference to (a) a third individual human body, and (b) a formal universal meaning.

Therefore,

C3.a. Levinas equivocates between (i) *transcendental* (idealist) categoriality and (ii) *ontological* (realist) conceptuality; between transcendental and empirico-metaphysical intuition. He performs ii in his anti-concept claims for original ethical meaning, he performs i in his anti-realist claims for original ethical meaning. Whether in realist or idealist mode, Levinas performs conceptual generalizations necessary to the face's own expression.

C3.b. Levinas's own descriptions ("face" and "paternal effectuation") perform a circular grounding of individual human bodies/experiences premised in an inherently equivocal account of "theory."

C3: By way 1a, 1b, and 2a, Levinas must perform O3.b to achieve 2b (my O1 and C2.b). By way of 1 and 2b, Levinas must perform O3a to achieve 2b (my O1 and C2a).

O4. Levinas's equivocal method and general claims are premised in the *unanalyzed* judgment: *concepts are inherently "violent."*

O4.a. Without justifying this judgment, the claim lacks warrant.

O4.b. Levinas in fact offers no justification for this judgment, or even directly analyzes it. He simply assumes it is true.

Therefore,

C4: The claim "concepts are inherently violent" is unjustified.

General Conclusion: Given O1, O2, and O3, Levinas's method is incoherent and his general claims unjustified. Given O4, the motivational ground for Levinas's project in *TI* lacks explicit warrant.

Chapter 4

Ontology and Ethics in *Otherwise than Being*

The true work of God is all good, since it is existence.

—Moses Maimonides

There can be a return of the repressed only if a traumatic event actually took place.

—Paul Ricoeur

Language is the possibility of an enigmatic equivocation for better and for worse, which men abuse.

—Emmanuel Levinas

Pure sensibility, released from any relation to content, would no longer be intuition, but rather "thought."

—Theodor Adorno

I. Introduction

The results of my critique of *TI* are clear. Levinas's actual methodological practice renders his own description of the face question begging. The analysis he actually performs internally relies on either transcendental categories or generalized empirico-metaphysical concepts, such that face's expression precisely fails to be *purely* self-referring, and hence, it makes no sense to assert that linguistic mediation is "violent" per se. In this chapter, I turn to Levinas's second major work, *Otherwise than Being, or Beyond Essence* [hereafter *OB*]. I have opted to treat this text as an independent philosophical proposal for two reasons: (i) there has been much good work done on the development of Levinas's oeuvre and Derrida's role in this development;[2] and (ii) my aim here is to ascertain what Levinas means by "responsibility" and "disinterest" in order to test their overall coherence and evaluate his allegedly Eurocentric statements in their light. I therefore set aside purely philological questions and continue with my immanent critique.[3]

In what follows, I analyze Levinas's mature philosophical position and seek to evaluate it from the perspective of his own account of what it means to be *disinterested*. This strategy is interesting for three reasons. First, to evaluate Levinas's philosophy on Levinas's own terms is to do him the justice of not performing purely external criticism. I seek to avoid at all costs importing another normative perspective in order to dismiss Levinas's through contrast. Next, Levinas's account of disinterest constitutes the absolute core of his ethics. As such, if it can be shown that his account is defective in some irremediable way, we will have to fundamentally rethink his approach. Finally, Levinas's account of disinterest is in part a response to Husserl and Heidegger's respective accounts of the phenomenological reduction. Given the problem of chauvinism and disinterest, this is perhaps the most interesting aspect of my approach. For phenomenology, the reduction is the methodological technique—or existential/ethical event—said to yield a non-distortive perspective *on the world as it is*. In other words, it's held to yield a *true, authentic*, or *just*—and as such, *self-justifying*—form of context-transcending universality. In part 1, I reconstruct Levinas's own account of what it means to be disinterested, focusing on what I call (a) *motivational purity*, and (b) *justified context transcendence*. In part 2, I perform an immanent critique of his position. I demonstrate (1) if taken on its own terms, Levinas's account of (a) is self-defeating; (2) will and concept in fact show up in Levinas's positive description of ethical selfhood, such that his account of (b) is ultimately question begging. I argue that the failure of (a) and the question-begging character of (b) are concealed by alternate and viciously circular appeals to *sensuous* and *semantic* immediacy, and that despite a few small augmentations, his method in *OB* is functionally identical to *TI*. I conclude by showing that Levinas's analogizing appeals to the play of philosophy and skepticism ultimately render "ethics" and "ontology" reciprocally imbricating on his own terms.

II. Levinasian Disinterest

For Levinas, disinterest is fundamentally construed as a "suspension" or neutralization of self-interest.[4] By "suspension" he means a moment in which self-interest ceases to determine the orientation of an act or perspective by producing a specific sort of self. Self-interest, here, is understood in at least two senses: (1) in the mundane sense of tainted or impure motivations in our dealings with others, and (2) in the special sense of our naive absorption in the everyday doings of the world, including extant reflective grasps of those doings, or philosophical accounts that purport to underwrite, clarify, or explain them. Disinterest, by contrast, consists in precisely the opposite possibilities: (1a) the possibility of pure giving, and (2a) the possibility of achieving a truly self-justifying perspective for considering the world as a whole. I call (1) *motivational purity* and (2) *justified context-transcendence*.

II.a. Motivational Purity

In ethical election, or what Levinas also calls "proximity," the Other "cores out," "de-substantializes," or "uproots" the embedded, self-interested subject of ontology.[5] This "uprooting"—an obligation to give without limit, beyond my extant capacities (even unto death)—occurs *against* my spontaneous will-*to-be*. Levinas describes responsibility as always painful, always "despite ourselves," always *against* our spontaneous inclinations and interests. The event of responsibility is said to produce an ethical self that is an "absolute" or "pure passivity."[6] So described, the ethical self is literally *incapable* of self-interest, in the following senses: such responsibility is (i) unpleasurable, and hence cannot be mistaken as appealing to or being in line with our natural inclinations, (ii) powerless with respect to itself, or incapable of escaping or modifying what it is (qua limitless responsibility), and (iii) structurally or "descriptively" distinct from all agency, that is, unrelated to agency such that the will contributes nothing to the meaning election opens or the giving that occurs through it. If the authentic ethical self is indeed not active, not "substantial," or not dependent on a larger context for its meaning; if the ethical self is indeed nothing other than an effect or "echo" of the other's affective demand, and if, as a relation, the ethical self is nothing but an indeclinable "coring out" of the self-interested ontological subject—a total giving-over to the other—then Levinas has apparently succeeded in giving a particular account of disinterested giving.[7] Levinas presents various illustrations of the sort of giving he has in mind. For instance, he often commented on Vassily Grossman's *Life and Fate*:

> [T]oward the book's end, when Stalingrad has already been rescued, the German prisoners, including an officer, are cleaning out a basement and removing the decomposing bodies. The officer suffers particularly from this misery. In the crowd, a woman who hates Germans is delighted to see this man more miserable than the others. Then she gives him the last piece of bread she has. This is extraordinary. Even in hatred there exists a mercy stronger than hatred.[8]

Over-against her hatred of the German officer, Grossman's devastated Russian woman gives the officer her last precious crust of bread. She acts against her quite understandable and spontaneous hatred in an act of kindness that puts her own survival at greater risk. Such is the meaning and possibility of disinterested giving Levinas has in mind.

II.b. Justified Context-Transcendence

II.b.i. Levinas's Critique of Tradition

To get at what "justified context-transcendence" precisely means, I must briefly review Levinas's ontology and his critique of tradition. A thorough treatment would take us too far afield for my purposes in this chapter, so I simply sketch its broad outlines here. Also, Levinas's own take on disinterested context-transcendence turns on his accounts of "substitution" and "the third party." Before turning to his own account, it is necessary to get a hold of what he objects to in the tradition, so as to more clearly grasp his alternative.

Levinas's account of disinterest turns on what he calls the Saying/Said distinction. Saying names the "approach" or "proximity" of the other, or the manner in which the alterity of the other comes to bear on the subject, and as such produces an ethical self of the sort sketched above.[9] The Said, on the other hand, is said to name the conscious domain of being and thought, or what Levinas calls "ontology." Ontology, here, has a rather wide berth, and involves essentially two aspects. First, for Levinas, ontology refers to any discourse that purports to describe or explain what human beings *are*. Ontology "thematizes," that is, *talks about* human beings in such a way that depends, explicitly or not, on a third-person point of view.[10] It involves generality, in other words, and the categorial specification of individuals as belonging to this or that class, with this or that meaning, and so forth. Levinas's constant protests against "paganism," "mythology," "theology," and traditional "philosophy" all revolve around this very basic point: they *identify* the other in some way, treat the other as a member of a class, an instance of a general term, or in some way determined by a larger context of relations.[11] Even Kantian philosophy falls under "ontology" here, insofar as Kant treats morality as originarily a matter of *law*, wherein actual selves and others are treated as instances or bearers of a transcendental subject in general, and not the unique ones they in fact are. Success in Kantian morality involves consistency in the performance of the categorical imperative, not pure giving to the other *as other*, and in just this way is "ontology" in the broad sense Levinas has in mind.[12] Ontology in this sense is the primacy tradition grants—whether as irrational "mysticism," cultural narrative, or rational construction—to identity over alterity in specifying the meaning individuals.

Next, the primary sense of ontology Levinas has in mind involves his own explicit characterization of being as *conatus*. Ontology is the self-interested perseverance of beings in their being. Being as a whole is said to exhibit this self-orientation, and Levinas variously refers to Spinoza, Heidegger, and even Darwin to gloss what he means by ontology.[13] Ontology in this sense emphasizes the universal propensity of beings to act for their own sake.

Finally, combining these two senses, Levinas regards ontology as always more or less prejudiced. Ontology is "violence" because it identifies alterity and remains polluted by the self-interest of the ontologist.[14] Ontology can never attain the authentic or pure universality it aspires to. The properly *lived* meaning of ethical selfhood—irrupting in Saying and in the pre-predicative affective life of the subject—is occluded by "thematizing," that is, in moving from *talking to* to *talking about* him or her, and the inevitable interpellation of concepts and categories this involves. When ontology posits general rules or norms and treats them as the proper domain of ethics, it distorts the true meaning of responsibility as it's *lived* in the face-to-face, and as it plays out in our pre-conscious affective life.

We are finally in a position to provisionally elaborate the second sense of disinterest in Levinas's work, what I call *justified context-transcendence*. As Levinas describes it, ontology is incapable of providing the true or unprejudiced universality it aspires to, because it fails to *justify its own practices in a non–question-begging way*. For instance, Levinas's persistent criticism of Husserl is his alleged "theoretical prejudice." Husserl putatively privileges knowing and theoretical practice as opening the exemplary form of human responsibility, and in such a way that allegedly distorts what authentic responsibility really is.[15] Husserl construed phenomenological practice as self-justifying, or the best and most rigorous candidate for authentically human responsibility in general, when contrasted with, for example, fascism, or the metaphysics of tradition.[16] Or consider the Heidegger of *Being and Time*. For Heidegger, responsibility ultimately emerges over-against the conventional norms and illusions of the mundane social world. *Angst* allows the world to be seen as it is—*temporal*—and enables Dasein to seize its *self* from absorption in convention, and the distortive philosophical perspectives that underwrite it. Levinas regards Heidegger's position as ultimately "pagan."[17] Heidegger allegedly not only fails to provide an unprejudiced context-transcending perspective, but he also fails at presenting anything that might qualify as a candidate for ethical responsibility. Setting aside the question of whether Levinas in fact does justice to Husserl and Heidegger's respective positions, his criticisms here allow us to catch sight of what he means by disinterest. Levinas believes he has succeeded in avoiding "ontology" and its problems because he believes he has succeeded where tradition, for example, Husserl and Heidegger, fails: *justifying his own practices in a non–question-begging way*. In short, Levinas's ethics apparently *justifies* practices of knowing because knowing is necessary for *justice*. Levinas asks:

> Why would proximity, the pure signification of saying, the anarchic one-for-the-other of beyond being, revert to being or fall into being, into a conjunction of entities, into essence showing itself in the said? . . . Why know? . . . Why philosophy?[18]

Levinas gives an answer to the question "why know?" by accounting for the origin of consciousness and concern for justice, and does so by grounding it in that which is held to be necessarily prior to justice and fundamentally not a knowing: ethics. In just this way, Levinas believes he has *justified* practices of knowing, and hence has attained an authentic context-transcending perspective that can apprehend the world as it is and provide guidance on how it should be. Apparently unlike Husserl, Levinas believes his account is disinterested or non-viciously universal, because it respects the alterity of the other and the uniqueness of the self by not originally treating them as of a piece, or determined by a larger determinative identity. His ethics, then, apparently succeeds at not conceptually "violating" the other at its most basic level of description. Moreover, by virtue of ethics, the ethical self qua just analyst always already *owes everything*, and hence necessarily excludes all reference to her or his own "ontological" needs in the accounting she or he renders of *who owes what to whom, in what order, and why*?[19] Apparently unlike Heidegger, authentic responsibility is absolutely for-the-other. Authentic ownness, the singularity of self, irrupts in an exceptional responsibility, not the banal self-interest shared with being as a whole. Against Husserl, disinterest originally is not a kind of pious pursuit of "fulfilled intentions." Disinterest involves a radical non-indifference to the other in his or her sufferings, an animation against injustice. And against Heidegger, disinterest proper is not necessarily some holdover of epochal theoreticism, but empowers a fair accounting of how things stand and how they might be improved. In order to evaluate Levinas's own position on Levinas's own terms, we have to review the transition he describes from singularity to universality and the justice it is said to open. Only then will we be able to judge if Levinas has achieved a truly disinterested universal perspective or non–question-begging form of theoretical practice, hence succeeding where he claims others have failed. This should allow us to fairly determine whether instances of apparent Eurocentrism in Levinas's political and religious writings are merely all-too-human mistakes or whether they follow from some defect in his philosophical position.

II.b.ii. Substitution

Ethical election occurs in "proximity" to other, or a pre-conscious affective "contact" that recurs each time I address or am addressed by another person.[20] This "contact" institutes a special sort of relation: it produces and identifies a self as "this responsible one." The relation established is irreducibly one-way, producing a self as "chosen" or "elected" for a limitless responsibility to the other. The ethical self can in no way decline, divide, or escape itself as inordinate responsibility, hence Levinas's apt determination of it as a "pure" or "absolute passivity."[21] Election is unpleasant, painful, and registers solely within our affective life. Levinas variously describes the self in terms of "persecution" and "obsession," and the elected one as a "hostage."[22] Such descriptions are meant to dramatically emphasize the unpleasant and unchosen character of the relation, and its purity from ontological agency or will. The sense of proximity involves does not end here, however. If responsibility is genuinely limitless, the ethical self is not only responsible *to* the other, but also responsible *for* the other, even responsible for her or his responsibility. As such, the ethical self *substitutes* itself for the other, becomes responsible *for* her or his responsibility.[23] And in so doing, Levinas claims, the self becomes responsible for *all* (for the entirety of the determinate world and the multitude that populates it). This is precisely why the ethical self is said to be a "pure passivity": it is called to take responsibility for a world not of its making, a world it did not produce. In substitution, self and other do not thereby "merge" or become completely identical, because the ethical self cannot allow itself to be substituted *for*. As Levinas insists: "no one can substitute their self for me, who substitutes my self for all."[24] Levinas describes the movement from proximity to substitution as a kind of unfolding of the sense or meaning the ethical self *is*, in stark contrast to the self-interest of the ontological subject.

With this account of substitution in hand, Levinas believes he has successfully described a disinterested *context transcending perspective*. The non-substitutable or irreplaceable character of the self as *more* (limitlessly) responsible than all the others concretely delineates its uniqueness, while the other apparently still remains veritably other or free from all determination. He has now also described a transition from singularity to universality. In the unfolding of sense from proximity to substitution, the ethical self moves from being responsible *to* the other to being responsible *for* the other, and for the "all." Insofar as responsibility is limitless, one-way, and unsullied by the violence of will, he appears to have also described a form of determination pure of "ontological" interest. This judgment is premature, however, because at this point we have only considered the self and the other, and not the multitude of other others to which the universality yielded in substitution must somehow reckon. If Levinas and Levinas *alone* claimed universal responsibility, his account would be uncontroversial. The question of disinterest and of a non-pernicious context transcending perspective becomes most acute when such responsibility is distributed, and produces norms *valid for all*.

II.b.iii. The Third Party, Justice

Judging by the voluminous literature, Levinas's account of the third party is well-known. The usual way we explain his take on the third party goes like this: if I, the ethical self, give all to the other, as my limitless responsibility to her or him initially suggests, I will have nothing to give the other other, to the *third party*. With the entrance of the third, concepts, calculation, and language—in a word, *justice*—become necessary. While this indeed does clarify one aspect of justice in Levinas—the just ordering of resources so as to address the needs of all—it does not tell us the precise meaning of the third. For instance, the other in proximity performs something the self cannot: it elects and produces a self as a limitless responsibility. The ethical self *cannot do* this (it is not self-caused or self-produced). Likewise, the ethical self is *not* the other of proximity, for it is nothing but limitless responsibility. Even if we posit some sort of responsibility in the proximate other, the ethical self always has "more" of it, and this "more" always remains to distinguish self and other. With this distinction in mind, what precisely does it *mean* to be a third party, and what does the third party contribute to Levinas's descriptions here? So as not to distort his account in my analysis, I quote him at length:

> If proximity ordered me to the other alone, there would have not been any problem, in even the most general sense of the term. A question would not have been born, nor consciousness, nor self-consciousness. The responsibility for the other is an immediacy antecedent to questions, it is proximity. It is troubled and becomes a problem when the third party enters. The third party is other than the neighbor, but also another neighbor, and also a neighbor of the other, and not simply his fellow. . . . The third party introduces contradiction in the saying whose significance before the other until then went in one direction. It is of itself the limit of responsibility and the birth of the question: What do I have to do with justice? A question of consciousness. Justice is necessary, that is, comparison, coexistence, contemporaneousness, assembling, order, thematization . . . Thus one would understand, in proximity, in the saying without problems, in responsibility, the reason for the intelligibility of systems.[25]

On the basis of this passage alone, we are unable to determine the precise meaning of the third party. Whereas the other of proximity and the ethical self remain relatively distinct, nothing here tells us what sense the third party holds in its own right. I set aside this problem and give a provisional interpretation to try to reconstruct what he might have in mind.

Levinas seems to be suggesting that the quantitative addition of another other gives rise to a qualitative change, and hence the emergence of a question for the self: *who owes what to whom, in what order, and why?* The "who" in question here is *not* the ethical self (the ethical self *just is* limitless responsibility: it owes *everything*); the "who" rather refers to the multitude of others for whom the self takes responsibility. Justice necessitates "comparison, coexistence, contemporaneousness, assembling, order, thematization," and "control, a search for justice, society, and the State."[26] With the entrance of the third, all the protocols and practices of typical intellectual and practical life find their justification. Yet the equality introduced by justice does not mitigate the excessive responsibility of the ethical self, but is said to *increase* it:

> In no way is justice a degradation of obsession, a degeneration of the for-the-other that would be produced in the measure that for empirical reasons the initial duo becomes a trio. . . . The equality of all is born by my inequality.[27]

Levinas claims that the ethical self, in its turn toward justice, cannot and ought not take into account its own needs, desires, and so forth in the consideration of what is just. It is in fact structurally excluded from such consideration. The ethical self never coincides with its ontological subject. Proximity/election *recurs*, repetitively "coring out" the ontological subject, such that it "suffer[s] through the augmentation of [an] ever more demanding" responsibility.[28] Levinas calls this recurrence and augmenting increase *infinition*: "the more I discover myself to be responsible, the more just I am, the more guilty I am," and hence: the more responsible I am obligated to *become*.[29] Each time I address or am addressed by others, proximity/substitution recurs, producing an ethical self distinct from the ontological will it is "cored" from. The subject is hence originally split: "fissioned" between an ontological conatus and an authentic ethical self. Levinas terms this fundamental split and the ethical *infinition* it recurs as *diachrony*. It is described as restlessness, a "gnawing away at oneself," wherein the subject proceeds as a kind of temporally extending parallax: thrown back and forth between the perspective of justice and the perspective of ethics, between the *presence* that characterizes justice and thought and the irrecuperable *past* that delineates the other as other, or finally and concretely: between a well-calculated apportionment of my resources to every other, and a pull to give everything to a specific other I might happen to face.[30]

With this account of the third party in hand, Levinas believes he has succeeded in providing a genuinely disinterested and hence justified *con-*

text-transcending perspective. His accounts of *motivational purity* and *justified context transcendence* describe a self whose obligations and perspective remain fundamentally unmoored in the will, and hence can potentially give to others and analyze its world without its own "ontological" desires polluting the result. These possibilities are what Levinas's ethics fundamentally seeks to describe. Now we must ask: is he successful?

III. Critique

III.A. Purity and the Will

As I hinted above, Levinas does indeed give us a particular account of disinterested giving. He does this by turning our usual understanding of the question of motivation on its head. In his own descriptions, "motivational purity" can no longer be understood in terms of *pure motives* for acting, but rather as a "giving" that is *pure of all willing*, that is, motivation no longer matters, because the ethical self is a *pure passivity*. If willing in general is self-interested by definition, as Levinas's account claims, then, indeed, responsibility cannot "be preached": no one can be praised for practicing limitless responsibility or *blamed* for not practicing it.[31] Any particular act we might regard as "good" must necessarily be construed as *involuntary*. This lends virtuous or noble acts a complete air of inscrutability. *Who acts?* We cannot say "the ethical self," because it is *nothing but* a *pure* effect or "echo" of the proximate other's demand. Nor can we say "the other acts through me," because Levinas denies that the other should be construed as an agency.[32] We cannot say "the ontological will from which an 'ethical me' is 'cored' does the actual acting, but does so at the behest of the other and the ethical self it forms," because the will is totally left behind—*irremediably* "ontological"—in his actual descriptions. We cannot say what Levinas often implies: that "ethical me" or proximate other *steals from* or *dispossesses* the ontological subject, because they fundamentally lack the "hands"—*the agency*—to do so. By characterizing the ethical self as an *absolute passivity*, as the obverse or "otherwise" than the will, we are left with the enigma: *how does any particular self manage to actually give anything to anyone?* If we simply accept Levinas's descriptions at face value, any "good" we might happen to do or might happen to witness is nothing short of a *miracle*. Ascribable to no particular will, "good" deeds become inscrutable: erratic events akin to bolts of lightening.

Even if we set aside his actual descriptions ("absolute passivity") and take him to mean that the proximate other or ethical self *can* somehow prevail upon the ontological subject to give, the problem of will remains. At minimum, the self-interested desire *to be remembered* as a moral hero, as an authentic exemplar for others to imitate—*the desire to win moral glory*—is at work in his position. This is not meant as a *moral* criticism: self-sacrifice for others with whom we don't wholly identify is indeed noble, and the self-interest involved in seeking to win recognition for it is perhaps the *best* sort of self-interest we have. But self-interest is there nonetheless. Again, I am not attempting to deflate the moral rigor of Levinas's position: indeed, I grant that giving to those with whom we don't wholly identify—at the limit: even an enemy—is noble, and if someone acts from this self-interested motive in *actually performing self-sacrifice*, they remain worthy to be regarded as noble. Think of Gandhi. Once acquainted with his biography, it is clear he aspired to be regarded as kind of spiritual guru or mahatma long before Tagore and others ascribed this status to him.[33] But does this desire impugn the moral exemplarity of his deeds? There comes a point where his own self-interest, though always there, simply does not matter next to the moral grandeur of the deeds he performed. This is one reason we remain relatively indifferent to skeptical "exposés" that point out his all-too-human flaws. His failures do not seem to matter considered next to his noble deeds, and those failures in fact render his deeds that much more exceptional. As this case suggests, Gandhi's self-interest is there, and we regard it as a potentially *good* form of self-interest, a form of self-interest that also aims at empowering others and humanizing enemies, and hence is not purely "selfish." This example suggests, perhaps, that the more self-sacrificial I am with respect to others, the more likely I might become to succeed in winning socially recognized glory for it. Even if my self-sacrifice seems to be failing to win me the recognition I desire, and it appears more and more improbable that this recognition can be won in a particular context, I might keep practicing it anyway because I regard prioritizing others over myself as good in itself. In this case, it is important for me to either (a) potentially be remembered by future generations as an authentic moral hero, or (b) remain noble in my own eyes alone. Any way we slice it, self-interest seems always operative in our dealings with others. Even if we were to distinguish between *giving for its own sake* and the self-interested desire *to win recognition for it*, this distinction would address itself *to our will*. Comparing Gandhi's moral failures with his glorious deeds does *not* suppose an active "ontological subject" that sometimes overtook his "absolutely passive" ethical self. If we did interpret in this way, Gandhi *could be praised for or "exemplify" nothing*: his glorious deeds would be mere involuntary, erratic, inscrutable events attributable to no will whatsoever. In this light, Levinas's attempt to construct an account that structurally excludes the "ontological" from the "ethical"—activity from passivity, will from affect—fails on his own terms, because self-relation and self-interest remain at work in self-sacrifice: stripped of all "ontological" agency, *nothing exemplary remains*. Indeed, if we take Levinas's account to succeed, no giving ever actually gets done: a "pure passivity" *can give nothing*.[34]

How do we deal with this? We cannot, for example, point to the transcendental character of Levinas's description to ward off this problem. Unlike Kant, Levinas is not dealing in pure a priori concepts. We *cannot* distinguish the purity of concepts from impure empirical cases to explain this problem away. Rather, Levinas claims his account "remains faithful to intentional analysis, insofar as it signifies the locating of notions in the horizon of their appearing . . . The said in which everything is thematized . . . has to be reduced to its signification as saying . . ."[35] Saying absolutely excludes the will, and this is the entire problem. The "diachrony" of Levinas's "fissioned" subject—ethical self and ontological subject—casts them as absolutely *disjunctive*, and hence, ultimately *unrelated*. If we take his descriptions seriously, we must conclude that there is no such thing as *good will* in Levinas. The moral and the will absolutely exclude one another.

Apparently unaware of this problem, Levinas believes he has successfully described the possibility of a disinterested, morally exemplary self. Therefore, it is reasonable to predict that the will *must* show up *within* his larger description of ethical selfhood, that is, must appear in his positive description of ethical responsibility and not only in the negative contrast his account of ontology provides. Let's look at his description again with an eye toward this problem.

III.b. Responsibility and the Will

In his vigorous descriptions of election, Levinas repeatedly claims that "the subject which is not an ego, but which I am, cannot be generalized, . . . we have moved from the ego to me who am me and no one else [sic]." Or, alternately, "To say that the ego is a substitution is then not to state the universality of a principle, . . . but quite the contrary, it is to restore to the soul its ego*ity* which supports no generalization."[36] Leaving aside here the telling question of whether the self *is* or *is not* an ego, in substitution, the ethical self qua responsibility is *nothing other* than *generalized*. In substitution, the elected self must attribute or *posit* responsibility in the proximate other. There are two possible interpretations of the generalization in play: (1) because the only form of responsibility thus far described has been *limitless* responsibility (the third party has apparently not yet arrived), the responsibility attributed to the proximate other must also be limitless. This will not work, however, because such would efface the uniqueness of the self and the alterity of the other by implying they jointly *share* in a "common concept" of limitless responsibility, or something of the sort. To avoid this, we are left with: (2) in substitution, the self *posits* responsibility in the proximate other and takes responsibility ("substitutes itself") for it. The self demands uniqueness, and as such it *refuses* to let itself be substituted for. The self hence prohibits the other from assuming "more" responsibility: *refuses the proximate other a share in what it is*. To posit *limited* responsibility in the other is, in effect, to cast her or him as originarily *ir*responsible. It were as if the "ethical self" *resented* the other for saddling it with such excessive responsibility, *blames* the other, and exacts its *revenge* by denying her or him a *share* in the authentic responsibility that it is. We are left here with a choice between abandoning our singularity by attributing limitless responsibility to the other, and of forever casting the proximate other as *ir*responsible by selfishly refusing to *share*.

As we turn to the third party, the situation becomes even more interesting. Levinas writes: "The third party is other than the neighbor, but also another neighbor, and also a neighbor of the other, and not simply his fellow."[37] Setting aside the question of what it might mean for *two* "absolute" alterities to confront me, if the third party can indeed count as (a) a *neighbor* (a proximate other the self is limitlessly responsibly for), (b) a *neighbor of the other* (an "absolute alterity" for my proximate other constituting her or him as a limitlessly responsible self), and (c) *other than the neighbor* (veritable third party), then all the relations become *reversible* and *reciprocal*. Here, responsibility moves beyond its generalization in substitution and becomes genuinely *universal*. We are left with the same choice we confronted in substitution: do we (1a) distribute the self's "limitless" responsibility or (2a) the other's "limited" responsibility? (1a) If the third party, and with it: *all others*, are indeed "other than the neighbor [*and*] a neighbor of the other, . . . not simply [fellows]" then they are necessarily *also* "limitlessly responsible" selves. As such, it appears a "community of singularities" is indeed possible, or in other words: a community of *what lacks all community*—a singularity. Levinas's own description yields an *absurd multitude* of "infinite responsibilities," of "insubstantial uniquenesses" all absolutely identical with one another.[38] Though his own descriptions include this possibility, Levinas once again decides otherwise: (2a) "The third party . . . is of itself limit of responsibility . . ."[39] The self not only posits *limited* responsibility in the proximate other, but also in all the others: "In no way is justice a degradation of obsession, a degeneration of the for-the-other . . . The equality of all is born by my inequality."[40] To protect its singularity, the self prohibits every other from potentially participating in authentic responsibility. Though the self had a choice to allow all others to *share* in authentic responsibility (option 1 and 1a above), it projects its *resentment* of the proximate other onto every possible other. All others are determined by and as limited responsibility, and hence: they are all *irresponsible*.

Perhaps this analysis is too strong. After all, Levinas also claims that the self's responsibility can also be limited, if momentarily. He writes:

> The relationship with the third party is an incessant correction of the asymmetry of proximity . . . There is a weighing, thought, objectification, and thus a decree in which my anarchic relationship with [other] is betrayed, but also a new relationship with it: it is only thanks to God that, as a subject incomparable with the other, I am approached as another by the others, that is, "for myself." "Thanks to God I am another for others. . . . The passing of God, of whom I can speak only by reference to this aid and this grace, is precisely the reverting of the incomparable into a member of society.[41]

If this is the case, Levinas's "god" is a strange one. This god somehow enables and apparently excuses a momentary lapse of responsibility. Given his actual descriptions, he never explains how this is possible, and the introduction of god-talk here seems somewhat arbitrary. But exactly two paragraphs later, he *also* insists:

> In no way is justice a degradation of obsession, a degeneration of the for-the-other that would be produced in the measure that for empirical reasons the initial duo becomes a trio. . . . The equality of all is born by my inequality.[42]

Justice *both* "corrects" the asymmetry of proximity *and* does not "degrade obsession," and both *simultaneously*. There are two possible interpretations here: (i) the self is, impossibly and simultaneously, *torn from itself* and *for itself*, or in other words: *a masochist*; or (ii) the "grace of God" or the third party commands a very brief forgetting of its authentic self—as crushing responsibility—by ordering it to coincide with itself or blanch in itself as *conatus*. This "grace" is somewhat miserly, however, in that the initial "inequality" of first-person responsibility *recurs*, eviscerating *conatus* once more, and so on *repeatedly*. Here, the ethical self is simultaneously *chastised for* and *summoned to* conceptually "violate" the other, is "persecuted" *for the very violence it was just enjoined to perform*, and will be enjoined to perform *again*. In this case, this self is a victim of caprice, the cruel joke of an eminently *sadistic* "*god.*" Is it any wonder the ethical self is so vengeful? Given its plight, the only consolation it allows itself is the illusion that it, and it *alone* (as an "absolute singularity"), *is* the "most" responsible self in the world. Horton tries to soften these implications through a quite suggestive analysis of "Desire as a gift that is the condition of possibility of joy," while arguing that, "paradoxical as it may seem, being a hostage to the Other is actually liberating."[43] Her analysis is creative and quite suggestive from multiple angles, but she ultimately fails to read OB on its own terms. By contrast, Kearney and Westphal's respective worries seems apt: the text approaches a nearly "theo-erotic masochism" that gives Levinas's ethics a "grimness it does not need."[44]

On the terms Levinas lays out, when the ethical self claims, "the more responsible I am, the more just I am, the more guilty I am," she is also claiming, "the more responsible I am, the more just I am, the more guilty I am, *the more innocent I become of the irresponsibility of all others.*" What if we avoid this by generously allowing all others to participate in authentic responsibility (option 1 and 1a above)? Perhaps we might summon contemporary mathematics, and talk of different orders of infinity to avoid annulling the uniqueness of the members of this absurd class? But this clearly would miss the point: *responsibility is not a "thing,"* not material, not a *quantity* we can have "more" or less of *when stripped of all relation to the will*. When we speak of someone being "more" responsible for some specific incident, we mean that his or her actions are more decisively implicated in precipitating the event, *not* that he or she has accrued more "stuff" called responsibility. When we speak of being obligated for a context or situation we did not create (as in environmental ethics, for example), we are, say, recognizing intrinsic value, not claiming to be "bigger"—infinitely more "massive"—than that context.[45]

As I predicted above, the will does indeed show up in Levinas's larger account, and the place where it shows up is utterly significant: *in the move from proximity to substitution*. The self must *posit* responsibility in the "absolute" other. The move from proximity to substitution necessarily involves willing in the form of *positing*. Moreover, by *positing* responsibility in the proximate other, Levinas is surreptitiously relying on a third-person point of view precisely *before* the entrance of the third. This means substitution does not purely follow from proximity or *purely unfold as* the implicit sense of proximity. The description depends on a position outside of proximity where self and other are *both* viewed as *two* "responsibilities."[46] The fact that Levinas *assumes* the proximate other's responsibility is *limited* in substitution, and does *before* the third arrives to perform its limiting function, demonstrates this dependence. This dependence is also evident in his broader account of the affective self. Levinas's entire description consists of insisting that the sheer immediacy of an *occurrent* feeling—unmediated pain—is *simultaneously* the "identifying recurrence"[47] of an elected self, and is such *repeatedly*. In other words, he is claiming "occurrence *is* recurrence," that the subject of sheer, unmediated pain is *absolutely identical* with the ethical self he is "describing." Whether or not this is the case, we can only arrive at this identity through the *mediation* of thought. It certainly does not spring whole from our affects, and Levinas's attempt to present it as such seems disingenuous. He in fact is *positing* an identity between them, and in so doing, performs a surreptitious judgment: occurrence *is* recurrence.

The problem of recurrence raises other issues for Levinas's position. For example, when he speaks of "augmentation," infinition, and diachrony, he gives the impression that some sort of active change or variation is in play. In fact, the function of diachrony in his descriptions does precisely the opposite. Recurrence yields no variation, but rather repeatedly proceeds as the self-same other ("pure alterity" putatively stripped of all determination) "coring" a self-same "me" (as pure responsibility) from an ontological subject. His talk of the "diachrony of time" and the rhetoric of "*becoming* more responsible" is apparently Levinas's way of trying to maintain his own distinction between ontology and ethics. But in what sense can a responsibility already determined as infinite "grow"?

The significance of Levinas's repeated recourse to both will and concept *within* his own account of the affective self and substitution should by now be obvious: on his own terms, his account of ethics is "ontological"; that is, the very distinction between ontology and ethics *is itself* an *ontological* distinction. Levinas need not and indeed *cannot* "unsay" anything, here, *because he has already Said it all.*

III.c. Levinas's "Method"

My analysis is sufficient to demonstrate not merely the question-begging character of Levinas's position, but also the unintelligibility of his claims. Nevertheless, what I have performed thus far is not quite enough. Levinas has attempted to construct his position in such a way so as to preempt just the sort of criticism I've performed, and does so by once more staging points of indeterminacy. What Levinas calls "pre-ontological" is *dependent* on a *transcendental* distinction, namely, empirical, non-reflective life "prior to" philosophical consideration of its necessary and enabling conditions. Levinas's various archeological appeals to Husserl disclose the problem.[48] If we unhinge Husserl's ur-impression, passive synthesis, and so forth from active position-taking and active constitution, we annul the phenomenological character of the passive dimension and concomitantly lurch into the natural attitude. This has the unfortunate effect of *also* annulling the distinction between ontology and "pre-ontology," and with it: claims to supply transcendental conditions for "meaning in being" in general.[49] What Levinas takes from and criticizes in Husserl annuls the basis for his own central methodological distinction. Rather than biting the bullet on these implications, and owning either the ontological description or empirical reconstruction this leaves him, Levinas rather entitles himself to present what amounts to a *realist theory* of the unconscious as a *transcendental description* of the conditions for meaning in general. Moreover, whatever we might think of Heidegger's contributions to phenomenology, he does not appear to perform the question-begging leaps Levinas practices here.[50] The distinction between authenticity and inauthenticity is *not* a distinction between *pure* "ontology" and *pure* "theory," and does not obtain in wholly independent or *purely* disjunctive experiences. Inauthenticity is held to occlude an allegedly more fundamental relation to being, but authenticity is only a *modification* that retains its reciprocal dependence on co-original being-with.[51] Inauthenticity amounts to misapprehending the *derived* as if it were *original.* The structure of Levinas's "argument" tracks Heidegger, while depending on explicitly Husserlian distinctions. When Levinas appeals to "pre-ontology," he is actually claiming the processes and performances of *pure* transcendental life. Conversely, when Levinas claims a "pure sensibility" over-against consciousness, he is actually appealing to *impure* and mutually *dependent* ontological structures. By finally casting his proposal in terms of an unconscious affective structure, Levinas finally annuls the necessary or determinative phenomenological status of the meaning he posits. Unlike Husserl and Heidegger, Levinas casts ontology and ethics as wholly independent psychic occurrences and *wholly* disjunctive regions of "meaning." This is ultimately why Ricoeur, for example, rightly claims that Levinas's "reduction" must be understood in a fundamentally "non-Husserlian sense."[52]

III.d. Arbitrarity

Levinas's entire project in OB is premised on an initial positive and universal determination: *the being of* all *beings is* conatus. Clearly, Husserl does not posit the natural attitude as an unmodifiable ontological fact; nor does he claim that any and all self-interest is unjustifiable in principle. Levinas simply declares "the said" to be totally and irremediably characterized by obdurately vicious self-interest, and then opposes "saying" to it. Because self-interest is cast as an unalterable ontological fact, and disinterest is posited as completely pure of the will, Levinas has rendered for us a fatal world of necessary violence we are ultimately powerless to "suspend." The clearly arbitrary character of Levinas's method in OB subverts his own positive project.

That election is not a pure affection becomes especially clear when we review the contrasting sins Levinas attributes to ontology. Consider:

> [D]espite all the simultaneous forces in its union, being cannot eternalize. The subjective and its Good cannot be understood out of ontology.[53]

Here, being's impotence or incapacity to render itself eternal is held to be a defect. Being's lack of eternity entails that the "subjective and its Good" cannot be grasped within it. Eternal presence, here, is held to be a virtue that Being lacks, and that ethics will apparently supply us. Yet we are also told,

> [O]ntological thought, where the eternal presence to oneself subtends even its absences in the form of a quest. . . .

unconvertible into a history, irreducible to the simultaneousness of writing, the eternal present of a writing that records or presents results.[54]

Now we are told that the eternal is not a virtue, but a vice. And not merely a contingent vice, but irremediably inherent to what being in general is. The temporality of a particular life, or of history in general, or even the deconstructive writing that seeks to subvert this history, are irremediably infected by eternal presence, and ethics will be summoned to "disrupt" this eternity. Levinas is once more taking aim at multiple targets at once (pre-Kantian philosophy, Heidegger, Derrida, etc.), and however interesting those debates might be, they are irrelevant to assessing what he actually presents us. Ontology is attacked because it is declared to both lack and have eternal presence, and both simultaneously and by apparent necessity. On the one hand, when Levinas holds eternal presence to be a vice that being has, he summons what are presented as pure, unmediated sensible oc-currences to "disrupt" this frozen eternity. On the other hand, when Levinas holds eternal presence to be a virtue that being lacks, he summons what are presented as pure, unmediated semantic re-currences to supply a stable meaning. If Levinas's analysis evinces arbitrariness at this most basic level, we should not be surprised to discover that his account of justice in OB does too.

As I noted above, Levinas never precisely specifies the meaning of the third. He seems to treat it as a quantitative addition of another "absolute alterity" to the allegedly more basic self/other scene. Yet at other moments in the text, he rejects the empirical reading and straightforwardly calls the third party "God."[55] Alternating references to both empirically present human bodies and to something non-empirical recur throughout the text, sometimes in the span of a few paragraphs. For example,

> It is not that the entry of a third party would be an empirical fact.

And

> for empirical reasons the initial duo would become a trio.[56]

Here he is once more circling between an empirical and divine presence, arbitrarily switching between sensible and semantic immediacy.

III.e. Oc-currence versus Re-currence

The entire issue resides in a series of equivocations all grounded in the circular utilization of what I have called "oc-currence" and "re-currence." Insofar as Levinas himself asserts that being both lacks and has eternal presence, ethics must be summoned to simultaneously supply and "disrupt" this eternity: "oc-currence" and "re-currence." I stress, this issue does not only consist in the performative contradiction he grants us he is performing, that is, that "the indescribable is described"[57] in what is presented as an unrepresentable unconscious structure. The issue also consists in rendering suffering inherently *meaningful*, couched in a simultaneous assertion of its absolute non-meaning. Suffering in itself becomes pure meaning, while still and simultaneously asserting it to be pure non-sense, and his "ethics/ ontological" distinction simply collapses. Quite against his own intentions, and in such a way that escapes his attempt to *frame in advance* all dissent through appeal to the play of skepticism, Levinas's own account of diachrony necessarily fails on its own terms.

When proximity, or the inaugurative moment of election, is being described: the ontological subject is presupposed as she who is being "de-cored." Here, the subject is cast as pure inertia, pure self-presence, and Levinas summons what I have called "occurrence": empirical contingency, empirical time and space, empirically exposed bodies, and events of empirically immediate pain are being descriptively utilized. This is immediacy 1: sensuous immediacy of a sensible subject and sensible moment, what Levinas designates as "*this* moment."[58] This "this" is meant to tell us that this is a real sensuous moment that allegedly escapes the "thematizing presence" of ontology. Here, we actually undergo something alleged to resist full description. Nevertheless, the empirical reference is there and is performing the methodological work at this level. The "reality" in these references means sensible/affective force, "empirically real," or "actually occurring yet not fully describable." Yet when proximity transitions to or "unfolds" as "substitution . . . at the basis of proximity," the sense of immediacy changes, and allegedly "becomes" the "sense of sensibility."[59] Here, the other is presupposed as "always the first on the scene," as that which "makes possible" meaning in being in general.[60] Levinas is not only explicitly performing an identification, here, he is performing an absolute identification. All his talk of otherness, "alteration," and affection over-against sameness and "ontology" becomes mere rhetoric.[61] Nothing "really" changes. The "oc-currence" of sensibly occurring pain, faces, and skin "becomes" the "re-currence" of an essential meaning: responsibility. The contingent time of empirical experience "becomes" a purely formal repetition of an eternal meaning. For "oc-currence," being is cast as eternal nonsense (il y a) that ethics comes to "disrupt," and this "disruption" occurs as a sensuous/affective event. For his "re-currence," the ethical self is described as an absolutely singular and necessarily recurring "one," as a me "formed" by "an Individual prior to all individuality," in remote history: the Immemorial, Absolute Other: "God."[62] When we point out: "disruption" by the other presupposes the ontological subject to be "disrupted," Levinas will assert, "the other is always first on the scene," and point to an eternal meaning over-against the asserted nonsense of "ontology."[63] When we respond: but this eternal meaning belies the claim that being is irremediable senseless, Levinas will assert: "suffering is the surplus of non-sense over sense by which the sense of suffering is possible."[64] *Senseless suffering makes suffering make sense. Suffering's sense makes suffering senseless.*[65] This is the self-annulling knot on which the whole text turns. Levinas's whole account only works by positing an absolute identity between sense and sensibility, or in other words: in performing the very thing for which ontology stands accused. A closer look at his so-called "diachrony" and "the instant" further corroborates this.

III.f. "Diachrony"

Levinas's question-begging switch between sensuous and semantic immediacy subverts his own account of diachrony. Levinas's "diachrony" is a synchronic structure. In its basic structure, diachrony is an alleged "diastasis or dephasing of the instant."[66] When Levinas is in "oc-currence" mode over-against the asserted "eternal presence" of ontology, diachrony is described as occurring between three distinct "exteriorities":

> the [sensuous or semantic?] proximity of the other in his face the materialization of matter, altered by the [sensuous] immediacy of contact.
>
> the other in the same, where [semantic] inspiration arouses respiration.

> It is only in ["this" or these?] way[s] that the absolutely exterior other is near to the point of obsession. Here there is proximity.⁶⁷

Here, proximity occurs as three distinct relations: (i) "between" my individual body and another human's individual body (faces), (ii) "between" my internal urge "to be" and an "other" urge "to give" (conscience), and (iii) "between" my own individual body and the sheer fact of exposure to time and change ("exposedness" in general). In all cases, "diachrony" names a moment of "disruption" that strikes the "inert self-assertion" of the ontological subject "from the outside."⁶⁸ The change is not from one moment or state to another, but from one eternal meaning to another: from the eternal nonsense of being to the eternal meaning of ethics. As Guenther very aptly notes, diachrony names a "turning point" or a "hinge" between two co-eternal meanings.⁶⁹ While sensuous immediacy inexorably implicates contingent time and actual "alteration," semantic immediacy remains always and forever The Same: marking a "switch," where contingent empirical experience "becomes" an "inevitably," "not accidental," "unconditionality [that] confers meaning on being itself."⁷⁰ On the one hand, appeals to sensuous immediacy necessarily imply that meaning is derived from experience, and is in some sense mediated by our experience of the world. On the other hand, semantic immediacy posits an underived meaning, and in this context is held to "condition," "make possible," or "confer . . . meaning" on being in general, rendering intersubjective relation inherently mediated.⁷¹ Levinas here repeats his circular account of the genesis of meaning, alternately utilizing transcendental and psycho-metaphysical genesis. This necessitates what clearly is, on his own terms, incoherent:

> proximity, a possibility included in the unity of the face and the skin. It is the immediacy of a skin and a face, a skin which is always a modification of a face, a face that is weighted down with a skin.⁷²

The "and" in "skin and face" renders the conjoined terms mediated, and supposes either an empirically perceived common quality, transcendental subsumption under or constitution of a common idea, or ontological belonging to a common category. When he ascribes "skin" to the face, once more, he is ascribing to it a capacity to suffer in a way like the ego suffers: by either analogy-perception to the "me's" own suffering, or to an original co-belonging implied by his general appeals to "exposedness" and "the materialization of matter."[73] As above, Levinas alternately summons and denies the empirical. On the one hand, he must affirm it, because he has charged being in general with inertia, and has untaken to alter it by affectively striking it "from the outside," that is, by way of the sensuously immediate. On the other hand, he chides being in general for failing at eternity, and so must deny the empirical. He does not want responsibility to be mediated or derived; he therefore has also described the other as ("pre-") originally "in the same," that is, as an eternal presence, "identifying recurrence," or semantically immediate.[74] Because this running circularity is hard to consciously sustain, he must finally and arbitrarily declare:

> And it is because the third party does not come empirically to trouble proximity, but the face is both the neighbor and the face of faces, visage and visible.[75]

This "both/and" turns on gratuitous, simultaneous, and mutually exclusive appeals to "empirical reasons" (other human bodies) and to a non-empirical or pure "God."[76]

III.G. "Freedom"

Once we have identified the absolute identity Levinas posits ("oc-currence *is* re-currence"), the text is thoroughly demystified. Just as this both necessitates and subverts Levinas's equivocal appeals to the "empirical," it also explains his equivocal appeals to freedom. In his Total Judgment against being in general, ontology "presupposes a freedom and the imperialism of a political . . . ego."[77] Any perspective that involves an originary freedom remains inexorably chained to the "synchronism" and "determinism of war and matter."[78] War and "synchrony" are identical: "War is deed or drama of essence's interest."[79] Yet he'll elsewhere say,

> This condition or unconditionality of being a hostage will then at least be an essential modality of freedom, the first, and not an empirical accident of the freedom, proud in itself, of the ego.[80]

This is why he must ceaselessly circulate between casting responsibility as (i) opposed to or a "persecution of" freedom, (ii) "prior to freedom," and (iii) a "modality *of* freedom."[81] For ontology, freedom is cast as illusory, imperious, arbitrary, and determined. For ethics, responsibility first "persecutes" freedom, strikes it from "outside" and from all sides: by faces, conscience, and time in general. Then ethics becomes "prior to" to freedom, or an internal or unconscious semantic determination that "conditions" freedom, and which empirical experiences of conscience instantiate. Finally, once ethics has moved from empirical "oc-currences" to transcendental "re-currences," ethics becomes "an essential modality *of* freedom," that is, an ontological determination, or creative repetitions of an original "gift" from a quite active, ontological other.[82] Levinas terms this threefold movement "the plot of the Infinite,"[83] and by this movement he fully ontologizes ethics on his own grounds. Nowhere is this more evident than in his various treatments of violence.

The text opens with an indictment of "philosophy which does not see beyond being, and reduces, by an abuse of language, saying to the said."[84] Yet the singularity Saying forms can only be named "me" or "I," "[a]s an exception, and by abuse of language."[85] Ontology and ethics both apparently require the "abuse" of language. We are not presented here with a choice of whether or not to abuse, but with apparently "better" and worse types of abuse.[86] One must yield to responsibility if "one is not to abandon oneself to violence."[87] Apparently, the "goodness of the good is alone able to counterbalance the violence of . . . choice."[88] How does the good counter this violence? It persecutes it, and as Levinas insists: "Persecution is trauma, violence par excellence."[89] Ethics and ontology both involve violence and abuse. The good occurs as "a disinterestedness imposed with a good violence."[90] Ethical violence is presumably better than ontological violence because it "enable[s] one to first catch sight of and conceive value."[91] Yet he'll say that "being Good, it redeems the violence of its alterity, even if the subject has to suffer through the augmentation of this ever more demanding violence."[92] The self is prohibited from enjoying whatever value it might subsequently "catch sight of," because its destined to re-undergo violent persecution in the recurrence of its "me." It is as if the Good were an actor in the war of all against all, and not an exception to it. Rather than distinguishing between violence and abuse, ethics and ontology both involve it, and apparently "necessarily" so.[93] We finally learn: "Justice, society, the State and its institutions, exchanges, and work are comprehensible out of proximity. This means that nothing is outside of the control of the responsibility of the one for the other."[94] Ethics remains, after all, an origin, an *arche*, a principality that rules by rendering "comprehensible" or "confer[ing] meaning on being" as a whole.[95] The entire text moves on these mutually exclusive and contradictory determinations: ethics is simultaneously "anarchically a relationship with singularity without the mediation of a principle," and the "kingdom of an invisible king," "nothing is outside the control of the responsibility of the one for the other."[96] These descriptions[97] seems to render an apparently necessary, "transcendental," and eternal conflict.[98] Levinas must and does stand above ethics and ontology to achieve his panoramic view of "self/subject" as an internally divided whole (ontological subject + ethical self = empirical ego). Being and Ethics conduct their conflict in the theater of human affects, where the "plot of the Infinite" and the ontological "time of the narrative" ultimately and necessarily *become one*: "a plot without beginning," a narrative "without finality and without end."[99] Levinas is describing what amounts to a conflict of *conscience* in a particular way, but how he does so is self-subverting. Conscience intrinsically relies on an assessment of how things are ("being") and how they ought to be ("ethics") presupposed by other commitments Levinas himself in fact defends.

III.h. Reason and Skepticism

Levinas appears to perform the impossible: to successfully both affirm and deny the meaningfulness of suffering. Absent a criterion that permits a distinction between, say, the gratuitous and the tragic, the intentional and the accidental, the criminal and the relatively neutral, etc., the attempt fails. The attempt is moreover premised in a fundamentally equivocal methodological use of the empirical:

> My substitution for another is the trope of a sense that does not belong to the empirical order of psychological events.
>
> In opposition to that, we suppose that there is in the transcendence involved in language a relationship that is not an empirical speech.
>
> These are not events that happen to an empirical ego.
>
> . . . the very pneuma of the psyche, precedes this empirical order.[100]

When Levinas writes, "equivocation, in the enigma whose secret [the ethical one] keeps,"[101] he is nodding to ancient traditions of esotericism utilized widely across different cultures and traditions. This was one way marginalized communities sheltered their internal commitments, and was often utilized in pedagogy to separate good educational needs from more complex, higher-order questions treated by specialist. In the wake of the Shoah, it's certainly understandable that Levinas employed this writing technique. But is it best practice in modern liberal societies?[102] Given how Levinas's work has been appropriated by the fashions of our day, the question seems pressing. Wherever one stands on reason and skepticism, neither the self-critical philosopher, nor the skeptic with intellectual integrity, arbitrarily leaps back and forth to the position they are respectively criticizing, arbitrarily claiming and disavowing philosophical authority as it suits their rhetorical needs. This is how appropriations of Levinas's work seem to function in quarters of philosophy today, and in contrast to TI, what Levinas himself seems to do in OB.[103] As Inukai notes, following Chalier: "Although [Levinas] criticizes rhetoric in general, he adopts a philosophical method called emphase (emphasis), which derives from rhetoric."[104] It must be said that OB as a whole falls to Levinas's own early critique of rhetoric.

IV. Conclusion

When Levinas asks us to construe our own experience of bodily pain *as if* they were creative events of moral meaning, he is asking us to adopt a particular conceptuality, one that necessarily *subsumes* the entirety of existence under a particular theological semantics. If we follow him, the meaning of humanity *as a whole* becomes *derived* from an absolute creative God, and hence: all other humans are constituted *with me* by God's actual creative activity. Other faces are not "intermediaries," here, but rather individuated *expressions* of original creaturehood fundamentally dependent on originary divine creation.[105] By presenting moral election as an "identifying recurrence," and by declaring his so-called "diachrony" to be "necessary," Levinas presents what in effect remains a formal, indefinitely recurring universal structure that is *unalterable in principle*.[106] As I've tried to show: by casting theory as irremediably determined by "ontology," and by declaring moral meaning to be absolutely pure of the will, he renders a world of sublime, fatal, and eternal *conflict*. This does *not* seem to be what Levinas intended to do.

Levinas ultimately succumbs to his own critique of phenomenology. If Husserl and Heidegger's respective performances of the reduction are to be accused of begging the question, Levinas's own so-called "reduction" quite clearly succumbs too. Levinasian "disinterest" does not "suspend" interest, but performs it, and all because he adamantly refuses to tell us the methodological norms by which we should fairly assess his claims. Levinas is of course perfectly free to posit a theory of the affective unconscious, or to propose a fundamental ontological or theological ethics. He is not free to assert that language is inherently "violent" while disavowing the larger consequences of this assertion for his own discourse. Rae has independently confirmed my point on Levinas's treatment of violence, concluding that "Levinas's affirmation of 'good' violence perpetuates the ontological and physical violence that he criticizes ontologically inspired politics for perpetuating."[107]

As should also be clear, Levinas repeats here his circular and question begging appeals to contrasting transcendental and empirico-metaphysical accounts of the genesis of meaning. While *OB* abandons *TI*'s attempt to present an independently individuated ego by a reformulated, yet no less aporetic, theology of creation, he nevertheless repeats just the deck flipping I've diagnosed above.[108] When we point out that an "absolute past" beyond memory is essentially utilizing a notion of *empirical* absence still dependent on an "invisible" semantic presence, Levinas will assert that this presence "does not belong to the empirical order of psychological events," and proceed to talk of "inevitably," "not accidental," "unconditionality [that] confers meaning on being itself."[109] When we point out that if such affection does not actually empirically or psychologically occur, then he is essentially trading in a purely theoretical theological semantics, Levinas will assert that "[t]he psyche [is] a uniqueness outside of concepts," and proceed to talk of a "feeling" of "undergoing," or "pain," that "imposes" upon and "alter[s] my contemporaneousness with the other," and so forth.[110] Crucially, *OB* not only performs this question-begging switch, but it appears to be premised on the same unanalyzed assumption I identified in *TI*, namely, that conceptual, categorial, or linguistic mediation in general is "inherently violent." As I have shown, self-sacrifice depends on the interrelation of giving and self-interest for its general intelligibility. Insofar as his account of disinterest is premised on an arbitrary *universal determination* (the being of *all* beings is *conatus*) that declares self-interest unjustifiable in principle, Levinas can only judge self-interest and "the said" *by performing them*. The entire Levinasian project is premised on a climactic and totalizing concept inclusion or a categorical judgment he never even attempts to justify.

As we are about to see in more detail, the contradictory performances and protocols at the core of Levinas's method are very relevant to assessing the problems in his political and religious writings, and specifically: his Eurocentric statements.

Chapter 5

Levinas, Eurocentrism, Justice

The arrival on the historical scene of those underdeveloped Afro-Asiatic masses who are strangers to the Sacred History that forms the heart of the Judaic-Christian world.

Europe, that's the Bible and the Greeks. It has come closer to the Bible and to its true fate. Everything else in the world must be included in this. I don't have any nostalgia for the exotic. For me Europe is central.

The yellow peril! It is not racial but spiritual. Not about inferior values but about a radical strangeness, strange to all the density of its past, where no voice with a familiar inflection comes through: a lunar, a Martian past.[1]

—Emmanuel Levinas

I. Introduction

As my prior chapters have demonstrated, Levinas's method proceeds by alternate and circular appeals to empirico-metaphysical and transcendental accounts of necessary conditions. Whether in the form of contrasting appeals to "the idea of Infinite" and divinely "effectuated" Paternity (*TI*), or in a like, self-annulling identification of sensuous and semantic immediacy (*OB*), in both cases he positively depends on conceptual generalizations in the midst of describing what is asserted to be an absolute "sensuous" immediacy. In both cases, these generalizations are performed *before* the explicit entrance of the third. This demonstrates that on Levinas's own grounds: concepts, categories, or linguistic mediation in general cannot coherently be construed as inherently "violent." Nevertheless, in Levinas's own positive descriptions, the central equivocation relevant to assessing his problematic political and intercultural judgments shows up precisely in his treatment of the third. If we boil the problem down to its bare structure, it comes to this: Levinas's third is alternately and equivocally cast by reference to (i) *empirical human bodies* and (ii) a *non-empirical, disembodied Other*. In *TI*:

1. Levinas justifies the generalization of the face to "all of humanity" (including "oneself") by initial appeal to *kath'auto* "revelation," or the absolute self-reference asserted to issue from a particular human body that faces the ego.

2. Levinas also posits biologically mediated, divinely "effectuated" fraternity as a condition "for the face to appear as face."

3. The circularity (and inherent mediation in play in both directions) is clear, but what must be noticed is that the "third" is simultaneously cast as (i) a generalization grounded in and justified by the originary face-to-face, and (ii) a generalization grounded in and justified by originary divine paternity.

In (i) a particular other's human body functions as the ground to criticize the "violence of concepts," and in (ii) a creative God functions as the ground to justify the conceptual/categorial comprehension of humanity in general. In *OB*:

1. Levinas declares being and thought in general to be irremediably senseless and viciously self-interested by definition through appeal to empirical and temporal—*sensuous*—events of pain.

2. Levinas declares "ethics" to be the *condition* for any meaning in being in general by appeal to non-empirical and "eternal"—*semantic*—moral meaning.

3. Levinasian "diachrony" is ultimately a *synchronic structure*, such that the eternal meaning he posits is in no way put at risk of *diachronic change*, and this is performed in his attempt to frame all questions *in advance* by analogizing appeals to philosophy/skepticism. In this riskless game, the third is simultaneous cast as necessitated (iii) "for empirical reasons" and as (iv) "not . . . an empirical fact."

When Levinas appeals to (iii), he is referring to other individual human bodies. When Levinas appeals to (iv), he is referring to an invisible "God."[2] In both of Levinas's major philosophical works, his account of the third is premised on equivocal appeals to human and divine *presence*, that is, to *pure* "singular" bodies and *pure* "universal" meaning.

As should be clear, the problem is not necessarily that Levinas has decided to perform a theology, or a religiously informed philosophical ethics, but rather that he necessarily performs the very thing he criticizes in other philosophers and other traditions. One's ethical and political commitments can of course involve reference to, say, Reason, Nature, Dharma, Dao, God, the Mandate of Heaven, Ancestors, Spirit, or the like. Such references don't a priori invalidate a norm or a meaning, or by themselves constitute sufficient grounds for dismissing an account as non-meaningful. Any philosophy or critical theory, religious or not, owes the targets of its criticism a coherent justification of its practices and judgments. This is where Levinas seems to fail. The intrinsic indeterminacy built into to his method is precisely reflected in long-identified problems in his political writings, and specifically: his apparently Eurocentric statements. Let us see how.

II. Political Justice

Moral election is *simultaneously* held to both anarchically "disrupt" and potentially "justify" the ordered, conceptually mediated activity of knowledge and institutions.[3] Clearly, if ethics justifies an order and the ordering activity of knowledge and institutions, it is most certainly *not* a pure, anarchic disruption, and the activities it is said to validate can surely not be said to be inherently violent or totalitarian, but confirmed or underwritten as validated. On the one hand, when one claims ethical justification for a specific disciplinary or institutional practice, ethics necessarily functions as a *ground* or a *presence* and not a disruptive or anarchic non-presence. On the other hand, when one claims ethical justification for resisting specific disciplinary, legal, or state formations, ethics *still* seems to function as a *ground* or a *presence*, which "disruptively" opposes the perceived injustice of this or that alleged "totalitarian" practice or policy. Is an individual's conscience infallible? States certainly are not. How is a particular state or a particular individual to know when they are performing overreach? Take the recent controversy over revoking military service exemptions for the ultra-Orthodox in Israel. Let's assume it's true that compulsory military service can be read as an ethically legitimate policy, where citizens are required to "serve the Other" in a particular polity's defense. Let's further imagine a daring ultra-Orthodox yeshiva student who has read his Levinas to say something like this: "My conscience objects. This policy is totalitarian, and it assumes that military service is the only way to serve my country. My Torah study is 'for the Other,' that is, it helps me to be a better Jew and a better human being. Moreover, it empowers me to serve my country by keeping its moral singularity and religious culture alive. I therefore refuse to comply with the state on this matter." On Levinasian grounds, both the Israeli state and our yeshiva student can equally claim justification, the latter charging the former with "secular" totalitarian overreach, the former charging the latter with exempting himself from a social burden that should be shared by all. On Levinas's own terms, we have no way to decide the conflict. A Levinasian statist can appeal to the exposed human bodies of co-citizens to supply a justification of Israel's revoking religious exemptions for mandatory military service. A Levinasian anarchist can appeal to a determinative divine meaning and collective religious culture to justify his or her noncompliance with a "totalitarian" state policy.

While this particular case can perhaps be read as a potentially necessary tension, a good tension that deprives both parties of purely good conscience, the question is partly determined by *internal* debates within the Israeli nation-state and within the global Jewish community, that is, among a variety of Jews on the meaning of Jewish identity in general. The indeterminacy of Levinas's "account" of justice becomes more pressing when the potential conflict is not over *internal* state policy, or an *internal* debate among a particular polity or people, but rather, say, over the proper mode of political organization in general. As both Wolff and Rae have questioned, because Levinas grants that it is sometimes necessary to kill some others for the sake of other others, how are we to determine when such killing is justified?[4] Imagine a group of anarcho-federalists who take Levinas's rhetoric a bit too literally. Say they decide to violently revolt against a nominally liberal state because they judge it to be "totalitarian" and to do a terribly wretched job of freeing its citizens to be ethical. On Levinasian grounds, both liberals and anarchists can claim justification for the violence they perform. Levinasian "justice" provides no way to decide what form of political organization best serves "the Other," and no principled way to decide or answer the questions: *who owes what to whom, in what order, and why?, and how are these debts to be discharged?* On the one hand, the Levinasian statist can justify the state's monopoly on violence, and its violent defense against anarchist revolutionaries, by both negative utilitarian calculations ("liberal institutions and the coercive practices at their disposal have historically proven the least violent form of government, and it protects us from Hobbesian ontological anarchy") and positive normative commitments ("human rights grounded in the divine spark formally recognize the ethical self, and rightfully limits state-power, that is, burdens the state to respect and protect the free undertaking of individual strivings for the good"). On the other hand, the Levinasian anarcho-federalists can justify their revolutionary violence "for the Other" by appeal to both alleged historical facts ("the complicity of the state with capitalist forces and entrenched power that in fact enforces the rule of the few on the many") and to normative theoretical judgments ("The state is 'totalitarian' by its very nature"). For the Levinasian anarchist, the proper mode of political formation "for the Other" is local, participatory, and direct democracies where responsibilities and decision making occur immediately in both work place and town square, finally ending the violent and arbitrary generalities, hierarchies, and violences that constitute states qua states. Both our Levinasian liberals and our Levinasian revolutionary anarchists can appeal to exposed human bodies (or to God) to construct contrasting political philosophies to justify their own oppositional coercive practices "for the Other."

As should be clear, the Levinasian debate between statists and anarchists has no easy access to "necessary tension" arguments that might be claimed for the military exemption question above.[5] Were such a hypothetical to actually occur, Levinasians would be forced to decide, and outside Levinas's occasional pieces and plainly ad hoc opinions on related issues, there is nothing internal to Levinas's account of justice that allows us to decide such questions. As Larocco aptly asks, "If the face of the third is 'an incessant correction of the asymmetry of proximity, in which the face is looked at,' how is one to think through that insight in the frictions and alliances between politics and justice?"[6] In my view, Bergo's conclusion seems unavoidable, "Levinas' remarks on politics are rare and . . . idiosyncratic."

For all the problems that attend Levinas's treatment of politics and justice, his formal insistence on an ethical ground for public life is not among them. Larocco engages Levinas to qualify Ophir's explicit (and Baliber's implicit), baldly Gnostic view of political life as "an order of evils." Such a view not only begs the question (by what right or good is political life judged "evil"?), but it implicitly identifies *burden* with *harm*.[7] Levinas's description of the face has problems that will continue to be debated, but one feature of its analysis will certainly endure: the inexculpable tie he presents between height and destitution, sovereignty and vulnerability, freedom and obligation. Any nominally "critical" political philosophy that treats sovereignty as pure chimera, or ignores it entirely, is either naive or authoritarian; naive because the constitution of a polity necessarily involves the codification in law of the duties and prerogatives of citizens qua citizens, and failing to treat both of these leaves power undetermined. Such is authoritarian for essentially the same reasons: political belonging is left adrift to the whims of mere custom or fashion, which minorities or dissidents must constantly negotiate, and indeed: *suffer*. Quite clearly, law can be wielded as a tool of oppression. It can also liberate, and is the only stable, yet augmentable, vehicle we have for securing the regularity and flexible order necessary for individuals and groups to enjoy basic well-being. If we decide for a liberal-statist interpretation of Levinas, which entails a concomitant rejection of anarchist "disruption" talk, then, as Bell rightly argues, "[The face] gives a way of understanding what states are responsible for, providing a criterion for judgment of political action and the meeting of their obligations to human beings."[8] Even still, as I've shown: the problem of indeterminacy haunts Levinas's own politics and talk of justice, but his analysis of the face can provide a necessary starting point for meaningful political thought and a way to critically assess the seriousness of any putative political theory.

In contrast to debates over the normative foundations of politics, or to internal debates within the Jewish community over Israeli state policy, and distinct from higher-order questions of the proper mode of Levinasian political organization or the justification of political violence "for the other," sadly, we face other realities that are decidedly *not* hypothetical. Moreover, we also have Levinas's actual commentaries on these realities, which bring into relief the stakes involved in the indeterminacy of Levinasian justice. No one has better identified the problem on the political question than Jason Caro.[9]

II.a. Levinas and the Palestinians

Any treatment of Levinas's various comments on the Israeli-Palestinian situation ought to take Eisenstadt and Katz's "The Faceless Palestinian: A History of an Error" as its point of departure.[10] I don't necessarily endorse every turn in their analysis, but in general they are spot-on about too easy and indiscriminate judgment on this matter. Though my own project in this book is gratefully indebted to Judith Butler's relevant analysis in *Giving and Account of Oneself*, she has since mounted the much more ostentatious claim that "[Levinas said] in an interview that the Palestinian had no face, that he only meant to extend ethical obligations to those who were bound together by his version of Judeo-Christian and classical Greek origins."[11] Chaouat, Eisenstadt, and Katz are spot-on: Levinas never actually said or wrote this.[12] As I discuss in more detail below, there is an important difference between the explicit endorsement of doctrinal ethnocentrism—straight-up *fascism*—and the *desire for recognition* involved in defending one's own indigenous culture or standing for, exemplifying, and contributing to its historic achievements. The former warrants careful, ongoing, and resolute resistance. As we will see, the latter is an affect every single person must contend with and take responsibility for. It can be said categorically that *Levinas was no fascist*, as his own critique of the jingoistic and land-worshiping quarters of Zionism make absolutely clear.[13] Though this is an important, and indeed central, point, it must be said that managing not to be a fascist does not exempt one from critical evaluation. I moreover share Eisenstadt and Katz's regard for Caro's handling of this matter, to which I now turn.

As has been widely noted in the scholarship, in response to Malka's question, "for the Israeli, isn't the 'other' above all the Palestinian?," Levinas responds:

> My definition of the other is completely different. The other is the neighbor, who is not necessarily kin, but who can be. And in that sense, if you're for the other, you're for the neighbor. But if your neighbor attacks another neighbor or treats him unjustly, what can you do? Then alterity takes on another character, in alterity we can find an enemy, or at least we are faced with the problem of knowing who is right and who is wrong, who is just and who is unjust. There are people who are wrong.[14]

Here, Levinas treats "alterity" as *universal determination*, a property or ascription of moral worth to all individual exposed bodies without regard to their concrete history or particularity. Here, taking sides with Israeli violence over-against Palestinian violence is apparently justified by a *purely universal meaning*. Yet at other times, Levinas holds that

> . . . [i]t is the position of an armed and dominant State, one of the great military powers of the Mediterranean basin facing the unarmed Palestinian people whose very existence Israel refuses to recognize! But is that the true state of affairs? Is not Israel, in its very real strength, also one of the most fragile and vulnerable

> things in the world, poised in the midst of unopposed nations, who are rich in natural allies, and surrounded by their lands? Land, land, land as far as the eye can see.[15]

And

> This conflict has been acute since the creation of the State of Israel on a small piece of arid land which had belonged to the children of Israel more than thirty centuries before and which . . . has never been abandoned by the Jewish communities. . . . But it also happens to be on a small piece of land which has been inhabited by people who are surrounded on all sides and by vast stretches of land containing the great Arab people of which they form a part. They call themselves Palestinians [*se dénomment Palestiniens*].[16]

Here, Levinas appeals to a particular people ("children of Israel") and concrete history ("more than thirty centuries") over-against Palestinian grievances, quite legitimate grievances if considered in light of international law and universal human rights. As Caro rightly notes, here Levinas stuffs Palestinians into a larger category: "Arab," casts the empirical nation-state of Israel as besieged on all sides, and hence apparently relieved of its excessive responsibility to particular Palestinian others. Israel is instead entitled to its just portion of land within an expansive sea of "Arabness."[17] Caro, with and better than many others, underlines the clearly equivocal character of Levinas's rhetoric of justice.[18]

What Caro and existing scholarship do not do is thoroughly diagnose this arbitrarity in light of Levinas's substantive philosophical proposals and intrinsically equivocal method. The indeterminacy of Levinas's "account" of justice is ultimately rooted in the indeterminacy inherent to his method, and specifically in this context: his alternate and circular appeals to empirical *human bodies* and non-empirical *universal meaning*. As my above examples illustrate, *within* the Jewish community, the tension between particular practices and universal meaning is held to be necessary and productive; *within* a settled commitment to the justification of the liberal state on Levinas's philosophical premises, the tension between particular practices and universal meaning is also held to be a necessary and productive tension. Yet as soon our anarchist claims Levinasian justification for the violent overthrow of the state in a naive bid to bring about its abolition, the liberal and anarchist have no way to adjudicate their conflict on Levinas's own grounds, and must ultimately *fight it out*: each killing the other "for the Other." That they kill each other with a bad conscience is certainly better than if they did so with a purely good conscience, but this sheds no light on the larger problem: *Levinasian "justice" devolves to the rule of pure force in the "justification" it enables for and against the state.* He essentially appeals to alterity in two distinct and mutually exclusive ways: 1) as a *universal* property or attribution of moral worth to *all* human bodies *in general*, and 2) as a substantive identity and determinate history of an empirically *particular* people. In the first appeal, the particular and empirical are excluded; in the second appeal, the particular and empirical are claimed.

I do not want to be unfair to Levinas in this analysis. Indeed, in light of concrete history, and of the millennial crimes of "Christian" Europe, and especially the Shoah, his defense of the particular is not in itself unjustified. We ought not and cannot condemn the clear self-interest involved in Levinas's defense of Israel, even if we might question how this defense is performed in light of his own philosophy, or its cogency in light of non-arbitrary political norms. Nor should the legitimate grievances of Palestinian struggle, and the justified self-interest it involves, be ignored or set aside here. Indeed, in the face of all the complexity of the situation—and the culpable missteps of all relevant parties, above all: the historical crimes of European states—a viable solution cannot fail to reckon, register, and redress the legitimate grievances and justified self-interest on all sides; and this will require not only formal rigor and existential strength in adjudicating matters truthfully, but also a concrete, creative, and sustainably evidenced commitment by all parties to being reliable partners for a peaceful and prosperous collective future.[19]

Moreover, despite Levinas's inadequate treatment of very difficult political questions of his day, he also perpetually strove to differentiate purely cynical political Zionism from one that is ethically or religiously guided, that is, normatively oriented and morally constrained in its dealings with others in fidelity to Judaism's own prophetic tradition. While Levinas's account of justice might be determinate enough to safely criticize Netanyahu or Jewish Home fascism, it remains structured by the inherent contradiction I have diagnosed in his core philosophical proposals. Finally, a full diagnosis of Levinas's Eurocentric statements must finally look at how Levinas conceived and treated the relation of ethics to Judaism.

III. Judaism and Ethics

First, we cannot take Levinas to represent Judaism in general or as a whole, whether this "in general" is construed in terms of religion, religious civilization, or purely ethnic belonging. Cleary, Levinas is intervening in and performing a creative proposal within a long and continuing debate. Nor can or should non-Jews demand an absolute accounting from a complex, internally differentiated, and living tradition that Judaism in fact is. Levinas and Levinas alone is responsible for his written opinions. But because Levinas has entitled himself to a normative interpretation of Judaism in general, and therefore utilizes a distinction between Judaism and other traditions, we are justified in analyzing these distinctions. Moreover, scholarship in religious studies has long wrestled with the issues I analyze above. As Herzog notices, there are "significant contradictions in Levinas's treatment of the relationship between philosophy and Judaism," and "not everything about the relationship between Athens and Jerusalem is clear."[20] In this light, when I refer to "Judaism" below, I mean "Levinas's specific normative interpretation of Judaism," and *not* "Judaism the ancient and internally variegated religion and moral culture." Because Levinas most closely identifies as a Jew, a brief review of his treatment of the Jew/non-Jew distinction is required to fully assess his allegedly Eurocentric statements.

Levinas sees himself as supplying not only the universal meaning of humanity (in general), but also of Judaism as a particular moral community. In and of itself, of course, this is not viciously self-interested or "chauvinist." Indeed, anyone who belongs to a long-standing religious, philosophical, and ethical tradition conducts just this sort of analysis. Judaism is an ancient and *open* tradition, that is, continually renews and critically assesses its own identity through internal debate and contest, in conversation with other traditions, and in light of contemporary problems it faces. Judaism involves certain norms, and does indeed give account(s) of genuinely universal norms held to be binding for both Jews and non-Jews, and a more rigorous and specific set of norms it assumes for itself that distinguishes it from other traditions. This, I take it, is a relatively uncontroversial description of traditionality. Whether we choose to analyze a particular tradition in terms of practices or meanings, each tends to involve a self-consciously defined range of practical and semantic commitments. Though traditions often include considerable internal contest and variety, there nevertheless tends to be at least one decision point by which a tradition distinguishes itself from its others. By belonging to such a tradition, one is not ipso facto chauvinist.

Is a Buddhist "chauvinist" because she believes her tradition gives a true or authentic account of what we are (or are *not*) and the obligations this involves? Can we blame a Buddhist *for being a Buddhist*, in other words? Most of us would say no. Whether a Buddhist is judged chauvinist or disinterested depends on precisely *how* he or she relates Buddhist tradition to other traditions. When we review how Levinas conceives his Judaism with respect to other traditions, serious questions emerge.

III.a. Singularity and Particularity

When Levinas claims to speak "in the name of original responsibility, in the name of this Judaism" and of "Israel—or the humanity of the Human," he in fact confuses singularity and particularity on his own terms.[21] He seems to claim that the meaning yielded in his philosophical account of ethics *just is* the meaning of Judaism. Here, there is no difference between the two: the ethical self as limitless responsibility *just is* the teaching of Judaism and the meaning Jewish community signifies, both to itself and for non-Jews. Here, Judaism is both "singular"—*more* responsible than other traditions— and "universal," or an exemplar for those traditions to follow. On this interpretation of Judaism, for non-Jews to be considered fully human, *they must convert to Judaism*, or must necessarily abandon their own histories, narratives, practices, and beliefs and adopt specifically Jewish ones. This seems wrong, however, and Levinas apparently refuses this implication by reminding us that Judaism rejects proselytizing; it does "not turn into an imperialist expansion that devours all who deny it."[22] He seems to suggest that anyone who actually commends and practices other-responsibility, quite apart from whatever else they might culturally practice, can legitimately count as a Jew, that is, as human. This implies it is *not* necessary to participate in Jewish ritual, Torah study, Halakhic practice, and so forth in order to count as Jew, that is, as human. If this is the case, what is the point of ritual, Torah study, and Halakha, if we can be Jewish by simply affirming and practicing limitless other-responsibility? If we take Levinas's generous universality seriously, we must answer: *nothing*. Those who in fact do take up limitless responsibility by prioritizing other's needs above their own, while carefully apportioning their resources to serve as many others as possible, are Jewish, that is, human. Yet this, too, seems wrong. For Levinas, the traditions and practices of historic Judaism absolutely cannot and ought not be discarded: *they are* essential, *in all their varied expressions, to what Judaism is*.[23] When Levinas recognizes non-Jews who do not convert to Judaism *as* Jews, he is recognizing both (i) their humanity, and (ii) that they are lacking something that "full" Jews do not lack. What do they lack? Namely, participation in traditioned Jewish community and the concrete history, practices, and beliefs that constitute it. Throughout Levinas's writings, he switches back and forth between these two positions. For example, "The ritual law of Judaism constitutes the austere discipline that strives to achieve [justice]. Only this law can recognize the face of the other which has managed to impose an austere role on its true nature."[24] Here, Levinas seems radically exclusivist: *only* Jewish ritual law can "recognize" the face of the other. This implies that ritual law is *not* a contingent cultural practice from which non-Jews can be excepted, and hence: practicing ritual law is the *only* way we may properly "recognize" the other as other. This seems to commit him to a position wherein all non-Jews must explicitly convert to Judaism to *fully* realize their humanity. Yet elsewhere he resists this implication. For example,

> . . . a Jew can communicate just as intimately with a non-Jew who portrays morality—in other words, a Noachide—as with another Jew. The rabbinic principle by which the just of every nation participate in the future world expresses not only an eschatological view. It affirms the possibility of ultimate intimacy, beyond the dogma affirmed by one or another, an intimacy without reserve.[25]

This "intimacy without reserve," as described here, suggests that (1) the specificities of a particular non-Jew's native tradition—their histories, narratives, practices, and beliefs—*count for nothing*, so long as they are "just" from Judaism's perspective, which for Levinas fundamentally means: "limitlessly responsible"; and (2) for a particular Jew, the specificities of Jewish tradition—its histories, narratives, practices, and beliefs—*count for nothing* in this "intimacy" with a non-Jew, because it is an intimacy "without reserve." There is "no reserve," *nothing held back*, no *difference* that counts between a Jew and a just non-Jew, that is, traditioned Jewish practices and beliefs are *not* necessary to Judaism's universal meaning. In the entirety of Levinas's corpus, he switches back and forth between these two mutually exclusive positions. We cannot say, "the Jew is more responsible," hence distinguishing the Jew from the non-Jew, because the non-Jew is "just," or shares this "more" with the Jew. It would be tempting to appeal to the different native histories and traditions that distinguish our "intimate" Jew and non-Jew to negotiate this ambiguity. In this case, the non-Jew must be construed as having her or his own "ritual law"—or set of traditioned practices and beliefs analogous to Judaism's own—such that both Jew and non-Jew participate in distinct and particular communities held to strive *for the same justice and truth*. In this account, there can be an "ultimate intimacy, beyond the dogma affirmed by one or another." Our Jew and non-Jew can recognize the uniqueness of each other's respective traditions, without those differences necessarily functioning to exclude either from "the future world," or rather: a genuinely universal meaning. As attractive as this account might be, Levinas rejects it. Such an account necessarily renders Judaism merely one traditioned community among others, construes it as subject to a universal justice or general truth that encompasses *all* particular communities, and as such impugns Judaism's "radical singularity." Such a move would render Judaism's uniqueness *relative*, in other words, and this he cannot accept. Though at times he shows some hesitation, his actual treatment of other traditions leaves little doubt: under no circumstances will he countenance any perspective that relativizes "the unique role that devolved upon Israel among the nations."[26]

Levinas ultimately becomes ensnared by his own logic in attempting to think the traditional *theological belief* in Jewish election by analogy to the *moral election* his ethics asserts. Here, Jews are *called out* from the nations and the idolatry they are allegedly inurned in. The nations function as the *negative horizon* on which Israel qua Israel acquires meaning, just as "ontology" functions to fundamentally contrast ethical self from the ontological subject. As such, Levinas's Judaism may be able to count non-Jewish *individuals* as Jews, that is, human, but on his terms cannot admit the non-Jew's native tradition as providing anything like a corollary to Jewish practice. There can be no relative equivalence between them on any terms (pedagogical or otherwise).[27] In other words, there can be an "intimacy without reserve" from Levinas's perspective because the non-Jew is logically forced to abandon her native traditions to be considered fully "just," and the Jew is not. Even if our non-Jew has abandoned her "idolatrous" traditions, the question of whether traditioned Jewish practice is normative for our Jewish non-Jew is never resolved.[28] Levinas's position perpetually switches between the two mutually exclusive alternatives above: traditioned Jewish practice both *is* and *is not* necessary to count as Jew. It is required for Jews; it is not required for "Jewish non-Jews," without us ever learning why this is the case or what the *difference* might be. The point, of course, is that because Levinas is *judging* the nations, he owes them an account of the norms by which they are being judged. If the nations are prohibited from judging Israel by a universal standard, and stand accused for impugning its "singularity," is Levinas justified in holding the nations to a universal standard?

As the attuned reader has no doubt noticed: there is something strange about ascribing "singularity" to a *community*. In moving from his analysis of the ethical self to his analysis of Judaism, Levinas introduces a new sense of "singularity." Namely, he moves from describing an individual, absolutely "singular" body to describing a *collective*. While "singularity," here, retains its function of specifying something unique (a particular tradition), in the move from describing a self to describing a collective, the concrete terms in which singularity is considered *change*. Judaism is *not* an individual self, but a *whole* community. Judaism is *not* an "absolutely passive" body (it is not *dead*), but an *active* and living tradition. Judaism is *not* called to completely and utterly sacrifice itself for its others—*not* obligated to *die* for the nations, thank God—which is precisely to say: *Judaism is not "infinitely" responsible.* And beyond the merely formal problem in play, if one examines the critical concepts by which Levinas distinguishes his own tradition from other traditions, problematic cases emerge. Under the heading of "the singularity of Israel," his Judaism is entitled to all sorts of allegedly "irresponsible" goods denounced as "ontology" in non-Jewish cultures:

Against Participation:

[False] transcendence . . . is already (or still) participation, submergence in the being toward which it goes, which holds the transcending being in its invisible meshes, as to do it violence.[29]

For Participation:

Has not the history of the nations already been in a sense that glorification of the Eternal in Israel, a participation in the history of Israel, which can be assessed by the degree to which their national solidarity is open to the other?[30]

Against Ecstasy:

The intervention of the unconscious, and consequently, to the horrors and ecstasies that it feeds . . . all this is linked ultimately to violence.[31]

For Ecstasy:

To transcend oneself is to leave one's home, to the point of leaving oneself, is to substitute oneself for another.[32]

Against violence:

[The] goodness of the good is alone able to counterbalance the violence of . . . choice.[33]

For violence:

The surprising saying which is a responsibility for another . . . [is] disinterestedness imposed with a good violence.[34]

Against mystery:

Nothing, in fact, is more opposed to a relation with the face than "contact" with the Irrational and mystery.[35]

For mystery:

The excellence of an exceptional message, even though it is addressed to all. This is the paradox of Israel, and one of the mysteries of the spirit.[36]

Against *jouissance*:

[Ethics] does not conform to the scheme of our normal relations to the world, in which the subject knows or absorbs its object like a nourishment, the satisfaction of a need.[37]

For *jouissance*:

[Ritual law] carries its own joys, which nourishes [Jewish] religious life and the whole of Jewish mysticism.[38]

Against roles:

> Does obeying God involve receiving a role from Him or receiving an order? We distrust theater, the petrification of our faces . . .³⁹

For roles:

> [Mendelssohn heralded] the unique role that devolved upon Israel among the nations.⁴⁰

Against representation:

> What is left for me to say . . . to get to the sources of the idolatries, . . . which there must be exposed and condemned some secret closing up of the soul, which is satisfied with I know not what fetish, symbol, or representation taken for a concept.⁴¹

For representation:

> [Singular responsibility] is what is represented by the Jewish concept of Israel, and the sense that it is a chosen people.⁴²

In each of these cases, Levinas will claim that for his Judaism, such notions or experiences are "ethical," whereas for other traditions, they are "ontological." In fact, Levinas evaluates other traditions by reference to the strict account of ethical singularity his philosophy asserts, whereas for his Judaism, all sorts of substantive attachments are admitted as an inherent feature of its "singularity." Levinas's Judaism carries its history, community, rituals, beliefs, and attachments with it in its "election to the good," while all others get a priori reduced to "ontology."

> The challenge of an ontological reversal! The original perseverance of being in its beings, . . . and of the soul, the "owner and interested party" Bossuet speaks of, . . . is reversed into "Thou shalt not kill," in the care of one being for another.⁴³

Levinas's Judaism *alone* exhibits this care. All *others*—religions, cultural narratives, and philosophies—are "mythological," "theological," "Sacred," or some particular species of "ontology" Levinas's Judaism *alone* "reverses."

When "mystery" is used to describe the character of the being of our common world, or to defend a particular non-Jewish cultural narrative, it is "the sacred" or "mythology." Yet mystery is considered an apt term to sanctify the paradoxes of Israel. When "ecstasy" is used to describe an aesthetic, religious, or social experience of belonging, it is "paganism." Though as "inspiration" and "substitution," not to mention the feeling of belonging participants in Jewish community in fact feel, it is the "glory" of the good. When Judaism appears as a character in a historico-cultural story, it rejects (as in Hegelian History, for example) such stories are "violent" and "ontological," but non-Jews should apparently be grateful for their role as a priori exemplars of idolatry and "ontology," that is, as Israel's *eternal antagonists*. As Butler notes,

> It's curious that Levinas should here extract "persecution" from its concrete historical appearances, establishing it as an apparently timeless essence of Judaism. If this were true, then any historical argument to the contrary could be refuted on definitional grounds alone . . . The problem, of course, is that "the Jew" is a category that belongs to a culturally constituted ontology (unless it is the name for access to the infinite itself), and so if the Jew maintains an "elective" status in relation to ethical responsiveness, then Levinas fully confuses the preontological and the ontological. The Jew is not part of ontology or history, and yet this exemption becomes the way in which Levinas makes claims about the role of Israel, historically considered, as forever and exclusively persecuted.[44]

Levinas's ethics and treatment of other traditions does not seem in each case disinterested. The most basic point in his entire philosophy—the distinction between ethics and ontology—already rigs the game. When Levinas moves to describe or evaluate any other tradition, he will find them lacking *by necessity* because of the question-begging "reduction" Saying performs and by his identification of this reduction with the theological doctrine of Jewish election.[45]

III.B. "Ethics" and "Ontology" in Intercultural Context

Not only is Levinas's actual account of Saying *not* "ethically" *pure*, as my analysis above demonstrates, but his tendentious treatment of other cultures *necessarily follows from* this impurity: his ethics/ontology distinction is *necessarily ontological on his own terms.* Levinas's ontological ethics performs an originary description of the *determinate meaning* of the being of the ethical one, and of the categories and relations that articulate it. His description vigorously stipulates that each self must shoulder the relevant responsibility *as* his or her own individual person, but this does not impugn the general character of his project. We *know* that Levinas is not simply describing *his own* "ethical self," but the meaning of ethical selfhood in general. He is "thematizing" *us*, thematizing *for us*, while strangely and simultaneously forbidding us to "thematize." If ontology is "violent" because it thematizes "the non-thematizible other," thereby "annulling the link between persons by making beings participate, albeit ecstatically, in a drama not brought about willingly by them, an order in which they founder," then Levinas's own ethics and his treatment of other traditions eminently count as "violence" and as "ontology."[46] We cannot say "ethics is *better* than ontology" without specifying what this might mean and why this is so.[47] Say a homeless man asks me for food. It would indeed be better for me to *actually give him food*, rather than, say, give him a lecture on Levinas's ethics. Here, giving is indeed better than "thematizing," but this does not tell us *why* Levinas's ethics is "better" than other accounts of ethics, or preferable to competing ontologies. He cannot abstractly appeal to alterity or singularity, because his own ethics already *generalizes* and tells us a very particular story about what it means *to be* ethical. Say our homeless man is Hindu and regards both himself and me as particular manifestations of transcendent Braham. As we enjoy lunch together, I proceed to tell him that Hindu philosophy is "ontological" and "mythological," that it does "violence" because it regards us both as instances of a larger identity, and hence is not "ethical." "What violence?" he might respond. "Have I harmed you? My religion teaches me that I'm obliged to practice virtue toward Hindus and non-Hindus alike. I take strong exception to your purely external and plainly ignorant critique of my religion. I thank you for your material generosity, and hope you can extend this practice by treating my tradition seriously and fairly."

The most basic presupposition of Levinas's entire philosophy is this: mere *thinking*—conceptually "violating" the other—is *bad*. We never really learn why this is so. His distinction between ontology and ethics, and the incessant appeals to abstract alterity, singularity, and affection, are failed attempts to establish a structural priority his own descriptions fail to yield. Abstract alterity does not obviate the problem, in other words. Consider Levinas's statement:

> The yellow peril! It is not racial but spiritual. Not about inferior values but about a radical strangeness, strange to all the density of its past, where no voice with a familiar inflection comes through: a lunar, a Martian past.[48]

If alterity, all by its lonesome, invested me with infinite responsibility, Chinese communism would apparently invest the "most" infinite responsibility possible! When he claims, "The ritual law of Judaism constitutes the austere discipline that strives to achieve [justice]. Only this law can recognize the face of the other which has managed to impose an austere role on its true nature,"[49] he admits what we already *know*: alterity is always already "recognized," *identified, known* in a *particular* way, and this knowing plays its part in motivating us and forming us in the moral practices we perform.[50] To relate oneself to other cultural traditions in a disinterested way, one would have to analyze moments in them that internally require obligations toward non-participants. For example, Buddhist doctrine holds that those who lack faith (*aśraddhā*) are subject to bad karmic consequences that determine their status in posthumous rebirths, but it does *not* command compassion toward only those who believe it. The Buddhist is obligated to practice compassion to all sentient creatures, whether or not they happen to be Buddhist. On Levinas's grounds, we must conclude that Buddhist *truth* is "violent ontology" because its claims have universal import, and hence can apparently be dismissed out of hand. On these terms, and without further ado: Buddhism must be judged "unethical" simply *because* it has a metaphysics. To take Buddhism seriously, one might fail to be convinced by the metaphysical story it tells, but one can come to *respect* the compassion Buddhism requires toward all non-Buddhists. Buddhist compassion, Islamic hospitality, Hindu *ahimsa*, Christian enemy-love, and traditional African *ubuntu* all involve non-contingent obligations universal in scope and effect. They also present specific *truths* and differing, sometimes mutually exclusive, stories of the ultimate meaning of our unfolding human drama. What is Levinas's own story?

> The challenge of an ontological reversal! The original perseverance of being in its beings, of the individualism of being, the persistence or insistence of beings in the guise of individuals jealous for their part, this particularism of the inert, . . . particularism of the enrooted vegetable being, . . . and of the soul, the "owner and

interested party" Bossuet speaks of, . . . is reversed into "Thou shalt not kill," in the care of one being for another.[51]

And when other traditions manage to produce some insight, they do so by their proximity to Levinas's story:

> Attentions to the reflections of the light of the Torah itself, illuminating the seventy nations through Christianity and Islam. And in the suffering, disdain and blood brought down upon the carrier of the Torah by so many triumphant bursts of its *borrowed light*, Israel has been able to see . . . a closer relationships than those derived from concepts.[52]

Other monotheisms—and presumably, whatever might shine in non-theist traditions—*borrow* their "light" from Levinas's ethics, here given religious expression. Levinas's ethics remains, hence, the *origin* and *proprietor* of the very meaning of the human, or in other words: "the owner and interested party" of an election described as the *impossibility of ownership and the transcendence of self-interest*. Levinas affirms his own story by claiming that other stories lack what they in fact do *not* lack: explicit accounts of non-contingent obligations owed to non-participants. Levinas denies other stories by claiming that his own story lacks *what it in fact has*: namely, *a story*, an *ontology*, a *particular* account of the overall meaning of our unfolding human drama.

IV. Conclusion

> *I often say, though it's a dangerous thing to say publicly, that humanity consists of the Bible and the Greeks. All the rest can be translated: all the rest—all the exotic—is dance.*[53]

The point of this chapter is not to deny Levinas his Jewish story or to attack election as a Jewish *theological belief or motif*.[54] My point is rather that there is *no outside a story* (*il n'y a pas hors-récit*).[55] As I suggest more specifically below, Levinas's position ultimately evinces what Nussbaum calls "normative chauvinism," not because he is committed to the sufficiency of Judaism, or even that he believes it tells the *best* of all stories, but rather for arbitrarily chastising participants in *other* stories for doing *nothing other than this.* On Levinas's own terms, the specificities of all actual intra-worldly struggles—be it feminist-, LGBT-, class-, minority religious-, or anti-racist-struggle—are a matter of relative indifference. The Levinasian self is only responsible to others stripped of all their worldliness, of all the *stories, practices, memories, hopes, and attachments that* make *each of them what they are.* Because it is simply impossible to refrain from or sustainably resist all linguistic mediation, when we speak of alterity, we do not really mean what Levinas wants it to mean. Responsibility for others in an irreducibly plural world must involve just, sympathetic, and critical attention to each other's stories. It also means revising our stories in light of criticism. In the face of violence and injustice, we can distinguish between stories that share a non-contingent commitment to others' holistic well-being and those that do not. As contemporary social, moral, and political struggles in fact show: people of diverse stories can struggle as comrades to create a world where injustice and gratuitous suffering are less ubiquitous.

In the last analysis, problems both in Levinas's method and his more specific analyses are not only relevant to the matter of his few Eurocentric statements. As Herzog notices, even historic Judaism may ultimately fall prey here:

> Is it possible that Torah is not pure holiness but rather a mixture of holiness and sacredness, of infinite "saying" and logical "said"? Could it be that the sacred is necessary in order to make the holy rationally and emotionally perceptible? If, as Levinas writes, "The Word of God, supreme meaning, is without insistence—it flies away like a dream. . . . Idolatry is real reality, natural reality," there is no way to record or even to perceive the word of God without turning it into idolatry . . . Thus, no idolatry at all would be equivalent to no perception at all of the word of God.[56]

As such, Levinas's take on "ontology" and the alleged "violence" of mere thought requires a fundamental revision, or in other words: *we must rethink his ontology as a whole.*

Chapter 6

Levinas: A Life

> Levinas survived the Second World War under difficult and humiliating circumstances, while his family, with the exception of his wife and daughter, perished. These experiences may well have shaped his sense that what is demanded of us is an "infinite" willingness to be available to and for the other's suffering.[1]
>
> —Hillary Putnam

What lives on in Levinas's philosophy? A cogently performed immanent critique terminates in a relatively precise specification of the normative potentials that remain in the texts or forms of life under analysis. As such, allow me to finally remove the rigorous brackets I've placed around all but Levinas's texts and relevant scholarship. I stress at the outset that the care I've taken to treat Levinas philosophically, and hence do him the justice of not vulgarly psychologizing his philosophical arguments, ought to still remain in force. His psychological motivations by themselves can neither vindicate nor undermine his philosophy, but they can shed further light on matters that must be consulted to thoroughly evaluate the life of the man himself. In some cases—take Heidegger, for example—such a procedure can yield deeply ambiguous conclusions, such that the banal and even vicious dimensions of a person's choices and personality actively haunt the serious task of independently assessing their philosophy.[2] Unlike Heidegger, Levinas was a deeply decent man. His life was quite remarkable, a testament to the triumphs and horrors of an age. No treatment of Levinas's philosophy would be complete without treating his life as a whole, and no critical evaluation would be complete without treating its problem in the properly human relationality of its historical context. His life remains, in his own words, "*dominated by the presentiment and the memory of the Nazi horror.*"[3]

I. Early Years

Emmanuel Levinas was born on January 12, 1906, in Kovno (Kaunas), Lithuania.[4] The oldest of three brothers, the Levinas family belonged to the city's historic and robust Jewish community. Though the family spoke Russian, Levinas's parents also spoke Yiddish, and he learned Hebrew as a boy reading the Bible and commentaries. He moreover grew up reading the titans of Russian literature: Gogol, Turgenev, Tolstoy, Dostoevsky, Pushkin, and so forth. During WWI, the Levinas family became refugees when the Germans took Kovno. They were refused entry into Kiev and resettled in Kharkov. Here he was one of the first Jews admitted to the Russian *Gymnasium*, and he experienced firsthand the tumult of February and October 1917. In 1920, the family resettled back in Kovno, where Levinas was enrolled in a Hebrew *Gymnasium*.[5]

In 1923, Levinas attended the University of Strasbourg. He studied Bergson and the philosophy of mind, and himself cites Charles Blondel, Maurice Halbwachs, Maurice Pradines, and Henri Carteron as his four most influential teachers (Levinas dedicated his first book on Husserl to Carteron).[6] It was in Strasbourg that he met and began a lifelong friendship with Maurice Blanchot. On the advice of another classmate, Gabrielle Pfeiffer, Levinas began a study of Husserl's *Logical Investigations*.[7] At this time, he met former Husserl student and close friend of Alexander Koyré: a Protestant theologian in Strasbourg's religion faculty, Jean Héring. Héring enthusiastically nurtured Levinas's growing interest in Husserl. After he obtained his *Licence* in philosophy in 1927, Héring helped arrange for him to study with the Master in Freiburg.

Levinas set off for Germany in July 1928. He attended Husserl's last seminar and Heidegger's first as chair of philosophy. While there, it seems Levinas became friendly with the Husserl family. In a letter to his friend, the Polish phenomenologist Roman Ingarden, Husserl wrote: "Héring has sent me a very gifted Lithuanian student." He even asked Levinas to give private French lessons to his wife.[8] In retrospect at least, and from the point of view of philosophical interest: this seems an exciting time to have studied in Freiburg. Levinas had not yet heard of Heidegger prior to his arrival, as he later wrote: "I went to Freiburg because of Husserl, but discovered Heidegger."[9] He arrived about a year after *Being and Time* was first published, and just a few months after Arendt and Heidegger ended their affair. He studied in Freiburg at the same time as Eugen Fink, Karl Löwith, Herbert Marcuse, Jean Wahl, and Hans Georg Gadamer, all at different stages of their education and early careers.[10] Levinas apparently caught Heidegger's eye too, as Kleinberg reports:

> Heidegger was very impressed with the young Lithuanian scholar from France and invited him to attend a philosophical retreat at Davos in 1929. Heidegger wrote a letter to the organizers of the Davos conference and to the Department of philosophy at Strasbourg, recommending that Levinas be sent as a representative of the French Universities.[11]

Davos was the occasion for the now (in)famous Heidegger/Cassirer debate. Levinas attended the philosophical meeting with others such as Léon Brunschvicg, Jean Cavaillès, Maurice de Gandillac, and Rudolf Carnap. Levinas eagerly sided with Heidegger, incurring the indignation of Frau Cassirer after satirizing old Ernst at an after-party *soirée*, an episode he later deeply regretted.[12]

In 1929, Levinas published his first article on Husserl's *Ideas I* in *Revue Philosophique*, and on his return to Strasbourg defended his dissertation, *La théorie de l'intuition dans le phénoménologie de Husserl*. His work won a prize from the Institute of Philosophy and was published the next year by Vrin in Paris. Through this and later writings, he helped introduce phenomenology to a new generation of philosophers. Paul Ricoeur once described Levinas as "the founder of Husserl studies in France." As Davis notes, "in 1932 Raymond Aron returned from Berlin to Paris and told fellow students Jean-Paul Sartre and Simone de Beauvoir about his discovery of Husserlian phenomenology. Sartre . . . 'turned pale with emotion,'"[13] and it was Levinas's earliest work that Sartre consulted to inaugurate his own turn to phenomenology. As Levinas later winks, "It was Sartre who guaranteed my place in eternity by stating in his famous obituary essay on Merleau-Ponty that he, Sartre, 'was introduced to phenomenology by Levinas.'"[14]

In 1930, Levinas moved to Paris. Thanks in part to his old friend Héring, he was about to land an important translation gig. As Dupont recounts, in 1926–27, Héring and Lev Shestov conducted a widely followed published debate on the phenomenological method that Husserl himself read.[15] Lévy-Bruhl published Shestov's critique of Husserl in the *Revue Philosophique*, and Héring—no doubt eager to please his former teacher—responded in Husserl's defense in the pages of the German-language *Philosophischer Anzeiger*. After a few exchanges, Dupont reports,

Shestov met Husserl only after the publication of his essays had earned him the reputation of being one of his chief antagonists. Their first encounter was at a philosophical congress in Amsterdam in April 1928. Shestov astonished Husserl by offering to arrange for him to speak in Paris, at the Sorbonne.[16]

Thus the *Cartesian Meditations* was born. Levinas attended Husserl's lectures, and Héring enlisted him and Gabrielle Pfeiffer to translate them into French with Koyré's editorial assistance.[17] As Critchley notes, "Levinas was responsible for the Fourth and Fifth Meditations, which contain Husserl's famous discussion of intersubjectivity."[18]

Over the next ten years, Levinas became a French citizen, married Raïssa Levi (his childhood sweetheart from Kovno), taught at the Alliance Israélite Universelle, and participated in Paris's bustling intellectual life.[19] He published the first article on Heidegger to appear in French, and in 1932 began a book on Heidegger's philosophy. He abandoned the project the next year when he learned that Heidegger joined the Nazi Party. He frequented Gabriel Marcel's Saturday-evening *soirées*, where he met Sartre and other avant-garde intellectuals. Shortly after Hitler took power, Levinas published "Reflections on the Philosophy of Hitlerism" in Emmanuel Mounier's avant-garde Personalist magazine: *Esprit*, an important journal on the Parisian scene that over the years also published original work by Ricoeur, Hannah Arendt, Frantz Fanon, Jacques Maritain, Leopold Sedar Senghor, and other notable intellectuals.[20] Levinas intermittently attended Kojéve's Hegel lectures, where he met Jean Hippolyte and others. Kojéve's lectures had a transformative impact on the French philosophical scene and were variously attended by Georges Bataille, Jacques Lacan, Raymond Aaron, André Breton, Merleau-Ponty, Koyré, and others.[21] Levinas's last interwar publication was an original phenomenological essay—*De l'évasion*—in Émile Bréhier's journal *Recherches Philosophiques*.[22]

With the advent of war in 1939, Levinas was drafted and served as an interpreter in the French army until their defeat at Somme in 1940. Captured by the Nazis, he was initially imprisoned at Rennes, but was later transferred to Fallingsbotel near Magdeburg in Northern Germany for the duration of the war. I quote at length Critchley's report on the Levinas family's horrific ordeal:

> Because Levinas was an officer in the French army, he was not sent to a concentration camp but to a military prison[]

camp, where he did forced labor in the forest. His camp had the number 1492, the date of the expulsion of the Jews from Spain! The Jewish prisoners were kept separately from the non-Jews and wore uniforms marked with the word "JUD." Most members of his family were murdered by the Nazis during the bloody pogroms that began in June 1940 with the active and enthusiastic collaboration of Lithuanian nationalists. Although it is not certain, it would appear that his brothers, mother, and father were shot by Nazis close to Kovno. The names of close and more distant murdered family members are recalled in the Hebrew dedication to his second major philosophical work, *Otherwise than Being or Beyond Essence*.

Levinas's wife and daughter survived the war thanks to the courageous humanity of many. Critchley continues,

> Raïssa and Simone Levinas were initially protected by a number of brave French friends, notably Suzanne Poirier, M. and Mme Verduron, and Blanchot. It would appear that Levinas somehow got a message through to Blanchot from the prison camp in Rennes. Blanchot lent his apartment to Raïssa and Simone for some time before Simone received an extremely courageous offer of refuge from the sisters of a Vincentian convent outside Orléans. Raïssa Levinas was supported financially throughout the war by the Alliance Israélite Universelle. She stayed in hiding in Paris until 1943 when she joined her daughter, adopting the name "Marguerite Bevos." Raïssa's mother, Amélia Frieda Levi, who had been living with the Levinas family before the war, was deported from Paris and murdered. There exist *carnets de guerre* from this period, as yet unpublished. Levinas vowed never to set foot on German soil again.[23]

As far as I'm aware, this is a vow he understandably kept.[24]

At the conclusion of the war, the Levinas family reunited in Paris. With the help of René Cassin, Levinas was appointed director of École Normale Israélite Orientale (ENIO). The Levinas family lived in an apartment above ENIO until 1980.[25] Critchley recounts well what seems to me the profound though everyday nobility of Levinas's own lived response to the Shoah,

Levinas did not have a university position until 1964 when he was in his late fifties. Because of his professional position and his pedagogical commitments, he dedicated a number of essays to the problems facing Jewish education and the need for a renaissance of Jewish spirituality after the catastrophe of the Shoah. This also explains why in this period Levinas's growing importance in discussions of Jewish affairs was not matched by an equal prominence in philosophical circles. These interests are well reflected in his 1963 collection, *Difficult Freedom*. The ENIO corresponded to and fostered the vision of Judaism that Levinas would defend with increasing vigor in the post-war years: rigorously intellectual, rooted in textual study, rationalistic, anti-mystical, humanist, and universalist. However, it should be recalled that most of Levinas's professional life was spent as a school administrator with extensive and rather routine responsibilities for the day-to-day welfare of ENIO students. Levinas took responsibility for Talmudic study in the ENIO and gave the famous public "cours de Rachi" on Saturdays which were followed by smaller study groups where Levinas would as readily discuss Dostoevsky or an article in *Le Monde* as a Judaic theme.

Levinas resumed the everyday routines—with all the joys and tedium they involve—necessary to the ongoing birth of Jewish futures.[26] Just after the war he met a medical doctor named Henri Nerson. He and Nerson spent time together on nearly a daily basis, and he soon became Levinas's best friend. It was Nerson who introduced him to the somewhat mysterious Talmudic scholar Monsieur Chouchani. They became so close, that some seven years after Nerson's death, Levinas would say, "I miss him every day."[27]

Just after the war, Levinas published an original work of phenomenological ontology, *De l'existence à l'existant* (1947). Written in captivity at Rennes and Fallingsbotel, it deepens and refines the themes he had treated in his 1935 *De l'évasion*.[28] During this period, his old friend Jean Wahl invited him to lecture. Wahl was professor of philosophy at the Sorbonne prior to the war (and again until his death in 1974), and himself had a quite noteworthy wartime experience.[29] After the war Wahl founded the Collège Philosophique, intended to be an avant-garde institute for aspiring French philosophers and intellectuals, and an alternative to the stodgy'ol Sorbonne. As Levinas recalled in his interview with Richard Kearney, "I had . . . frequent contact with [Merleau-Ponty] at Jean Wahl's [Collège]," and other notable French intellectuals were involved in the experiment.[30] Levinas's four lectures were published the next year as *Le temps et l'autre*.[31] As Critchley notes, its "initial publication was famously criticized by Simone de Beauvoir in the preface to *The Second Sex* for its understanding of the feminine as the other to the masculine."[32] Throughout the remainder of the 1940s, Levinas maintained an active intellectual life. In addition to his important duties as ENIO's Head of School, he penned a controversial critique of art, "Reality and Its Shadow." It appeared in 1948 in Sartre's recently launched, and now storied pages of, *Les Temps Modernes*; and, as Kavka notes, "with a cutting unsigned prefatory note by Sartre [himself]."[33] He also released a collection of unpublished prewar research under the title *Discovering Existence with Husserl and Heidegger*. Another significant publication of the period appeared in *Revue de Métaphysique et de Morale* a few years later, "Is Ontology Fundamental?" Here Levinas first makes explicit his ethical critique of Heidegger.

One of the most interesting events in Levinas's life in the 1940s was his encounter with the mysterious Monsieur Chouchani. Little seems to be known about the man, except that he mentored two of the most important Jewish intellectuals of the twentieth century: Eli Wiesel and Levinas himself. Wygoda recounts their initial meeting,

> In 1945 Levinas closest friend, Dr. Henri Nerson a Jewish obstetrician, told him about an outstanding and quite bizarre individual he came to know during the years of the War in the area of Vichy. The man was so unusual that even his real name was not known. He used to be called Chouchani but this was more of a nickname than his true one. His external appearance was quite unpleasant, some say even repugnant. However, according to Nerson his knowledge was phenomenal. Nerson, who was known for his sober way to apprehend people and situations, was clearly in a state of excitement as if he would have become an adept of some sect. He strongly recommended to Levinas to meet Chouchani, but for two years Levinas refused. . . . Levinas was quite suspicious as to what this "clochard" looking man could contribute to him. Finally in 1947 Levinas agreed to meet Chouchani. We know very little about the meeting itself. But there exists a myth. The myth suggests that they met for an entire night, and in the morning Levinas said to Nerson as he was about to leave: "I cannot tell what he knows, all I can

say is that all that I know, he knows." But the accuracy of this myth as it may, one fact remains undisputable. From then on, Levinas became interested in the study of Talmud to a point where most of his free time, he would devote to studying it.³⁴

As Wygoda notes, however we assess the reliability of this account, Chouchani quite clearly impressed Levinas. Critchley reports that he lived with the Levinas family for two years and played a central role in guiding Levinas—who remained famously skeptical of anything smacking of irrational religious devotion—into the serious and rigorous study of Talmud as a text worthy of thought. In my view, Chouchani may have aided him in finding a specifically religious and Jewish response to the Shoah in the everyday doings of school life. ENIO's students would learn not only out of the pages of Dostoyevsky, *Le Monde*, or the French and European classics to which Jews also contributed; but also out of Judaism's own treasured sources and ancient literary heritage. Wygoda continues,

> For the next five years Levinas studied at length with Chouchani. Alone, with Nerson and in a weekly study group that would study Talmud and which included in addition to them a small group of friends. In 1952 Chouchani left France for Israel, and came back in 1956 for about six months before leaving Europe definitely for South America where he remained until his death in 1968. After he left, the study group continued for many years, with Nerson leading and preparing the text and Levinas often suggesting his own way of reading it.³⁵

Chouchani became Levinas's *maître* (or religious teacher) for an important season of his life, and as folks who have experienced this style of mentorship know with a smile: Levinas ever remained a plucky and relatively autonomous mentoree, though he ever and always referred to *l'maître* with warm respect.

II. *Totality and Infinity*

The 1950s was a relatively quite period in Levinas's publishing life, no doubt because of his intense research and writing of what we today know as *Difficult Freedom* and *Totality and Infinity*. Between his research and daily labor at ENIO, Levinas here enjoyed both personal and civic honors.

In 1952 he took his first trip to Israel, and would return more often to lecture there in the 1970s and 1980s. In 1956 he was elected *Chevalier de la Légion d'honneur,* the highest French order of merit for military and civilian accomplishment. The only publication of this period of research, "Philosophy and the Idea of Infinity," does not emerge until 1957 in the pages of *Revue de Métaphysique et de Morale*. As Critchley rightly notes, the "essay is the best overview of Levinas's work in the 1950s, . . . developing Levinas's appropriation of the concept of infinity from Descartes." In the same year, Levinas participated in the founding of the Les Colloques des Intellectuels Juifs de Langue Française. Launched as a branch of the World Jewish Congress, the organization exists to this day, and it's where he later gave well-attended lectures on Talmudic themes. As Critchley underlines—and as those who've enjoyed the pleasure of Levinas's stylistic *esprit* outside the bounds of his major works already know well—these discussions were no dreary or merely pious affair:

> . . . these commentaries often see Levinas using the Talmud to discuss the intellectual and political events of the time. As well as exemplifying a highly rationalistic hermeneutic approach, inspired by Chouchani, the commentaries are also noteworthy for their informality and for their often wry humor. For example, his 1972 commentary, "Et Dieu créa la femme," alludes to Roger Vadim's 1957 film, starring Brigitte Bardot.[36]

Other well-known French intellectuals also frequented the meetings, the likes of Vladimir Jankélévitch, André Neher, Jean Wahl, and Jean Halpérin, among others.[37] Levinas remained actively involved with the college until the early 1990s.

Totality and Infinity is the fruit of a near decade of intensive research. The text is a classical and canonical light in the lived and ongoing unfolding of the phenomenological tradition. Bettina Bergo, whose *Stanford* entry in my view remains the best concise, holistic treatment of Levinas's work that exists, aptly characterizes the text as a "highly original" work.[38] Levinas initially intended to publish the text as an independent book, but Wahl persuaded him to submit it as a doctoral thesis. As Critchley reports, "In addition to Wahl, Vladimir Jankélévitch, Gabriel Marcel, Paul Ricoeur and Georges Blin were members of the jury, which was also due to include Merleau-Ponty, who died one month prior to the event." Gallimard passed on Levinas's manuscript, to the eternal shame of the relevant editor. A Dutch publishing house, Martinus Nijhoff, published *Totality and Infinity* in 1961 "under the patronage of the Husserl archives in Leuven and with the crucial support of Father Herman Leo Van Breda."[39] Levinas's magnum opus was the eighth monograph to appear in the Phaenomenologica series, launched by Van Breda as a companion to the Husserliana (Husserl's collected works).[40] Eugen Fink's *Sein, Wahrheit, Welt* (1958) launched the book series that went on to showcase—beyond Levinas and Husserl—work by Jan Patočka, Roman Ingarden, J. N. Mohanty, Alfred Schutz, Jacques Taminiaux, Nam-In Lee, William Richardson, Babette Babich, and Dan Zahavi.

With the publication of *Totality and Infinity*, Levinas's star began to rise. The book was reviewed almost immediately by Quentin Lauer in Canada, Anna-Teresa Tymieniecka in the United States, and Raymond Vancourt in France.[41] In 1961, Blanchot published three texts "more or less directly inspired by" *TI* in *La Nouvelle Revue Francaise*.[42] Albert Dondeyne and Adriaan Peperzak were the first to do serious work on Levinas's magnum opus. Dondeyne was a Belgian Catholic priest and professor of metaphysics at Leuven. A vigorous progressive and advocate for church reform, he and his work played a role at Vatican II.[43] In conversation with Buber and Marcel, he developed a "dialogical" approach to religion and embraced *TI* as an authoritative expression and development of this approach. According to Roger Burggraeve, Dondeyne taught the text in both Dutch and French in his metaphysics course and supervised the first master's theses on Levinas's work. One of Dondeyne's students, Luk Bouckaert, wrote the first dissertation on Levinas in any language. As far as I've been able to ascertain, Rudolf Gerber and Dondeyne respectively published the first substantive articles on *TI* to appear in any language.[44] Meanwhile, Adriaan Peperzak encountered *TI* shortly after its publication, and was so impressed that he assembled the first conference ever organized on Levinas's work. He also visited the National Library in Paris and published the first anthology of Levinas's extant articles, in Dutch translation. Published as *Philosophy of the Human Face*, the book made a mark outside philosophical circles on the broader Dutch intellectual scene, enjoying seven successive editions.[45]

In 1964, Levinas was appointed professor of philosophy at University of Poitiers. This same year, Jacques Derrida published his justly acclaimed "Violence and Metaphysics: An Essay on the Thought of Emmanuel Levinas" in *Revue de métaphysique et de morale*. Republished three years later in *Writing and Difference*, Derrida's piece played a significant role in the ongoing reception of Levinas's work. As Critchley rightly notes, "this essay—effectively a monograph—was one of Derrida's first essays, and would for a long time be the most extensive discussion of Levinas's work." Levinas himself published "Meaning and Sense" in *Revue de Métaphysique et de Morale* this same year. The text "shows the beginnings of the philosophical transition from *Totality and Infinity* to *Otherwise than Being*."[46] Throughout the rest of the 1960s, Levinas continued developing the main lines of his later work. In 1965 he joined the steering committee of l'Amitié Judéo-Chrétienne de France. Two years later, he gave lectures in Brussels, published the following year as "Substitution" in *Revue Philosophique de Louvain*. In 1967 he was appointed professor of philosophy at University of Paris-Nanterre, where, as Critchley notes, "his colleagues included [Mikel] Dufrenne, Paul Ricoeur, and Jean-François Lyotard in philosophy and Alain Touraine, Henri Lefebvre, and . . . Jean Baudrillard in sociology." Ricoeur was a newly installed administrator at the time, and as he later recalls, "I was very proud to have lured him to Nanterre, because he had not completed his *agrégation* . . . [T]here was a prejudice to overcome, and I succeeded in doing so with what little power I had." Levinas distanced himself from the student movement in May 1968, publishing a series of articles criticizing the then-fashionable anti-humanism of prominent strands of structuralism and post-structuralism: "Humanism and Anarchy" (1968), "Judaism and Revolution" (1969), and "No Identity" (1970). In 1968 he also published *Quatre lectures talmudiques* (Jérôme Lindon).[47] The end of the decade saw the material beginnings of English-language Levinas studies, with Alphonso Lingis's English translation of *Totality and Infinity*.

III. *Otherwise Than Being*

The turn of the decade continued Levinas's rise to international philosophical prominence. In 1970 he was awarded an honorary doctorate at Loyola University of Chicago, the same day as Hannah Arendt and the only time the two personally met. As Peperzak recalls: ". . . I got the impression that they were not on the same wavelength. They spoke of Judaism and of Israel. Not of Heidegger, that was too delicate."[48] More honorary doctorates followed, "from the universities of Leiden, Holland (1975), Leuven, Belgium (1976), Fribourg, Switzerland (1980) and Bar-Ilan, Israel (1981)."[49] He was appointed to a visiting professorship at Fribourg, where he taught intermittently through the decade. In 1971 he was awarded the Albert Schweitzer philosophy prize; in 1973 he was appointed professor of philosophy at the Sorbonne, and in 1974 he was elected *Officier de l'ordre national du Mérite*.[50]

Throughout the early decade, he continued research, writing, and developing the major themes of his late work. In 1972 he published *Humanisme de l'autre homme*, followed up by his second major work, *Otherwise than Being or Beyond Essence*, published by Nijhoff in 1974.[51] This same year, Edith Wyschogrod published the first monograph on Levinas's work to appear in English: her beautifully written and highly influential *Emmanuel Levinas: The Problem of Ethical Metaphysics* (Nijhoff). By the mid-1970s, Levinas's influence was such that talented students began to seek him out for philosophical conversation. Two such students, quite well-known to Levinas studies, were Roger Burggraeve and Richard A. Cohen.

A philosopher, theologian, and Salesian priest, Burggraeve completed a thesis on Levinas's work for his *Licentiate* in theology at Leuven in 1972. He was present when Levinas was awarded an honorary doctorate by Leuven's Higher Institute of Philosophy four years later. Burggraeve recalls,

> I met him for the first time face-to-face. I went to speak to him, almost literally pulled at his sleeve, when he was on his way along with the other togati from the Saint Peter's Church towards the University Hall on the Naamsestraat where the honorary doctorates were to be awarded in the Promotion Hall. He remained standing and we talked briefly, until he was fetched in order to again take his place in front of the procession. When I made clear to him who I was, he remembered the extensive letter with five exhaustive questions (and sub-questions), which I sent to him the year before on the 10th of July 1975 and to which he sent an equally comprehensive and handwritten reply already on the 4th of August. However short and interrupted the conversation with Levinas on the 2nd of February 1976 had been, he invited me promptly, and with a certain decisiveness, to come over to Paris.[52]

Eager to visit with the master, while also wanting to respect his time, Burggraeve continues,

> I waited some four to five weeks before contacting him. When I called him on the telephone, it seemed clear that he kept our brief face-to-face in Leuven constantly in mind, for he invited me again to come to Paris and visit him at his home. He suggested

that we would meet on Monday, not on Saturday on account of the Shabbat, and not on Sunday (because for me as a Christian this is a holy day).

They met at the end of March 1976, the first of what became "an entire series of Monday afternoon meetings that went on for years, up to the beginning of 1993."[53] Deeply inspired by Levinas the man, Burggraeve went on to author a nearly 2,000-page (!) doctoral dissertation on his work, and to date has published more than 450 books, articles, and contributions in English, Dutch, French, German, and Italian on various philosophical and theological themes, explicitly on Levinas's work or deeply influenced by it.

Richard A. Cohen grew up in Staten Island, New York, and Allentown, Pennsylvania.[54] He first read Levinas with Alphonso Lingis as an undergraduate student at Penn State University. Cohen's first reading of Levinas was something of a personally decisive existential event, as he reports: "'This is *true*,' I thought, in contrast to all the philosophies and philosophers which are *fascinating* or *provocative*."[55] While doing summer work at Bethlehem Steel, he went on to graduate study under Don Idhe at SUNY Stony Brook. As he approached the completion of his coursework, Cohen recalls, "It occurred to me: Levinas is not merely a name, but alive, well, and still engaged in active writing and teaching. I immediately began making the necessary arrangements, and informed Don that I was leaving for Paris." Cohen enrolled in all of Levinas's courses for the 1974/75 academic year, the second-to-last year of his tenure as a full-time professor at the Sorbonne (Cohen moreover had originally arranged to also do a master's thesis with Ricoeur, who agreed to supervise him).[56]

On his arrival, Richard was understandably quite eager to meet *le maître*: "Though I knew full well that the Sorbonne doesn't assign books, I phoned Levinas and asked to meet with him about it. He graciously agreed." The first of two meetings took place on September 14, 1974, at the Levinas's apartment above ENIO: "Mme. Levinas welcomed me, and showed me into Levinas's study. The apartment was lovely though modest, and his study was peppered with stacks of books and scattered papers. After a few moments, Levinas himself entered. We shook hands as he welcomed me kindly." Richard asked him about the assigned texts for the class, and afterward Levinas inquired about his school (he had not yet heard of Stony Brook). At the time Richard nursed a grad school interest in Foucault, and asked Levinas a question about their proximity. "My thinking is very different from Foucault," Levinas rejoined. Over the next half hour, they discussed a variety of topics, from Hegel to Judaism: "Hegel is an example of the same," Levinas insisted. "Being Jewish is a state of alertness." They enjoyed such a pleasant meeting that Levinas invited him back the next week. Richard recalls,

> Mme. Levinas served little cakes and Cointreau, and over small talk Levinas even asked my opinion about titles he was considering for a book of essays on Blanchot. I cherish the brief time I was able to spend with him. I mean, here was one of the most important philosophers of the century, willing to share his time and kindness with me: an unknown American grad student! He was not only a great philosopher, but also a superlative human being.

Throughout the rest of the academic year, Richard attended each of Levinas's seminars, including "Being and Being Given," "Ontology and Transcendence," and "General Philosophy." Ever the plucky American, he even once transgressed Sorbonne convention by daring to ask an in-class question, to Levinas's surprise and the giggles of classmates. Levinas, with intentional care and kindness, answered Richard in detail and at length, as if to model for the entire class what welcome to the stranger means in the humdrum of everyday university life.

Firsthand anecdotes like these (and the hundreds more known to Levinas scholars) give a unique window into the character of Levinas the man.[57] As Burggraeve rightly marvels,

> I have always been amazed that such a great thinker, who must have been sought after for interviews in all sorts of ways, was so very much accessible. This was confirmed when I found out from other "visitors" how he received them all hospitably.[58]

Both Cohen and Burggraeve kept in active contact with Levinas over the years. Cohen often exchanged books with him, and they liaised on various projects. Burggraeve continued on with their Monday meetings through 1993 and once ferried his own seminar students down to Paris, where Levinas warmly received them at his home.[59]

IV. Later Life

In the late 1970s, Levinas retired from full-time teaching while maintaining a vigorous professional life. He published *Proper Names* (1976) and *Du sacré au saint. Cinq nouvelles lectures talmudiques* (1977). The turn of the decade saw the first edited collection on Levinas's work: *Textes pour Emmanuel Levinas* (1980), with contributions by Blanchot, Derrida, Lyotard, Ricoeur, Edmond Jabés, and others; and the publication of Lingis's English translation of *Otherwise than Being or Beyond Essence* (1981). In 1982 he appeared on French radio for a series of conversations with Philip Nemo, eventually published under the title *Ethics and Infinity* (1985), translated by Richard Cohen. This same year, Catherine Chalier edited a volume of Levinas's work on the feminine: *Figures du féminin: lecture d'Emmanuel Lévinas*. In 1982 and 1983, Derrida sought out Levinas's counsel as he was cofounding the College International de Philosophie (an institutional experiment intended to reform the teaching of philosophy in France). Derrida recalls,

> [F]rom the very beginning—and I can bear witness to this—Emmanuel Levinas gave his support to this institution. I remember visiting him on the rue Michel-Ange in 1982 at the time we were preparing to found the College. I had gone there to ask for his advice, his approbation, and even for a promise of participation.[60]

Levinas periodically lectured at the college, notably delivering the paper "Dying For" (1987). As Critchley notes, "This is a wonderfully measured paper on Heidegger given at the hysterical height of the Heidegger affair in Paris."[61] This same year, Levinas was awarded the Karl Jaspers prize in Heidelberg.

By the 1980s, Levinas had achieved recognition as a philosopher of international import. His thought deeply impressed even the Pope. Karol Wojtyla (Pope John Paul II) was a student of Husserl's friend, the Polish phenomenologist Roman Ingarden. He wrote a thesis on Scheler in 1959 and later read Levinas's own work. As Peperzak recalls,

> The pope read him, and I suspect that he probably took him to be the best Jewish thinker. I cannot prove this, and undoubtedly he met other Jews. But knowing a bit of what the pope wrote,

there is no doubt to my mind that Levinas was, for him, the model of a great Jewish thinker.[62]

Levinas first met the pope in Paris in 1980, and later that year he wrote an essay on "The Philosophical Thought of Cardinal Wojtyla."[63] He was later invited to participate in a series of conferences at the Papal summer residence. As Malka reports: "Originally, it was the idea of Pope John Paul II to gather thinkers around him in order to reflect on the future of the world."[64] Levinas gave a paper, "Transcendence and Intelligibility," at one of these meetings. Ricoeur also participated, and on one occasion Levinas was not able to attend. Malka reports: "Pope John Paul II took [Ricoeur] aside to confide in him, 'Would you please give my regards to Levinas and tell him of my respect and admiration.'"

One of the more surprising events of this period took place in Brussels. As Malka notes in more detail, thanks to Dondeyne, de Dijn, Peperzak, and Burggraeve: "Levinas was adopted by [Leuven]." A Leuven alumnus, Robert Vandeputte, had gone on to become minister of finance and later honorary president of the Bank of Belgium. Vandeputte had studied philosophy and was an avid reader of Levinas. As a part of the bank's anniversary celebration, he proposed a series of distinguished lectures. Vandeputte and Burggraeve traveled together to Paris to invite Levinas, "who was initially surprised by their approach, but let himself be convinced." Malka recounts,

> [On] December 10, 1986, at the Palace of Congress, [Levinas] obliged the investment bank group with a long-awaited lecture that he delivered before a distinguished audience of politicians, economists, and academics, as well as the prime minister.

Levinas refused an honorarium for the talk, and afterward was an official guest at the royal palace, where King Baudouin received him.[65]

In 1985, Levinas was elected *Commandeur des Arts et Lettres*. A year later, Jean Greisch and Jacques Rolland organized a ten-day conference in Levinas's honor at Cerisy-la-Salle.[66] This same year, Cohen edited one of the most important volumes in the history of English-language Levinas study: *Face to Face with Levinas* (1986), with contributions by Blanchot, Robert Bernasconi, Luce Irigaray, Theodore de Boer, Lyotard, Peperzak, and Levinas himself, among others. Over the next several years, Levinas continued writing and publishing: *Collected Philosophical Papers* (1987),

Outside the Subject (1987), *The Hour of Nations Published* (1988), *Entre Nous: On Thinking-of-the-Other* (1991), *Les imprévus de l'histoire* (1994), and *Alterity and Transcendence* (1995). By the turn of the decade, Levinas had earned recognition as one of the most important philosophers of the twentieth century.

Thanks to the yeoman's work of Dondeyne, Derrida, Peperzak, Wyschogrod, Lingis, Burggraeve, Cohen, Chalier, Bernasconi, and others, the 1990s and beyond saw a veritable explosion of interest in Levinas's work among a new generation of scholars.[67]

Folks like Bettina Bergo, Simon Critchley, Tina Chanter, Enrique Dussel, John Llewelyn, Diane Perpich, Robert Gibbs, Merold Westphal, Jon Drabinski, Jeffrey Bloechl, and Claire Katz carried Levinas studies into the new millennium.[68]

V. Death and Legacy

In September 1994, Raïssa Levinas died. All who knew and spent time with the Levinas family tell of the power of their love and the abiding force of her presence in the life and work of her partner. In a special way, they were a team. Ricoeur recalls,

> I got to know Mme. Levinas, and to witness the depth of their intimacy and attachment. Levinas did not travel to any conference without Mme. Levinas. It's why I understood the extent of his pain when she died. I truly valued and understood all those admirable pages in *Totality and Infinity* on domestic grandeur, and the beautiful page on the caress.[69]

Burggraeve, who for nearly twenty years spent more time with Levinas than perhaps any other professional colleague, remembers:

> Those Monday afternoon meetings always took place "in three's," namely with his wife who was constantly present as if the third person who heard and listened to what was being said between two people not only gave resonance to what was being said but also raised it to another level and to a certain extent made it public.[70]

To my knowledge, no research exists exploring in depth the impact of Raïssa's love on Levinas's life and work; a project I dare to call forth here as worth our time and attention.

After a long struggle with ill health, Emmanuel Levinas died on December 25, 1995, fourteen months after his wife.

Exploring Levinas's philosophical legacy would require the effort of an entire monograph. To all intimately familiar with the unfolding of late twentieth- and early twenty-first-century European philosophy, the broad strokes of his enduring contributions are well-known. In my judgment, these can be specified under four main headings: phenomenology, Jewish theology, post-structuralism, and Christian theology.

Levinas's contributions as a Husserl specialist, critic of Heidegger, and himself a highly original phenomenologist, are self-evident and indisputable. As I specify in more detail below, for all its distinctive methodological problems: *Totality and Infinity* stands as a living and enduring light in the ongoing unfolding of the phenomenological tradition. The book will remain an irreplaceable and necessary companion to *Being and Time*, and taken with Husserl's oeuvre: abides as an unsurpassable pillar of phenomenological ethics and a contribution to the social ontology of normative commitment.

Levinas's contributions to Jewish theology are also well-known. These take the form of posing new questions and proposing new ways to understand the inherited assumptions of various received traditions. He has helped engender renewed interest in Talmud as a text worthy of thought, as evidenced by the growing engagement with the text in the work of a younger generation of scholars nursed on Levinas's work. Importantly, he has generated new debates and contests among the diverse fields and orientations that constitute Jewish theology in its living movement;[71] all centered on the emphatic themes of ethics and, according to Levinas himself: *holiness*, which remains a primary meaning at stake in his insistence on the priority of the Other.[72]

One of the more ironic achievements of Levinas's work is to have supplied the cluster of thinkers we generally label "post-structuralist" with, at the very least, a *rhetoric* of "ethics." Ironic, because Levinas himself was a staunch critic of post-structuralism and a vocal defender of critical humanism. There is no need to cite specific examples, but ever-expanding literatures exist—which can be fairly described as "apologetics"—among Derrida and Foucault's more theatrical of respective readers, all of whom keep Levinas ready-to-hand to defend their own master's schtick. As I've shown above, Levinas takes aim at too many antagonists *at once* in *OB*, but he clearly and unmistakably takes aim at the very core of Derrida's own methodological game there.[73] Moreover, Levinas did not judge Foucault a serious enough interlocutor to even bother criticizing him, though it would be fair to assume that he considered the latter implicated in his own critique of Nietzsche and Heidegger.[74] Though for empirical, institutional, and political reasons phenomenology and post-structuralism are often classified together under the banners of "post-phenomenology," "Continental philosophy," and so forth, they nevertheless involve radically distinct methodological commitments, and Levinas's contributions to both fields of research will continue to be both rightly recognized and internally debated.

Finally, Levinas has enjoyed a growing influence within Christian theological circles, across the widely diverse traditions it involves, in both conservative and avant-garde styles.[75] To my knowledge, there has been next to no work surveying the relevant literature, and hence I cannot fairly characterize it here (I once more dare to call forth this task as worth our time and attention). As a general trend, Levinas's work has contributed to the post-Shoah Christian movement of actively revaluing the faith's Jewish roots, evident across the widely diverse ecclesial streams that constitute actually existing Christianity. Levinas himself personally played a role in this, in his service on the committee of l'Amitié Judéo-Chrétienne de France, in his various friendships and dialogues with Christian colleagues, and in his numerous thematic essays on Jewish/Christian relations. In terms of more specific scholarly interests, he has contributed to reanimating reflection on the concept of revelation, revaluing the import of historical tradition overagainst purely systematic approaches to religious philosophy, and of course: has been an ongoing dialogue partner in thinking through the demands of both Christian ethics and political theology in light of the challenges of today. In my humble opinion, the single greatest dimension of Levinas's work that is attractive to Christian scholars is his steadfast commitment to at least the *possibility* of theological realism. The methodological structures of both *TI* and *OB* firmly defend "an Individual prior to all individuality," accessible to the emotional life of the subject (or *as* the very occurrence of that life).[76] In my view, and in contrast to a lot of hay that passes for philosophy of religion today: *God is at stake* in Levinas's texts, and this is of obvious interest to the practice of Christian theology.[77]

VI. Conclusion

Levinas's life was extraordinary. He has indelibly marked the entire trajectory of postwar European thought. In my view, his work has played a nearly singular role in reorienting some of the more tedious absurdities of so-called "postmodernism" (I apologize for even uttering the term, but its mention invites reflection on just how the profession has changed since the early 2000s).[78] When I entered university, a book titled *Against Ethics* was still considered a fashionable, vaguely scandalous literary gesture, in (a perhaps self-caricaturing) "Nietzschean" style. Not today.

I want to close this chapter by underlining the universal witness to Levinas's kindness and generosity as a man and colleague, though we should not ignore both his famous sense of humor and the feisty austerity to which he was sometimes given. Malka recounts a hilarious episode that reflects both of these aspects of his personality. In the 1960s, Levinas became friends with Bernard Dupuy, a Dominican priest and scholar of modern Jewish philosophy. They met at a local colloquium, and Dupuy went on to attend Levinas's Shabbat classes on Rachi at ENIO, every week for four years. "Levinas once invited him to his home, one time with Gershom Scholem." Dupuy reports,

> I recall the situation very well because I paid a price for it. It was for a *shabbat*, and the previous day he said to me: "I'm inviting Scholem to lunch, if you'd like to come." I was very honored, as you can imagine! . . . In fact, I drove [Scholem] around in Paris. I was his host. He had his habits. He stayed at the same hotel. I drove him around every day in my own not-so-comfortable two-horsepower vehicle. One time, he wanted to go to the municipal archives of Nanterre to examine some documents. I wasn't very smart. I went to pick him up at four o'clock . . . and we got stuck in a traffic jam. He began to groan, "It's impossible, we will never arrive there! What would you have me do?!" In the end, the documents were not there and we returned empty handed, again in the same heavy traffic. He cursed. "I have never seen such an ugly city," he said, "yet I know Tel Aviv . . ."

As Malka reports, Dupuy was not able to follow through on Levinas's invitation to lunch. He haplessly overscheduled, and was already committed to give a talk at a conference. Dupuy continues, "I agreed to go [to the conference], it was set and I couldn't cancel. I explained this to Levinas. . . . Even so, he insisted." Malka offers: "I venture to suggest that he insisted thus so as to not remain alone with Scholem."

"Ah, but I will surprise you! The one who had more respect for the other was Levinas for Scholem." Nevertheless, Dupuy winks: "I would have to pay a price for missing that lunch."[79]

Scholars of phenomenology above all are quite well acquainted with Levinas's wry humor and at times acerbic wit. His writing is peppered with subtle and quite funny barbs, delicious to those aware of their broader context of belonging, for example: "the ontology that grasps the being of the existent is a spontaneous and pre-theoretical work of every inhabitant of the earth."[80] This is a maestroly swipe at Heidegger's early heroism, and in such a way that forces a critical shift in perspective, disclosing the more ridiculous dimensions of Heidegger's own carefully cultivated personae. What is so interesting about Levinas's treatment of Heidegger is how he masterfully modulates both a frank, uncompromising critical posture wedded to a perceptibly sincere gratitude, and he never failed to openly acknowledge Heidegger's genius (Levinas famously listed *Being and Time* as one of the five most important books in the history of Western philosophy, alongside Plato's *Phaedrus*, Kant's first *Critique*, Hegel's *Phenomenology*, and Bergson's *Time and Freewill*).[81]

Ricoeur and others convey well Levinas's delicious sense of humor, periodic severity, and abiding human solidarity. At one of the Vatican conferences they jointly attended, Ricoeur recalls,

> I had to go four times, I believe. . . . The pope attended the discussion twice a day, remaining completely silent. He would invite us to share a meal, and I recall one of these occasions. We were invited, Levinas and I. Levinas said, "You sit at the Pope's right, and I'll sit on his left." I said, "No, the other way around." We had a little skirmish over prerogatives, and each of us understood what is meant.[82]

Derrida also tells of Levinas's subtle wit:

> One indication of this historical shock wave is the influence of this thought well beyond philosophy, and well beyond Jewish thought, on Christian theology, for example. I cannot help recall the day when, listening to a lecture by Andre Neher at a Congress of Jewish Intellectuals, Emmanuel Levinas turned to me and said, with the gentle irony so familiar to us: "You see,

he's the Jewish Protestant, and I'm the Catholic"—a quip that would call for long and serious reflection.[83]

Levinas moreover was admirably consistent and nonsectarian in dispensing both his good humor and critical attention. He served on Richard Kearney's dissertation jury:

> Levinas telephoned me the day before my defence to relay a sense of the questions he would pose. I'll never forget his caring initiative. Though at one point he surprised me! "Leave out Martin Buber," he stated firmly. "Buber was not a real philosopher."[84]

Levinas could sometimes be a bit severe on questions he considered especially important, a trait noted by a variety of colleagues. He was famously impatient with all-things-mystical. On one occasion Malka visited Scholem in Jerusalem, and they discussed Levinas's work. "With a mixture of tenderness and cruelty," Malka reports, Scholem said: "[Levinas] is more *litvak* than he thinks."[85] Though Levinas could dig in his heals on some questions, the kindness and solidarity that characterize his life always overflowed the bounds of his own areas of explicit interest. For example, in 1972 Enrique Dussel led a cadre of students to engage Levinas on the question of colonialism. Dussel recalls,

> I asked [him]: "What about the fifteen million Indians slaughtered during the conquest of Latin America, and the thirteen million Africans who were made slaves, aren't they the other you're speaking about?" Lévinas stared at me and said: "That's something for you to think about." . . . At the end of the meeting, he said to us: "I see all of you as though you were hostages." I didn't grasp what he meant. Shortly after that, while I was reading *Otherwise than Being*, I understood. As a group of young teachers and students, obsessed by our Latin American victims, Lévinas saw us as hostages in Europe; that is, Europe took us as hostages for our distant and oppressed peoples. I didn't know if he was insulting us by making this observation, but as I read *Otherwise than Being*, it dawned on me that it had been a vast, undeserved, and encouraging appraisal of us.[86]

This episode discloses one of the abiding tensions pervading Levinas's work as a whole, namely: his complicated relation to Europe. He remained both a staunch critic of European barbarity and a staunch defender of its best historical legacies. As Ricoeur noted,

> [Levinas] . . . gave a speech about Europe to the European parliament, and another one on peace. He advocated a European sentiment based on culture rather than simply on the power of the marketplace, but a sentiment informed by real history, including its abysses. . . . yes, he was a great European.[87]

Later, Levinas and Kearny sat together for a paper by Jean-Luc Marion at a conference they jointly attended. Kearney recounts: "at one point in the talk, he turned to me, and with emphasis exclaimed, 'this is the French university!' He held Marion in high regard. Levinas was very ecumenical." His famous love for France stands as a testament and symbol to his own most basic, tenacious, and unsurpassable philosophical commitment: welcome to the other. But it must also be said that Levinas did not merely remain France's "other," but himself became—not merely by "official" citizenship, but in his explicit commitments, and the very style of his unfolding person—a true Frenchman. Such that today we rightly recognize him as one the enduring lights of twentieth-century French philosophy. As Marion suggests,

> [If] one defines a great philosopher as someone without whom philosophy would not have been what it is, then in France there are two great philosophers of the twentieth century: Bergson and Levinas.[88]

A disputable claim, but one can certainly *not* dispute Critchley's exquisite response to it: "Of course, this is hyperbole, isn't it?"[89]

To close, I give Derrida the last word: unequivocal words. Their meaning evinces an unshakable finality, clarity, even a twinkling of the Eternal:

> By means of discreet though transparent allusions, Levinas oriented our gazes toward what is happening today, not only in Israel but in Europe and in France, in America, and Asia, since at least the time of the First World War and since what Hannah Arendt called *The Decline of the Nation State*: everywhere that

refugees of every kind, immigrants with or without citizenship, exiled or forced from their homes, whether with or without papers, from the heart of Nazi Europe to the former Yugoslavia, from the Middle East to Rwanda, from Zaire all the way to California, from the Church of St. Bernard to the thirteenth arrondissement in Paris, Cambodians, Armenians, Palestinians, Algerians, and so many others call for a change in the socio- and geo-political space—a juridico-political mutation, though, before this, assuming that this limit still has any pertinence, an ethical conversion.

Emmanuel Levinas speaks—indeed, already long ago began to speak—of this distress and this call.[90]

Indeed, this witness will Stand through whatever unheard-of fashions—who like gentle fireflies, quaintly enchant as they come-to-pass those with the courage to actually live out the call, and stand for a world of which authentic prophets and poets—of every tribe, tongue, and tradition—to this day ache and dream. For surely, Derrida writes his last word: "Let us leave the last word to Emmanuel . . ."[91]

Chapter 7

Levinas Today

"I wanted to see a place where reconciliation is possible."[1]

—Jean-Luc Godard, *Notre Musique.*

Language is the possibility of an enigmatic equivocation for better and for worse, which men abuse.

—Emmanuel Levinas[2]

I. Signs of the Times

Again, what lives on in Levinas's philosophy? To even suggest answers to this question requires some attention to our wider world and the relevant contexts toward and out of which his philosophy can still speak. As I noted at the outset, Levinas's work has achieved a near canonical status in European philosophy today. The literature is vast, spanning from familiar treatments in philosophy, ethics, and religious studies to more specialized applied fields, such as nursing and organizational management.[3] His popularity moreover bursts the bounds of the academy. As Atterton and Calarco have noted, Levinas's work has "inspired religious leaders, writers, dissidents, statesmen, and artists the world over."[4] When the breadth of influence encompasses such disparate regions of culture glossed by Pope John Paul II, Vaclav Havel, and Jean-Luc Goddard, we certainly do seem to be approaching a wide signature. From its relatively humble migration among specialists in European philosophy through the 1980s, the scholarship saw a veritable explosion of new work throughout the 1990s.[5] Indeed, growth in Levinas scholarship has coincided with the accelerated rhythms of our post-1989 world. By February 12, 2000, then secretary-general of the United Nations Conference on Trade and Development, Rubens Ricupero, delivered an opening address to UNCTAD's 10th Session. His opening paragraph is worth quoting in its entirety, and from its first word:

> A little after the crumbling of the Berlin Wall, the philosopher Emmanuel Levinas was asked whether he thought that the democracies had won. "No," he said, "I think they lost, and lost a lot. Despite all the horrors and excesses, communism had always stood for hope and waiting. Hope that it would be possible to redress the evil done to the weak, waiting for a more equitable social order. Not that the communists had a solution, nor were they preparing it. On the contrary. But there was the idea that history had a meaning, a direction, that living was not senseless, absurd. It was an idea that people in the West had had since the eighteenth century and which, thanks to Marx, had taken firm root in the twentieth century. I do not believe that to have lost this idea forever amounts to a great spiritual conquest. Until yesterday, we knew where history was heading and what value we should give to time. Now we roam aimlessly and lost, asking ourselves every few minutes: 'What time is it?' In a fatalistic way, a little bit as some people keep asking in Russia: 'What time is it?' No one knows any longer." This beautiful text of Levinas is a good starting point.[6]

A good starting point the world over. For perhaps obvious reasons, that the secretary-general of UNCTAD should summon Levinas at this precise time, on these precise themes, for these precise reasons, seems concentrated with saturated significance. Why Levinas? Why these themes? And why these reasons? Setting aside his own psychological motivations, and without pretending to an exhaustive account, Ricupero supplies a good opening into our problematic.

Why Levinas? Levinas's work creatively repeats what might be called a *deep grammar* inscribed in the ethical imaginary of the West. At a conceptual level, he retrieves and redeploys Plato's "Good" and Descartes's "Infinite" in an innovative way. At the level of rhetoric, image, and affect, his discourse evokes storied intuitions shared across widely diverse sectors of our culture and politics. The "epiphany of the face," the "widow, orphan, and stranger," "election to the Good," "messianic time," and so forth reach past philosophical concepts to Sinai, the Prophets, and the Gospels. Indeed, when Levinas above speaks of meaning in history as "an idea that people in the West had

had since the eighteenth century," he is being a tad coy. The "messianic" and "prophetism" his texts variously thematize are other names for the meaningful time at issue, a sense that reached beyond its strictly religious iterations to storm the Bastille and occupy Uprising Square. The idea *that the world can be changed*, that oppression can be overcome, that sustained peace and plenty are possible, and that each person can play a unique role in bringing this future about stands at the basis of anti-oppression struggle, and was why Levinas counted the collapse of twentieth-century socialist promises such a loss. Levinas moreover performs this in creative and critical participation in the avant-garde philosophy of his day (Husserl, Heidegger, Rosenzweig, Sartre, Ricoeur, Derrida, etc.), and at a time of grappling with two World Wars, new Cold Wars, decolonization, and above all: the Shoah. His wide appeal has much to do with how he powerfully evokes and critically rearticulates these living sources of ethical imagination. In this light, it is not surprising that Ricupero should summon Levinas while casting UNCTAD's development vision.

But why these themes, precisely? The turn of the millennium was a unique moment. The collapse of the Soviet Block accelerated already extent processes of globalization. In the throes of an information revolution, the year 2000 saw smartphones hit the mass market, and the Dot Com bubble burst; saw the Human Genome mapped, and the Camp David Summit fail; saw Al Gore win the US presidential election, and George W. Bush take office. On January 5, nearly a decade into Fukiyama's *The End of History*, an al Qaeda planning summit took place in Kuala Lumpur. In the reveries of this pre-9/11 moment, a new generation of scholars was denouncing, celebrating, and re-litigating the merits of so-called "postmodernism."[7] Ricupero's Levinasian invocation speaks to the mélange of ennui and hope, loss and possibility of renewal, and a general sense of disorientation that—to this day?—characterized the historical moment. It is not surprising that Levinas's work found warm welcome in an era when we became newly and radically saturated with 'otherness' in our day-to-day lives, news cycles, and social medias.

But why these reasons? Ricupero's address occurred a month after the UN's Millennium Summit. The largest gathering of world leaders ever convened, the General Assembly adopted the "Millennium Declaration, committing its nations to a new global partnership to reduce extreme poverty and setting out a series of time-bound targets."[8] Dubbed the Millennium Development Goals (MDGs), the framework was the result of a decade of collaborative work by NGOs and UN conferences. It moreover reflected the impact of the neoliberal critics and popular activism of the time, pledging to "ensure globalization becomes a positive force for all, acknowledging that at present both its benefits and its costs are unequally shared."[9] Indeed, as Ricupero took the podium that day in Bangkok, he registered the ambivalence of the moment: the Asian Crisis, global inequality, spiritual ennui, and the perils that attend economic integration. In each case, he countered with an aspirational confidence that collaborative liberalization, universal solidarity, and shared responsibility can win a better future. He summoned Levinas to mark the epochal shift that occurred with the end of actually existing socialism and to frame the questions that open up UNCTAD's moral vision: "to provide common people . . . with realistic, credible, practical, reasons to hope for a future that will be better than the cemetery of utopias and illusions that we left behind."[10] Though Levinas would of course complicate Ricupero's too naive brand of liberalism, his work nevertheless inspires for the *social and material processes* it speaks to, the *cultural legacies* it repeats, and the *ethical mission* it calls forth.

As should be clear, Levinas's wide appeal contains a tragic irony, an irony that haunts in a parallel way Ricupero's UNCTAD address. The very reasons for Levinas's popularity are also the source of problems that have attended his work, and specifically: the problem of Eurocentrism. What do we do with the fact that notions of "ethical mission" are implicated in the worst crimes of the West's history? Crusades, colonial conquests, revolutionary terrors, and white supremacy are in some sense the fruit of the West's habit of viewing itself as the apex or vanguard of human history. Are its cultural legacies irremediably marred by these moral disasters? And as urgently, the techno-social and material processes now transforming our world were brought to birth on the backs of indigenous genocides, Black slaves, exploited labor, and colonial subjects. The inequality Ricupero mentions is partly structured by this history. Moreover, do the neoliberal trade regimes now dominating and destabilizing our world in some sense work as a neocolonial stalking horse? Despite quite meaningful development gains and the sincere work of aid organizations over the last thirty years, the distribution of global wealth remains radically asymmetrical. Can Levinas be read as repeating ideological cover for an implicit form of conquest and domination? Does the very discourse of "the other" execute simply another round of missionizing plunder premised on an occluded stance of Western supremacy?

These are big questions. I broach them to mark the wider significant contexts of not only my inquiry, but also of our geopolitical present. In our unfolding season of globally resurgent neonativism, it is important to know what intercultural respect and solidarity mean, how they should be concretely practiced, and how a plurality of traditioned commitments can ground an effective, intergenerational, and working-class politics capable of *actually advancing global justice struggle*. Some good work has been done treating Levinas from a post-colonial perspective, and no doubt more work remains to be done. But much of the vast interdisciplinary literature treating Levinas remains structured by the ambiguities I've treated above. In order to specify with relative precision the living potentials Levinas hands us, I turn to a sketch of where we stand today.

II. The Post-1989 Left

Identity politics. This conjuncture of terms has become the *near* universal scapegoat of our political times: denounced by serious conservatives, articulate liberals, and a variety of radicals the world over.[11] In order to avoid unfairly singling out idpol for the failures of the past generation, I begin with a brief review of what the left has gotten right. Of the various tribes that constituted left-politics in the post-1989 era, no single group has more achievements to speak for it than our comrades in identity politics.

II.A. The 1960s Coalition

Socialist struggle is not all the left was up to in the twentieth century. The ongoing success of the Black Civil Rights Movement in the United States formed an international node of solidarity and collaboration during the unfolding season of decolonization. Fueled by Gandhi, King, Khan, Malcolm X, and others, new conversations began to occur between emerging voices with the ongoing work of Franz Fanon, CLR James, Che Guevara, Léopold Sédar Senghor, and others; and in dialogue with European comrades like Sartre and Merleau-Ponty. In South Africa, Nelson Mandela, Bishop Tutu, and other leaders helped mold a coalition of cultural conservatives, social justice liberals, and radical socialists into a mass democratic movement that, with blood-soaked struggle, succeeded at rending the veil of putative Afrikaner "respectability," exposing the bald white supremacy Apartheid had codified. In the United States, with contributions by the "beat generation," Black Civil Rights activism helped spark the student movement of the 1960s, which gathered around anti-racist, free speech, anti-war, and labor activism, this in the relatively immediate wake of McCarthyism, and with the participation of various Euro-Atlantic intellectuals, notably Noam Chomsky and Herbert Marcuse. Moreover, thanks to the work of Simone de Beauvoir, Betty Friedan, Mary Daley, Maya Angelou, and others, various iterations of second wave feminism radicalized feminist struggle, carried forward by folks like Ella Baker, Mary King, Casey Haden; carried on by Audre Lorde, Gloria Steinem, and others within the network of solidarity that Black Civil Rights activism hosted, and under the explicit and newly emerging discourse of "human rights." The moral élan, tactical success, and new conversations Black Civil Rights involved formed the historical ground and growing political consciousness that exploded in the Stonewall riots, helping to midwife the queer liberation movement. With very important exceptions, the general culture of political militancy in left-wing social movements throughout the 1960s began to gradually decline throughout the 1970s and into the 1980s, in part because of some stunning political successes, in part because of shifting conditions in the global economy that attended decolonization and innovations in communications technology, and finally in part because of the more decadent threads of the 1960s coalition itself. But the left-wing culture born in the furnace of the 1960s grounded further advances, from anti-fascist Latin American struggle symbolized in Oscar Romero, to the immigrant, civil, and labor rights organizing and activism of Dolores Huerta and Cesar Chavez; unto the humble beginnings of left-wing Evangelical activism by Jim Wallis, Sharon Gallagher, and Ron Sider. With allies in the ruling class, over-against truly demonic foes in the working class, and premised in its labor and civil rights antecedents of the New Deal era, the solidarity, collaboration, and courageous struggle of the 1960s coalition gave us much: Executive Orders 8802 and 9981, *Brown v. Board of Education*, the Little Rock Nine, Civil Rights Act of 1957, *Bailey v. Patterson*, the repeal of sodomy laws, Equal Pay Act of 1963, Executive Order 10988, Vivian Malone and James A. Hood; and under the emblematic power of Dr. King's speech at the March on Washington, amid Bloody Sundays: the Civil Rights Act of 1964; Voting Rights Act of 1965; *Loving v. Virginia*; Service Contracts Act of 1965; Age Discrimination in Employment Act of 1967; UN International Covenant on Economic, Social and Cultural Rights of 1966; Fair Housing Act of 1968; the dismantling of Jim Crow; the Equal Employment Opportunity Commission ruling of 1968; Christopher Street Liberation Day; Occupational Safety and Health Act of 1971; the Equal Rights Amendment of 1972; the Congressional Black Caucus; Lambda Legal; an end to the Vietnam War; American Psychiatric Association removal of homosexuality from its list of mental disorders; folks like Shirley

Chisholm, Kathy Kozachenko, Barbara Jordan, Elaine Noble, Andrew Young, Harvey Milk, and Patricia Roberts Harris; the criminalizing of marital rape; *University of California Regents v. Bakke*; the Pregnancy Discrimination Act of 1978; the Federal Service Labor-Management Relations Statute of 1978; National March on Washington for Lesbian and Gay Rights of 1979; and what else? These are merely some of the achievements a relatively united left actually won, grounded in commitments to the universality of labor, to the power of communication and covenant, and to *solidarity* in and with individuated yet *collaborative collective struggle*.

It should be stressed that the left didn't accomplish these victories all by itself. Socialist radicals and social justice liberals were joined by hoards of cultural conservatives eager to advance the struggle for justice. Black Civil Rights as a near whole was birthed and bore by the Black Church, in its historic alliances with white abolitionists, the labor movement, and others. Its leadership was peppered with clergy: Andrew Young, Fred Shuttlesworth, Wyatt T. Walker, Joseph Lowery, Jesse Jackson, and of course, Dr. King. Rep. John Lewis, who was a seminary student at the time, was one of the founding leaders of the Student Nonviolent Coordinating Committee. He and many of the Black youth activists who led the way cited their Christian conscience as a primary motivator.

There was wide Jewish participation in the civil rights movement too. Secular Jews peppered the vanguard of nearly every front of the 1960s coalition, but religious Jews also played a crucial and ongoing role in the movement. Rabbi Abraham Joshua Heschel locked arms with Dr. King at Selma and publicly advocated for civil rights throughout his career. A vice chairman of the Union for Reform Judaism, Kivie Kaplan, served as the national president of the NAACP from 1966 to 1975. Drafts of the Civil Rights Act of 1964 and the Voting Rights Act of 1965 were actually written in a conference room at the Religious Action Center of Reform Judaism.[12]

Catholics and Muslims also played a quite significant role in Black struggle. As early as 1948, activists and lay leaders initiated various commissions—notably, Southeastern Regional Interracial Commission (SERINCO) and the Commission on Human Rights (CHR)—to end segregation within Catholic churches. In 1956, Archbishop Joseph Rummel of New Orleans began a process of integrating all the city's Catholic schools, churches, and hospitals. In 1961, Father Albert Foley brokered a deal with Joseph Langan, the Catholic mayor of Mobile, Alabama, to desegregate downtown restaurants.[13] Radical Catholic activists such as Dorothy Day, Daniel Berrigan, Peter Maurin, and others were leaders in the 1960s coalition. The Islamic faith of Malcolm X, H. Rap Brown, Askia Muhammad Toure, Max Stanford, and Clara Muhammad, among others, played a central role in the militancy of the day.[14] Islam contributed a universalizing dimension to the Black Nationalist movement, as Malcolm X's late though very important turn to the Sunni tradition—and to human rights—makes clear.[15]

So the historic achievements of the 1960s coalition do not merely belong to socialists and liberals, but also to the best quarters of the cultural conservatism of the day. Indeed, churches and synagogues have been central to advancing the ball on a variety of fronts, especially in queer activism. In 1971, the United Church of Christ ordained the first openly gay minister in all of church history, followed the next year by Beth Chayim Chadashim, the world's first LGBTQ synagogue recognized by Reform Judaism. The involvement of religious communities in left struggle is thankfully an abiding reality to this day.

II.b. The Berlin Wall

In a way that Millennials (and even Gen Xers, who were youth at the time) cannot fully know or understand, especially for the pre-internet context: the collapse of the Soviet Block radically shocked the entire world. The closest formal analogy to the momentous nature of the event is probably 9/11. Leftists above all—both in the West and the Non-Aligned Movement—were flummoxed. Thanks to Arendt, Solzhenitsyn, and others, few had any illusions about the radically oppressive character of the Soviet system, but its very institutional reality grounded a hope that genuinely democratic alternatives to both Western capitalism and Soviet tyranny *were actually possible*. This was in the wake of strategic experiments in economic liberalization by socialist actors: Brezhnev and Deng liberalized agriculture and other sectors, ultimately necessitated by chronic underproductivity in their respective systems of collective enterprise; but also among central-European economists and states looking for ways to actually bolster their economies.[16] Developments like these were in the background for left analysis and strategy across the globe throughout the 1980s, where a new generation of scholars and activists sought ways to counter the pushback of the Reagan administration and integrate the best among the real options then on offer. Moreover, after successful decolonization, the Non-Aligned Movement had positioned itself to try to realize an alternative of just this sort, with the solidarity of Western leftists and reformist factions in the Soviet CPSU. The collapse of actually existing socialism left a gaping void in the professional projects and motivational life of leftists. Marxist analytic philosopher G. A. Cohen gives a sense of the struggle in that time:

> It is true that I was heavily critical of the Soviet Union, but the angry little boy who pummels his father's chest will not be glad if the old man collapses. As long as the Soviet Union seemed safe, it felt safe for me to be anti-Soviet. Now that it begins, disobligingly, to crumble, I feel impotently protective toward it.[17]

Fashionable chatter about "the work of mourning" that became popular in 1990s was *in part* a response to this, what Christine Sypnowich describes as "a real sense of loss among democratic socialists in the West when the Soviet Union came apart."[18] This is one reason "post-1989" remains a meaningful—indeed, central—signifier in the unfolding history of left-politics and global justice struggle. The more crotchety of elderly Leninists aside, the surprise occasioned a real crisis of Left self-identity: how did we not see this coming? What is Marxist analysis worth in light of what seems its historical death? What in God's name do we do now?

Into this precise breach, Levinas's philosophical work stepped. Left intellectuals throughout the entire world began a process of experimental coping: searching for alternative analytic resources for understanding what took place also capable of funding egalitarian social struggle. The 1990s saw the beginnings of a renaissance in American pragmatism, the growth of "continental philosophy" from its outposts among Stony Brook, Penn State, Boston College, and elsewhere to other distinguished programs throughout the humanities, a consolidation and flowering of new, very serious work in feminist philosophy, Black studies, and post-colonial theory, widely growing engagement with the work of Rawls, Rorty, Kripke, and other comrades in analytic philosophy, and thanks to the yeoman's work of David Rasmussen, Martin Jay, Nancy Fraser, and others: growing engagement with the Frankfurt School. In a very real historical sense: 1989 hosted an eruptive crisis for Marxist analysis that in truth *is still unfolding*.

Youth across the world watched Berliners destroy the Wall from their living rooms, participating in the mediated collective euphoria with a mix of joy and ambivalence: watched adults weep and listened to them fumble to make sense of the miracle. Outside of leftist households and regimes propped up by Soviet aid, the mood was clear: "Good God Almighty, 'freedom' won!'" We'd no longer go to bed worrying about the real possibility of global nuclear holocaust (my first memorable nightmare as a child was about nuclear war). But what happens now? Liberals in the West had been paying close attention to the real economics unfolding unto the event and had watched socialists for more than a decade take on liberalizing reforms.[19] In US politics, the so-called "New Democrats" were thrust to the front of the Party, seizing the day for the electoral moment. One can't fully describe the institutional and ideologically tumultuous realignment that 1989 sparked globally. In 1992, Bill Clinton rode that wave into the White House, eventually touting a so-called "Third Way"; merely so-called because it seemed an enthusiastic declaration of Reaganomics wholly triumphant, and began a process of negotiating the mere pace of dismantling social safety nets and labor protections the 1960s coalition had worked so hard codify, while only gradually compensating Jane Q leftist with advances on non-economic fronts.

As 1989 unfolded, this generation of youth sparked their very own explosive countercultural moment. Nursed on the best aesthetic and political legacies of the twentieth century, and mediated by more proximate antecedents, the early 1990s saw an eruption of popular creativity: the Golden Age of rap and hip-hop, Grunge, a new generation of folk, cute new suburban "punk," new iterations of Gospel, electronica, the rebirth of some politically conscious country music, "alternative rock," mainstreaming metal, Spike Lee, Kathryn Bigelow, a veritable renaissance in indie film spearheaded by Miramax Films and others, and what else? The spiritual ambivalence of the moment is clearly legible in the contrasting hues of angst and optimism that capture the mood of the era, generously peppered with its own unique decadence appropriated from boomer parents. Public Enemy and NWA landed contrasting blows against the complacency of the day, as Snoop Dog became the uncontested King of the party. Dr. Dre himself and Wu Tang Clan sparked whole new stylistic traditions of still unfolding popular poetry, even as A Tribe Called Quest and Queen Latifah preserved its authentic roots. The local music scenes in Seattle; Chicago; Athens, Georgia; and elsewhere were taking the world by storm. Nirvana expressed the angst of an entire generation, as the Smashing Pumpkins showed us how to transform it into the birth of new sonic worlds. Eddie Vedder and Chris Cornell helped to mediate all the overwrought teenage self-absorption by keeping Grunge connected—if somewhat indirectly—to the political struggles of the day. Grunge bled into unfolding traditions of art rock, post-punk, and goth—under the banner of "alternative rock," from the vulnerable queer beauty of The Cure, R.E.M., and The Smiths, to the defiantly boyish garage-band noise of Dinosaur Jr. and Sonic Youth, from the drug-laced though searing opera of Jane's Addiction, to the maturing experiment in modulating lament and protest of Radiohead.

The era moreover hosted new and now iconic voices of women and queer empowerment. One of the most important folk artists of all time, with her signature mix of rage, vulnerability, and joi de vivre: Ani Difranco singlehandedly landed a death blow to the patriarchy inhabiting the psyches of her male fans across a generation. Janet Jackson evolved into a tasteful and unapologetic defense of Black women's sexuality, even as Tori Amos thrust rape culture into popular consciousness. The Indigo Girls reminded us that politics is always subtended by *everyday life*, and that being queer is not only about being seen and heard as the individuals we are, but also seeing and hearing all the grubby others; queer power has always been as much a collective festival of love, art, and the precious in everyday life as it has been about the collective fight against oppression.

Even outside the avant-garde eruptions of the day, mainstream pop music was registering the magnitude of the moment. As canny a working-class shaman as ever, Billy Joel's "We Didn't Start the Fire" (1989) clumsily played pop music's Joyce in a candied expression of "now what?" Garth Brooks and Reba McEntire took serious career risks to speak up for queer love (however staid their gestures may appear in retrospect). Springsteen started writing about tunnels of love and lament, with "The Streets of Philadelphia," the soundtrack to Demme's own *Philadelphia* (1993), where Denzel and Tom spiritually channel over a decade of queer pain, activism, loss, and struggle for a whole new generation, and in my view to ultimately game-changing effect (do Springsteen and Demme jointly disclose a key link between queer and working-class struggle?). Lenny Kravitz reminded us that being Black and Jewish are not mutually exclusive, as Spielberg defied the moronic orthodoxy of his faux-chic critics in the well-heeled professoriate: daring to break convention by crafting one of the most accomplished works of film history. *Schindler's List* (1993) brought popular consciousness of the Shoah to proper cultural prominence, presiding over an unfolding and sustained season of collective mourning and debate across the Euro-Atlantic and Israel. Just a few years later, the release of Swoboda and Kasprzyk's respective renderings of Górecki's Symphony No. 3—*Symphony of Sorrowful Songs*—mingled in this moment. As it played over the radio, popular reception produced countless testimonies: folks pulling to the side of the road overflowing with tears, even the odd decision against suicide (swapping stories about one's first listen is an actual thing). From the standpoint of a proper, culturally embedded reception theory: in its variegated musical, sociological, historical, psychological, and theological totality, Górecki's piece musically incarnates the concept of *holiness* to near absolute perfection. Its melodic simplicity and sonic texture, woven across droning scales of simultaneous ascent and descent, creates a place of emotional safety. Like my grandmother's embrace at my pap's wake, with modesty, tenderness, and dignity: it opens a dimly lit portal to the Throne of the Most High. As if God shimmied from her seat to lay down in nearness, close enough to hear one's cry and respond to an embrace, yet far enough that all the pain and love and loss surging up within me can count as properly *my own*. But not only or merely my own. There, in a secrecy rendered visible in the gentle glow of the innumerable assembly, in whose sacred solidarity: one may grieve. Kilanowicz's soprano becomes my own voice. In it, one grieves freely; grieves all the personal and world-historic moral disasters that constitute the dust of every tragic-comic human spirit.

But grieving is not all that we must do. To the selfish chagrin of hard-core fans, Metallica's *The Black Album* (1991) brought metal into the mainstream. From the perspective of band biography and popular reception, the album is comparable to the Beatles' *White Album* (1968), at least for the debate it generates among the faithful. Hated by Mustainey purists and Burton aficionados—I count myself among the latter—as a "sellout" to fashion, debating the piece at the time could easily degenerate into an actual, all-out *brawl*, at least in very certain corners of the fandom, and depending on how much Jack was left to swill. If evaluated on its strictly musical merits, the album certainly lacks the apocalyptic punch of prior offerings, but in a way that seems entirely intended. From a politically informed cultural point of view, *Black* is daring in its operatic sweep, tastefully modest in swagger, though stout in its proud display of tough-guy vulnerability (that the rest of the known multiverse saw in the genre from the get-go). If *Kill 'Em All* fairly distills the threat of getting jumped by a gang of flamingly pissed nerds, *Black* represents those same white boys come-of-age: they'll still kick ass if context requires, but there are better things to do. If an intruder breaks into the house or it's time to win Santa Clara, it's nice to have a few crazy white dudes around to aid in the fight; though it's also cool if they can chill enough to not needlessly tussle or stalk every sister at the collective party. Such was Metallica's discographical journey, at least from an angle that values the more defensible dimensions of "normality," say: common human decency (and of course, nothing after

Black really counts as truly Metallica). James and the boyz seemed to be saying: *the world is big enough for all of us to shine*. To those socialized in the culture of the early 1990s, this sentence really was in the air, with the much-maligned birth of so-called "political correctness" eagerly embraced by the lot of us, though with a signature willingness to resort to irony should one tribe get too rambunctious. This was the case even in the peculiar fields of popular Christian music.

What has popular Christian music to do with the genealogy of left politics and Levinas's roles in it, you ask? More than you might think. As it happens, parents who by force limited their kid's aesthetic education to DC Talk and MC Hammer were the very same moral guardians who forged an alliance with Newt Gingrich and Bill Clinton. Such are the perils of elevating a disincarnate Plato above the prophet Isaiah and St. Paul. For all the stupidities of so-called "postmodernism," it really did do some culturally necessary work in its time. At her stout best, the self-avowed "postmodern Christian" is actually embodying cultural code, a solemn public plea: "I am not a fascist, please be my friend," even if authentic fidelity to Christianity's best legacies cannot be intelligibly articulated within the teenish bounds of official postmoderndom.[20] In the immortal words of Matthew Linder, writing for Patheos's *Christ and Pop Culture*: "Music Matters: In Search of 90's CCM that Doesn't Suck."[21] Treasure hunters exist for a reason, though sometimes tragically. There are a few jewels amid this pre-internet Wasteland, but most of the musical creativity of the period took place outside the commercial and near-vacuous theological policing of the Evangelical *Stasi* of the day.

One must stress a few very important facts to contextualize my selection process here. First, these were days when Bono's religious credentials were still subject to explosive contest between Dads and kids, with Moms trying to hold the apocalypse at bay. Many a pastor have their U2 stories to tell: family trips to the church office, combing with rabbinic vigor every word in liner lyrics to try to safely determine if Bono—in fact—was "hip with Jesus." A true Irishman, Bono himself didn't always help matters much, at least at that time, and this did nothing but fuel adolescent passions all the more. U2's oeuvre stands on its own merits, but Gen X Evangelicals feistily defend it primarily because of the suffering expended in the—in some cases—*years* of trench warfare it took to get them passed parental censors. Our good elders instinctively knew: "if we say 'yes' to this, the universe will probably collapse." To this day, you can measure the fascism of a self-avowed Evangelical by their position on Bono's religion.[22] You must pry beneath merely formal showings of critical disinterest: any living Evangelical qua Evangelical socialized prior to the year 2000 in the United States has quite definite views on U2. Within the tribe, the very possibility of counting as "cool" is premised by a willingness to defend U2's bona fide Christianity, while dismissing them as culturally compromised remains a way to tout one's own religious purity. This yields a relatively clear picture of where the intersection of true rebellion and rooted love resided for staunchly conservative, especially middle-class Evangelicals of the 1990s.

But that's not all. Evangelicalism is a diverse and theologically contentious movement. Its current iteration came to birth during World War II, as a variety of American Protestants tried to differentiate themselves from bald fundamentalists on the one hand, and theological liberals on the other.[23] It was launched as primarily a religious movement, without any major political aims beyond shared agreement on keeping godless commies at bay (they took the doctrinal atheism of vulgar Marxism, and Stalin's tyranny, quite seriously). Though always culturally conservative in character, and as hard as it is to imagine: in relative terms youthful Evangelicalism was as politically as it was religiously diverse:

> In 1968, *Christianity Today* published a special issue on contraception and abortion, encapsulating the consensus among evangelical thinkers at the time. In the leading article, professor Bruce Waltke, of the famously conservative Dallas Theological Seminary, explained the Bible plainly teaches that life begins at birth: "God does not regard the fetus as a soul, no matter how far gestation has progressed. The Law plainly exacts: "If a man kills any human life he will be put to death" (Lev. 24:17). But according to Exodus 21:22–24, the destruction of the fetus is not a capital offense . . . Clearly, then, in contrast to the mother, the fetus is not reckoned as a soul.[24]

A big tent movement, it eventually gathered the near whole of the quantum mass of American Protestantism under its wing, because even theological conservatives in mainline Protestant denominations self-consciously identify with the movement. Its theological *Leitkultur* was constituted by an unstable pact between broadly "Reformed" (Calvinists and Lutherans) and broadly "Anabaptist" (Baptists, Mennonites, Methodists,[25] etc.) theological orientations, grounded in a common commitment to what Stanley Grenz dubs "convertive piety."[26] The Reformed camp consists of a spectrum: on its right wing, the Stalinist doctrine of God worshiped by TULIP fascists, and on its left wing, folks like Herman Dooyeweerd and comrade Barth, and the ecclesial cultures that produced them. One has many a theological bone to pick with John Knox, but his Presbyterian polity is an enduring gift to the history of democracy, compliments of tribe *Jean*. This spectrum is determined by the degree to which the theologies in play reject apathy, fatalism, and authoritarianism, and actually call forth, ground, and collectively practice a historical egalitarian community. Shockingly, Calvinists and Lutherans of various stripes always had more money and organized institutional power, and they've tended to set the terms of theological debate for Evangelicalism as a whole.

The Anabaptist camp also consists of a spectrum: on its right wing, we have Independent Baptists, more insular iterations of Mennonite, Holiness churches, conservative Quakers, the more stern corners of Methodism, and its most radical exemplar: the precious Amish. On its left wing, we also have Independent Baptists, less insular iterations of Mennonite, Holiness churches, less conservative Quakers, the more gracious corners of Methodism, Moravians, and among its best exemplars: the Social Gospel movement. One might have a few theological bones to pick with John Wesley, Richard Allen, Sojourner Truth, and Walter Rauschenbusch, but the embedded, socially active ecclesiologies they develop and put to work are an enduring gift to history. This spectrum is determined by the degree to which the theologies in play reject insularity, sanctimony, and authoritarianism, and actually call forth, ground, and collectively practice a historical egalitarian community. Not so shockingly, Anabaptists tended to be working class, self-perpetuating, ceding more arcane theological questions to others as they got busy surviving and helping the community.

So what's the punch line here? In short: Jerry Falwell. Before Evangelicalism sold its soul to the Republican Party, it was a politically diverse religious movement focused on maintaining lively churches and doing service in local communities. Its various ecclesial participants have political traditions with roots in progressivism, various labor movements, abolitionism, urban social activism, women's suffrage, and so forth—traditions at daggers with Falwell's own good 'ol boy white Baptists of Southern yore. The perverse irony of Falwell's 1979 political coup is that over the course of the 1980s into the early 2000s: "religious right" political commitment slowly became the central unifying thread binding Evangelicalism together. Given the class-rooted historical antagonisms between Reformed and Anabaptist wings of the movement, Falwell's revenge was to have co-opted both all those respectable suburban Calvinists who had generationally peered down their snoots at him, and historically working-class political antagonists, for his own good white man's fundamentalist culture war.[27] Desperate for cultural legitimation, movement Evangelicalism did the deed with Jerry Faust, embracing a theological and cultural enemy under a quite thin banner of "Christian unity," over-against the evil leftists. Such is the etiology of today's idolatrous Christian nationalism.

The near total Wasteland of early 1990s pop Christian music discloses the spiritual vacuity people faced at the time. Falwell's coup began a homogenizing trend, and movement guardians rigorously enforced certain doctrinal and stylistic boundaries. I don't want to overstate the case, because this was still a pre-internet context when a good bit of local culture escaped the notice of mainstream pop. But when Kirk Franklin or Jars of Clay scored a crossover hit, one could hear the collective rejoicing across the three or so blocks that separated Easton Mennonite and Shiloh Baptist church. The best new trends in Christian music of the period emerged out of more marginal local traditions. It's not always complex, musically speaking. But it cuts a stark contrast to the overproduced, cookie-cutter kitsch Evangelical bean counters were churning out through the early decade. It was earnest, participatory, and emotionally authentic. Folks like Yolanda Adams, Delirious?, Donnie McClurkin, or the path-breaking pillar of smoke and fire blazed by Vineyard worship. Anyone today managing to soldier on to Charles Jenkins and Fellowship Chicago or Hillsong Worship stands on a multitude of giants, who each in their own way populate that great consummation of our age. If Tasha Cobbs Leonard and Steffany Gretzinger aren't gigging the Renewal of All Creation, who among us is?

II.c. Post-1989 Left Struggle

Thanks to the invention of cable television, innovative programming and new experimentation in part drove the indigenous counterculture of the early 1990s. Initially, this was a welcome and even helpful phenomenon. When MTV actually still played music, programming allowed everyone to access cutting-edge offerings across genres: *Yo MTV Raps*, *120 Minutes*, *Headbangers Ball*, *Alternative Nation*, and so forth, though still primarily grounded in locally based fan cultures. Zines, local music stores wired into the nearest urban metropolis, the latter themselves connected with the art and music pages of urban and regional newspapers, were still a nationwide reality. As late as 1995, one could buy coveted bootlegs—out of Chicago,

Seattle, Athens GA, Rio, Tokyo, Wembley, and so forth—from a locally owned music shop in southside Bethlehem, Pennsylvania. Both College and local-scene radio were still thriving. These material, communicative networks functioned very much like an informal "minor leagues" to the Show, and helped drive a playful struggle for excellence among aspiring artists: East versus West Coast rap, Seattle versus Chicago, and so forth. These locally based networks gave fans and well-placed critics leverage over music industry executives. Music criticism and connoisseurship was itself a field of playful popular contest, between conservative localists and cosmopolitan formalists: maintaining a creative tension between local histories and the formal originality and technical excellence of particular acts. This dynamic played out in the homespun precincts of "Hood-" and "Mall-" rat cultures, across streets, malls, pool halls, twenty-four-hour diners, coffee houses, bars, clubs, and small-venue concert halls throughout the United States These networks of working- and lower-middle-class culture gave fans real collective power to fuel the rise of chosen artistic heroes and diss the rise of chosen villains; and this in turn created a field of aesthetic contest record company and TV executives were forced to take seriously.

The early days of cable television hosted a nearly utopian moment for the cultural and political consciousness of a generation. The polite polish and restricted forms that formerly dominated the mainstream airwaves gave way to a period of creative risk and experimentation. Artistic creation decisively grounded in local cultures found a wider national audience. Arsenio Hall, MTV, *The Simpsons*, *In Living Color*, *Buffy*, *Twin Peaks*, and so forth reflected the coming of age of what I'm tempted to call—with a nod to Rev. Jackson and then emerging queer power: "the rainbow generation." Every evolving niche culture in 'hoods and high schools across the country participated in the moment, and this molded the consciousness of an entire generation. MTV's initial experiments in dramatic programming were political in character, though rooted in the everyday experience of the youth of the day. The first few seasons of *Real World*, *My So-Called Life*, *Daria*, and so forth brought feminist, queer, and wider multiracial consciousness to new audiences. Moreover, *MTV Unplugged* was born. The show was inspired by a single performance at a music awards show airing in the late 1980s, in the traces of Springsteen trickling through Bon Jovi's glam. Jon and Richie performed a stripped-down, acoustic version of "Living on a Prayer" that electrified a nationwide audience. *Unplugged* was launched soon after. One cannot too quickly reach for "false immediacy," here. *Unplugged* corresponded to an active, nationwide coffee-house culture, where local artists interspersed cover songs with their own material (I myself frequented The Ferry St. Café). Moreover, artists took a real risk in the gig. It showed how their musical chops stood up by itself, without the help of studio producers (a risk that did not always end well). Over the course of the decade, we watched an intergenerational troop of artists get intimate with fans: Elton John, Clapton, A Tribe Called Quest, McCartney, Mariah Carey, Dylan, Maxwell, Pearl Jam, 10,000 Maniacs, Stevie Ray Vaughn, De La Soul, Oasis, Nirvana, Lauryn Hill, and so forth.[28] *Unplugged* helped an entire generation connect the creativity and politics of the day to the ongoing struggles of yore.

The LA riots once more radicalized Black struggle. Fueled by the more draconian dimensions of Reagan's so-called "war on drugs," Rodney King raised popular consciousness of existing networks of local oppression by police and law enforcement across the country; this during the slow growth of the private prison industry. Amid the struggles of the day, the Golden Age of rap and hip-hop was only one field of what became an explosive renaissance in Black art. BET helped drive the expansion of cable, and in 1991 it became the first Black-controlled TV company to be traded on the NY Stock Exchange.[29] Spearheaded by Spike Lee and *Do The Right Thing* (1989), with others like Neema Barnette, John Singleton, and Darnell Martin, the decade saw a flowering of Black film: *Boyz in the Hood* (1991), *Jungle Fever* (1991), *Juice* (1992), *Malcolm X* (1992), *Poetic Justice* (1993), *Above the Rim* (1994), *Friday* (1995), and so forth. In the artistic explosion of the era, Black creativity had a transformative impact on the pop culture of the time. Party cultures in multiracial neighborhoods and high schools across the country were integrated, multicultural affairs.

As the theoretical and normative foundations of the 1960s coalition migrated from classical Marxist analysis toward left-cosmopolitanism, institutionally established networks of activism and their allies in the Democratic Party pressed on, though in a radically transforming political environment. The shock of 1989 lent an air of legitimacy to the Reagan years and breathed life into a fast-growing Movement conservatism. Within the Democratic Party, "New Democrats" were thrust to the forefront. Any overly staunch retrospective judgment on Democrats of the time that fails to treat this unfolding empirical situation is ungrounded. The situation was fluid throughout the globe. Because of the success of a determined, intergenerational, indigenous, and international collective struggle, and without any actually existing Stalinists to use as cover for bald white supremacy: the Apartheid regime in South Africa collapsed. It's fashionable these days to lob purely abstract Marxist critique at Mandela and the post-Apartheid system the ANC founded. What was the alternative?[30] The defensible dimensions of Castro's pre-1989 narrative used to justify his specific critique of US hegemony—not to mention his own domestic political repression and incompetence at economic experimentation—collapsed with the Berlin Wall. This was historically corroborated by Chavez's complete and utter mismanagement of Venezuela's economic (non-) development and historically evolving democratic culture. However grateful we must be for his aid to the Venezuelan peasantry, that aid doesn't justify Chavez's tenure as a demagogue who appropriated Cuba's best legacies—with a cynicism comparable to Pablo Escobar—to ruin his own country's institutions and stultify its economy, as he enriched himself and obedient toadies, selling it all to global civil society as reprising *Fidel!*

The emerging neo-liberal global order took on a life of its own for a period. Vladimir Tismaneanu does not overstate the "world-shattering revolutionary consequences" of 1989, which "generated a fluidity of political commitments, allegiances and affiliations that signaled a general crisis of values."[31] Though Naomi Klein contributes an indispensable critical perspective on what she dubs "disaster capitalism," it can't be retrospectively applied without qualification.[32] As Marx taught us, and over-against right- and left-wing anti-Semites: there is no George Soros or council of mustache-twisting boogey-men behind the scenes plotting to destroy other nations and cultures. Capitalism itself eagerly welcomed the commodification of suffering and the academic hierarchies it funds, and still warmly embraces ethnic studies and indigenous cultural production. One index of the fluid character of the immediate post-1989 situation is not only the slow and ongoing decay of labor activism, but also a lack of vision by liberals of the day who failed to take political economy seriously. Despite serious efforts of Clinton's foreign policy team, and largely due to GOP indifference and cynicism: policy toward post-Soviet states was weak and ineffective. Had something more than an economic wild west taken hold in the birth of the Russian Federation, Vladimir Putin would not have been possible. Had multilateral, interculturally embedded human rights activism and accountability been higher on everyone's agenda, Xi's politically Stalinist and expansionist reappropriation of Mao's legacies would not be unfolding today. The only constituency more responsible than George W. Bush for Putin and Xi's realist, geopolitical pivots is none other than the global left. Who rallied around grounded left-analysis of the unfolding situation? Who out social-scienced the neoliberal analysis of the day, marking the probable social and institutional consequences of then current policy toward post-Soviet states?

These questions and the concomitant judgment may be too staunch, because the left itself was reeling in the unfolding fluidity. As academics took to the *jouissance* of "postmodernism"—bathing in the baldly vacuous character of Derrida's so-called "New International"—a ragtag, teeming mass of incommensurable constituencies gathered under the banner of the "Anti-Globalization Movement." Driven in part by conspiracy theories in every sector of the political spectrum, the movement housed a carnival of difference: anarchists of infinite variety, mom-and-pop vulgar Marxists, right-wing nationalists, the decaying remnants of organized labor, even religious traditionalists, all gathered under a banner of pure "*No!*" to globalization. The Battle for Seattle became a dramatic symbol and harbinger for since-unfolding geopolitics in its near totality: the eternal return of declaring anarchist (pyrrhic-) victory over-against the implicitly conceded Gnostic necessity and omnipotence of global capital—if only one's own "*no!*" gets noted in the news cycle. The death of the 1960s coalition—and the failures of its more fanciful threads—dramatically announced itself at the thirtieth anniversary of Woodstock. At Woodstock 99, Generation X theatrically repeated the negative conclusion reached by the global left when analyzed on then inherited frames. Corporate sponsorship, exploitative concessions, ecological indifference, and an explosion of antisocial animus came to the same end disclosed in the Battle of Seattle. As *Wikipedia* recounts,

> Violent actions occurred during and after the Saturday night performance by Limp Bizkit; they included fans tearing plywood from the walls during their performance of the song "Break Stuff." Several sexual assaults were also reported in the aftermath of the concert. The band's vocalist, Fred Durst, stated during the concert, "Don't let anybody get hurt. But I don't think you should mellow out. That's what Alanis Morissette had you motherfuckers do [Morissette's *MTV Unplugged* album is lovely, btw]. If someone falls, pick 'em up." Durst said during a performance of the band's hit song, *Nookie*, "We already let all the negative energy out. It's time to reach down and bring that positive energy to this motherfucker. It's time to let yourself go right now, 'cause there are no motherfucking rules out there." In contrast, partway through [their song] *Break Stuff*, Durst encouraged the crowd to be angry.[33]

As fun as sex, drugs, and rock-and-roll are, and whatever their role in the eros of progressive politics, they don't by themselves get anything specifically political accomplished; and can in fact fund self-destructive and politically dubious modes of desire fulfillment (as we already knew well from the darker corners of punk, metal, goth, country, etc.). By 1999, the early decade's indigenous explosion of creativity and political consciousness gave way to the increasingly unilateral hegemony of media executives, as the internet presided over the decay of material networks of local cultures that grounded fan (and labor) power. As neoliberal economic theory became a global reality, activists carrying forth the best legacies of the 1960s coalition doggedly soldiered on to their best lights.

As the labor movement increasingly withered, new digital media became a veritable identity market: a too often zero-sum battleground of political performativity that slowly became the primary medium of political engagement, in general and as such, exemplified by the popular emergence of the slogan "the personal is political." Across the abyss of 1989 and the unfolding of these transformations, it was precisely comrades in identity politics that continued advancing the struggle where it mattered most: the threefold engine of legal policy transformation, the production of culture, and grassroots mass mobilization around anti-racist, feminist, queer, and minority-religious causes. With the courageous leadership of Barney Frank, among others in prior generations, Gen X activists of the 1990s and beyond gave us the Americans with Disabilities Act of 1990, the Civil Rights Act of 1991, the Family and Medical Leave Act of 1993, the 1993 March on Washington for Lesbian, Gay, and Bi Equal Rights and Liberation, *Lawrence v. Texas*, the Gender Equity in Education Act of 1994, the Violence Against Women Act of 1994, Clinton's naming of the first-ever White House Liaison to the queer community, The Million Man March, *United States v. Virginia*, Title IX, South Africa's 1997 constitutional ban outlawing sexual-orientation discrimination, *Burlington Industries,* Ellen DeGeneres's explosion of the closet, *Inc. v. Ellerth* & *Faragher v. City of Boca Raton*, Coretta Scott King's plea for solidarity between queer and anti-racist struggle, *Will & Grace*, the United Kingdom's 1999 and 2000 bans on discrimination against queer folk, Vermont's 2000 legalization of same-sex civil unions, the Massachusetts Supreme Court's 2003 ruling on the unconstitutionality of DOMA and subsequent legalization of queer marriage, anti-Iraq II popular uprising, *Jackson v. Birmingham Board of Education*, New Zealand's 2005 legislation protecting queer identity, the 2005 reauthorization of the Violence Against Women Act, the Employment Non-Discrimination Act of 2007, Iran's 2009 Green Movement, the Matthew Shepard Act of 2009, Lilly Ledbetter Fair Pay Act of 2009, Occupy Wall St., Obama's 2010 repeal of Don't Ask, Don't Tell, The Affordable Health Care Act of 2010, *United States v. Windsor*, the

Arab Spring, 2013 reauthorization of the Violence Against Women Act, the 2013 revoking of the ban on women in combat, Hong Kong's "Umbrella Movement," Black Lives Matter, spontaneous mass-protests across the Euro-Atlantic to Trump's proposed "Muslim Ban," the grassroots emergence of sanctuary churches, synagogues, mosques, temples, and cities over-against Trump's ICE brown shirts, the Women's March, and what else? These are merely some of the achievements the post-1989 left actually won in areas of consistent, intelligible, impassioned, and tactically aware individuated yet *collaborative collective struggle*.

II.D. POST-1989 LEFT CHALLENGES AND MISTAKES

For all its stunning successes against generational conservative pushback, both the ongoing justification for and the limits of identity politics became evident on two specific dates: January 7 and 26, 2015. Across these nineteen days, and against the backdrop of the entire post-1989 era: the fortunes of idpol became crystal clear to anyone with eyes actually paying attention.

II.d.i. Charlie Hebdo

On January 7, 2015, at about 11:30 local time, Al-Qaeda operatives Saïd and Chérif Kouachi stormed the offices of the satirical magazine *Charlie Hebdo* and murdered twelve of its employees. Truth be told, those employees died not only at the hands of youth radicalized by a deviant sect far from orthodox Sunni (and other) Islamic traditions, but, among other salient factors, also by a very unique form of white privilege peculiar to France (with relevant corollaries elsewhere, including the thoroughly puritan United States). This form of white privilege is exemplified in the historical life, relevant scholarship, and the cultural meanings surrounding the Marquis de Sade. This might seem to be a provocative claim, especially in the context of an absolutely unjustifiable criminal tragedy. So that there is no implicative confusion, I will be clear.

The French Libertine tradition is a complex cultural and literary phenomenon. As Bradley Reichek has shown, it cannot be reduced to its more widely known and baldly masculinist iterations. Reichek complicates the too stark classification of relevant literature between "libertine" and "sentimentalist" variants, showing areas of important overlap that include both consensually transgressive forms of experimental sex, though ultimately grounded in genuine interpersonal affection.[34] Next, Sade was in some sense a product of his culture, and this is what makes him an interesting and controversial historical and literary figure. As such, a specifically moral analysis is not the only sort of analysis one should perform in treating the Sadean personae. With qualifications, I think Foucault's move in analyzing Sade, as a critical historical moment of confronting the overly repressive sexual culture of the day, is basically right. But much Sade scholarship also fails to tell the whole story, often succumbing to the duel temptation toward the romantic idealizations characteristic of the Sade mystique and overtly caricatured vilifications of the contexts Sade confronted. I must emphatically stress that one cannot and ought not implicitly identify Sade himself with the moral culture of BDSM communities, despite contingent lexical overlaps. As French historian Olivier Blanc notes,

> Persons who practice BDSM respect conventional codes regarding limits not to be overstepped in consensual games of sexual domination. These enshrined practices, whose practitioners belong to organizations, apparently have nothing to do with the unrestrained and deadly sexuality of Sade, but the paradox is that his name serves as well to designate BDSM practices and games deemed "safe."

Finally and unequivocally: verbally insulting, aesthetically caricaturing, and morally criticizing other people or cultures in no way justify murder. But moral assessment and cultural critique are a two-way street, so I explicate the point.

The artistic and lifestyle work of the Marquis de Sade is part of what is generally called Libertinism. Libertine art and literature are characterized by staunch anti-clerical, counterculture, and erotic—indeed, boldly pornographic—themes. Beyond Sade, it includes authors and artists like Claude de Crébillon, Denis Diderot, Choderlos de Laclos, Andrea de Nerciat, Claude-Louis Desrais, and others. As an aesthetic movement, it played a significant role in the ferment of the French Revolution. Pornographic art was a prominent mode of popular criticism at the decadence of the French ruling class, often depicting priests, nobility, and the royal family engaged in explicit sex acts, at times with gothically perverse flourish. The second sentence of *Wikipedia*'s entry for the "Libertine novel" reads: "The genre effectively ended with the French Revolution."[35] The equivocity of this sentence reflects the sentiments of much of the literature on Libertinism, from the hagiography characteristic of some French avant-garde treatments, to a more conservative reticence to even treat the matter, perhaps grounded in a worry that it might taint the nobility of French revolutionary ideals and achievements. This contrast informs my proposal that variants of Libertine tradition—and Sade, above all—involve a very specific form of white privilege.

Angela Rene Nacol well represents the more celebratory wing of hermeneutic work in Sadean tradition. She presents Sade and Desrais as artistic and political revolutionaries utilizing "sexualized bodies [as] political tools that critiqued traditional orders and reflected societal disorder."[36] She describes "a close relationship between sexualized violence, pornography, and the political upheaval during the Revolution."[37]

Hunt further evidences this, documenting the "very intimate connections" between pornography and the revolutionary ferment of the day.[38] Leading revolutionaries like Mirabeau and Saint-Just were themselves pornographic authors, and Hunt suggests that the genre reaches a kind of apex in Sade. The internal tensions of the Revolution itself, exploding in the moralistic and chaotic Reign of Terror, suggests Robespierre as a sort of puritanical counterpoint to Sade. So one cannot, as a veritable reactionary tradition likes to do, try to tar the Revolution itself as a degenerate specimen of mere sexual liberality. Nevertheless, the Libertine influence did worry folks on all sides in the period. A well-known literary figure of the time—the republican, anti-militarist, centrist member of the Convention, and one of the inventors of the literary Black Spartacus figure that anticipated Toussaint—Louis-Sébastien Mercier, comments on this. As late as 1798, he complains: "Some people display nothing but obscene books whose titles and engravings are equally offensive to decency and good taste. They sell these monstrosities everywhere."[39] Many treatments of the Libertine phenomenon tend to present any sort of dissent to it as a homogenous piece of overwrought morality the authentic Revolution sought to overflow. This of course is too simplistic.

Nacol documents and describes what was at issue here. Newspapers widely reported on the more peculiar dimensions of popular activity in the revolutionary era. As the *Edwards's Baltimore Daily* observed,

> A woman was flogged by the women in the market called La Halle, for wearing the national cockade, which was torn from her. She went away heartily cursing her assailants, and had hardly proceeded 600 yards father, when she was again attacked by another set of ferocious women, who beat her for appearing without the cockade![40]

This must have been more than a marginal occurrence. Anonymous etchings of the period depict scenes of women publicly attacking each other. One depicts a woman being thrashed, bare-bummed, by other women, to the gawking eyes of male onlookers and as a nun tries to intervene.[41] Some of the etchings have splendidly concrete titles:

> Anonymous, *Patriotic Discipline or Fanaticism Corrected: The Period begun during the Week of the Passion, 1791, by the Women of the Market. According to an Exact Count, there were 621 Buttocks Whipped: 310 and one-Half Butts, since the Treasurer of the Miramion(s) Has Only One (Cheek)*, 1791, Bibliothèque Nationale, Paris.[42]

Claude-Louis Desrais, a student of Casanova's brother, is a more famed pornographer of the era. Among his less lighthearted offerings, his work includes "acts of sadism by groups of women whipping each other or a single male with cat-o-nine tails," or "a member of the clergy strapped to a table where a group of women flog him with cat-o-nine tails and irons, while another woman is under the table performing oral sex," even the obligatory "a woman defecating on a plate, and a man bleeding from lacerations on his back, while sitting on a toilet as two women insert hot pokers in his ears. Another image shows a man with bruised and bloody buttocks as he ejaculates in a woman's face."[43] As Nacol explains,

> cat-o-nine tails or brooms are the predominant form of sexual relations in Desrais's suite of drawings. The use of cat-o-nine tails, fringed whips with bent nails or other flesh-tearing mechanisms attached at the tips, are synonymous with Sade's form of sadism and differ from more common depictions of broom-like whips, which are less painful.[44]

Desrais and Sade, true to the patrician origins of Libertinism, sought to out-radical popular "restraint" in doling out the social criticism of the period.

Nacol's admirably frank analysis of Sade and Desrais's debauchery is keen to stress that they "promoted counter-hegemonic ideologies," though she also points out Sade's "hatred for [both the] *ancien régime*" and "the Jacobins."[45] A brief review of his literature leaves one wondering just what these counter-hegemonic "ideologies" amount to. Without endorsing every turn in their larger analysis, Adorno and Horkheimer seem right that Sade exemplifies a will to "understanding without [any] direction from another," a valorization of instrumental rationality deaf to the pleas of comrades and the cries of its victims,

> . . . like the gymnasts' pyramids in Sade's orgies and the formalized principles of early bourgeois freemasonry—cynically reflected in the strict regime of the libertine society of the *120 Days of Sodom*—prefigures the organization, devoid of any substantial goals, which was to encompass the whole of life.[46]

Nacol's analysis seems to fall prey to something like this problem. She notes how Sade's dehumanizing violence is radically steeped in a reactive hatred that would have made Nietzsche himself blush. For example, Nacol writes,

> Many scholars claim that Sade hated women, which was corroborated by his acts of violence against women. However, he did act out his political views like a performance artist and a protestor of conventional sexual behavior and Christian morals.[47]

Even misogyny and nonconsensual sexual torture can be "excused" if framed as acts of *blasphemy*.

The Marquis de Sade was a real-life psychopath and moral monster. He was known for luring working-class women back to his flat under the pretense of maid service. Once there, he imprisoned them, perpetrating sexual and other forms of bodily torture for extended periods of time. He's rumored to have murdered many. There are law-enforcement records of the time that bear testimony of a few who managed to escape Sade's "counter-hegemonic" practices. Though one can certainly question the more empirically ungrounded moments of Andrea Dworkin's critique of male sexuality, and wonder if she doesn't overstate an otherwise grounded worry about the nature of pornography, she is spot-on about the character of the Sadean personae; and this is why Reichek rightly distinguishes it from the very human, sentimentalist variants.[48] Adorno and Horkheimer capture the semantic core of the relevant Libertine, in general and as such:

> It is the weak who are guilty, according to Nietzsche's doctrine, since they use cunning to circumvent the natural law. "It is the diseased who imperil mankind, and not the 'beasts of prey.' It

is the predestined failures and victims who undermine the social structure, who poison our faith in life and our fellow men." They have spread throughout the world the Christianity which Nietzsche hates and abominates no less than Sade.[49]

Though Nacol notes that Libertine aesthetic and lifestyle culture was the primary province of patrician men, she suggests that Sade "walked a fine line between being a Revolutionary and an aristocrat in the manner of a true libertine."[50] This, of course, is hagiography in action. According to French historian Olivier Blanc,

> The revolutionaries expressed their reservations about the duplicity of the former marquis, who had succeeded in being elected president: "From August 10, when he arrived at the section, he has never ceased to play the patriot. But these (patriots) here were not fooled." Biographers of Sade, notably Maurice Lever, have abundantly shown that Sade was neither a defender of new ideas nor an admirer of the Revolution. And no one, in 1792, was in fact fooled by his claimed republican convictions, nor the writings of circumstance which he published after the fall of the monarchy.[51]

The point, of course, is not to burn Sade's books or refuse to read and understand them for what they are. They are a testament to the pathologies of an era, above all to the failings of church leadership, the monarchy, and the nobility who itself gave birth to the darker corners of Libertinism to begin with; all of whom presided over an ocean of poverty and suffering among common folk. As one sociologist put it, "leading indicators of a severe deterioration of social organization and the ultimate collapse of the legitimacy of authority."[52] We should therefore resist conservative attempts to summon the more ridiculous corners of the culture of the day to tar the Revolution's achievements. The point is rather that some "hegemonies" are splendidly good, for example: a culture that actively values the parity, privacy, and leadership of women. Difference isn't a necessary good or politically progressive by definition, and this is why sincere communication about the values and rules we use to govern ourselves is so important, and why a free society is one where mutual respect and conflict resolution are actively practiced by all. Beyond the boldly psychopathic dimensions of Sade's character, Wiccan blogger Sabina Becker pinpoints his other primary trait: "The Marquis was the quintessential spoiled brat, debauched from an early age."[53] This is what I mean by "white privilege" above.

We should neither endorse the Libertine romanticism of some avant-garde literary treatments nor summon its teenish character to pronounce a wholesale pox on these literatures. The fact is, the less gothic pornography of the period serves as a kind of mirror for understanding some of the more peculiar features of France's revolutionary tumult, including the violently moralistic dimensions of Robespierre and the Reign of Terror. Above all, anyone utilizing pornography to tar the Revolution as a whole ought to be confronted as to what they are: puritans blind to the plight of commoners in the *ancien régime* and to the genuinely revolutionary contributions of France to normative and institutional histories in the unfolding arc of global justice struggle.

At their most violent and radical, both the Libertine and the Puritan are in an *eternal* struggle-to-the-death, an unending cycle of degenerative and destructive conflict that is one face of *hell* itself, and that only erupts historically in the breakdown of the culturally embedded, differentiated *phronesis* that is necessary to a flourishing social life. This is one reason for the truly global resurgence of neo-nativism today due to the disruptions introduced by postmodern economic globalization. The task, of course, is not to return to the too-scrubbed repressions of yore, but rather to find modernities grounded in an *authentically liberatory repression*, freeing each other to true creativity, service, and self-governance in a political eros that properly values, collaboratively limits, and creatively channels our bodily desires for more than our own singular goods. In truth, queer folk well exemplify what everyone must do better, in the creativity they deploy in constructing community codes and collective conventions that help everyone pursue their desire and enjoy difference together, in ways that are safe, sensitive to others, and empowering for all. Consciously or not, doing this involves a core virtue of monotheism in general, witnessed in Levinas's work, the Talmudic tradition, St. Paul, Thomas, base ecclesial communities, and especially in the authentic everyday meaning of the Islamic concept of *jihad*, namely: firmly educating the will-to-power *in me*, such that repression becomes merely one moment in a movement of letting eros be ethically *oriented*, within a community of others, toward an excellence that creates and innovates without exploitation or at the cost of the needless suffering of others.

But clearly, blasphemy is not an intrinsic good, and the teenish style of those who imagine it one is quite clear. One can only truly blaspheme either (1) my own religion, or (2) the religion of one who is actively, empirically oppressing me. Even the latter must be qualified, because religious minorities in functional societies know all too well the various fault lines that separate the aggressively oppositional from the collaboratively amicable among majority religionists in a given context. The originary theological meaning of "secularity" implicates the redemption of *this world*, and across various traditions: the participation of all citizens in its unfolding event. Much good work has been done excavating the darker corners of Europe's monotheist traditions. I've laid out here the outlines for a similar project with regard to France's *laïcité*, and its historical and postural links to the darker interplays between conservative and licentious sexuality, between formal public pieties and self-oriented occult spiritualities; dynamics that play their own roles in the eternal return of Stalinism/fascism in the pathologies of liberal capitalism.

In the context of *Charlie Hebdo*, my point could not be clearer. France's Muslim population is by no means a privileged minority, but rather working-class folk forced to cope with integrating as who they are into the broader rhythms of French society. Moreover, and especially at that time, French Muslims were striving mightily as a community to fight the radicalization of their youth. *Charlie Hebdo*'s blasphemous depictions of the Prophet Mohammed, peace be upon him, made the earnest work of French mothers, fathers, and imams that much harder, adding needless stress to a community that deserves our solidarity as we collectively practice what feminist philosopher Lisa Tessman calls "burdened virtue."[54] Moreover, the highly patriotic character of the national response to the tragedy involved sacred odes to the *laïcité*, and a defense of Becker's "spoiled brats" that in this case were certainly *not* punching up, but rather bullying already marginalized co-citizens. *Charlie Hebdo*'s cultural sadism of course in no way justifies murder, nor should we waver in our defense of free speech. But we can utilize our free speech to criticize the officially sacralized white privilege on display throughout the tragedy; a sacralization historically performed in and by the more amusing quarters of the French avant-garde, in their fanatical devotion to the Sade mystique. Revered as what Kendrick aptly calls "the Prophet of our Disorder," the etiology of Sade's depravity lay not in popular struggle, but rather, with Adorno and Horkheimer: in "an old bourgeois heritage."[55] Such is the "radicality" of those "sycophants of Sade who conflate sexist violence, murderous sexuality, and literary audacity," and as feminist philosopher Linda Martín Alcoff notes, "a fact that persists across [Euro-Atlantic] cultural differences."[56]

The *Charlie Hebdo* tragedy clearly discloses the ongoing reality of identity politics, even as we must distinguish between better and worse iterations of it. Indeed, the eruption of spontaneous mass protests across the Euro-Atlantic in the face of Trump's "Muslim Ban" is an enduring legacy of the best in idpol traditions. Thanks to the ongoing leadership of social movements across the political spectrum, civil society's "*no!*" to Trump's ban was not the vacuous gesture of theatrical skeptics, but rather grounded in an originary "*yes!*" to Muslim co-citizens qua Muslim co-citizens: "*you are one of us—you are us—as who you uniquely are!*" Without the voluntary collaboration and everyday work of activists, journalists, scholars, rabbis, pastors, priests, and imams—all daring to risk rallying with and around neighbors to stand against the hate of cynical politicians and the idolatry of Christian nationalists, where would we now be? This indigenous, grassroots resistance to global capital's dangerously useful idiots in the United States, Europe, Israel, the Middle East, India, Brazil, China, and nearly everywhere else is *lighting up the way to a better global future*.

Given the complicity of "big powers" and colonial history in the problems of the Middle East, global citizens owe it to Muslim neighbors and comrades to learn about not only the past gifts, debates, and problems that constitute Islamic history, but also its ongoing contributions to global democracy and human culture. We are presently in the midst of a veritable, worldwide renaissance in Islamic culture, that, in view of Eduardo Mendieta and Jürgen Habermas, is one "form of multiple modernities [among] the great world religions [in their] great culture-forming power . . ."[57] Led by social activists, Muslim feminists, cutting-edge writers, and more traditional scholars whom major media rarely mention, these folks are carrying forth the best in their tradition over-against the worst in every corner of our world.

Malala Yousafzai will continue to stand as a trailblazing youth for the moral power of Muslim women. Popular writers like Irshad Manji and scholars like Ingrid Mattson should increasingly find a global readership. Folks like Tawakkol Karman, Mohammed Salah, El-Farouk Khaki, Nabeel Rajab, Youssef Msakni, Saleemah Abdul-Ghafur, Loujain Al-Hathloul, Maliha Khan, Ayman Mohyeldin, Simon Shaheen, Karim Benzemaand, Mohammed Al-Modiahki, and scores of others are leading the way as exemplars of excellence in peacemaking, feminist, queer, anti-poverty, and human rights advocacy; popular scholarship, education, courageous reform, athletics, arts, media, and so forth. In the United States, Reps. Ilhan Omar and Rashida Tlaib carry forth the best legacies of Kubra Nurzai, Benazir Bhutto, Tansu Çiller, Toujan al-Faisal, Halimah Yacob, and Abraham Lincoln.

Even in regions of more traditional scholarship, cultural conservatives and cultural liberals together are confronting infidelity and corruption in corners of their own communities, leading the Ummah past those perverting the nobility of Islam. Building on the spirit of indigenous voices of Islamic modernity—folks like Syed Ahmad Khan, Muhammad Iqbal, Begum Rokeya, and examples like Abdul Ghaffar Khan, Farid Esack, and Ahmed Kathrada—a culturally diverse group of intellectuals and activists are at the leading edge of engaging contemporary global problems. Iranian philosopher Seyyed Hossein Nasr is a leading environmental thinker. American philosopher, legal scholar, and co-founding editor of *Hypatia* Azizah Al-Hibri does important work on democracy and woman's rights. Jordanian philosopher Prince Ghazi bin Muhammad is a global interfaith leader, authoring the very important "A Common Word Between Us and You," addressed to Christian leaders, initiating neighborly religious dialogue for the twenty-first century. Kuwaiti legal scholar Khaled Abou El-Fadl has done important work in human rights law and Islamic jurisprudence. American feminist philosopher Amina Wadud has done important work on gender in Islamic theology and has led the way—to considerable controversy—in advocacy for integrated prayer. Syrian refugee and accomplished scholar Muhammad al-Yaqoubi has been an important pastoral figure, leading the popular fight against ISIS ideologists in defense of Sunni orthodoxy. Morocco's Tahar Ben Jelloun is an accomplished French-language poet, novelist, essayist, and critic; his work has been translated into forty-seven different languages. Black American Islamic scholar Warith Deen Mohammed achieved quite significant reform in Black Muslim communities and has advanced important proposals for developing locally led schools of Islamic jurisprudence. A variety of scholars have spoken up for interfaith peace and cooperation throughout conflict-prone regions, for example: Egypt's Ahmad Muhammad Al-Tayyeb and Nigeria's Sa'adu Abubakar. Leaders in Abu Dhabi have taken bold new steps in interfaith cooperation, with Ali Al-Jifri's contributions to "A Common Word," and quite significantly: Crown Prince Mohammad Bin Zayed Al-Nahyan's initiative in gifting land for the construction of a Hindu Temple, joining Muscat and Sultan Qaboos bin Said Al-Said's leadership in hosting the region's only Hindu houses of worship.

Throughout the world, everyday scholars and imams of note are leading their communities into the future. They include Colombia's Munir Valencia, Germany's Seyran Ateş, Australia's Nur Warsame, France's Mohamed Bechari, the United States' Qamar-ul Huda, New Zealand's Ibrahim Abdul Halim, Russia's Ravil Gaynutdin, the United Kingdom's Abdal Hakim

Murad, Canada's Yasin Dwyer, and Imam Yao Baoxia among the trailblazing women of China. Important work by Sufi scholars committed to Islamic orthodoxy are enriching human culture and leading for world peace. Yemen's Umar bin Hafiz is a truly global leader in Islamic research, spirituality, and intercultural cooperation. The feisty scholarship of Lebanon's Sheik Hisham Kabbani—declared an "apostate" by ISIS ideologues—combats domestic abuse, distortions to the concept of *jihad*, blind denunciation of Israel, and other ongoing challenges. He's moreover played a leading role in promoting charitable work, interfaith dialogue, and research in Sufi spirituality. Cyprus's Nazim Al-Haqqani is a prolific Sufi scholar, a vocal critic of extremism, and an important Islamic missionary, with a following throughout Europe, notably by John G. Bennett in the United Kingdom.

If I may be so bold, I want to nominate two specific Sufi Islamic scholars for the title of authentic *genius*: Iran's Seyyed Hossein Nasr and Malaysia's Syed Muhammad Naquib Al-Attas. Professor emeritus of Islamic studies at George Washington University, and dubbed a "polymath" by Egbert Giles Leigh, Nasr has authored, edited, and translated more than forty books treating "philosophy, religion, spirituality, music, art, architecture, science, literature, civilizational dialogues," ecology, and even two books of poetry.[58] He was the first non-Western and Muslim scholar invited to give the prestigious Gifford Lectures, and was a recipient of a Templeton Religion and Science Award. Malaysia's Syed Muhammad Naquib Al-Attas also has an impressive vita. Author of twenty-seven books across various disciplines, he did groundbreaking research on indigenous Malay Sufism and substantially contributed to the development of the modern Malay language. He's done interesting work across a variety of disciplines, including religious sociology, educational theory, Islamic epistemology and metaphysics, and is an accomplished calligrapher. A Member of the Royal Academy of Jordan, he has lectured worldwide on a variety of topics of public concern.[59]

Beyond the work of notable individuals, a group of Turkish scholars has played an ongoing and leading role in the collective *ijtihad* of emerging Islamic modernity. In 2013, the "Ankara School" of Sunni Islam released a new seven-volume edition of commentary on *hadith*, or the "sayings" of the Prophet Mohammed. As Heneghan reports,

> 100 authors have selected a few hundred of the about 17,000 reported quotes from Mohammad to examine Islamic views on God, faith and life in terms that the average modern Turk can understand. "We don't live in the 20th century anymore," said

Mehmet Ozafsar, director of the project and vice-president of Ankara's Religious Affairs Directorate, or Diyanet, a state agency. "We needed a new work with Islamic beliefs in the perspective of today's culture."[60]

According to Heneghan, the Ankara School adopts "what they call 'conservative modernity,' a Sunni Islam true to the faith's core doctrines but without the strictly literal views that ultra-orthodox Muslims have been promoting in other parts of the Islamic world."

Another important Turkish reformer worthy of note is intellectual, activist, and educator Fethullah Gülen. Described as an "influential Ottomanist, Anatolian panethnicist, Islamic poet, writer, social critic, and activist–dissident developing a Nursian theological perspective that embraces democratic modernity," he was a Turkish state imam for more than twenty years.[61] A centrist figure, the civil society movement he helped build drew accusations from both sides of traditional Turkish politics: secularist parties deemed him a religious threat, and Islamicists attacked him as a secularist. He has lived in exile in the United States since 2002 (as it happens, a twenty-minute drive from where I now sit). In a 2015 *New York Times* op-ed, Gülen openly challenged Erdoğan's rightward drift:

> The core tenets of a functioning democracy—the rule of law, respect for individual freedoms—are also the most basic of Islamic values bestowed upon us by God. No political or religious leader has the authority to take them away . . . Speaking against oppression is a democratic right, a civic duty and for believers, a religious obligation. The Quran makes clear that people should not remain silent in the face of injustice: "O you who believe! Be upholders and standard-bearers of justice, bearing witness to the truth for God's sake, even though it be against your own selves, or parents or kindred."[62]

The next year, Gülen was accused of plotting a coup, and the state shut down his civil society groups across Turkey. In 2017, Erdoğan betrayed a century of Turkish republicanism with a constitutional referendum of questionable legitimacy. Gülen observed,

> In Turkey or elsewhere, authoritarian rulers have exploited the differences within the society to polarize various groups against

each other and maintain their stronghold in power. Whatever beliefs or worldviews they have, citizens should come together around universal human rights and freedoms and be able to democratically oppose those who violate these rights. . . . In contrast to claims by political Islamists, Islam is not a political ideology, it is a religion. It does have some principles that pertain to governance, but these account for, at most, five percent of all Islamic principles. To reduce Islam to a political ideology is the greatest crime against its ethos.[63]

Debates in Islamic political theology aside, for more than four decades Gülen has been a tireless voice in the diverse constellation of a burgeoning Islamic modernity. His work merits wide attention and engagement.

The politics of identity aren't going anywhere, and as our Muslim comrades beautifully suggest: non-Muslims should at least *try* to achieve the excellence of Islam's brightest lights. In the words of Abdallah Bin Bayyah, a Mauritanian professor of Islamic studies at King Abdul Aziz University in Jeddah, Saudi Arabia, and over-against lovers of Sade wherever they happen to reside: "I call to life, not to death."[64] Yes.

II.d.ii. The Euroleft

If the *Charlie Hebdo* tragedy discloses the ongoing necessity of well-motivated and competent identity politics, another date discloses its limits. These limits became crystal clear on January 26 of 2015 with Syriza's victory in Greek parliamentary elections. Every responsible social scientist and geopolitical analyst immediately knew that Tsipras and Co. had exploited the hopes and struggle of the working class they claimed to represent by promising way too much, way too fast in an egregiously irresponsible gambit willing to risk the very existence of the EU itself as a transnational political reality. Ultimately grounded in a series of blunders by technocrats in Brussels and Athens' political class (with the greedy aid of Wall St. predators), and various other flaws and institutional problems that have attended the EU experiment, Syriza effectively pitted the Greek public against German and Scandinavian populations bearing the fiscal brunt of then economic, political, and institutional dysfunctions across southern Europe. This was in the immediate wake of Putin's declaration of a New Cold War by breaking an explicit covenant through annexing Crimea, the collective sigh of relief that attended the tensions of the 2014 Scottish Referendum, and new public awareness these both raised over Moscow's civil society lobbying for and material aid to then emerging right-wing parties, EU skeptics, independence movements beyond Scotland in Catalonia, Wallonia, and so forth. Various leaders in the Syriza coalition had close financial and ideological ties with Moscow.[65] The latter are even more worrying than the former, in the burgeoning solidarity between fascist quarters of the Orthodox tradition with the bald ethnocentrism of Alexander Dugin, a charlatan who without exaggeration exploits the worst in the late-Heidegger's negativist equivocations for his own proud Russian fascism.[66] As Tsipras pronounced a pox on the sanctions imposed by international allies on Russia for violating its commitments and bullying Ukraine, so-called leftists throughout the world actually celebrated Syriza's victory. I witnessed self-avowed Marxists valiantly ignoring the emerging constellation of financial, ethnocentric, and institutional geopolitical dynamics we now recognize as "global neo-nativism," reaching for purely doctrinal ex post facto apologetics to defend Syriza from firmly grounded cosmopolitan and liberal-internationalist criticism. In her retrospective treatment of the movement, activist Helena Sheehan rightly notes, "Syriza was a horizon of hope. Now it is a vortex of despair."[67] This despair was the wholly predictable result of irresponsible promises not grounded in serious economic and geopolitical analysis, as debate at the time shows.

A nearly identical fiasco unfolded with much higher stakes during the 2017 French elections, where Mélenchon's utterly despicable demagoguery reprised so-called "Marxist" flirtation with homegrown fascism and anti-Semitism. Mélenchon exploited and indirectly helped to legitimize Le Pen's racist nationalism and Euro-skepticism by lending it ostensive left-wing imprimatur. While all this ultimately implicates failures by Brussels itself, it nevertheless suggests that blind invocations of purely negative anti-capitalist contest are no longer adequate to the popular politics of our day. In a joint press conference, snug at Putin's side, Tsipras told reporters: "We have repeatedly said that the vicious circle of militarization, of Cold War rhetoric, and of sanctions is not productive. The solution is dialogue."[68] *Dialogue.* Exactly what should be discussed he didn't immediately specify, as the farce of a Crimean referendum unfolded against the backdrop of radically destabilizing Russian military deployments, the paramilitarization of Ukrainian politics, deeply serious alterations in established patterns of Russian nuclear deterrent, and its open support for any regime or domestic political movement willing to bid adieu to international norms under populist calls of "the nation!" Thanks to the precedent set by Bush and Blair's geopolitically catastrophic Iraq II cynicism, Putin went on to exploit Obama's anti-war platform, foiling and directly challenging the latter's earnest attempt to reorient US foreign policy toward a multilateral coalitionism headed by international actors, as Xi followed Putin's lead in the unfolding saga in the South China Sea, bullying Vietnam, Japan, and other immediate neighbors, the walking back of prior promises to Hong Kong, and new draconian crackdowns by the Han majority on various cultural minorities, on Muslim Uyghurs above all. In the United States at least, one of the most damning embarrassments of the left today is its blindly contextless criticism of Obama's foreign-policy performance, lending aid and comfort to his neo-con critics and the good ol' fashioned racist isolationism of Rand Paul, Paul's allies among fellow anarcho-careerists like Glen Greenwald, not to mention ideological cover for the exploitative corruption of Maduro, Iran's nuclear ambitions, the more glittering inanities of Tulsi Gabbard's hapless "diplomacy," and so forth. All of this played an ongoing background role to Hillary Clinton's defeat by Donald Trump.

Contrasting blogs and popular commentary captured the collective mood across the political spectrum during the unfolding carnival of the 2016 US presidential election. As shock-activists at *ConservativeMomma* put it, with folksy suburban charm: "I am so over people saying that Trump and Hillary are the same, . . . ummm not in the slightest."[69] Even the indefatigable editors of *Counter Punch* let a recent piece of earnest, socially located, and basically sound analysis past its more theatrical censors: graduate student Nick Pemberton humbly complicates the racial dynamics of the electoral day, noting how "[w]e spent months basically saying that Trump and Hillary are the same and that identity politics are a sham. Not entirely true, obviously."[70] In the lead-up to 2016, academic politics exploded in what Edward Erwin aptly dubs "The New McCarthyism": the Kipnis affair, scholars sacked or blackballed on mere rumor, the absurd monstrosity of Rachel Dolezal (and concomitant *Hypatia* kerfuffle at Rebecca Tuvel's complex treatment), campus anti-racist activism that seemed—in stark contrast to the Black Civil Rights tradition—barely able to formulate a serious demand or functional reform proposal, the pitiful farce of the punching-Nazis "debate," itself driven by a culture of shock-careerism and mob-machismo among putatively leftist academics exploiting ongoing injustices and deep racial, intercultural, and gendered wounds for a status-seeking bump in professional capital; around newly crystallizing, unvarnished hierarchies erected by the giddy commodification of human suffering and grievance.[71] And what else? When well-meaning and earnest Black Lives Matters youth activists disrupted a rally of democratic socialist and Black civil rights veteran Bernie Sanders, the collective shoe had already dropped.

The ongoing apologetics for the more curious aspects of late-Millennial activist tactics by left intellectuals and journalists began to fray. By inverse contrast to the vanguard of the 1960s coalition, where courageous, self-disciplined, and highly articulate student activists lead the way—by their moral *esprit*, functional demands, intelligent tactics, and through a meaningful debate between principled non-violence and *a political violence governed by principle*—in *forcing* politicians and intellectuals of the day to take notice and respond seriously, today's youth activists have been ill-equipped by educators. The contributions of grassroots youth activism across various fronts of struggle cannot and ought not be denied or demeaned; quite the reverse. The problem does not reside with youth—reducible to mere fallout of generational change in culture or leadership—but rather with their educators and the pitch of social justice media and education untethered to serious social science, policy platforms, or a coalitional political program. For all the ongoing successes of post-1989 identity politics, and partly fueled by the understudied effects of post-internet processes of socialization, idpol is also saddled with the general *infantilization of activist political culture*. Until Bernie's improbable rise as a force in US electoral politics, the near total lack of real-time and methodologically cogent class and institutional analysis rendered the problem acute, an issue not addressed with by-now formulaic nods to the jargon of Marxologists or anarchist appropriations untethered to empirically serious sociology. The responsibility for this rests primarily with *Marxists themselves*. Outside of ongoing serious work by a few historians, aesthetic theorists, geographers, and sociologists, post-1989 Marxism beat a swift retreat to the libertarian wing of sacred tradition, and could manage little more than predictable analyses of a world that longer exists on the technological and institutional terms assumed by holy writ. In the midst of reemerging Alt-right zombies, a veritable rainbow coalition of putatively left-wing activists, celebrities, journalists, academics, and self-avowed socialists endorsed none other than Putin chum and recipient of Moscow largesse Jill Stein for 2016: Oliver Stone, Medea Benjamin, Susan Sarandon, Camilla Page, Chris Hedges, Harvey Wasserman, Cornel West, Kevin Zeese, Richard Wolf, Jesse Ventura, Marsha Coleman-Adebayo, the Internationalist Socialist Organization, Richard Stallman, Socialist Alternative, editorialists at Russia Today, and more. Rampant and ostentatious anti-Hillary vitriol among left-wing academics across social media legitimated the popular journalistic chorus of "they're both the same," itself peppered by generational conservative misogyny and anti-Hillary vilification, that quite likely exerted a climatic effect for depressing progressive turnout.[72] As *Vox*'s Tara Golshan succinctly distills,

> In Michigan, Wisconsin, and Pennsylvania, one could . . . blame third parties for the outcome. In Michigan, Clinton lost by less than a percentage point, a deficit she could have recovered from with half of Stein's votes. Again in Wisconsin and Pennsylvania, where Clinton lost by one point, Jill Stein's votes would have covered her loss. Had Clinton won all three states, she would have won the election.[73]

There is of course universal electoral blame to pass out for the Trump disaster, but the only corners of US political cultural that seem most immune to relevant critical self-reflection are those who, in fact, are most immune to relevant critical self-reflection: Trump's racist loyalists and their hapless allies among the self-baptized "radicals" in left-wing identity politics.

I don't want to overstate the complicity of Marxist criticism in the post-1989 identitarian transformation of left politics so much as emphasize the objective and still unfolding crisis it involves. Cogent critical and ongoing work by Marxist scholars include well-known contributions by Keenga-Yamahtta Taylor, Aijaz Ahmad, Fredric Jameson, Ueno Chizuko, Benita Parry, Terry Eagleton, Nikita Dhawan, Slavoj Žižek, Asad Haider, Nancy Fraser, Cornel West, David Harvey, and Vivek Chibber, among others. Yet for all the sound dimensions of Eagleton's infamous swipe at Gayatri Spivak, his frequent use of the "reformist/revolutionary" binary never quite comes to what exactly a revolutionary politics could be today, or what footballers should expect of a global socialist revolution.[74] For all of Žižek's masterfully contrarian comedy as the epochal analyst of the more fanciful corners of the post-1989 left psyche, he has singularly fueled the most symptomatic of its vacuous gestures: defiant calls to imagine alternatives to capitalism without anyone ever managing a functional proposal. The touché of intramural jousts among intellectual celebrities has become a central organizing dynamic of political consciousness today, in its ecological links with periodic bursts of popular anarchism notably lacking in any specific policy orientation, let alone the gumption to seize institutional levers outside the immediate lights of the news cycle. To seize levers, one must care enough to do more than join in a collective "*no!*" now and then. To seize levers takes actual and relatively holistic knowledge, teamwork, and understanding the difference between tactics, strategy, and the normativity that informs them. For all that, still: few have more consistently and effectively challenged the more questionable assumptions of unfolding left struggle than comrades like Eagleton and Žižek.

As emerging critical voices like Asad Haider and Chi Chi Shi contribute to the unfolding conversation, one may retrospectively peer at what now seems quite crucial critical insight in youthful work by today's veterans, for example: Cornel West and Nancy Fraser, both deploying normative resources inaccessible to classical Marxism. As early as 1985, West's own Marx-peppered Black pragmatism took aim at "[t]he Foucaultian model" of left critique, because it zeros in on "power-laden discourses in the service of neither restoration, reformation, nor revolution, but rather of revolt."[75] Fraser echoes West in a parallel way, by a soberly prescient critique of Derrida's more aspirational fantasies. In 1991, she confronted deconstruction's pretense of methodological profundity, in general but here for specifically legal analysis:

> Attempts to understand the relationship of violence and law through, say, critical social theory, political sociology, or cultural studies will be deprivileged as merely empirical and hence, comparatively superficial.[76]

West and Fraser jointly pinpoint the central, defining characteristic of post-1989 left analysis and culture, baptized in the name of poor ol' Gramsci, incoherently worshiped by Hardt and Negri, and rendered operational by Laclau and Moffe, namely: *the alliance between the respective normative negativisms and legal nihilisms of Nietzschean and vulgar-Marxist vintage.*

Perhaps the most professionally tragic living scholar in the world today, Christine Sypnowich's untimely *The Concept of Socialist Law* (Clarendon) holds the singular honor of mounting the only piece of positive and relatively coherent Marxist legal philosophy *in all of world history* (and with Hermann Cohen and Hermann Heller, one of only three I'm aware of in broader socialist tradition). In the best tradition of analytic Marxism (though not without internal philosophical problems), the book was published in 1990 just as history rendered its institutional context of immediate relevance moot. One central front of socialist politics today lay in engaging Sypnowich's path-breaking work for the ongoing renewal of social democratic popular politics. Her sober review of actual Soviet legal practice yields a stinging rebuke to left cynicism and naiveté on this front: "injustice of these practices may prompt the conclusion that law had indeed 'withered away' in the Soviet Union, though not in the sense forecast by Marx and Engels."[77] Muslims in China or Myanmar today might agree.

An economic correlate to Sypnowich's work emerged in the scholarship of a new generation by sociologist Johanna Bockman. Her *Markets in the*

Name of Socialism: The Left-Wing Origins of Neoliberalism (Stanford, 2011) argues that the neoliberal reconstruction of the post-1989 world order appropriated and exploited the novel ideas of central European socialist economists. Against the classical Marxist critique of capitalism, and its reliance on the labor theory of value, these socialist economists contributed to developments in neoclassical economic theory. Bockman goes on to show how these theoretical developments were put into practice through experiments with social ownership, worker self-management, competitive leasing, and even "contractual socialism." Over-against both its Marxist and Keynesian critics, Bockman holds that neoliberal appropriation of neoclassical ideas harbors "decades of radical democratic and socialist experiments."[78] On Barker's perhaps too expansive reading, the quite startling takeaway of Bockman's analysis is that "there is no inherent affinity between neoclassical theory, market institutions, and capitalism."[79] Debatable, to say the least.

Among Bockman's contributions is to have underlined a central lacuna running through—with important exceptions—the near totality of post-1989 traditions of neoliberal critique. North Korea and the radicalized state capitalism of the Chinese Communist Party aside, and without any actually existing industrial socialisms to meaningfully compare, Bockman pinpoints the near total lack of *an intelligible theory of democratic institutions* that her own Polanyian premises don't specifically treat. On the one hand, she seems to endorse Yugoslav and Hungarian experiments with "decentralization," and "competitive market[s]," as a means "to expand . . . individual freedom" and "loosen" centralized state power. On the other hand, she holds that "disembedding the market from the state obscures the very clear argument these economists made for particular state and corporate institutions necessary for markets to thrive."[80] She summons markets, as a potential site of social self-determination, against state power, and summons the state against unfettered markets as a condition for their just function. This forms a relatively clear companion problem to Sypnowich's critique of legal nihilism.

Finally, Sypnowich and Bockman's contributions should be put in conversation with the impeccable scholarship of perhaps the sole surviving methodologically and politically serious Marxist on planet earth today: Vivek Chibber (an honor I hesitate to bestow as a bearer of bad tidings to the more blind fancies of an era). No competent reader can fail to note Chibber's deflationary—and in my view, quite promising—attempt to rescue empirically grounded, sociologically serious Marxist analysis from all the fun destroying its credibility; while putting it to politically serious work in well-grounded popular writing at *Jacobin* and elsewhere. His sound critique of classical determinism, and concomitant defense of a modest though meaningful explanatory role for "productive relations" within the theory of social forms, already funded his groundbreaking work on the contrasting fortunes of postwar "developmental states."[81] His signature mix of analytic perspicuity, argument force, rich engagement in empirical detail, theoretical modesty, and rhetorical humility was on full display in his *Postcolonial Theory and the Specter of Capital* (Verso, 2013). A calmly executed demolition of some core empirical and theoretical claims of Subaltern Studies, it generated an amusing—though also disappointing—uproar among mandarins in the left intelligentsia. Chibber quite successfully defends the universal dimensions of science and politics, though Spivak is certainly right that social-scientific theory engages unique contexts and that political commitments find unique expressions across cultures. Insofar as post-colonial theory is itself a normatively oriented, interdisciplinary social science, the hubbub was a tad anticlimactic. Chibber and Spivak embody two necessary and complementary poles essential to the practice of good social science: theoretical rigor and sensitivity to empirical situations and materials; and debates like these help all participants recalibrate and refine their respective models, tools, and fields.

One of the more interesting dimensions of the Chibber-Spivak debate is what it discloses about us as scientists—*people of truth*, and partisans—*people who care*. A good dust-up now and then can help clarify the stakes involved between our own specializations and the broader ends to which we are jointly committed. Louis Proyect's report on a debate between Chibber and Partha Chatterjee presses the point. As Proyect narrates,

> Chatterjee outdid Chibber with a Marxist purism calculated to make Chibber look like an utter piker by comparison, including a jibe that his critic appeared committed to Rawlsian contract theory, a charge to which Chibber plead guilty.[82]

The more athletic dimensions of tribe Marx aside, Proyect's jab at Chibber's Rawlsian interests is revealing.[83] If Chatterjee is indeed a Marxist purist, the jab works. But then Proyect must concede that Chatterjee is doing universal Marxist "science" and thus not bound by specifically moral and political modes of justification—only scientific modes of justification. This would seem to confirm one of Chibber's own arguments in *PSC*. But Marxism is not only a social science, but also a political practice, and as such owes justification to others with different political commitments. If Rawls helps

Chibber do just that, and in such a way that is grounded in good Marxist social science, why is it a problem? Say Chibber was religiously committed. He'd perhaps then access a different discourse and procedure of justification, but justification would here again get done. Is Chibber ridiculed because he's a Rawlsian on normative justificatory questions, and not something else? What precisely does it mean to be a "Marxist purist" on normative justificatory questions? Proyect never mentions. And truth be told, for the library of literature that constitutes the expansive archive of team Marx, the question itself enunciates one core dimension of Marxism's crisis, especially in the post-1989 era.

Sypnowich, Bockman, and Chibber all contribute something new and unique to the Marxist and more broadly socialist tradition. First, that they are socialists at all is enough to know *they care*. Next, as scholars, they beautifully exemplify what it means to be self-critical. Because they care about socialism, they want it to pass muster on practical, scientific, moral, and political grounds, and therefore deeply engage both the best and worst in socialist tradition in light of the problems and possibilities of the day. Their willingness to undertake the *discipline* of substantively criticizing a tradition they love *shows* that they actually care and are really committed to socialism (and are not merely deploying jargon to adorn themselves with a mantle of "radicality"). Finally, all three have demonstrably focused all their creativity toward contributing something relatively *new*, but also intelligible on broadly traditional socialist commitments. Without having engaged in the discipline of working through the tradition in light of the present, they would have never been positioned to *actually* innovate. If Marxist analysis and socialist politics are to have a meaningful future, we all must do what Sypnowich, Bockman, and Chibber are doing, which of course does not necessarily mean endorsing all their conclusions or unquestionably taking on their innovations. But it does mean this: if you want to be a socialist today, you must contend with their work, and meet it with more than a stern defense of holy writ, erudite lectures on the opinions of comrades of yore, ridicule, or theatrical displays of purely tactical *je ne sais quoi*

Chibber especially is worth our engagement.[84] In his own way, he integrates both Sypnowich and Bockman's contributions within an actually functional, theoretically modest, social scientific explanatory paradigm, using all the best tools the social sciences have refined for more than a century. Because Marxism is not only social science, but also political practice, it can countenance an intelligible spectrum of normative plurality, and in fact needs that plurality to move forward and keep it a living tradition that enriches human culture with good science and a smart politics that actually empowers the working classes. Whatever your indigenous culture and the wisdom it hands down, if you yourself see that it can sing with Marx and the broader socialist tradition, then you yourself can bring something both new and ancient to the tradition and politics of Marxism.

One the varied tasks of post-colonial theory is not merely the good ongoing work of documenting past crimes and analyzing their structuring role in current geopolitical social problems, but also equipping the populations of both former colonies and former colonizers to actually communicate and jointly work through the highly complex issues in play. The socialist tradition forms a ground for transnational solidarity and coordinated action. To even contemplate certain possibilities for advancing global justice, for example: reparations for colonialism (a proposal I support), requires preparing publics for it, and no one is better placed than Marxist comrades in post-colonial theory to do this. As a normatively oriented, interdisciplinary social science, the explicit commitments and grounding presuppositions of post-colonial theory self-designate a set of very important tasks, as: (1) *encultured comrade*, a morally and politically committed, creative human being who cares about others; (2) *critic*, positioned to competently identify and exhaustively document moral harms and social injustices across at least two distinct cultures; (3) *scientific analyst*, able to competently classify and assess information relevant to (i) identifying causes and motivations culpably at stake in a moral harm or social injustice under analysis, (ii) understanding, with a relative though grounded holism, the debilitating effects of the harm for victims first, and victimizers second, (iii) formulating hypotheses for how those effects can be effectively treated for the relevant class of patient (including, of course, each patient's own story and the histories it documents), and actually testing them; (4) *healer*, with morally grounded solidarity, in culturally competent idioms, collaboratively apply the testably best remedies appropriate to a region of effective harm in question; (5) *translator*, the ability to communicate universally intelligible information to at least two culturally distinct populations; (6) *encultured comrade*,[2] aiding at least two culturally distinct moral and political polities by equipping them with the knowledge, communicative resources, and practical direction needed to voluntarily practice mutual acknowledgment, working-through, debate about fair restitution, forgiveness, memorialization, and joint comradeship for a collective future. Embodying these tasks and carrying them out will take time, but we already have a growing, maturing, and analytically rich post-colonial tradition to work with. But repeating the cycle will generate the ground for (7) increasingly determinate forms of cultural and material restitution that are meaningful and fair to each relevant, internally differentiated population. Post-colonial theory, done well as culturally embedded, normatively oriented social science, will finally (8) contribute vitally important context-bound information necessary to advance coalitional, international social democratic struggle. As it builds bodies of knowledge, responds to grounded criticism, and refines itself over time, post-colonial theory will increasingly play an irreplaceable role in the hard work of moving toward world peace, in helping broker bilateral and multilateral reparative policies, in negotiating fair and enforceable trade deals that codify win-win labor protections across different populations, refining serious intercultural curricula and pedagogies that empower publics to understand the best and worst of the past and the shared grounds for a better common future, and above all: help to shift the locus of global democracy from "great powers" hegemony to renewed and reformed transnational democratic institutions. This is merely an inkling of the high calling post-colonial theory has assigned itself, and we all should read, engage the scholarship and arguments, loyally criticize, and listen to all the best scholars and activists helping us win a better future. As a socialist, in my view we'll have no shot of even approximating the long-forgotten dreams of the left: world peace, global economic parity and prosperity, ecological justice, and a free world stewarded by every living tradition that inhabits our planet, without the irreplaceable contributions of Marxist and post-colonial comrades.

This noted, Sypnowich, Bockman, and Chibber are in a certain sense the bearers of bad news (depending on one's style of socialist commitment). In truth, they each confirm in different ways a central problem that deeply worried G. A. Cohen, motivated some of his best work, and occasioned his own consideration of the possibility of "market socialism."[85] Sypnowich highlights the well-known problem that Marxism, in fact, has no normative legal theory. Bockman highlights two important and well-known problems: (1) as all competent economists know, the labor theory of value is defunct; and (2) Marxism, in fact, has no normative political theory. Fully aware of this, Chibber marks out what is enduring in Marxist theory, demonstrates its value by putting it to cogent and innovative use, and utilizes Rawls and the best of current economics to defend Marxism's analytic relevance, and to ground its current political, pedagogic, and experimental tasks. All these comrades complicate current inherited assumptions and popular habits in the tribe, but they blaze a way forward to renew an insightful, innovative, popularly embedded, normatively oriented, and practically effective socialist politics.

Altogether, they confirm that leftists mourned for a reason in the immediate wake of 1989, and as observers of China already know well: core parts of classical Marxist theory died with the Soviet Union. But Cohen, Sypnowich, Bockman, and Chibber also demonstrate by their own innovative scientific and normative work that mourning is but for a season. We really do have a functional and relatively programmatic way forward. I encourage you all to read them. However absurd it will appear to dogmatists and painful it will seem to activists, and grounded in a critical dialogue with all four theorists: I nominate Chibber's *Our Road to Power* as a rallying point and fragile beginning for a new era in Marxist theory and practice.[86] An era that scours social networks, the internet, and library databases for every faithful comrade who has been thinking, organizing, and acting creatively throughout the desert of high "postmodernism," and think with them, argue with them, and improve them. Exclude any perspective or proposal that doesn't justify itself in light of the necessarily transnational scope of the democratic control of capital. Study everything that seems to work, and evaluate why it works, and if it ought to work that way. Economic nationalism and reactionary fascism are two heads of the same beast. That beast is in part loosed by the recurrent pathologies of liberal capitalism and the economic injustice it involves, but we can no longer treat democratic institutions, legal architectures, and moral justification as mere bourgeois contrivances. The biggest lessons of 1989 are these: (1) markets aren't going anywhere, and Stalinism has proven that we probably shouldn't want them gone; markets are a common good; (2) capital is an inherently international phenomenon, and as such deliberative democracy at local, national, and transnational levels aren't going anywhere, at least if capital is to actually become subject to global, multilateral, and democratic control; and (3) normative and legal nihilism are chimera, because it's precisely through normatively justified and legally structured, transparent, and codified international agreements that we will tame the beast and multilaterally monitor and enforce democratic control, reinstitute labor protections, enact innovations in corporate law to incentive worker ownership, enact Piketty's surcharges on stock trades across every market to finance sustainable development and reparative policies to reduce ongoing wealth asymmetries between Global North and South, and co-organize the working class into constituent blocks capable of wielding real power in electoral politics. Such is the horizon of authentic Marxist theory and practice today. It will take innovative and experimental work in economics, political theory, organizational systems theory, legal philosophy, cultural theory, international relations theory, post-colonial theory, and much else. As Bockman shows us: it was socialist economists who supplied

Chicago-school libertarians with some of the tools they used to help defeat actually existing socialism. Now an insurgent socialism will seize back those tools—and anything else of good use—with new and renewed competence in the project of advancing our originary project: sustainable economic and ecological justice for all the people actually doing the work of keeping this good world dancing.

II.e. Whence and Why Neo-Nativism?

Trump, Xi, Putin, Modi, Bolsonaro, Netanyahu, Bumbling Boris, Zwelithini, Le Pen, Rouhani, Abe, Okamura, Duterte, Meuthen, Erdoğan, Macri, Wilders, Bedie, Salvini, Maduro, Kaczynski, Piñera, El-Sisi, Hlaing, Åkesson, politicians in South Africa (for example, Maimane, Lekota, and Mkongi), Abascal (with an assist from Forcadell, Sànchez, and other stooges for the Catalan bourgeoisie). Beyond the exploitive games on display in the worst corners of cultural performativity, why global neo-nativism? Welcoming, of course, finer-grained calibrations for each particular context, political scientist Jan Rovný suggests the beginnings of an answer to this question. With focus on European contexts, he asks, "What happened to the left?"[87] Insofar as neo-nativism is a truly global phenomenon, and considered historically names a singularizing event that calls for explanation, the deeper structural components of Rovný's analysis are generalizable.

Analyzing the collapse in popular support for historic socialist parties, he looks beyond more immediate catalysts to "the consequences of a structural development that we have been witnessing for at least three decades." He writes,

> The weakening of the political left has been long in the making. It has been largely caused by deep structural and technological change that has altered the face of European societies, changed the economic patterns of the continent, and given a renewed vigor to politics of identity. In this process, traditional left-wing parties have lost not only the grasp of their main political narrative, they have lost much of their traditional electorates. These electorates did not so much "switch" away from the left, they have rather disappeared as a comprehensible social group.

On Rovný's account, the electoral power of the pre-1989 left politics was grounded in relatively stable and intergenerational social formations. Its success at winning labor protections, protections for minorities, meaningful redistributive policies, the expansion and improvement of public education, the (once) universal accessibility of higher education, played a role in eroding the very base of its electoral success. He explains,

> Somewhat paradoxically, the left's success precipitated its own demise in a dialectic fashion. First, the emancipation of the working class—primarily the extension of access to higher education—changed the working class and its dependence on left-wing subcultures and organizations. Second, the left's enabling of the search for rights allowed younger generations to seek personal liberation from traditional hierarchies, including those of the left. The traditional working class as we imagine it from the times of Henry Ford does not exist anymore. . . . Today's working class is much less visible, and much more atomised. Today's working class are the masses of unskilled service workers who predominantly cook, clean, or drive. Often, their jobs are short-term or part-time, and low-paying. These people do not come into contact with each other nearly as much as the traditional factory-floor workers did. They are more often than not from diverse minority backgrounds, and thus are separated by cultural boundaries. In short, these people have significantly reduced ability to organize, and they do not. . . . [T]heir political belonging is weak, and—in the absence of a formative subculture—it is malleable. The extension of access to higher education has increased the individual ability of people to process more complex information and make their own choices. As education also brings better jobs, this process has created more cognitively and financially independent citizens. In the context of the changing working class and the developing political supply, the traditional left parties became parties of the new middle class— . . . it slowly but surely abandoned the new "precariat"—the new service working classes and those in poor or irregular employment.

In the United States and United Kingdom, over-against more sunny evaluations of low unemployment statistics, those numbers include the category of "involuntary part-time work," for example, folks who want stable full-time jobs but are forced to contend with poor paying, precarious part-time gigs. Involuntary part-time work is a whopping 40 percent higher than it was in 2000.[88] Rovný seems right that "the traditional left opened a political breach—a gaping political vacuum around those seeking economic protection, and a certain cultural traditionalism." He moreover grounds his analysis in the growth of "transnationalism," for example, postmodern economic globalization.

Globalization has generated a systemically structured antagonism between cosmopolitan, urban metropoli, and traditionalist rural peripheries, dividing societies into

> those who, while happily consuming cheaper products, earn their income in either sheltered (public) or internationally competitive sectors on the one hand, and those, on the other hand, whose livelihood is threatened by foreign competition in the form of imported products, and imported laborers. Transnationalism thus creates economic winners and losers, who are increasingly keenly aware of their status in our globalised societies.

Crucially, Rovný continues, "Transnationalism redefines the political space by dissociating economic progressivism from socio-cultural openness. . . . In doing so, [it] effectively shatters the old electoral coalition of the left." Forced to politically compete with neo-nativist entrepreneurs and demagogues, "the west resembles the east, and the mainstream left everywhere is left out in the cold." The withering of social democratic left politics "has been long in the making," and has been "largely caused by deep structural and technological change that has altered the face of . . . societies, changed the economic patterns . . . , and given a renewed vigor to politics of identity." To leftists actually doing their jobs in the post-1989 era, Rovný's diagnosis is not exactly news. But it's an extremely valuable contribution that explicitly connects actual social and labor-market dynamics to the sociology of left politics today. He achieves an analysis that should inform strategies for mass mobilization, pedagogy, and policy construction.

I have said little about the internet in this chapter's genealogy, for a few good reasons. Noting the ongoing good work by open net activists, and the novel ways it has empowered organization for mass protest, the left-anarchist promises of yore for its revolutionary potentials have never actually materialized, and if anything have helped empower authoritarian actors to better manage populations and threats, while providing new ways to destabilize democratic processes. The role of the internet in post-1989 processes of socialization and popular politics remains ambiguous and as yet ill understood. Rovny's analysis of the "precariat" suggests an apt analogy between domestic labor-markets throughout the globe—with the urban/rural dynamics it involves—and the internet's transformation of the music industry. On the one hand, the internet has in one sense democratized the industry: anyone can create music and market it without the mediation of record labels and other middlemen. The way enfleshed, brick-and-mortar, pre-internet fan cultures functioned has in one sense been replicated online: hosting a teeming mass of musician and fan niches that power the occasional rise of artists from relative anonymity to a popular market-wide audience. On the other hand, file sharing and cognate problems have made it nearly impossible for artists themselves to be fairly compensated for their labor and the intrinsic quality of their art. The internet has presided over the balkanization of communicative cultures, grounding the rise of eisegenic echo-chambers partly to blame for the breakdown of serious national debate, exploited by Faux News, corporate-funded disinformation, "alt-fact" peddlers, demagogues like Glen Greenwald, and his allies in Russia's FSB. The internet cannot do what brick-and-mortar culture once did: require fans and artists to communicate, directly and in person, with other members of a diverse local community in organizing and coordinating relevant events. Thanks to the laws of physics, biosocial reality, and creative moral desire, the internet excludes concrete information that less canny writers—most working folk—cannot always convey in online discussion: even political enemies are human beings with whom we must co-construct publics capable of stewarding meaningful debate, and that recognizes the best voices and marginalizes the worst. This might be less of a problem in diverse urban metropoli, where daily working life presses this same education. Admitting variability for national contexts, this is probably why the fiercest resistance to insurgent nationalisms resides in big cities. In the less socially diverse rural margins, populations in national demographic majorities feel marginalized, aggrieved, and excluded from both the economic benefits of globalization and from a recognizable place in mainstream public cultures.

Aspiring artists today correspond to Rovny's "precariate" in the analogous structural obstructions that impede their ability to effectively organize. Outside those able to leverage artistic success for lucrative Netflix deals, even successful popular artists have been forced to expand tour schedules to compensate for the paltry revenue generated from royalties by record deals, radio, and streaming services. Forced to cope directly with the realities of the market, and with analogues in gamer culture: aspiring artists primarily participate as hobbyists in virtual communities in whatever spare time left them after working three jobs. Aspiring artists *are* the precariat, and their objective situation will require creative policy architectures and specifically legislative remedies supported by organized and feisty civil society advocacy, in order to help collaboratively empower their own self-organization. For that to happen, it'll take a lot more than a generalized politics of negation. God bless Bernie Sanders and Liz Warren, they and various social movements are lighting up a serious and functional way forward.

II.F. FORWARD!

Before concluding, I want to point out who has consistently been on point on crucial matters, both intellectually and within social movements. Having already detailed major and widely known threads and blocks of the actually existing left, I focus here on too often overlooked participants and contributors. Having already defended the irreplaceability of Marxist and post-colonial theory in the folding project of left-struggle, it must be said that some of the core issues I highlighted were identified long ago by Adorno, Horkheimer, and Habermas on the one hand, and Husserl, Heidegger, Arendt, and Levinas on the other. Before acknowledging their insights, I briefly treat others of note.

II.f.i. Light's of Russian Modernity

Nineteenth- and twentieth-century Russian literature stands as one of the most accomplished literary archives in the world. It can be read as an unfolding study in the cultural dynamics of modernity. Levinas's favorite poet, Alexander Pushkin, led the way in a literary ethos that includes Gogol, Dostoyevsky, Tolstoy, Chernychevsky, Turgenev, Chukovskaya, Gorky, Zamyatin, Sholohov, Pasternak, and Solzhenitsyn. It reflects a uniquely Russian style of syncopated romanticism and realism, mediated by a nearly mystical sensibility. It forms a spiritual tapestry that is intertwined with long-stifled Russian democratic political traditions. From a historical point of view, Russian citizens have endured centuries of bad governance and sublimely horrific suffering. Some of the dissident and defeated among its political traditions are worth more of our time.

The mother of Russian modernity was a member of the pre-October Constitutional Democratic Party, colloquially dubbed the *Kadets*. They supported worker's rights, Jewish emancipation, universal suffrage, and the transfer of local governance throughout the empire from appointed heads to local representatives. After the Bolshevik's demagogued and co-opted February of 1917, the *Kadets* disbursed or emigrated when Lenin disbanded the Duma. Prominent *Kadets* include noted poet Konstantin Balmont, Crimean political leader Solomon Krym, historian Pavel Miliukov, and activist and philanthropist Sofia Panina. Though she hailed from the aristocracy, Panina was a practicing Christian and at the vanguard of the progressive struggles of the day. According to *Wikipedia*,

> In 1903 Panina built one central building to house all of the diverse services she and Peshekhonova had started in the 1890s, known as Ligovsky People's House (Narodnyi Dom), for working-class residents of the same impoverished district on southern outskirts of Saint Petersburg. . . . Its evening courses and literary circles provided a meeting-place for working-class men with socialist sympathies, and during the 1905 Revolution, Panina opened Ligovsky People's House to various political groups for meetings and rallies. On 9 May 1906 Vladimir Lenin addressed his first mass meeting in Russia there. Panina also was a co-founder and major financial supporter of the Russian Society for the Protection of Women in 1900, an anti-prostitution organization. In addition to building schools and hospitals on her various estates, she also provided assistance to countless individuals. In 1901 she loaned her Crimean estate, Gaspra, to the novelist Leo Tolstoy, then suffering from a life-threatening illness; Tolstoy and his family lived at her estate for almost a year.

After February of 1917, she became vice minister of State Welfare and vice minister of Education for the provisional government and played a central role in trying to stave off Bolshevik cooptation of the democratic revolution. She was among the first victims of what became a long and venerable tradition: Bolshevik show trials. Before a panel of seven male judges and a gawking crowd, she denied the transparently bogus charges. According to Adele Lindenmeyr, a comrade interrupted the farce and asked to address the court:

> [He] identified himself as N. I. Ivanov, a factory worker by occupation and a Socialist Revolutionary by political affiliation. . . . Ivanov passionately defended Panina's educational and cultural work during the years of tsarist repression. This count-

ess, undeterred by the "people's sweat and smoke," personally conducted classes for them, "lighting in the working masses the holy fire of knowledge." Emphasizing her maternal dedication and love for the common working people, he told the court how working people found "light and joy" at her Narodnyi Dom, while their children received more affection there than in their own families.[89]

This man's testimony probably saved her life. She eventually settled in New York City and collaborated with Tolstoy's daughter in founding the Tolstoy Foundation.

One of the brightest stars among the comrades of Russian modernity stands Orthodox priest and tireless union organizer Father Georgy Gapon. In 1904, Gapon organized the *Assembly of Russian Factory and Mill Workers of St. Petersburg*, a reformist union that grew to twelve active branches throughout Russia. The obdurate authoritarianism of Russian capitalists and aristocracy radicalized him, and he began collaborating with revolutionaries. In 1905, he organized a worker's march appealing to the tsar for improved conditions, fairer wages, and an eight-hour workday. As the crowd marched toward the Winter Palace, they donned religious icons and sang patriotic songs, appealing to the tsar's sense of justice as a leader and supposed religious benefactor. When Gapon and the workers reached the Palace, the police opened fire. Thousands were killed. It was dubbed "Bloody Sunday," the first of too many in the twentieth century. This event shocked the population of the Russian Empire, undermining the tsar's legitimacy, and helped generate the conditions for February of 1917. In response to the massacre, Gapon anathematized the tsar and called on workers to take action against the regime. Forced to flee St. Petersburg, he spent time in Geneva and London, meeting other revolutionary Russian émigrés like Georgy Plekhanov, Vladimir Lenin, and Peter Kropotkin. Henry Nevinson of *The Daily Chronicle* called Gapon "the man who struck the first blow at the heart of tyranny and made the old monster sprawl." According to *Spartacus Education*,

> When he heard the news of Bloody Sunday Leon Trotsky decided to return to Russia. He realized that Father Gapon had shown the way forward: "Now no one can deny that the general strike is the most important means of fighting. The twenty-second of January was the first political strike, even if he was disguised

under a priest's cloak. One need only add that revolution in Russia may place a democratic workers' government in power."[90]

Gapon's first loyalty was to the worker's welfare above all. On his return to St. Petersburg, he was willing to work with members of the regime if allowed to continue his trade union activities. For this, he was murdered by his own socialist "comrades," a harbinger of the fate of millions of Russians throughout the twentieth century.

Over the intervening decade, with ongoing tsarist oppression and the catastrophe of WWI: the Russian people had enough. On February 23, 1917, on National Women's Day: a spontaneous mass uprising erupted in Petrograd. The city's "governor, AP Balk, said they consisted of 'ladies from society, lots more peasant women, student girls and, compared with earlier demonstrations, not many workers.'"[91] Women led what became a more than 200,000 strong mass protest demanding an end to food rationing, the war, and the tsarist regime itself. The city's garrison mutinied and joined the revolution, and Nicholas abdicated a few days later. A Provisional Government was formed to restore order and prepare a Constituent Assembly, with power shared between the Duma and the Petrograd Soviets and led by a coalition of progressives with collaboration between *Kadets* and Mensheviks. In a state of national crisis, the coalition managed a stunning array of legislative achievements. Forced to deal with unfolding chaos, implementation of these policies was slow and interrupted by a variety of problems. Vice-Chairman of the Petrograd Soviets Alexander Kerensky details what the Duma and Soviets were in the process of instituting. I quote him at length:

> Everything that generations of the Russian people had dreamed about during their century-long struggle for freedom, right and justice was given to Russia at one stroke. . . . First of all, of course, the Provisional Government granted a full political amnesty and abolished capital punishment . . . The government likewise did away with all extraordinary courts, making trial by jury the only form of justice for both criminal and political offences; it abolished all religious, national, and class limitations; proclaimed full liberty of conscience; restored the independence of the Orthodox Church from the State; introduced completely equal rights for women; immediately called a special commission to draft the electoral law for the Constituent Assembly;

abolished punishment by exile; promulgated absolute liberty of the press, union, and assembly, and the inviolability of the individual; abrogated all the measures which infringed on the independence of the judicature; urgently drafted new standing orders for the election of urban and rural local authorities, based on universal suffrage and proportional representation; did away with all political and economic discriminatory measures against the peasantry; extended the rural self-government principle down to the "volost" . . . ; re-established the constitution of Finland; proclaimed the independence of Poland; appointed a commission for the introduction of self-government in Lithuania, the Ukraine etc.; reformed the administration of Turkestan and the Caucasus. . . . The eight hour day was introduced at all the government works and factories, as well as in private undertakings; works' committees were formed; industrial arbitration was instituted; labor representation on the Board of Trade was introduced; a Ministry of Labor was set up; a grain monopoly was established, and prices for essential commodities were fixed; a new law concerning the co-operatives was prepared, which gave the movement exceptional possibilities; the entire military code was revised.[92]

Then Lenin and Uncle Joe showed up.

In contrast to the hundreds of thousands who participated in the February uprising from across Russian society,

[In October,] [p]robably no more than 10,000 Bolshevized soldiers, sailors, and workers participated, seizing key governmental institutions in Petrograd and arresting the ministers of the feckless provisional government. There were no more than a handful of casualties. The Bolsheviks' seizure of power was deliberately timed by Lenin to immediately precede the convening of the national Congress of Soviets—the bodies of worker, peasant, soldier, and sailor representatives that had sprung up across the nation in the wake of the Tsar's fall.[93]

Julius Martov was one the most widely esteemed socialists of the day and leader of the Mensheviks. There had been a constant struggle for movement leadership between him and Lenin. For years he too graciously opposed

Lenin's authoritarian vision of Party structure and leadership, instead endorsing wide popular participation. He was in exile in February, and initially opposed Menshevik participation in the Provisional Government. This was partly due to his struggle to counter Lenin's demagoguery and defend his own revolutionary credentials. After the Bolsheviks seized power, Martov immediately called for a " 'united democratic government' based on the parties of the soviet. His proposal was met with 'torrents of applause.' "[94] According to Meyerson, "[Martov] encouraged the new government to reach out to other groups and social forces."[95] For this, Trotsky publicly humiliated him in a theatrical denouncement at a subsequent meeting of the Council of Soviets. Martov walked out. According to the scholars at *Wikipedia*, just as he cleared the last row, a young man spoke up: " 'And we amongst ourselves had thought, Martov would at least remain with us.' Martov stopped, and with a characteristic movement, tossed up his head to emphasize his reply: 'One day you will understand the crime in which you are taking part.' " Lenin later abolished the Menshevik party altogether, and Martov became a near total pariah. Later, "when a factory section chose Martov as their delegate ahead of Lenin in a Soviet election, it found its supplies reduced soon afterwards." A comrade to the end, Martov died in exile just after launching the newspaper *Socialist Messenger*. Stalin finished Lenin's good work, conducting a Menshevik Trial during the Great Purge in 1931.

Peddled by fascists and leftists alike, the notion that Russia is somehow immune to democracy or illiberal by nature is a *lie*. Its own organic democratic experiment and burgeoning modernity were disrupted by the remnants of Tsarist decadence, the horrors of WWI, brutal oligarchs, and the sadistic thuggery of Vladimir Lenin, Joseph Stalin, and Vladimir Putin. In the immortal words of comrade Mikhail Gorbachev, "People, human beings with all their creative diversity, are the makers of history. So the initial task of restructuring . . . is to 'wake up' those who have 'fallen asleep.' " Indeed.

II.f.ii. Feminist Philosophy

The future will judge post-1989 Feminist Philosophy as a veritable Golden Age for women in the profession, grounded by the historically unfolding eruption of second-wave feminist social movements and the intergenerational and organizational work of philosophers across various streams of the discipline. The diverse community that feminist scholarship hosts is so rich and well populated that it's impossible to canvas every voice in the short space of this chapter, but I'll do my best. Alison Jaggar's co-founding of the Society for Women in Philosophy (SWIP) in 1972 marks an important moment in the history of English-language feminist philosophy. SWIP established a beachhead and point of origin for confronting white-male hegemony throughout the profession and a site of collaboration and solidarity for women and allies. As Joyce Trebilcot recalls, "almost as soon as SWIP was formed, its members began to discuss the idea of a journal."[96] These discussions terminated in the 1980 birth of the most important feminist journal of our time: *Hypatia*. As Gruen and Wylie note, this involved a troop of well-known and by now venerable grandmum-titans:

> The initial Editorial Board, assembled by Ann Garry and Jacqueline Thomason, included Sandra Bartky, Candace Groudine, Sandra Harding, Sarah Hoagland, Alison Jaggar, Helen E. Longino, Linda L. McAlister, Kathryn Morgan, Janice Moulton, Connie Crank Price, and Joyce Trebilcot. . . . Longino was to coordinate journal activities and joined Azizah al-Hibri in over-seeing publication of the initial WSIF special issues; Hoagland was responsible for developing editorial policy; Harding was to formulate a plan for "sustaining the journal financially;" Garry and Thomason were to explore options for its publication; Moulton would investigate what the legal status of the journal should be; and Bartky and Trebilcot undertook to coordinate a meeting of the board for the following spring. At this meeting (spring 1979 in Denver), the Editorial Board endorsed the plans thus far set out in correspondence with SWIP members and adopted a proposal to appoint Azizah al-Hibri as founding editor.[97]

Throughout the 1980s, SWIP and *Hypatia* helped empower a new generation of important feminist voices, and intertwined with existing and newly emerging streams of anti-oppression feminist scholarship; from trailblazers in Black feminist thought like bell hooks, Barbara Smith, Cheryl Clarke, and Kimberlé Crenshaw, a vanguard in Latin American feminism like Gloria E. Anzaldúa, Aurora Levins Morales, and Linda Martín Alcoff; to important liberal feminists like Diane Meyers, Susan Moller Okin, and Martha Nussbaum; to specialists in European philosophy like Bat-Ami Bar On, Luce Irigaray, Judith Butler, Jessica Benjamin, and Nancy Fraser. One cannot overstate the import of ongoing work by movement veterans for the advancing archive of feminist philosophy, folks like Sandra Harding, Marilyn Frye, Nel Noddings, and Alison Jaggar. Harding's work in the philosophy of science is as important as her activism and consultancy at the United Nations. Frye blazed a path for methodological diversity in ongoing feminist scholarship. Noddings's care ethics trailblazed one of the most fertile and important fields in the running agora of team *Féministe*. Jaggar's work, if considered from the holistic point of view of both historical and scholarly achievement, might be the single most important philosopher to the origins of the English-language discipline. As Tong and Williams note, "If ethics is about human beings' liberation, then Alison Jaggar's summary of the fourfold function of feminist ethics cannot be improved upon in any significant way."[98] Moreover, SWIP and *Hypatia* continue to play a role in movement solidarity across institutional and scholarly lines, locking arms with the American Philosophical Associations Committee on the Status of Women and journals such as *Signs*, the *Women's Review of Books*, *Quest*, and *Feminist Studies*.

The collapse of the Berlin Wall coincided with Rebecca Walker and Kimberlé Crenshaw's leadership in the eruption of third-wave feminism. Both movement veterans and emerging scholars participated in the conversation. Iris Marion Young's important oeuvre unfolded across the course of the decade, as Bonnie Honig contributes to this day. Judith Herman's *Trauma and Recovery* (Basic Books, 1992) is without exaggeration an epochally transformative piece of psychological theory. Ann Ferguson advanced the ball in oppression studies, including co-editing with Ami Bar On the important collection *Daring to Be Good* (Routledge, 1998). As Joan Tronto questioned the division of ethics and politics, Maria Lugones highlighted the interwoven nature of misogynist and racial oppression. Important scholars in European theory also advanced some game-changing work, for example: Chantel Mouff, Wendy Brown, and Seyla Benhabib. In my view, Benhabib joins Nancy Fraser as two of the most important political theorists of our time. The philosophical work of Claudia Card also deserves special mention. After completing her dissertation under Rawls at Harvard, her oeuvre irreplaceably contributes to feminist, queer, and broader moral theory. In my judgment, her *Unnatural Lottery: Character and Moral Luck* (Temple, 1996) is one of the single most original and transformative contributions to ethical thought in the post-1989 era. Other important feminist voices of the 1990s and beyond include well-known work by Virginia Held, Rosemarie Tong, Ann Cudd, Sally Haslanger, Helen Longino, and Hilde Lindemann.

The new millennium saw the discipline grow beyond my ability to competently chart, but I'll identify whom I personally regard as absolute must-reads. Margaret Urban Walker is one of the most important philosophers of her generation. Her *Moral Understandings* (Oxford, 1998) and *Moral Repair* (Cambridge, 2006) will be studied for a long time to come. Movement veteran bell hooks' prolific authorship is a US national treasure: her *All About Love: New Visions* (William Morrow, 1999) and *Salvation: Black People and Love* (Harper, 2001) are a necessary gate for study in the history and phenomenology of love. Lisa Tessman's *Burdened Virtues: Virtue Ethics for Liberatory Struggles* (Oxford, 2005) is a necessary starting point for critically thinking through the dynamics of moral solidarity among advancing social movements. Anna Gotlib has done interesting work rendering narrative ethics fruitful for bioethics, personal identity, and the moral psychology of emotions. Folks like Sara Heinämaa and Marcia Sá Cavalcante Schuback stand at the forefront of rigorously phenomenological feminist work, and in my own specialist's judgment: Leslie MacAvoy is one of the best phenomenologists of our entire generation. Christine Korsgaard's unfolding oeuvre will fund debates and advances in normative ethics for at least the next few centuries, as Linda Martín Alcoff is fast earning a place among the single most important philosophers of the new millennium.

I should also point out the trailblazing role of feminist theologians and religious philosophers in the unfolding arc of feminist theory. In the pathbreaking wake of Mary Daly stand feminist veterans like Rosemary Radford Ruether, Elisabeth Schussler Fiorenza, and Phyllis Trible. In Jewish theology, veterans like Margaret Wenig and Rita Gross led the way in a tradition that includes Rebecca Alpert, Ahuva Zache, Rachel Adler, and Judith Plaskow; and philosophers and Levinas specialists like Catherine Chalier, Laura Duhan Kaplan, and Claire Elise Katz. SWIP and *Hypatia* trailblazer Azizah Al-Hibri led the way in Muslim feminism, followed by Saleemah Abdul-Ghafur, Amina Wadud, and Ingrid Mattson, unto a new generation of voices. Even our embattled leaders in Evangelical feminist theology deserve mention here, folks like Letha Dawson Scanzoni, Reta Halteman Finger, and Bettina Tate Pedersen. Some of the most interesting work being done in the post-colonial perspective over the past generation has been done by feminist theologians, led by the Mujerista and Black Womanist theologies of Katie G. Cannon, Ada María Isasi-Díaz, Jacquelyn Grant, and Delores Williams; and with voices in Asian theology like Kwok Pui-lan, Chung Hyun Kyung, and Grace Ji-Sun Kim. Feminists like Begum Rokeya, Urvashi Butalia, Vandana Shiva, Manasi Pradhan, and Malala Yousafzai led the way across the subcontinent; while Renya K. Ramirez, Paula Gunn Allen, and Crystal Ecohawk bring important Amerindian perspectives to the conversation. Lü Pin, Li Ang, Leta Hong Fincher, the Guangzhou Five, Weibo's now banned

Feminist Voices platform, Su-Mei Thompson, and so forth lead the way in China's embattled though burgeoning feminist movement.

Feminist theory is such a huge and diverse tradition; one can find much to learn from, think with, and argue about throughout. The only central unifying thread is shared solidarity in the ongoing fight against misogyny and sexism for the empowerment of women, girls, and queer folk. The voices of feminist theorists have exercised the leadership that led to many of the victories of the post-1989 era. Without the work of the philosophers mentioned here and so many more, nothing like the historic 2017 Women's March would have been possible. In the ongoing challenges of the day: Deborah's will lead us forward.

II.f.iii. Jewish Philosophy and Theology

Both traditional and cutting-edge work in the Jewish philosophical and theological traditions have been consistently on point on substantive questions that inform left theory and practice throughout the entire emergence of European modernity. In light of the enduring legacies of Saadia Gaon, Paquda, Maimonides, Crescas, and others, Moses Mendelssohn sparked what came to be known as *Haskalah*—or the Jewish "Enlightenment." One of the most important European philosophers of his day, Mendelssohn brought the prophet Daniel into the eighteenth century ("And the intelligent [*hamaskilim*] shall shine as the brightness of the firmament," Daniel 12:3).[99] A genius, Mendelssohn was largely an autodidact. His father was an impoverished scribe, and outside of a traditional religious education, members of the local Jewish community tutored him in languages and mathematics. As a young man, he mastered Latin by reading John Locke and won a prize for work in metaphysics—in one case beating out none other than Immanuel Kant, who came in second competing in the same essay contest. He also worked as a literary critic in his journey into the heart of the avant-garde philosophy of the day. In 1754, Mendelssohn met and become fast friends with literary giant Gotthold Ephraim Lessing. The two were regular chess partners, and Lessing must have been quite impressed with his new friend: a central character in *Nathan the Wise* is introduced at a game of chess.

Mendelssohn fast became an important public intellectual and an autonomous contributor to current debates in European philosophy, especially those surrounding Kant's epoch-making work. He was a perceptive though nuanced critic of Spinoza, noting his contributions to Leibniz's (and others') cutting-edge work. Mendelssohn moreover posed a relatively autonomous critique of Kant's idealism. His political theory—in a now classic contribution to European literature: *Jerusalem, or on Religious Power and Judaism*—sets out a case for the separation of religious and political power, defends the freedom of conscience, and underlines the import of future-oriented intergenerational solidarity for political life. *Jerusalem* can be fruitfully read alongside Locke's *Toleration* (and antecedents like Erasmus of Rotterdam, Huguenots like Sebastian Castellio, voices in the radical Reformation, etc.). Kant called *Jerusalem* an "irrefutable book." Though Mendelssohn is sometimes considered a threat to more traditional Jewish religious commitment (because of social factors at the time and some of the more radical *maskilim* that came later), he publicly defended Talmud and traditioned religious practice to Christian audiences largely ignorant of them, confronting the caricatures of inherited sectarian polemics in some cases of baldly anti-Semitic vintage. Moreover, and in contrast to Spinoza's shrill polemics, Mendelssohn can be rightly credited for sparking a creative internal dynamic between tradition and modernity that is still unfolding today.

Students of Jewish philosophy and theology know well that European Judaism is as intellectually diverse as any other culture. Mendelssohn started a conversation that tapped into ongoing debates over continent-wide processes of social change, though for Jews with the added stress of maintaining its culture as a minority religion (a plight shared by protestant dissident communities). One of the more interesting trends of the period emerged in Eastern Europe, involving Levinas's own Lithuania, namely: the uproar between Hasidic and Mitnagdim Judaism.

Hasidic Judaism was a religious revival movement that began in the early eighteenth century in the southeastern region of the Polish-Lithuanian Commonwealth, sparked by the charismatic Israel ben Eliezer, know by his followers as Ba'al Shem Tov ("Master of the Good Name"). An initially rural religious movement, it was grounded in "the loss of faith in traditional institutions of community leadership, including the rabbinate, which were increasingly identified with the interests of the Polish nobility."[100] The Jewish community was beleaguered in part because of the recent memory of the Cossack and Tarter pogroms, periodic Polish oppression, metropolitan indifference to rural peripheries, and an overemphasis in synagogue preaching on guilt and punishment at the time.[101] Moreover, a metropolitan snobbery seemed to be in play between city folk able to afford a good Talmudic education and rural folk who lacked the means and immediate access to such education. Movement leaders are rightly proud of *Besht*'s working-class origins. Before his religious calling, he worked as an assistant at a *cheder*, then as a laborer, and later as an innkeeper. Around 1736, he had a radical spiritual experience and felt called to do religious work in local Jewish communities. Though he engaged in the practice of spiritual healing, his teaching was far from the fanatical heterodoxy of the prior century's Sabbateans, with whom Hasidim were often compared. *Besht* was fond of quoting "God desires the heart" (*Sanhedrin* 106b), and renewed the art of the parable and aphorism in the Jewish literature of the day. The Hasidic movement can be characterized as a unique communalization of previously individualist, ascetic, and esoteric Kabbalist spirituality. *Besht* liberated Jewish mysticism for the collective practice of communal worship and prayer, though grounded in a commitment to normative traditions. The following quote gives a sense of *Besht*'s teaching:

> But this is the power of love and joy: When they prevail, they cause anger and fury to ascend upward toward their root. This is part of the secret knowledge, that these forces of anger and strict judgment are mollified only when they reach their origin, since at its origin, all is pure goodness. It comes out that anger and fury are healed and mollified through love and joy.[102]

As the revival spread across the commonwealth, it was viciously attacked by established authorities. One of those authorities was the famous Vilna Gaon.

Gaon was very important Talmudist, Halakhist, and Kabbalist; and commonly known as "the pious genius from Vilnius." Renowned throughout the region as an authority on Jewish law, his work was so respected he was often called on to resolve disputes by other Rabbis throughout Europe. When the Hasidic movement spread to Vilna, it encountered its most staunch opponent. As Immanuel Etkes narrates,

> In the late 1760s and the early 1770s, [Gaon] heard testimony on deviant conduct of people associated with the new Hasidism founded by the Ba'al Shem Tov. Hasidim were accused of unruly behavior during prayer, of altering prayer texts, and of establishing new prayer groups, thus disassociating themselves from existing synagogues. They were also accused of sinning by neglecting Torah study and of hunting for recruits to their movement among young students. The Gaon particularly condemned three practices: (1) Hasidim were said to turn somersaults prior

to prayer, an act of self-abasement that they claimed brought a person to modesty and humility; the Gaon, however, viewed the practice as idolatrous; (2) Hasidim were said to scorn Torah scholars (the Talmud refers to one who scorns Torah scholars as a heretic); and (3) he held that a new, Hasidic interpretation of a passage in the *Zohar* was a grave perversion of the meaning of the text. Based on these testimonies, the Gaon concluded that Hasidim fell into the category of heretics. Following this ruling, he and the leaders of the Vilna community assembled for an emergency meeting during the intermediate days of Passover 1772, and declared war on Hasidism.[103]

Gaon organized hostile resistance against the Hasidic community in collaboration with other traditionalists across the region. Rabbi Aryeh Yehudah Leib of Brody (Ukraine) published an anti-Hasidic screed titled *Zamir Aritzim* (1772), aiming "To cut off all the thorns which have risen among the Jews." The tract actually donned an *edict of excommunication issued by Vilna.*[104] While Gaon's scholarly brilliance cannot be denied, and acknowledging the recent memory of the Sabbatean debacle, his intemperance toward dissidents here is somewhat shocking. It's difficult for our secular minds to grasp the radically serious nature of this move. Gaon was willing to expel Jews from Eternal Israel on the basis of hearsay and with no effort to even talk to them, and for stated reasons that don't seem to justify the action.[105] Hasidic leaders sent emissaries to try to reason with him, but Gaon refused to even receive them. Moreover, this was not just a matter of religious quibbling across equal social footing. As Etkes elsewhere notes,

> During that time the Hasidim were the objects of persecution and oppression. Community leaders who took part in the campaign against Hasidism passed ordinances that led to the social ostracism of the Hasidim, interfered with their sources of livelihood, prohibited people from eating meat that they had slaughtered, and prevented them from holding prayers in the manner they wished. It is easy to imagine the suffering and humiliation of the Hasidim in the areas where they were persecuted.[106]

The Hasidim showed great courage and resilience throughout this and other bursts of periodic persecution. Movement leader Rabbi Schneur Zalman counseled the community, "We are obliged to remain silent, to tolerate and accept the torment with love."[107] This even in the face of his own arrest by Russian authorities "based on trumped-up charges of revolutionary activity concocted by jealous opponents."[108] The Hasidim persevered in their nonviolent approach to countering oppression by actively seeking peaceful reconciliation and by a determined resolve to *show*—in the conduct of their lives, by ethical action, Torah study, and prayer—the religious authenticity of their spirituality. One wonders if Tolstoy didn't have the Hasidim in mind as one exemplar of the pacifism he developed. This would historically implicate indigenous Jewish spirituality in the multicultural genealogy that informs Gandhi and King's contributions to culture and politics. In any case, after Gaon's death, the Hasidim suffered a last burst of persecution before "Ḥayim of Volozhin, the Gaon's leading disciple, openly admitted that the Hasidim were not heretics and reconfigured the struggle against them as a conceptual and educational one."[109] Hayim responded to Hasidic courage by ethically transforming the situation into a religious and cultural debate that went on to enrich both communities.

The Hasidic movement is of central importance for a variety of reasons. First, Rabbi Zalman composed one of the period's most original pieces of Jewish theology. *The Tanya* was written in the pastoral thick of a spiritually hungry and growing indigenous religious movement, and in the face of fierce sectarian persecution. Grounded in the Scriptures, Talmud, and Lurianic Kabbalah, Zalman synthesized an entire complex tradition with the teachings of Ba'al Shem Tov. The work presents a genuinely original moral psychology wedded to everyday spiritual and ethical practice, grounded in a mystical, theological metaphysics that remained faithful to traditional sources, while enriching the everyday spiritual lives of working-class and rural Jews. The Hasidim were, like the Mitnagdim of Gaon's generation, a pre-*Haskalah* community, and were as skeptical toward metropolitan fashions as the more Orthodox Judaism of the day.[110] But they enacted innovations in daily religious life that empowered Jews to not only renew their religious community, but also creatively revalue the normative traditions of historic Judaism. As Mendelssohn was contributing to the avant-garde European philosophy of the day, the Hasidim were forging a wholly indigenous avant-garde spirituality across Eastern Europe. Throughout the uproar, persecution got so bad that movement leaders asked political authorities for help. As Assaf notes,

> An important turning point in the history of Hasidism occurred when the Russian authorities agreed to allow the Hasidim to establish separate *minyanim* (prayer groups) and elect their own

spiritual leadership. Such *minyanim* had already been recognized in Galicia, then a part of the Austrian Empire, by the Toleranzpatent of 1789, but in Russia recognition came later, with the Jewish Statute of 1804. This official recognition of the legitimacy of the religious dichotomy in Jewish society dealt a further blow to the traditional community, ultimately enabling not only Hasidism but also other groups (such as *maskilim*) to break free of their previously enforced affiliation with the traditional community.

As paradoxical as it might seem, it was both Mendelssohn and the Hasidim who sparked an unfolding dynamic of modernity and tradition across European Jewry, and in such a way that the more Orthodox Judaism of the day could no longer simply ignore. Debates over the merits of modernity are legible in relevant work throughout the nineteenth century, for example, Naphtali Hirz Wessely, Samuel David Luzzatto, and Samson Raphael Hirsch.

By the later half of the nineteenth century, German Jewish culture produced yet another philosophical master: Hermann Cohen. Raised in a devout family, Cohen attended a German *Gymnasium* before enrolling in rabbinical seminary at Breslau. He decided not to become a rabbi, and instead studied philosophy under Adolf Trendelenburg at the University of Halle.[111] Kant scholarship at the time was embroiled in the "psychologism" controversy, between speculative idealists and empirical psychologists. Cohen cogently intervened in the debate, founding the historically influential Marburg School of neo-Kantianism. His work altered the debate in such a way that would significantly influence both Husserl and Frege, and hence helped to shape the entire history of twentieth-century philosophy (dare I say, even the immanent critique I conduct above). Cohen's critical work against both Hegelian speculation and materialist scientism uniquely positioned him to immediately grasp the more obviously problems in Marx, and his religious sensibility provided an inspiration for an idealist interpretation of classical Jewish messianism. He admired and committed himself to the socialist project and set out to ground it by developing Kant's ethics and political work. Cohen shows that both a normative orientation and set of specific institutional conditions were necessary to actually realize socialist aims. He advances one of the first sets of serious non-Marxist arguments for democratic socialism.

Beyond his philosophical work, Cohen opposed the death penalty and spoke out against racism:

Necessity, universality, is the logical means which ethics uses to guard against the possibility of exceptional cases. By the latter, politics is wont to confirm the general rule of the love of neighbor. The Negro, too, is a man, even before he has become a Christian.[112]

Cohen's Kantian socialism moreover influenced German politics, for example: "on socialist political leaders such as Eduard Bernstein, a social democratic member of the Reichstag."[113] The problem with Cohen's socialism is not its idealism per se, but its too optimistic practical appraisal of the pace of change, missing the role played by historical cultural and material processes in the birth or reform of relevant institutions. One need not endorse every detail in his particular system to fruitfully engage his work for socialist theory.

Cohen's ethical monotheism would exercise enormous influence in the development of modern Jewish philosophy, as a simultaneous mentor and critical foil for the likes of Rosenzweig, Buber, Scholem, and Walter Benjamin. Benjamin's famous critique of progress took aim at the common premise shared by both Cohen and Marx on the "necessity" of social change, grounded in an original mystical messianism informed by a quasi-historicist reinterpretation of Hassidic communitarian metaphysics. Benjamin's highly original work influenced Adorno, and they both developed a whole new style of social criticism that sought to redeem the particular and non-identical, those traces excluded and defeated in the historical march of "Enlightened" reason. One interesting area of potentially fruitful research is to properly distinguish Cohen's *methodological* insights from his too optimistic assessment of the power of reason for social change, at least when it's too radically abstracted from the cultural and historical life of particular peoples. This empowers a distinction between Benjamin's now historically corroborated critique of Marx's dialectical materialism on the one hand, and Cohen's absolutely indispensable insight that normative commitment holds consequences for how democratic institutions should be arranged. However one in the end assesses the justice of Scholem's reading of Cohen and Kant, his idea that Kant requires a historically linguistic and religious supplement speaks to the problem of Cohen's too naive optimism. Buber's work is highly interesting in his attempt to mediate the various threads of these ongoing debates.

Martin Buber needs no introduction. He's the single most important Jewish intellectual of the early twentieth century, and his influence has not waned with time. His authorship spans "from [Hasidic] mysticism to social philosophy, biblical studies, religious phenomenology, philosophical anthropology, education, politics, and art."[114] He and Rosenzweig produced a new German translation of the Jewish Bible, and Buber commented on and contributed perspectives to nearly every pressing question of the day. He contested Scholem's too uncritical and hermetic historicism in an attempt to "recapture a sense of the power that once gave [Hasidism] the capacity to take hold of and vitalize the life of diverse classes of people," and for its "faithfulness to 'the central truth of Judaism and Hasidism' [in] its ability to help 'our age renew its ruptured bond with the Absolute.'"[115] According to Agassi,

> Buber considered himself a religious socialist and communalist . . . He considered Marx's dialectical and historical materialism as voiding the human ability to be a moral force. . . . He deemed particularly absurd . . . Marx's irresponsible proclamation about the leap from the Kingdom of Necessity to the Kingdom of Freedom. This was Marx's prophecy that soon after the socialist revolution there will be a quiet withering away of the state and a leap into the ideal paradise of communist society. As to the disastrous influence of Marx's centralism on socialist theory and practice, Buber devoted his *Paths of Utopia* of 1945–1950 to it.[116]

Buber valiantly tried to renew pre-Marxist traditions of utopian socialism over-against the more questionable postulates of Marxist "science" at the time; and characterized his own authorship as an extended commentary on and expression of "sacramental existence."[117] This can be seen even in his Zionism. Buber's Zionist commitment not only shows the internal diversity of the movement from its very inception, but also reflects his overarching philosophical commitment to dialogical solidarity. He consistently opposed *realpolitik*, always recognized Palestine as a "land of two peoples," and publicly defended both active dialogue with Arabs and a binational state.[118]

Buber's intuitionism is a strength for his uncanny perception in grasping the spiritual power of creative religious practices for communal identity formation across the ritual, jurisprudential, theological, and critical differences that characterize all long-standing religious traditions, in this case indigenous Judaism. Buber, a "spokesman for Hasidism—the decidedly *communal* Jewish mysticism," inspired an entire generation of assimilated Jews to once more take up more traditional religious practice.[119] As Friedman reports, "'It was Buber,' writes Alfred Werner, 'to whom I (like thousands of Central European men and women devoid of any Jewish background) owe my initiation into the realm of Jewish culture.' "[120] His intuitionism moreover empowered an understanding of the moral potential of active solidarity in processes of both critically working through and creatively healing wounds between historically differentiated communities. For example, Friedman recounts,

> In the spring of 1952 Buber was awarded the Goethe Prize by the University of Hamburg for his "activity in the spirit of a genuine humanity" and for "an exemplary cultural activity which serves the mutual understanding of men and the preservation and continuation of a high spiritual tradition." In accepting this award Buber recalled the number of Germans whom he knew during the time of Hitler who risked punishment and death in order to help the German Jews. "I see this as a more than personal manifestation and a symbolic confession," he wrote, "and accept it as such." This award was indeed a more than personal symbol, but it was of great personal significance as well: Martin Buber is the only person who stands in such a relation to the Germans, the Jews, and the people of the world that he might receive such a confession for his people.[121]

Buber's gracious recognition of German repentance is a living legacy in the ongoing work of critical acknowledgement and creative solidarity, and remains an active reality in Israeli and German politics. He is an eternal witness to the ongoing moral power of Judaism in the living archive of Jewish culture, itself among the great Lights of all humanity.

But his intuitionism also bears well-documented and much discussed limits. Though he valued Jewish law in his youth, his theoretical and practical indifference to it throughout his authorship is not merely a religious problem, but a political one as well. Buber is spot-on in questioning the more ungrounded dimensions of Marx's work, and underlines the *moral power* of pre-Marxian traditions of culturally grounded socialism. But utopian socialism's cultural focus also contributed to the historical eclipse of socialist internationalism in the post-1989 era. History has more than buried the pretense of scientificity claimed by Marx's actual method (and the Bolsheviks will forever stand next to the cruel decadence of the *ancien régime* as an example of what not to be), but now more than ever we need sociologically serious Marxist analysis in the ongoing work of theory and practice for social democratic internationalism. This requires the contributions of historical religious cultures, but in such a way that avoids either explicit right-wing or hapless left-wing fascist appropriations. Buber's major contribution to twentieth-century philosophy is his phenomenology of *dialogical solidarity*. But as Levinas's critique underlines: without discursively rigorous philosophy and science, such solidarity runs the risk of being empty, or degenerating into the mere entertainment of enjoying culture "otherness" unhinged from people's actual moral and existential commitments and the political realities of the time. This bears on his problematic rejection of Jewish law.

Hillel Goldberg fairly diagnoses both the strengths and weaknesses in Buber's philosophy,

> Orthodox Jews are both attracted to and repelled by Buber's thought for other reasons. What repels Orthodox Jews is Buber's unbending personal and philosophical rejection of halakhah (Jewish law)—of the notion that authentic religious experience is received or achieved through fixed forms of behavior and ritual. Buber's own position that authentic religious experience is dependent upon both will and grace, both self-realization and the unpredictable, unevocable, uncontrollable gift of spirit that meets and thus consecrates one's will, is utterly removed from the Orthodox view of a commanding God who makes himself available to man through rigorously defined actions and attitudes whose time, location, and limits are clearly delineated. What makes Buber attractive to certain Orthodox thinkers is his emphasis on the integrity and feeling-tone that he sees as indispensable to real religious experience, and that a formalized religious system such as halakhah runs the danger of overlooking or suppressing. Orthodox thinkers, then, use Buber piecemeal, appropriating certain subjective elements in his thinking while rejecting his rejection of objectivity in religious ceremonial and interpersonal life.[122]

Buber's witness to the reforming power of religious creativity should be retained, but the onus always remains on participant-innovators, in the language game of particular traditions, to prove themselves in the conduct of their communal lives, and with articulatable arguments that preserve the nobility and contributions of relevant ancestors and essential extant practices. But Orthodox thinkers rightly join serious Marxists in a justified worry about "objectivity." We not only owe reasons to the future and the present, but also to the past. This is part of the substance of intergenerational solidarity, and is why Goldberg rightly claims that "the antagonism between Buber and halakhah [is] ultimately contingent, not absolute."[123]

In my view, Levinas and Buber jointly present the irreplaceable legacies of the Eastern European Jewry nearly annihilated by Nazis. Together, they disclose the interwoven unfolding of contraction and expansion, pain and joy, ethics and poetry, law and love, and so forth that makes *authentic traditionality and intergenerational solidarity what it is*. Both the Hasidic and Mitnagdim traditions retain a communally grounded, quasi-anarchist sensibility, informed by their historical disenfranchisement and marginality in "Christian" regimes across Eastern Europe. This might explain why both Levinas and Buber lack a functional political theory. Levinas privileges the solidarity of scholars. Buber privileges the solidarity of popular culture. And they both, Levinas's famous equivocations notwithstanding: utilize a quasi-anarchist notion of *divine kingship* as the central conceptual commitment that binds their respective work together. Neither common law nor popular culture is by itself sufficient to justify political authority. Hermann Cohen and other Jewish philosophers of note supply resources to rectify this lacuna, and in a way that doesn't erase or impugn Levinas's and Buber's respective contributions. Indeed, as I discuss with more specificity in the conclusion: critical issues in his work already noted, Levinas contributes a basic, unsurpassable, and living insight to the ongoing practice of moral and political philosophy.

With Buber, another deeply important philosopher of the period who deserves a lot more attention is Ernst Cassirer. A student of Cohen at Marburg, he taught at Yale and Columbia after the Nazis took power. A somewhat tragic figure professionally, his work has never received the full airing it deserves because of the historical eclipse of neo-Kantianism with the rise of Russell and Husserl. Close attention to the details of the famous Davos debate with Heidegger reveals still living methodological questions at play in *Being and Time*. A prolific author, Cassirer's oeuvre is unique for both its substantive philosophy of science and systematic philosophy of culture. His account of reason and philosophy of symbolic forms tries to stake out a path between Kant and Hegel in a philosophy that seriously rivals other twentieth-century attempts to properly value *both* the physical and human sciences. Cassirer's work remains highly relevant to the debates of our own time.[124]

Beyond the giants of modern Jewish philosophy, more attention should be paid to lesser-known lights in the Jewish intellectual tradition. Thanks in part to Cohen, Eduard Bernstein—who can justly be called one of the fathers of social democracy—courageously and publicly fought Lenin's Blanquism. To my knowledge, he mounted one of the first pieces of substantive criticism of Marx's pretense of "science," questioning the very ground for the then near universal appeal to the necessity of violence in socialist politics. His *Probleme des Sozialismus* caused an uproar in the SPD, and the later *Die Voraussetzungen des Sozialismus und die Aufgaben der Sozialdemokratie* was panned by nearly everyone—including all the good comrades who later spoke up against Bolshevik oppression—from Kautsky and Plekhanov to Bebel and Luxemburg. He was nearly ousted by the party for what should today count as genuinely courageous and prophetic criticism.[125]

Finally, I'd like to call attention to the fascinating work of Hermann Heller (which I myself just discovered in the last week doing research for this chapter). An English translation of Heller's *Sovereignty: A Contribution to the Theory of Public and International Law*, edited and translated by Daniel Dyzenhaus, came out just a few months back from Oxford.[126] Stop what you're doing and read it. My above case for the salience of Sypnowich, Bockman, and Chibber for Marxist theory underlined its central lacuna: its lack *of an intelligible and normatively oriented theory of state*. This is precisely what Heller theorizes, and in explicit critical contrast to the dueling legal positivisms of Hans Kelsen and Carl Schmidt.

It must be said that the popularity—at times theoretical, at times performative—of Schmidt's fascist legal philosophy among left-wing academics is a down right scandal, informed as it by the more fanciful quarters of post-1989 "theory." Unlike Schmidt,

> Hermann Heller was a Jewish socialist and militant opponent of the Nazis. He is hardly known outside of Germany, in large part because he died in exile in Spain in 1933. He was then in the midst of composing a definitive statement of his views, a book on state theory, which was subsequently published in a form revised by his assistant. *Sovereignty* is the major work that Heller himself brought to completion. Heller was one of the leading public lawyers and legal and political theorists of the Weimar era . . . In this work, he addresses the paradox of sovereignty. That is, how the sovereign can be both the highest authority and subject to law. Unlike Kelsen and Schmitt, who seek to dissolve the paradox, Heller sees that the tensions the paradox highlights are an essential part of a society ruled by law.

In an exploration of history, constitutional and political theory, and international law, he speaks clearly to our contemporary concerns, and shows that democrats must defend a legal idea of sovereignty suitable for a pluralistic world.[127]

My above call for renewal in Marxist theory and practice should not only read G. A. Cohen, Sypnowich, Bockman, and Chibber, but especially engage Jewish philosophical and theological contributions to the socialist tradition, above all the cutting-edge work of Hermann Cohen, Eduard Bernstein, Ernst Cassirer, Hermann Heller, and Martin Buber. With Levinas, they carry forth the unfolding legacies of Mendelssohn and the Hasidim as lights of the dynamic creativity of a traditioned Jewish modernity. We'll not move forward without them.

II.f.iv. The Frankfurt School

In my best judgment, across the populated fields of critical theory today no tradition has been more consistently on point and productively self-critical than the Frankfurt School. Taken with the best quarters of the phenomenological tradition, no single other methodological tradition has more consistently yielded relatively cogent and normatively informed social and political analysis. Horkheimer and Adorno consistently refused to yield to the twin chimera of a subject-erasing positivism and subject-valorizing volunteerism, in a dogged commitment to both serious social science and the non-identical uniqueness of concrete life in late capitalist societies. Benjamin and Adorno squarely faced the genuine paradoxes and losses that attended the capitalist transformation of more traditional ethical life, teaching us how to both properly mourn on the one hand, and to creatively retrieve history's best legacies for the ongoing struggles of the day. Though second-generation critical theory's worries about Horkheimer and Adorno's late and respective turns to a more theological sensibility are not without some warrant, it should be noted that even Habermas has concluded his career with an effort to constructively engage the relation between religion and modernity, in a way that keeps both the best in the past and the open possibilities of the present alive. The Frankfurt School has consistently carried forth one of Marxism's best legacies while soberly criticizing its worst. The tradition exemplifies what I'm tempted to name *the call of authentic critique*: to start from a rigorous and defensible critical assessment of where we actually are, alive to the extant normative resources that can be called on in the task of redeeming and co-creating a better world. Third-generation critical theorists have carried forth this legacy, and in my judgment present some of the best assessments of where we stand today.

Nancy Fraser tackles a core dimension of our plight today, what she cogently describes as a "[*frame problem*]: What, if anything, should delimit the bounds of justice?" Treating the figure of a blind and balance-toting Lady Justice, she writes,

> Today, however, the received image of the balance is stretched to the breaking point. Current conflicts exceed its template of a simple dualism of commensurable alternatives, as present-day claims for justice routinely run up against counterclaims whose underlying ontological assumptions they do not share. For example, movements demanding economic redistribution often clash not only with defenders of the economic status quo, but also with movements seeking recognition of group specificity, on the one hand, and with those seeking new schemes of political representation, on the other.[128]

This is perhaps the core problem postmodern economic globalization has yielded: how do we adjudicate conflicting claims of justice across social movements when the very substance of those claims is often itself in dispute? Moreover, how do we engage both urgent social problems and the higher-order issues they involve in such a way that can generate solidarity and cooperation for broader social change across local, national, and transnational democratic contexts? Fraser's question is acute because it goes to the heart of the *very possibility of communication*. This is *not* itself a transcendental question, because any such question necessarily presupposes or enacts communication, but is rather the challenge of creating shared understandings across widely diverse forms of life and interests, and a common ground for democratic deliberation and collective social action.

Axel Honneth has engaged this problem in a constructive reading of Levinas. While he critically defends the Kantian streams of the Frankfurt School tradition from its more theatrical critics, he grants that the "moral point of view of equal treatment . . . requires continuous correction and supplementation by a viewpoint indebted to our concrete obligation to individual subjects in need of help."[129] His work on mutual recognition provides a good starting point for showing how this works concretely, and his debate with Fraser provides a way into thinking about the questions of the singularity and plurality of justice in general. That debate holds important consequences for how we think about and practice social justice transnationally. Indeed, third-generation critical theory is unique for both its consistent defense of human rights as a legitimate paradigm of global justice struggle, while also soberly assessing the ways it can be misused by the unjust shape of extant transnational institutions and practices. As Christine Lafont notes,

> Global governance institutions such as the World Trade Organization (WTO), the International Monetary Fund (IMF), and the World Bank are particularly relevant institutional contexts in which the power differentials among member states can have very negative impacts upon the sovereignty of weak states, not to mention upon the protection of human rights in these states.[130]

Rather than wield these facts as an excuse to lurch into conservative realism or turn a blind eye to the dynamic harms and possibilities that characterize our world today, third-generation critical theory has consistently *tarried with our dilemmas*, and in a way that calls forth both serious sociology and a political theory with enough gumption to propel normatively ambitious calls for transformed and renewed transnational democratic institutions. Rather than reach back for a naturalistic conception of human rights, with Baynes we should perhaps embrace a properly political understanding: "human rights are international norms that attempt more generally to respond to the changing conditions of political inclusion and membership in an increasingly pluralist world."[131] Indeed, Seyla Benhabib is spot on the mark here, cogently arguing

> . . . that if we embrace skepticism about universal human rights (as many are now doing), we will have very few conceptual tools with which to oppose European right-wing populism, murderous Turkish nationalism, Hindu chauvinism, and a reactionary and racist American isolationism that aims to retain white hegemony by closing its borders to the brown and black people of this world.[132]

Of course, this will not be welcome news across the spectrum of today's academy. Third-generation critical theory is to be lauded for its methodological seriousness and normative courage in resisting the more theatrical fashions of the day.

In my judgment, one primary and crucial area of potentially fruitful work is to reexamine and rethink the role of religion in communicative reason and ongoing social struggle. Across the broad sweep of the social sciences today, it has become near common sense that the old secularization thesis is all but defunct. If it is defunct, what consequences does this hold for our operative understandings of modernity? Max Pensky explores these questions in an interesting and in some ways counterintuitive analysis of the role of religion in today's Europe. He argues,

> The secularization thesis . . . makes itself dependent on a normatively fraught, indeed a cryptically Jacobean view of religion, that now appears, at its most innocuous, as an unfortunate collective immaturity besetting otherwise sleekly modern political systems, and, at its most malign, a positive evil, an infamy that only civic religion, the cult of reason, can vanquish.[133]

Moreover, he frankly—and in my view, rightly—holds that "the secularization thesis is Eurocentric."[134] The problem of communication across cultures and social movements precisely implicates religion. Pensky goes on to question "American religiosity," underlining how

> [Religion] has deinstitutionalized to such an extent that many Americans are able to see faith in a sort of rational-choice manner, and religious institutions as something like a field of spiritual commodities from which the religious consumer is able to pick and choose, constructing a personally tailored religious portfolio. Brand loyalty is often trumped by the freedom to move from one church to another based on the maximization of personal spiritual utility, and churches find themselves obliged to compete in a "spiritual market."[135]

By contrast to the American model, religious belonging in Western Europe tends to be more climatic, more akin to "a public utility than a free market concern."[136] In my view, Pensky cogently describes what was likely at issue in much older debates between established and disestablished national religions, underlining how too radical individualization of religious identity generates its own set of potential pathologies on stark display in the American model. Pensky does *not* suggest that we ought try to revert the past, but he invites reflection on potential ways religious belonging and participation can be integrated into robustly democratic national and transnational institutions. In the United States, where religious establishment is constitutionally prohibited, what might happen if, instead of trying to ban public religious expression, we democratize it? For example, establishing a system where different community leaders do things like pray, chant, read poetry, and so forth before sporting and other special events on a rotating basis. The logic being: citizens regularly interact with people and symbols different from their own, ideally at local, national, and international levels. The import of first-person religious commitment cannot be reduced to a market model or wholly thought in terms of mere consumption, but it can and should be made answerable to democratic publics, and in a way that not only preserves that state's obligation to protect the democratic freedoms of all citizens, but that also invites religious participants to freely articulate their own political theologies and religio-political understandings, openly and explicitly. What if modern democracies created a cabinet-level department of religious life and made voluntary filing of political-philosophical public statements a condition for participation in public rituals like prayer breakfasts, opening prayer/chant/poetry at various public events (sports, graduations), and so forth? Such a process could potentially help national polities properly value and limit markets, on the one hand, and public utilities on the other, by making the diverse normative resources inherent to religious communication an explicit dimension of public debate. Religion has played an active and positive role in the emergence of modern democracy, and to this day stands at the forefront of various social movements. Processes like I'm proposing could moreover aid all citizens to forge mutual understandings, insofar as a matter of course it will differentiate democratic from nondemocratic religious and theological traditions within particular polities. They might help institute internal impediments to the occluded popular growth of sympathy for "European right-wing populism, murderous Turkish nationalism, Hindu chauvinism, and a reactionary and racist American isolationism" that Benhabib rightly worries about.

Indeed, no single more accurate and concise statement of where team global justice stands today exists than in Benhabib's recent piece in the *Boston Review*. She writes,

> The project of emancipation in a globalized world—one in which many different civilizations and life-worlds are continuously confronting one another, in which new subjectivities represented by women, gender, and sexual minorities and ethnic and racial groups

are expressing themselves through competing narratives—cannot ignore the lessons of genealogy, postcolonialism, and feminist theory, or neglect the ethical meaning of deconstruction [*if there is one!* —JM].[137]

Benhabib is clearly not out to quell the diversity of liberatory struggle or impose a whole new syllabus on us. But she is spot on that

> . . . none of these approaches succeeds in carrying out one crucial legacy of a critical social theory that Horkheimer identified: the critical theory of society develops, he said, an existential judgment of a "period which is approaching its end." Critical theory must also be a theory of crises. Restoring this link between critique and crisis in a theory of society has been one of Jürgen Habermas's many lasting contributions.[138]

What is coming to an end today, with Pensky, is the primary marker of Eurocentrism itself: the secularization thesis *as such*. As such, it requires going back to the drawing board on a whole set of assumptions and habits that are so deeply imbedded in the West's social imaginary and academy that they manifest even in research and discourses that explicitly question or criticize the secularization thesis. No other critical tradition that I'm aware of has more consistently fought for and defended the authentic gains of European modernity, while more honestly reckoned its limits and problems, than the Frankfurt School. Over the course of my entire education, it has remained fashionable to poke fun at old Habermas. One of course need not endorse his every move to properly appreciate his nearly unparalleled contributions to social and political theory today. As Benhabib rightly notes,

> Habermas's theory of communicative action has been criticized for its Eurocentrism. This critique misunderstands that concepts such as rationalization, system, and life-world describe processes that are not just Eurocentric but developments of a global modernity. The capitalist economy from the start had a worldwide dynamic reach. The modern state and its juridical and administrative apparatus became the universal aspiration of many former colonies that freed themselves from their colonial legacies. Theories of alternative modernity should not reject the analytical usefulness of these categories. *Alternative modernity*

models are most helpful when they inform us about the varying institutional and organizational configurations of states, markets, and civil societies in Western, non-Western, and global contexts. But historical descriptions of alternative modernities cannot substitute for a critical approach that tries to locate the emancipatory and oppositional potentials of these transformations. The charge of Eurocentrism misunderstands the methodological abstraction through which Habermas develops his system and life-world crisis theory. . . . The boundaries of the demos—of the self in democratic self-government—have not been formed democratically through the enfranchisement of the voice of all affected. The nation has been the privileged collective identity that has inserted itself into the gap between the ideal of democracy as the subjection to laws that come from *all who are affected*, and the reality of a closed demos founded on the privilege of *belonging* to the nation. This interplay between democratic voice and nationalist closure is a global process that we see in Turkish as well as contemporary Hindu nationalism, in Japanese as well as increasing German ethnocentrism. The West has no monopoly on the intensity of murderous nationalisms.[139]

As Benhabib's work—and the entire archive of third-generation critical theory—beautifully exemplifies, taking Horkheimer and Habermas seriously does not require quelling methodological diversity. It might require budgeting some of our time to talk to and think with them. Habermas and Co. provide a determinate yet flexible and open-ended method for, in Eduardo Mendieta's words: "retain[ing] a normative ground from which to criticize 'pathological' as opposed to 'healthy' process of rationalization."[140]

If modernity and rationality no longer exclude religion by definition, new practical and theoretical possibilities emerge. I critically endorse White's intuition that

> In the broadest methodological sense, Habermas's account of reason and action offers a new conceptual "core" to the research tradition of critical theory. It thus provides a means of generating coherence across a broad terrain of research in the social sciences.[141]

Generating ought to be underlined here. The task is not to impose a new meta-discourse per se, but rather to take normative justification more seriously.

Habermas's contribution is to have taken up and repeated a task well known to a variety of pre-modern traditions, and to Marxism and phenomenology especially, namely: *maintaining a productive link between theory and practice*. It's this very commitment that informs Benhabib's call:

> Today the post–World War II international order (or disorder) is in shambles. A new war of superpowers is announcing itself, disguised for the time being as trade wars. The left has always been skeptical—in many cases justifiably—of multi-national governance institutions such as the United Nations, the International Criminal Court, and the World Trade Organization. But it now finds itself on the sidelines of history, watching the clash between the U.S. and China on the one hand and the growing expansion of authoritarian populism from Hungary to Turkey, from the Philippines to Poland, from Russia to Singapore, on the other. And unfortunately, so far we have had very little to say about the shape of an alternative world in which freedom and justice can be housed in institutions that transcend murderous superpower confrontations. The left critique of neoliberal globalization will have to be extended to envisaging new global institutions for controlling capitalism on a global scale, for encouraging sustainable and ecological planetary growth among peoples, and for supporting the international human rights system.

Let's get to work.

II.f.v. Christian Philosophy and Theology

In the economy of left theory and practice, no culture is more often and abusively caricatured then the teeming diversity that constitutes the Christian tradition. There are many reasons for this, above all the objective and sometimes murderous oppression practiced in its name. In the United States and United Kingdom today, nothing is more responsible for the clownish abominations that are Donald Trump and Boris Johnson than the good ol' fashion idolatry of the billionaires' useful idiots: white Evangelicals and Catholics (including the more pale-faced corners of my own Pentecostal tribe). I'll have more to say about these failures in future critical work, but here I want to draw attention to the contributions of Christianity to unfolding traditions of global justice struggle.

Communities of Jesus people have been at the cutting edge of every progressive moral and political struggle since the birth of Christianity. No better testimony to this exists than all the women of Africa, Asia, and Europe mocked by second-century neo-Platonist and explicit anti-Semite Celsus: "only foolish and low individuals, and persons devoid of perception, and slaves, and women, and children" who disobey their esteemed elders, and "go [off] with women and little children, who are their playfellows, to the conclave of women, or to the shoemaker's or fuller's shop, that they may obtain perfection."[142] As Kroeger notes, Celsus's "contemporary, Bishop Cyprian of Carthage [and other patristic authors] acknowledged in his *Testimonia* that 'Christian maidens were very numerous' and that it was difficult to find Christian husbands for all of them. These comments give us a picture of a church disproportionately populated by women."[143] All of this is widely attested, and will only seem shocking to those nurtured on the propaganda that passes for historiography in some corners of European letters. Why on earth should women, slaves, and children feel *empowered* by Christianity? It may have something to do with the brutal realities of slavery and sexual exploitation that riddled pre-Christian European societies, among Norseman, Greeks, and Romans above all. The shoddy fiction that women were the stupid victims of crafty preachers promising riches in the afterlife for their submission today is an outright *lie*. Pre-Christian oral scripture—Virgil's poetry—had already moralized the Homeric epic, incorporating long-standing Platonic and other myths of posthumous punishment and reward within its ode to filial and civic piety. Pagan traditions created "crafty preachers" all by themselves, and this partly explains why Celsus was so peeved by the insubordinate gumption of Christian women. Women, slaves, and children flocked to Christianity because it improved their daily lives and empowered novel forms of popular self-organization, with the added benefit of morally improving the behavior of their most immediate oppressors: husbands, brothers, masters, and parents. Karl Kautsky's method notwithstanding, he was certainly right that aboriginal Christianity was an empowering, communitarian force for the abject of the day.[144] The spiritual and *moral power* embodied in the life, death, and resurrection of Jesus of Nazareth, exploding at Pentecost, knocked Saul of Tarsus off his horse, and fueled the growth of a movement initially led by peasants, fisherman, and tent-makers. Why on earth has it taken more than 2,000 years to win gender egalitarianism? Because European men really are patriarchal beasts. Christian men could accept a new set of new rules and creative practices transparently better than the class and misogynist realities of various pagan societies, but couldn't countenance being sissies in the eyes of their pagan male peers. Those days are over, and it's been too long in coming. It took Jewish, Christian, and pagan women two millennia to socialize European masculinity enough to win both legally protected equality and actual advances in material parity, witnessed in perhaps the greatest archive of women's literature among the world's great cultures.[145] The dialogue between more traditional and more daring forms of sexual ethics will continue on, because that debate is of central import to socializing people to be decent mothers, fathers, sisters, brothers, and co-citizens in a free society. But the days of women's formal and material subordination to male authority are over. The fight continues.

Beyond bettering the everyday lives of women, it bettered the plight of slaves too. Too much contemporary scholarship uncritically applies baldly anachronistic modern views to the past, failing to treat it in its actual contexts, as if the Declaration of Independence and the Declaration of the Rights of Man sprung whole from the Void. Slavery was a ubiquitous social institution throughout the entire world, up to and beyond the time of Christianity's birth. Spartacus and a few politically quietist Stoics had questioned it, but its social function in the ancient world was such that no one could yet imagine what a world without slavery could be like. Christianity's first literary and organizational genius—student of Gamaliel and son of Pharisaical Judaism—the Apostle Paul creatively intervened in the question of slavery, and in a way that reflects its problematic status.

Paul mounts one of the boldest egalitarian intellectual and social projects the world had known till that time: "for all of you who were baptized into Christ have clothed yourselves with Christ. There is neither Jew nor Gentile, neither slave nor free, nor is there male and female, for you are all one in Christ Jesus" (Gal. 3:27–28, see also 1 Cor. 12:3, Col. 3:11). Beyond simply declaring this *in abstracto*, and in contrast to Plato and Aristotle: Paul actively and performatively subverted the "slave/free" binary, "For the one who was a slave when called to faith in the Lord is the Lord's freed person; similarly, the one who was free when called is Christ's slave" (1 Cor. 7:22), "Though I am free and belong to no one, I have made myself a slave to everyone, to win as many as possible" (1 Cor. 9:19), and "because you know that the Lord will reward each one for whatever good they do, whether they are slave or free" (Eph. 6:8). Paul is radically extending here an ancient Jewish tradition that protected the humanity of slaves, laying down religiously enforceable rules for their fair treatment (Exod. 21:20–27, Lev. 19:20, 22:11; Duet. 24:7). Close attention to Paul's texts here clearly shows the complex and socially embedded understanding of the radical universality he was proposing. On the one hand, within the community of Jesus people: baptism united everyone as socially located individuals, "So you are no longer a slave, but God's child; and since you are his child, God has made you also an heir" (Gal. 4:7). This equality was not merely formal, but had active consequences for the everyday ethical life of the community:

> Were you a slave when you were called? Don't let it trouble you—although if you can gain your freedom, do so. For the one who was a slave when called to faith in the Lord is the Lord's freed person; similarly, the one who was free when called is Christ's slave. (1 Cor. 7:21–22)

This empowered slaves within the Christian community to assert their equal standing in the family of Jesus and as citizens of the Kingdom of God, and not merely as spectators in a context that reproduced social distinctions from wider non-Christian culture. The spiritual and moral practices described in the book of Acts was characteristic of the new Christian movement, and Paul went on to catalogue them throughout his letters, giving guidance on their responsible practice. They included prophecy, healing, words of wisdom, words of knowledge, discerning of spirits, speaking in tongues, and the interpretation of tongues (see especially Rom. 12, 1 Cor. 12, Eph. 4). One sees why slaves and women were so attracted to the movement! In stark contrast to the realities of the ancient world, in churches they could assert their equality by actively contributing to the liturgical life of the community on equal footing. The Christian Bible and early literature refer to various women and slaves as prophets, healers, and church leaders. Moreover, Paul didn't just declare all this from a villa in Tarsus, but traveled the Mediterranean as a tent-maker with a team of men and women, all actively building and pastoring the communities he helped to found.

But Paul was also aware of the brutal realities common folk of the day had to contend with in their everyday lives. The new empowerment attracted converts and caused friction in new Christian communities across the Mediterranean. Paul had no truck in calling out moral faults on a variety of issues, often listing negative exemplars of those who should be excluded from the communities of Jesus:

> We also know that the law is made not for the righteous but for lawbreakers and rebels, the ungodly and sinful, the unholy

and irreligious, for those who kill their fathers or mothers, for murderers, for the sexually immoral, for [pimps and pederasts], for slave traders and liars and perjurers—and for whatever else is contrary to the sound teaching that conforms to the gospel concerning the glory of the blessed God, which he entrusted to me. (1 Tim. 1:9–10)

Though Paul is often described as a gnostic and antinomian, his writings show a nearly dialectical understand of law and grace. He endorsed the moral teaching characteristic of Second Temple Judaism, but valiantly sought to extend the history and promises of the God of Abraham to gentiles, without annulling or forgetting Christianity's Jewish origins. One the one hand, "[h]ere there is no Gentile or Jew, circumcised or uncircumcised, barbarian, Scythian, slave or free, but Christ is all, and is in all" (Col. 3:11). On the other hand, of the people of Israel:

Theirs is the adoption to sonship; theirs the divine glory, the covenants, the receiving of the law, the temple worship and the promises. Theirs are the patriarchs, and from them is traced the human ancestry of the Messiah, who is God over all, forever praised! (Romans 9:4–5)

"Jews have been entrusted with the very words of God" (Rom. 3:2), Paul declares, and in the context of redemptive history, seems to have adopted a policy of "first for the Jew, then for the Gentile" (Rom. 2:10). So Paul's radical universality was not premised on denying Jews their heritage or the moral force of the law in general, but rather on situating the message of Jesus squarely in its tradition, inviting gentiles to share in its legacies and promises.[146]

Paul's policy on how to handle social differences presents another important contribution. The larger shape of his political theology aside, he constantly exhorted Jesus people to be Jesus people: to live as lights of a better way in their interactions with non-Christians. He fiercely opposed the sexual exploitation rampant throughout the Europe of the day. Confronting an incestuous relationship in the Corinthian church, he writes:

I wrote to you in my letter not to associate with sexually immoral people—not at all meaning the people of this world who are immoral, or the greedy and swindlers, or idolaters. In that case you would have to leave this world . . . But now I am writing to you that you must not associate with anyone who claims to be a brother or sister but is sexually immoral or greedy, an idolater or slanderer, a drunkard or swindler. Do not even eat with such people. What business is it of mine to judge those outside the church? Are you not to judge those inside? God will judge those outside. (1 Cor. 5:9–13)

Though Paul endorsed institutions of human government for restraining evil, he shows that early Christian communities were a hell of a lot less concerned with other people's business than the theocratic nationalism so popular among middle-class Christians today, above all in the United States. In the entire New Testament, there is no talk about or justification for theocratic government, only an insistent and determined call to imitate Christ and live out self-sacrificial love in the everyday conduct of public and communal life, even in the face of fierce persecution. I do not document here all of the testimony of Imperial sources at their consternation with the new social movement. It reflects Celsus's contempt, though in some cases with added self-description of the gothic methods used to quell the ethical rebellion. However overstated classical Christian hagiography remains, a critical review of both pagan and Christian sources clearly establishes the persecution of Christians as historical fact, from sunny Nero's use of Christians as actual torches (among other amusing methods), to Trajan's spectacular creativity in feeding folk to lions, to the great paragon of stoic Enlightenment: Marcus Aurelius's own mobs.

II.f.v.i. Imperialism

Another conventional canard that must be put to bed is the idea that Christianity invented the practice of proselytizing. As Sharma demonstrates, Hinduism's spread to the "*mleccha* barbarians" was informed by indigenous religious literary sources dating "from fifth century B.C.E. to the tenth century." They "combined with the [missionary] success of the heterodoxies of Buddhism and Jainism," establishing Indian religion beyond its indigenous border: "classical Hinduism provides an identifiable model of Hindu missionary activity."[147] Early Buddhism was as a prolific missionary faith as Christianity came to be. Under the eventual sponsorship of India's Ashoka the Great, Buddhism spread as far west as the Black Sea and as far east as Japan and China, where it firmly took root. Jewish missionary activity is also quite well attested, particularly among the Jewish communities that remained from the days of Babylonian captivity. "The Geonim actually set quotas," notes Perelmutter.[148] Jewish missionaries established communities among the Khazars in the Caucuses, tribes in southern Arabia, and the Falashas in the Aksunite Kingdom of Ethiopia. The Silk Road became a thriving reef of religious difference, utilized not only for economic trade but also by every religion of the day to spread its own good news, in the first great phase of the phenomenon of globalization led by Eastern empires.[149] Christian dissidents in the Eastern Church had ongoing success at resisting the control of the West, and by itself established communities in India and China as early as 635 CE. Moreover, the world Christianity was born into was a veritable religious market, populated by sects and schools of nearly infinite variety: mystery religions, Cynics, Essenes, Stoics, and so forth, all making their case in the public square of the day. As one might expect, freedom to safely operate on that ideological market was premised on paying homage to Roman religious supremacy. The state-mandated imperial cult was the largest across the empire, and the ideological market itself also hosted the cruel realities of sexual exploitation and the slave trade.[150] As N. T. Wright notes,

> it is increasingly apparent that to many ordinary people in Greece, Asia Minor, the Middle East and Egypt—with the exception of the last, the focal points of Paul's missionary work—the Caesar-cult was fast-growing, highly visible, and powerful precisely in its interweaving of political and religious allegiance.[151]

Pre-Christian Rome had already explicitly utilized its religion as a popular tool of Imperial rule, a common practice throughout the entire ancient world. The Silk Road not only funded the exchange of ideas, but, as the later and brutal success of the Mongol Empire shows, and in the wake of the Muslim conquest of India, reports of human trafficking in European and Jewish slaves are documented as far East as China, as late as the fourteenth century. Seriously evaluating the ancient world materially and ideologically requires considering better and worse forms of the (effective or explicit) political theologies in use, and not uncritically projecting modern categories in our processes of analysis and assessment.

In truth, one searches in vain for an ancient culture untainted by the evil of slavery.[152] As far as I've been able to ascertain, there are a variety of important exemplars of relatively enlightened reformers on this and related issues throughout ancient history. Cyrus the Great (590–529 BCE) conquered much of the known world and was admired for his comparatively liberal policies: praised in the Jewish Bible and in Greek literature by Xenophon and Herodotus. An important archeological find, the "Cyrus cylinder" seems to confirm some aspects of his literary portrayals as a great administrator with relatively tolerant policies toward some religious cults.[153] Though as Simonin points out, "But taking '(. . .) find rest (. . .) from their servitude (. . .)' (L.26) as an abolition of slavery, for example, is a total anachronism, as the existence of multiple kinds of slaves during Achemenid rule proves."[154] One of course ought not arbitrarily impose modern standards in the evaluation of Cyrus. Though popular portrayals are somewhat overstated, given the realities of common life in the ancient world, he certainly does stand out among the leaders of antiquity as a luminary and trailblazer for what we today call human rights.

Another great exemplar is one of India's brightest lights, Ashoka the Great (304–232 BCE). He established the largest empire in the history of the ancient subcontinent. Though his early reign is marred by conquest and brutality, sometime after 261 he halted expansionist military policies, expressed regret at the suffering his leadership had caused, and converted to Buddhism.[155] His famed Edicts sought to codify Buddhist teaching across the empire. They are a truly stunning example of enlightened rule that caused considerable domestic controversy at the time. They include prescriptions for familial, civic, and fiscal piety, public health, compassion toward animals and slaves, religious tolerance and cooperation, and much else. He instituted practices of transparency for state administration, and policies for both the domestic and missionary expansion of the Buddhist religion.[156] He moreover criminalized "[t]he selling and mortgaging by kinsmen of a sudra who is not a born slave and has not attained majority but is an Arya (free)."[157] As Sharma notes, this policy was restricted to only highest cast citizens, indicating the ubiquity of the practice at the time. Though classical Buddhist texts don't specifically mention slavery and even monasteries at the time held them, Ashoka's policies clearly promoted their welfare, instituting explicit norms for their ethical treatment. In my view, Ashoka and the traditions his edicts exemplify stand next to the Jewish Bible as one of the most important ethical legacies among human culture.

China's rich and complex history has produced a variety of important reformers. Political instability throughout its ancient history invested folk customs and traditions with an important stabilizing role in the life of commoners. Like many other cultures, some of those customs involved human sacrifice. As Mark Lewis shows, Duke Xian of the Qin Dynasty (424–362

BCE) can be credited with abolishing this practice at his ascension to the throne in 384.[158] Tung Chung-shu (179–104 BCE) was an important Confucian intellectual and writer. Around 140, he advocated for "the abolition of the threat of the arbitrary killing of slaves, which suggests that at that time masters had such a right."[159] Tung's literary influence may have played a role in subsequent history. Wang Mang (45 BCE–CE 23) was the nephew of Empress née Wang, and would have received a good Confucian education. As Pullyblank notes, he seems to have had a fiery social conscience: "[he] accused the state of Ch'in of having established markets in which slaves were penned like horses and cattle."[160] In 6 CE, "a portent appeared, supposedly sent by heaven, directing that Wang become emperor."[161] Wang took the throne on January 10, 9 CE, founding the Hsin Dynasty. Faced with a variety of problems, Wang instituted some truly radical reforms, including nationalizing land ownership and prohibiting the "buying and selling of private slaves."[162] Wang Mang is perhaps the first person in *all of world history to formally abolish the slave trade!* Because of opposition of the aristocracy, he had to rescind these policies three years later. In contrast to his early career, his imperial tenure was plagued by a variety of problems. He was deposed and killed on October 26, 23 CE. Wang's abolitionism must have made an impact, however. His eventual successor, Kuang-wu-ti, "declared that henceforth that the killing of a slave should be regarded as the same as killing an ordinary man [in 35 CE]."[163] Given the unstable character of Chinese political history, these policies didn't always take root. But the Confucian tradition produced a variety of important ethical lights to human culture.

As is widely noted in the scholarship, aboriginal Christianity was constitutively *both* anti-imperialist and transnational in character. As Wright notes, the literature of New Testament authors

> must have been heard in Rome, and that Paul must have intended it, as a parody of the imperial cult. . . . The thematic exposition [of Romans] concludes with 15:7–13, where the mutual welcome of Jewish Christian and Gentile Christian in the one family of God in Christ, producing united worldwide worship in fulfillment of scriptural prophecy, is the goal of the whole gospel. Paul builds up a careful sequence of scriptural passages to make the point, emphasizing on the way the universality of the rule of Jesus Christ, the *kyrios* (Ps. 117:1, quoted in v. 11, repeats "all": all the nations, all the peoples). The final quotation

is from Isaiah 11:10, one of Isaiah's great messianic passages, and Paul has chosen a passage which, in its Septuagintal form, looks right back to Romans 1:3f: "The root of Jesse shall appear, the one who rises up (*ho anistamenos*) to rule the nations; in him shall the nations hope." Jesus' Davidic messiahship, once more, is confirmed by his resurrection, and means that he is the true ruler of the nations. This cannot, I suggest, be other than a direct challenge to the present ruler of the nations, Caesar himself.

In a contrast that directly challenged the core of Roman religious ideology, and the very basis for its use of the sword for expansionist, imperial conquest: the good news proclaimed in the life, death, and resurrection of Jesus of Nazareth radically challenged the empire of its day. Though leaders endorsed the function of the state for the rule of law, Christian literature and community ethos adopted a fundamentally nonviolent approach to resisting empire through active, creative, and spiritually positive modes of engagement: "For though we live in the world, we do not wage war as the world does. We use God's mighty weapons, not worldly weapons, to knock down the strongholds of human reasoning and to destroy false arguments" (2 Cor. 10:3–4). What were these anti-imperial weapons? Paul elsewhere elaborates,

> Finally, be strong in the Lord and in his mighty power. Put on the full armor of God, so that you can take your stand against the devil's schemes. For our struggle is not against flesh and blood, but against the rulers, against the authorities, against the powers of this dark world and against the spiritual forces of evil in the heavenly realms. Therefore put on the full armor of God, so that when the day of evil comes, you may be able to stand your ground, and after you have done everything, to stand. Stand firm then, with the belt of truth buckled around your waist, with the breastplate of righteousness in place, and with your feet fitted with the readiness that comes from the gospel of peace. In addition to all this, take up the shield of faith, with which you can extinguish all the flaming arrows of the evil one. Take the helmet of salvation and the sword of the Spirit, which is the word of God. (Eph. 6: 10–17)

Paul's own critical theory took the form of demonology, the exemplification of forces oppressing individuals and communities, militating against their spiritual freedom as members of the family of Jesus and as co-citizens of God's kingdom. He sought to equip the church with the pedagogic and spiritual tools to help them flourish as individuals and as a community in the radically exploitative society of the day. All this wasn't merely the fine sayings of rich clerics, but corresponded to an active ecclesial life where all participants practiced the "gifts of the Spirit." The New Testament writers—mostly in the form of epistles—spent a good deal of time mediating disputes and laying out the shape of this creative form of popular self-organization:

> But to each one of us grace has been given as Christ apportioned it. This is why it says: "When he ascended on high, he took many captives and gave gifts to his people" [Ps. 68:17]. (What does "he ascended" mean except that he also descended to the lower, earthly regions? He who descended is the very one who ascended higher than all the heavens, in order to fill the whole universe.) So Christ himself gave the apostles, the prophets, the evangelists, the pastors and teachers, to equip his people for works of service, so that the body of Christ may be built up until we all reach unity in the faith and in the knowledge of the Son of God and become mature, attaining to the whole measure of the fullness of Christ. (Eph. 1:7–13)

Paul's quotation of Psalm 68 creatively develops an ongoing Jewish tradition of mystical political theology that involved a "divine assembly" in G-d's heavenly abode (see Isa. 6, Ezek. 10, Ps. 82, etc.). This quite ancient tradition sparked richly imaginative and interwoven traditions of popular myth that wrestled with deep theological questions such as the origin of evil, the structure of the cosmos, the critique and transformation of polytheistic traditions that underwrote exploitative social systems throughout the ancient world, and more (see the books of Isaiah, Ezekiel, Daniel, Enoch, etc.). When the psalmist writes, "you are all [children] of the Most High," (Ps. 82:6), s/he is addressing *spiritual powers* identified with the pantheon of near eastern "gods" of the day, asserting their status as *created* over-against the Creator. Popular interest in angels and demons was not the result of the stupidity of our ancient ancestors, but rather a creative way to analyze, resist, and creatively endure the political and social forces that affected their everyday lives. This tradition played a role in informing the various ways Jews thought about Israel as a historical polity across generations. Paul shared the Pharisees' skepticism and antipathy toward Rome, and in his own unique way built a religious counterculture comparable to the Essenes, though by contrast: an urban, socially engaged community. This traditional idea of "divine councils" or "spiritual assemblies" would play an ongoing role in Biblical monotheism, with both the Christian New Testament and the Jewish Talmud becoming sibling archives that embody the differentiation and democratization of divine political authority, materially grounded in a self-organized and self-perpetuating urban community life pioneered in parallel ways by the Church Mothers and Fathers and the Rabbis.[164] The democratizing streams of the "divine council" tradition emerged roughly parallel to the democracy of the Greek city-states, and the subsequent history that Philo and Paul develop and pass on can be read as debates in political theology among Christian, Jewish, and pagan monotheists on what "divine assembly" means for the economy of political authority, symbolized by the phrase "the Kingdom of God."[165] The use of democratic councils in movement leadership was a consistent feature of the early church.

The first council of church history is described in Acts 15, and as the church grew it regularly utilized regional councils to collectively consider matters of common concern: the Council of Rome of 155, the Council of Rome of 193, the Council of Ephesus of 193, the Council of Carthage of 251, the Council of Iconium of 258, the Council of Antioch of 264, the Councils of Arabia of 246–247, the Synod of Elvira of 306, the Council of Carthage of 311, the Synod of Neo-Caesarea of c. 314, the Synod of Ancyra of 314, the Synod of Arles of 314, and so forth. One ought not think of Christian leaders at this time as chaste old men in purple vestments reclining in castles or at rich estates funded by the public purse. As Christianity spread throughout the empire, members of the Roman aristocracy started to convert. The Roman Emperor Constantine saw political potential in the movement for his own maneuvering and possibly a renewal of Roman civic virtue. He began to court the Christian community. By Constantine's day, the church was a thriving intercontinental reality of locally organized and run communities unprotected by the state, from Spain and North Africa across the Mediterranean to Britannia in the north, to the Caspian Sea in the east and Iraq in the south. Critical treatments like to present caricatured accounts of the development of Christian orthodoxy through the lens of late-Medieval church decadence. By contrast, the church was still a self-perpetuating, largely urban movement with a growing body of participants across social classes, and still independent from the state. However arcane their theological debates appear, they represent a highly original and organic process of transnational debate and development among pastors and intellectuals with real stakes for everyday church life. Whatever Constantine's motives might have been, in 325 he invited 1,800 church leaders from cities across the world to a council: the Council of Nicaea.

Nicaea hosted community leaders from nearly every region of the Christian world to debate and collectively settle six practical and theological issues. The outcome of this particular assembly was the composition of the Nicene Creed.[166] The Nicene Creed became the first democratically debated and composed ecumenical document in the history of the Christian church. It gave the widely diverse cultures within Christianity a common liturgy—in Greek, *leito-* "public" or "people," and *-ergos* "work." Nicaea was followed up by councils in Rome (382 CE) and Carthage (419 CE) that formalized a widely recognized though relative consensus on the canon of the Christian scripture (by Augustine's death in 430, he considered the cannon closed). Six more ecumenical councils followed, in Constantinople I (381 CE), Ephesus (431 CE), Chalcedon (451), Constantinople II (553 CE), Constantinople III (680 CE), and Nicaea II (787 CE), with participation of community leaders and scholars across the world. Through a process of democratic and scholarly deliberation, the early church constructed what amounts to one of the world's first transnational religious constitutions, which came to be called "orthodoxy."

The achievements of Christian orthodoxy involved a vastly complex and long-term social process. In contrast to the caricatured myth of mustache-twisting clerics plotting to impose oppression on an innocent populace, the debates over various "heresies" were a community-wide affair involving quite substantive questions with important consequences for the conduct of everyday church life. In contrast to Arianism, a majority of Christian leaders defended the uniqueness and exemplarity of Jesus's life, death, resurrection, and eschatological renewal of all of God's good creation. In contrast to Nestorian and Adoptionist dualism, church leaders defended the singularity and originality of Jesus's nature as human and divine. In contrast to the anti-humanist spiritualism of Apollinarianism, Sabellianism, Docetism, and Monophysitism, Christian leaders defended the actual, material humanity of Jesus. In contrast to Pelagianism, church leaders defended human finitude, critical realism, and the necessarily social character of religious community as such. In contrast to Manichean asceticism and dualism, Christian leaders defended the goodness of creation and the organic unity of spiritual and material reality. In contrast to the stupidities of Gnosticism, the church defended the goodness of material creation within a critical realist stand-point that squarely faced the tragic side of life and the human capacity for radical evil. Christian orthodoxy incarnates a complex and living history of a popularly fueled and community organized exercise in public philosophy, centered on the person of Jesus and a progressive Trinitarian defense of the heritage of traditional Jewish and pagan monotheisms. Orthodoxy was the progressivism of its time. This liturgical and theological achievement stands to this day as the center around which Christianity gathers in all its unwieldy diversity. The ancient creeds are a multicultural and democratic heritage—achieved by Africans, Asians, and Europeans—of the church universal at the close of ancient history.

Constantine's Edict of Milan in 313 declared a general and legally enforceable policy of religious freedom and required restitution of Christian property confiscated during the persecutions. But Constantine himself did not promote Christianity to state religion; his successors did in 380 with the religiously catastrophic Edict of Thessalonica. This began a tide of politically motivated conversions that slowly inculcated elite Roman attitudes within the church and sparked a process of the slow, piecemeal, and internally contested integration of church authority and Imperial state power (early asceticism and monasticism were in part a reaction to the increasing imbrications of church and state). For all of Augustine's authentic contributions to human culture, his choice to endorse state power as an instrument of religious politics opened a floodgate that helps explain the later crimes of church history. He never was able to resolve the question of the right relation between religious and political authority. One cannot embrace a villainizing (or valorizing) narrative here: on the one hand, he represents the aboriginal church's commitment to the rule of law (and the literally Millennial debate it hosted between pacifists and just-warrists, until Urban II's betrayal in the run-up to the First Crusade); while moreover resisting the triumphalist, right-wing interpretation of church/state power by folks like Eusebius of Caesarea. Augustine presents both a realist view of human finitude and fallibility, held in resolute commitment to the radical possibility of redemption. On the other hand, his fateful choices on the use of sword were cited as an authority by nearly every Christian militarist and inquisitor since. For leftists especially, who must defend a theory and practice of political revolution: a serious, non-anachronistic, and interdisciplinary study of Augustine, the Donatist controversy, evolving orthodoxy, Gregory of Nyssa, and the plight of European Jews will contribute to the ongoing story of the problems and promises of democratic transnationalism. We should neither heroize nor villainize Augustine. As Markus has shown, his work—and his *City of God* especially—sets out the world's first *theology* *of the secular.*¹⁶⁷ Though not altogether self-standing, the text is still relevant for rethinking questions that face us today. But it remains true that Augustine endorsed—complexly—the slow yet increasing imbrications of church authority and state power that would eventually come to characterize the medieval world.

But Christianity's origins really did spark an unfolding debate about the nature of slavery. Beyond St. Paul's originary contributions, Bristow observes,

> According to Ignatius, a second-century bishop, church funds were used to buy freedom for a number of slaves (*Apostolic Constitutions* 4.9 [cf. *Ignatius' Letter to Polycarp* 4.3]). Some Christians even surrendered their freedom to ransom others from slavery (*1 Clement* 55). Marriage among slaves was protected, and non-Christians were urged to free their slaves or allow them to purchase their own freedom. Clement wrote, "Slaves are men like ourselves," and Lactantius added, "Slaves are not slaves to us; we deem them brothers after the spirit, in religion, fellow-servants." Ambrose argued that a slave might be superior to his master in character . . .¹⁶⁸

There is evidence that the Donatist controversy tapped into a living debate and caused widespread consternation and community-wide discussion of the question of slavery. In this unfolding context, Gregory of Nyssa spoke up.

Some of the scholarship on Gregory presents a wildly stunning determination to either skeptically occlude or systematically marginalize the audacious radicality of his preaching. J. Kameron Carter halts that nonsense, properly naming Gregory for what he is: "an abolitionist intellectual," whose "antislavery outlook surpassed all ancient intellectuals—pagan, Jewish, and Christian."¹⁶⁹ Denby follows up by asking "The First Abolitionist?," joining Carter's performative anachronism in order to confront the blind anachronism that structures some of relevant scholarship. None other than a small-town preacher in the Cappadocian countryside (central Turkey) produced the first unambiguous and philosophically articulate denouncement of slavery's very existence *in all of world history*. Jesus rocks. Denby goes on to counter the more scholastic handstands deployed to deny Gregory this honor, following Hart and Carter in underlining work beyond his famed *Fourth Homily on Ecclesiastes* to other attacks on slavery in his *Easter Sermons*. Denby finally shows that this wasn't merely an intellectual matter or a shiny exercise in rhetoric. Gregory was highly influenced by his sister Macrina, whom he often called his "teacher." Gregory writes,

> Macrina persuaded her mother to give up her customary mode of living . . . and the services of her maids . . . and to put herself on a level with the many by entering into a common life with her maids, making them her sisters and equals rather that her slaves and underlings.[170]

And Gregory was not merely an exception here. He stands next to John Chrysostom and others for what I call "Biblical liberalism," a tradition of social reformism grounded in local communities that defended the rule of law and the goodness of a common liturgy, but retained a skeptical distance toward Imperial power politics; often openly challenging the rich.[171] Post-Nicaean Christian literature evinces three distinct tendencies that would live on throughout church history: (1) the biblical liberalism exemplified by Gregory and others grounded in the scriptures and the ecclesial life of urban churches, (2) theocratic triumphalism wedded to state power willing to use the sword to enforce dictates, grounded in regional power politics, and (3) dissident movements friendly to formal orthodoxy but resistant to the increasing imbrications of church and state. The increasing proximity of church and state institutionalized both triumphalist state clerics and biblical liberals as the spectrum of then mainstream Christianity, to the exclusion and repression of radicals like the desert ascetics and the popular jihadism of proto-nationalists like the Circumcellion. As I see it, the task today for left-wing Christianity is to shift the center of the mainstream away from triumphalist nationalisms of whatever vintage to a "biblical liberal/experimental radical" spectrum that reclaims the radical roots of a creative materialist orthodoxy. Donald Trump is, among other things: divine judgment on the tradition of Christian political theology of Eusebius of Caesarea and his contemporary fascist acolytes. Instead of Eusebius/Gregory conversations, we should be having Gregory/Sojourner Truth conversations.

II.f.v.ii. Orthodoxy and Popular Struggle

As counterintuitive as it might seem, and in light of Pensky's insight into the tensive relation between popular religious individualism and public religious institutionalism, I want to propose a progressive defense of the heritage of

Christian orthodoxy. Noting parallel achievements in other religious cultures, and above all underlining the complex intertwinement of religious and state power throughout actual church history: Christian orthodoxy has hosted ongoing and popularly fueled moral and political debates since Nicaea. Orthodoxy to this day remains a field of nonviolent creative contest, and working through the very complexities, imperfections, and evils that mare the tradition can shed light on how the church evolved over time and yield insight for the tasks of the day. For every sin of church history rose dissenting communities that countered it, and tracing that history tells the story of popular struggle among Christian populations from late antiquity to our time. By the early modern era, nearly every locality touched by the barbarity of European colonialism themselves involved indigenous practices of slavery and often sacralized forms of classism. Wherever clerics issued putatively theological justification for conquest and slavery, nearly immediately other leaders rose to contest them. In the Spanish context, folks like Bartolomé de las Casas, Alonso de Montúfar, Tomás de Mercado, and Joaquim Nabuco actively stood with indigenous victims and openly challenged church authorities. One cannot even cast Catholic institutional leadership as unambiguous villains here, as the next generation of popes responded to this activism by trying to impose legal protections for indigenous populations on the political and economic actors directly exploiting them. This in itself shows the ambiguity and conflicted character of the forces and actors in processes of colonization. Latin Americans today defend their Catholic heritage for good reasons: that tradition was not only complicit in colonization, but actively sought to empower the indigenous over-against their more immediate political and economic oppressors.

Following in the footsteps of Catholic luminaries like Francisco de Vitoria and Alberico Gentili, Hugo Grotius (1583–1645) is considered one of the primary forerunners of international law: the idea of a community of nations governed by laws and covenants instead of war and brute force. A Dutch jurist, Grotius actively participated in the "Arminianism" theological controversy that dominated Dutch public debate in the early seventeenth century. Arminius was an internal reformer in the best tradition of Christian humanism, challenging the more Stalinist dimensions of the Protestant scholastic's own doctrine of God. His followers were called "The Remonstrance." Grotius intervened in the debate despite the serious risk it involved to his life and career. He took up the mantel of Erasmus of Rotterdam, arguing for religious tolerance and an irenic approach to religious differences; defending the peaceful coexistence of orthodoxy with differing views. He moreover argued that the church should be accountable to secular law. As a risk-bearing participant in the Arminian theological movement, Grotius is not only a trailblazer for international law, but also a spiritual legacy for later church movements (both Methodism and Pentecostalism robustly embrace Arminius as a theological antecedent and icon). By challenging the inherited shape of the theological idea of "predestination," Arminius and Grotius joined the Catholic humanists in distinguishing the *normativity* of law from the *actual course* of history, implicating human action and institutions as historically effective actors accountable for their conduct. His ongoing theological and legal-philosophical work exemplify the best tradition of biblical liberalism: the commitment to a community-grounded and open-ended orthodoxy, tolerant of dissidents, and conciliatory toward other faiths. He argued that the Dutch state should grant Jews freedom of worship, and actively corresponded with various rabbis of the day.

Among newly emergent Protestant countries, Christianity's indigenous abolitionism would come to find even more radical expressions. Over the course of Protestant modernity, a parallel internal contest unfolded between entitled elites actively profiting from slavery and conquest, peddling putative theological justifications for them, and religious dissenters actively challenging those justifications. From a historical point of view, the actual history of abolitionism in the United Kingdom and the United States is an important—even marvelous—phenomenon, the joint legacy of political radicals, social liberals, and progressive religious traditionalists and revivalists. Led largely by Quakers and Evangelicals, the abolition of slavery in the United Kingdom presents one of history's first victories for mass, religiously led civil society activism over-against the political and financial interests of the ruling class of the day. It's high time that story be told in all its glories and ambiguities, stripped of both the biases of Enlightenment historiography and the tendency toward hagiography one finds in popular treatments. Non-anachronistically sorting through the internal contests between abolitionist and pro-slavery theologies will tell the story of authentically traditional biblical progressivism over-against the cynical appropriations and ideology of the Protestant ruling class.

Indeed, our more immediate history well testifies to the inner link between authentic Christian existential commitment and popular moral and political struggle across Africa, Europe, and the Americas. Progressivism, abolitionism, women's suffrage, labor activism, civil rights struggle, liberation, feminist, and queer theologies, and so forth were in part propelled by relevant participants' Christian conscience, in solidarity with others in these irreducibly coalitional struggles. It is not accidental that much of the work being done today in post-colonial perspective is the labor of Christian theologians, repeating the transnational and multicultural legacies of evolving orthodoxy itself.

In contrast to today's conventional wisdom, the *question* of orthodoxy does not necessarily refer to necessitarian metaphysical systems or wholly contingent local traditions; it's rather a *living archive* of a transnational community's best guess in the ongoing critical and creative tasks of the day. It amounts to a religio-philosophical equivalent to *paradigms* in the practice of science and to the *constitutions* of political communities.[172] From a normative point of view, the very idea of "orthodoxy" concretizes the obligations we owe not only to the future and the present, but also to the past, in the context of a religious or life-philosophical commitment. Anyone who has *suffered* at the hands of defenders of orthodoxy knows all too well both its dangers but also its value as a reservoir of ongoing questions, practices, and understandings that are important to the political struggles of the day. One of my central proposals is that we should start reading the documents of traditional orthodoxies across every living religious tradition as *democratic achievements*—the fruit of millennia of experimentation by actually existing communities—that can be both challenged and creatively repeated by all willing participants.

III. Conclusion

In this chapter I have tried to show the problems and promises of post-1989 global justice struggle. This analysis will empower a more precise specification of the normative potentials Levinas gifts to us, despite the methodological problems at play in his work. Returning to Ricupero's opening address to UNCTAD's 10th session, and in light of the preceding analyses, can we actually say that Levinas supplies ideological cover for an implicit form of conquest and domination? *Absolutely not.* Indeed, the cultural legacies Levinas repeats and to which he creatively contributes informs one of Europe's own enduring legacies. Those carrying forth these legacies are precisely those participating with every non-European culture in the ongoing tasks of global justice struggle: those trying to *listen*, *give*, and *collaborate* in the urgent task of winning a better future for every individual soul and living culture actually doing the work of keeping this good world dancing.

Indeed, as I glossed above: religiously committed individuals and groups stand among the vanguard leading social movements today. Voluntary cooperation and solidarity in struggle across civil society is actively countering global neo-nativism in all its local iterations, across cultures and across the globe. In the face of Trump's hate, the spontaneous emergence of interreligious and civil society cooperation—mutual aid and support between mosques, synagogues, churches, temples, and activist groups—is not exactly mysterious. It's the production of the best legacies and ongoing creativity of social justice traditions and religious spirituality across cultures, which often plays a too invisible role in keeping our democratic institutions and best public traditions alive. It is everyday activists and adherents doing the hard work of ethically improving and vocationally innovating who are leading for a redeemed future. As usual, we philosophers and intellectuals have some catching up to do.

The reason I have focused primarily on the Euro-Atlantic in this chapter's genealogy is not out of a lack of interest in other local or regional contexts. Rather, pathologies in the Western academy and political culture are culpably at stake in the emergence of neo-nativism, in the irresponsible choices and habits that gave us Trump, Boris, and neo-fascism across Europe. My focus is therefore determined by the active responsibility I bear to counter as best I can the dysfunctions in the communities I actively participate in, and do the best I can as a philosopher, critical theorist, and theologian to help.

The truth is that one core legacy of European philosophy and religion is recognizing that human meaning is the *joint legacy and project* of every single religion, culture, and singular soul that walks this small planet; and that co-preserving and co-creating that meaning materially holds the promise of a redeemed future. That is the legacy Levinas defended. That is the ethical mission he called forth for our time. This is the legacy and promise we must live up to today, together.

Chapter 8

Conclusions and Beginnings

> We were more than the wars of our fathers.
>
> —Anonymous

> The idea of human rights and freedoms must be an integral part of any meaningful world order . . . If it is to be more than just a slogan mocked by half the world, it cannot be expressed in the language of [the modern] era, and it must not be mere froth floating on the subsiding waters of faith in a purely scientific relationship to the world.
>
> —Vaclav Havel[1]

> Yes, Levinas was a great European.
>
> —Paul Ricoeur[2]

I. The Shoah

On the night of June 24, 1941, Lithuanian Fascists began anti-Jewish pogroms in Levinas's hometown of Kaunas in advance of the German occupation. In one incident, forty to sixty Jewish men were rounded up and gathered at Lietūkis Garage, near the city center at 43 Vitautas Avenue. According to multiple accounts, "Lithuanian children were lifted onto the shoulder of their parents to catch a glimpse of the 'Death Dealer of Kovno,'" the latter "A young man—he must have been a Lithuanian . . . with rolled-up sleeves was armed with an iron crowbar."[3] A German army photographer witnessed the incident:

> At the beginning of the Russian campaign on the morning of June 22, 1941 I was transferred with my unit to Gumbinnen.

We remained there until the following Tuesday, June 24, 1941. On that Tuesday I was ordered to transfer from Gumbinnen to Kovno with an advance party. I arrived there with the head of an army unit on Wednesday morning (June 25, 1941). . . . Close to my quarters I noticed a crowd of people in the forecourt of a petrol station which was surrounded by a wall on three sides. The way to the road was completely blocked by a wall of people. I was confronted by the following scene: in the left corner of the yard there was a group of men aged between thirty and fifty. There must have been forty to fifty of them. They were herded together and kept under guard by some civilians. The civilians were armed with rifles and wore armbands, as can be seen in the pictures I took. A young man—he must have been a Lithuanian . . . with rolled-up sleeves was armed with an iron crowbar. He dragged one man at a time from the group and struck him with the crowbar with one or more blows on the back of his head. Within three-quarters of an hour he had been beaten to death the entire group of forty-five to fifty people in this way. . . . After the entire group [had] been beaten to death, the young man put the crowbar to one side, fetched an accordion and went and stood on the mountain of corpses and played the Lithuanian national anthem. I recognized the tune and was informed by bystanders that it was the national anthem. The behavior of the civilians present (women and children) was unbelievable. After each man had been killed they began to clap and when the national anthem started up they joined in singing and clapping. In the front row there were women with small children in their arms who stayed there right until the end of the whole proceedings. I found out from some people who knew German what was happening here. They explained to me that the parents of the young man who had killed the other people had been taken from their beds two days earlier and immediately shot, because they were suspected of being nationalists, and this was the young man's revenge. Not far away there was a large number of dead people who according to the civilians had been killed by the withdrawing Commissars and Communists . . .[4]

Similar barbarities unfolded over the next few days. Rabbi Ephraim Oshry recounts an event in a nearby suburb,

The rabbi of Slobodka, Rav Zalman Osovsky, was tied hand and foot to a chair, "then his head was laid upon an open volume of gemora (volume of the Talmud) and [they] sawed his head off," after which they murdered his wife and son. His head was placed in a window of the residence, bearing a sign: "This is what we'll do to all the Jews."[5]

By the end of the war, Lithuania's ancient, thriving, 200,000-plus-strong Jewish communities were effectively annihilated. In Vilnius, the capital of Levinas's Lithuania and once dubbed the "Jerusalem of the North," fewer than 500 Jews remained. Levinas's entire extended family was murdered by Lithuanian and German fascists.

II. Evaluating Levinas

Any assessment of Levinas's Eurocentrism that fails to treat the plight of Jews throughout European modernity—and above all: the Evils of the Shoah—is not merely distortive, but downright sanctimonious. Levinas was faced with the task of healing and rebuilding Jewish culture and institutions in the wake of a historically unprecedented catastrophe. Moreover, Levinas's complicated love for Europe reflects the attitudes of nearly his entire generation of intellectuals, and is therefore not some special vice he alone possessed. Europeans to this day are rightly proud of the traditions of science and philosophy it has contributed to the world, even as it confronts, repents, and makes restitution for its own internal barbarities unleashed on the world throughout the colonial era, two World Wars, Stalinism and the Cold War, and so forth. If Kant's racism and Husserl's Eurocentrism don't by themselves annul or invalidate the critical tools they've contributed to the ongoing task of resisting xenophobia, problems and tensions in Levinas's work certainly do not negate his enduring contributions to philosophy and culture.

Andrew McGettigan makes this last point especially evident with his critique of Levinas in "The Philosopher's Fear of Alterity."[6] Setting aside the more cynical dimensions of his analysis, McGettigan leaps on Levinas's use of religious language to argue, "the problematic of the face is at root mobilized in a valorization of the Judaea-Christian legacy against those who come from outside 'the West.' "[7] This, of course, is question begging. Quite unlike, say, Bernasconi's relevant work, McGettigan seems unaware of the grounds for the criticism he poses, premised on a robust and wholly moral sentiment that "chauvinism is bad," but without recognizing the implications of that very commitment for his own critical practice. Simply ditching religious language does nothing to ameliorate the problem of critique and the question of truth in intercultural context, because it's the very mark of "European" thought to hold to the possibility of culture-transcending validity. The fact of the matter seems to be that Levinas's worry about Merleau-Ponty's proposal in "Everywhere and Nowhere" remains our living plight: even while endorsing open and creative intercultural dialogue, if no "constructive principle is left in place which can give an orientation to existence—nihilism or the 'pure indifference of multiplicity' is the result."[8] There is not even the possibility of translation without reference to a context-transcending experience, norm, or principle. There is no exit from this fact, and Levinas is certainly not racist for noting it; nor are his proposals chauvinist for the mere fact that they are informed by Jewish traditions. If Levinas cannot justifiably be accused of racism or religious chauvinism per se, how can the moral problems in his work be fairly characterized?

Levinas ultimately succumbs to a temptation that attends every single soul who walks this small planet, and is certainly not restricted to the precincts of European philosophy, even if it is on prominent display there: what Martha Nussbaum calls "normative chauvinism."

> The evaluator judges that her own culture is best, and insofar as the other culture is unlike it, it is inferior. Normative chauvinism has a complex relationship to descriptive chauvinism. Both may, of course, be present: the describer may make the foreign culture look more homelike than it really is, and then proceed to criticize it for the differences that remain. But very often, normative chauvinism is grounded in descriptive romanticism: having made the foreign culture look different and strange, the evaluator condemns it for that very strangeness.[9]

Even this must be qualified, however, because Levinas himself often admits it when he knows little about a non-Western cultural tradition in question. His encounter with Dussel, and so many others, demonstrates conclusively that Levinas was neither racist nor indifferent to the plight of non-Europeans. But in my view, and noting his own situated ordeal as a Jewish educator and Shoah survivor: his Eurocentric statements are most fairly understood as a form of specifically *normative* chauvinism. As I hinted above, the *desire for recognition* involved in defending one's own indigenous culture or standing for, exemplifying, and contributing to its historic achievements is not intrinsically chauvinist, but it's precisely *how* we treat others in light of this desire that matters, and this is where assessment can and should be made in tough cases, noting important context considerations for the assessment to be fair.

III. Normative Potentials in Levinas's Work

Debates over his method are likely to be ongoing, but nevertheless: Levinas's phenomenological analysis of the Face will continue to Stand as a fundamental and unsurpassable contribution to phenomenological ethics and the social ontology of normative commitment. The inexculpable tie he presents between height and destitution, sovereignty and vulnerability, freedom and obligation should be taken as a starting point for political theory today. Any nominally "critical" political philosophy that treats sovereignty as pure chimera, or ignores it entirely, is either naïve or authoritarian; naïve because the constitution of a polity necessarily involves the codification in law of the duties and prerogatives of citizens qua citizens, and failing to treat both of these leaves power undetermined. Such is authoritarian for essentially the same reasons: political belonging is left adrift to the whims of mere custom or fashion, which minorities or dissidents must constantly negotiate, and indeed: *suffer*. Quite clearly, law can be wielded as a tool of oppression. It can also liberate and preserve, and is the only stable, yet augmentable, vehicle we have for securing the regularity and flexible order necessary for individuals and groups to enjoy basic well-being. If we decide for a liberal-statist interpretation of Levinas, which entails a concomitant rejection of anarchist "disruption" talk, then, as Bell rightly argues, "[The face] gives a way of understanding what states are responsible for, providing a criterion for judgment of political action and the meeting of their obligations to human beings."[10]

Axel Honneth has noted another important feature of Levinas's analysis of the Face. In contrast to Derrida's fun and games, and over-against fascists like Carl Schmidt, the tension between law and goodness laid out in *Totality and Infinity* need not be read as "violent." Indeed, Levinas "did not reduce the domain of the moral to a single perspective; rather he supplemented it at a second level with a further perspective that is supposed to be in permanent tension with the first."[11] Though, as Honneth rightly notes: "Levinas does not, however, clarify whether such a face refers only to the faces of those objectively in need of help, that is, 'the poor' and 'the strange,' or to the faces of all other human subjects."[12] Honneth pinpoints here the problems in Levinas's logic and method I treated above. But to retain the force of Levinas's analysis of the face does not entail giving up the tension between law and goodness, it only requires giving up the indefensible notion that concepts, categories, or linguistic mediation in general is "necessarily violent." For all the stupidities of "postmodernism," its single most important achievement is to have underlined the import of the concrete in the determinations of justice and for the serious commitment to the truth. As Honneth positively emphasizes, the perspective of universality requires ongoing openness and supplementation by the historically concrete social, political, and personal contexts that inform its meaning. Levinas stands nearly alone in the desert of high "postmodernism" for both his insistence on this point and his refusal to endorse the indifferent nihilism that results by the game of theatrical skepticism.

At the conclusion of this study, I must say that both Levinas's positive contributions to phenomenology, and critical issues in his method, have helped clarify an important methodological point for comparative philosophy and religion in general. Levinas's treatment of singularity consists of an implicit act of formal differentiation of *this body* that faces me from every other face that ever has or ever will exist. A finite singularity is, in short: *a totality*. For ontologies that take time and temporality seriously, a singularity is moreover *open*: actively unfolding as the life of a person, community, or world. As such, it's not quite true that a singularity is indescribable or that language necessarily does "violence" to it. The problem of language in this context is not a problem of language per se, but rather the issue of *finitude*, for example, that our descriptions can get things wrong; can be biased, distortive, or incomplete. The limits of finitude noted, Levinas's emphasis on singularity—when the ban on language is lifted—allows us to distinguish three levels of analysis for projects of comparative cultural, religion, and philosophy: (1) *the universal*, a practice or meaning in question that applies to or constitutes all units of analysis of a given type; (2) *the particular*, or the situatedness of a practice or meaning in question that expresses or realizes itself in a particular historical community; and (3) *the singular*, a person or tradition as differentiated and distinguished from every other person and tradition in a given world. These simple distinctions yield the means necessary for a person or tradition to (i) acknowledge what is universally shared, (ii) discover how what is universally shared can be articulated or realized in a multitude of ways, and (iii) to consider what a specific person or tradition presents that is unique to them alone, understood in its unfolding totality. This may seem a rather obvious, indeed: banal, point; but in light of both prevailing scholarly practices and global neo-nativism, it's a point we all need to take more seriously.

Corresponding to this threefold distinction is the unique treatment of temporality analyzed in various philosophical traditions, but most radically and cogently in Husserl, Heidegger, Levinas, and the broader phenomenological movement. The creaturely finitude analyzed in *Being and Time* and *Totality and Infinity*—read against the backdrop of Husserl's oeuvre—empowers the identification of three distinct *normative postures* of both epistemological and political significance: the normativity inherent to (1.i) the practices of science, (2.i) the ethical life of historical communities, and (3.i) the responsible commitments of individual conscience. In cultural and political contexts, these normative postures find determinate expression in both singular individuals and actual historical polities. If we indeed are finite, it means we cannot fail to in some sense be conservative, progressive, and liberal *at once*, insofar as we necessarily *do* repeat traditions, we *can* in fact innovate, create, or try to found new traditions, and we *ought to answer for* the various commitments we each take up, stand for, and defend across the varied contexts of our everyday lives. In the context of particular cultures and polities, we can hence functionally specify the political tasks of the authentic conservative, authentic radical, and authentic liberal in terms of the norms and capacities each involves, and in ways that empower both the public assessment of claimants to a particular posture, and collaboration across postures in the construction of healthy publics. Something like this seems necessary in light of the pathologies of our political present, when bald libertarianism can be mistaken for religious conservatism, the right-wing anarchism of an Assange, Gabbard, or Greenwald can be mistaken for left-wing radicalism, and where liberals, either out of fear or a complacent desire to merely appear "radical," fail to decisively intervene in public debate.

Authentic conservatives doing their jobs must assess the best and worse in particular traditions and histories to present possibilities actually *worth* publicly repeating, and serve as a critical check on radical proposals by probing potential normative, systemic, or other consequences out of view to creative radicals because of their orienting focus. Authentic conservatives *steward the grounds* necessarily at play in the projects of radical creation and public deliberation. Authentic radicals doing their jobs must assess the best and worst in the present to identify possibilities actually *worth* our time and risk in the experimental and organizational tasks of the day, and serve as a critical check on demonstrably ungrounded conservative skepticism of a project or policy in question, possibilities often obscure to the conservative by virtue of their orienting focus. Authentic radicals *steward the open* necessarily at play in the projects of preserving the grounds and public deliberation. Authentic liberals doing their jobs must assess the best possibilities for repetition presented by authentic conservatives, and the best possibilities for innovative creation presented by authentic radicals, and assess which are actually *worth* enacting in light of the normative commitments of democratic publics and the actual shape of public opinion, extant resources, and so forth; and serve as a critical check on unproductive or degenerative conflict to which conservatives and radicals often devolve by virtue of their respective orienting foci. Authentic liberals *steward communicative reason* necessarily at play in the projects of preserving the grounds and radical creation. As I underlined above, these postures are not hermetically sealed categories but rather *normative postures* that in fact are open communities of contest and debate. Together, they name the structural elements necessarily involved in collective democratic projects and historically unfolding cultures. In order to beat neo-fascism back to its abyss, as citizens, scholars, and activists: we must above all cooperate across postures to jointly steward meaningful—and today especially: merely intelligible—public debate, and foster broader productive cultures of differential inquiry, art, and activism. Thanks to Levinas, I will treat these matters in more rigorous detail in forthcoming work.

IV. Reemergent Anti-Semitism

At the conclusion of this study, I want to underline the dire import of the resurgence of violent anti-Semitism we've witnessed since 2014: Kansas City (2014), Jerusalem (2014), Belgium (2014), Copenhagen (2015), Nice (2015), Tel Aviv (2015), Paris (2015), Columbus (2016), Mt. Carmel Cemetery (2017), Gothenburg (2017), New England Holocaust Memorial (2017), Pittsburg (2018), Halle (2019), İzmir (2019), Poway (2019), Los Angeles (2019), and so forth. In synagogue attacks alone, more than forty Jewish worshippers have been murdered or maimed over the last five years, to say nothing about the desecration of and destruction to Jewish property, memorials, and so forth. Motivations for these attacks fall roughly evenly between Islamicist and White supremacist ideologies. The Poway terrorist, nineteen-year-old John Timothy Earnest, was a member of a theologically traditionalist Orthodox Presbyterian Church. His manifesto interweaves mainstream protestant doctrines with "white genocide" conspiracy theories, making him the first explicit case of alt-right Evangelical terrorism that I'm aware of. Earnest ought to be taken with absolute seriousness as a harbinger of what to expect if the Evangelical community in the United States fails to repent of its idolatrous nationalism and fails to begin taking both spiritual discipleship and a politics of the common good more seriously in religious pedagogy and media. Across Europe, anti-Semitism is on a frightening rise. As Thiessen notes, "In 2018, France reported a 74 percent increase in anti-Semitic attacks, while in Germany they grew by 60 percent."[13] It will take a determined and collaborative effort by state and civil society actors to confront and transform the situation.

Even more worrying is the spike in open anti-Semitism we've seen in left-wing groups and circles. Anti-Semitic attitudes—with tropes like "international Jewish bankers"—has an old left-wing pedigree, but was long marginalized throughout the postwar era. The spike in violence against Jews we've seen in the past few years has coincided with public displays of anti-Semitic attitudes among leaders of social movements, political parties, media, and so forth. Beyond the well-publicized incidents that attended the Occupy Movement, even the Women's March and Black Lives Matter have had to deal with anti-Semitism in movement leadership.[14] To their credit, these movements took serious steps to rectify the issues. But in light of terrorist threats to local Jewish communities and the increasing impunity of anti-Semitic gestures by highly visible politicians and media personalities, the situation is deeply serious. When Jeremy Corbyn consistently and publicly tolerates anti-Jewish demagoguery in his own party, and when folks like Steve King, Louis Farrakhan, Steve Scalise, Alice Walker, and so forth aren't held accountable for their racist attitudes and speech, we shouldn't be surprised when younger generations reproduce them.

Though I support in principle highly specific and targeted BDS action, irresponsible and distortive marketing by the movement and allied "scholars" is helping to instill left-wing anti-Semitism in a new generation. As all responsible critics of Israel's policy in and toward the territories have noted, there is a stark difference between conditions inside Israel and conditions in the territories (themselves not merely subject to Israeli state brutality, but also under explicit Palestinian jurisdiction and political leadership).[15] Israeli policy toward the territories—especially under Netanyahu's disastrous tenure—*can* be meaningfully compared to Apartheid, though while noting that Israel is *not* the sole responsible actor there. By stark contrast, Arab citizens within Israel are legally enfranchised and quite active in the nation's public life. A recent survey suggests that some 65 percent of Arab-Israeli citizens *self*-identify as "Israeli Arabs" or "Israeli Palestinians" (as opposed to just "Arab" or "Palestinian").[16] Moreover,

> . . . a sweeping majority of the Arab public—87 percent—wished to be involved in the political system and its executive branch, and was very much in favor of its representatives joining the government. . . . The obstacle it faces is the lack of leaders and parties that acknowledge these wishes.[17]

If BDS would simply acknowledge these facts, and calibrate its rhetoric and targeting accordingly, it might actually help the Palestinian people, and moreover could help to galvanize internal Israeli resistance to the right-wing of its domestic politics. As it stands, BDS allows itself to be utilized as a propaganda tool by Hamas and Islamic Jihad, who to this day still execute, endorse, and publicly praise terror attacks that target Israeli civilians. None of this of course justifies Ahab, or the abject violence and cynicism of Netanyahu's policies (and the institutionalization of fascist parties on the right-wing of Israeli politics he has enabled). Standing with and aiding the Palestinian people requires not only confronting the worst quarters of Israeli politics, but also the long-held and standing tactics of Palestinian political leadership, and those that finance them from Tehran to the worst corners of the Gulf. Until the left gets serious about the actual situation and confronts all the various actors involved, it will continue to adopt activist tactics that propel anti-Semitism abroad, isolate Israeli political allies, and exacerbate the polarizations exploited by fascist actors to the detriment of both the Palestinian people and Josi Q Israeli (who desires peace and reviles her governments policies, but rightly worries that she cannot trust Palestinian leaders to defend her own children and family).[18] In light of the inordinate violence and draconian cynicism of state policy in the Netanyahu era, activism is needed that confronts, calls out, and transforms the postures of mutual destruction, and calls forth and enacts trust-building links between Israelis, Palestinians, and allies abroad for peace, actively embracing a common and collaborative future for both peoples. Nothing less will actually help. Can Jews in Palestine reasonably expect to live securely and at peace with Arab neighbors in a future (two- or bi-national) state? In light of the explicit statements and ongoing tactics of Palestinian political leaders and other regional actors, the answer to that question is *no*. Until that changes, abstract denouncements of Israel and incomplete empirical treatments of the holistic situation will continue to put Jewish lives at risk throughout the globe. We know with great specificity what must change in current Israeli policy and practices, but until we also pressure relevant Palestinian leadership (and their supporters) to radically change course in tactics and public statements, the situation is not likely to improve. I want to applaud, here, courageous Arab leadership exemplified in the Arab Peace Initiative. It's as good starting point for re-starting negotiations and carrying forth the peace process. I moreover congratulate both Emirati leaders and Israeli national security professionals for the years of joint effort that resulted in the quite recent normalization of diplomatic relations between their great polities. Courage of this sort will win a future of multilateral justice, peace, security, and prosperity for the entire region, above all: for the Palestinian people.

The resurgence of anti-Semitic violence and generalized anti-Jewish sentiment should be understood as a deadly serious harbinger: if we don't radically, multilaterally, and collaboratively change course, unthinkable moral disasters may well recur. Queer folk in Russia and Chechnya. Muslims in China and Myanmar. Latin Americans in Trump's America. Jewish folk across the globe. Who else? Not on my watch.

V. Conclusions and Beginnings

> WHEREAS disregard and contempt for human rights have resulted in barbarous acts which have outraged the conscience of mankind . . .
>
> —Preamble, UN Declaration of Human Rights

> Where, after all, do universal human rights begin? In small places, close to home—so close and so small that they cannot be seen on any maps of the world. Yet they are the world of the individual person; the neighborhood he lives in; the school or college he attends; the factory, farm, or office where he works. Such are the places where every man, woman, and child seeks equal justice, equal opportunity, equal dignity without discrimination. Unless these rights have meaning there, they have little meaning anywhere. Without concerted citizen action to uphold them close to home, we shall look in vain for progress in the larger world.
>
> —Eleanor Roosevelt

> How is it that, once victory took form and the horrible spectacle of the extermination camps was revealed, we could have shamelessly broken the promises given to the peoples in those years of ordeal?
>
> —René Cassin

If there is a single most important—even Eternal—point Levinas's oeuvre articulates and to which bears witness, it is perhaps best spoken in biblical words: "you shall love your neighbor as yourself" (Leviticus 19:17, Mark 12:31, cf. Bhagavad Gita 17:20, Śāntideva, The Bodhicaryāvatāra 8:28, the Analects 15:24, Romans 12:21, Qur'an, Sūrah al-Duhā 9–10). The paradox of the priority of the Other is that it inexorably unfolds by reference to the self (however construed), such that the concrete act of putting others before myself—the everyday "after you, Madame," that Levinas so admired and fought for—*shines forth*. This simple point finds glowing witness in nearly every nook of human wisdom across the ages, in the words of an African proverb: "I am what I am because of who we all are," or in the Hawaiian injunction: "Recognize others, be recognized; help others, be helped." For the various methodological problems and moral questions Levinas's work bequeaths us, witness to the explosive and creative Goodness contained in simple everyday kindness Stands eternal as both his singular witness and the common legacy of the best in our encultured humanity. "Faith . . . is believing that love without reward is valuable," Levinas maintains, and doesn't *living out* Eleanor Roosevelt's challenge precisely require such a faith? A courageous faith: *living true* to the problems and promises of human rights in the face of people and interests who despise them? With Levinas and Cassin, do we not owe it to all peoples to creatively traverse problems in human rights, and to make good on its promises in every ecosystem in our world? The risk of *living out* and the challenge of *living true* are inexorably at stake in *living well* in our world today.

But to endorse "love without reward" is just to say that it is *worthy*, and that its worth is publicly recognizable and owed praise. As Levinas ceaselessly emphasized: love without reward means caring about the death of another more than my own death. To care about another's death is also and inexorably to care for her memory and possibility, her past and future; it is to creatively repeat a past in the defiant hope that death is not the final word and arbiter of human meaning. In the words of a Comanche song: "*We shall live again; we shall live again.*" This desire is an inexorable complement to love without reward. The task of our time calls forth the stewards of memory and hope across cultures, to unite us all as individuated persons and traditions to courageously and creatively meet the challenges of neo-fascism, climate change, wealth inequality, migration, sustainable development, and so forth; even as we work through the legacies and ongoing realities of conquest, oppression, and exploitation with enough courage and creativity to dare to hallow the legacies and realize the dreams inhabiting the UN Declaration of Human Rights, all of its signatories: *together*. For Justice. For Beauty. For Peace. In Truth. The best days of global justice and transnational democracy are before us. Let's shine, *together*.

> *Prophesy to these bones and say to them, 'Dry bones, hear the word of the* LORD! *This is what the Sovereign* LORD *says to these bones: I will make breath enter you, and you will come to life. I will attach tendons to you and make flesh come upon you and cover you with skin; I will put breath in you, and you will come to life. Then you will know that I am the* LORD.*'*
>
> —Ezekiel 47: 4–6

> *Leaving behind nights of terror and fear*
> *I rise*
> *Into a daybreak that's wondrously clear*
> *I rise*
> *Bringing the gifts that my ancestors gave,*
> *I am the dream and the hope of the slave.*
> *I rise*
> *I rise*
> *I rise.*
>
> —Maya Angelou

Notes

Introduction

1. Outside of philosophy and ethics, various disciplinary, subdisciplinary, and interdisciplinary treatments of Levinas's work are legion. Here's a sample: **Anthropology**: Bernhard Leistle, ed., *Anthropology and Alterity. Responding to the Other* (New York: Routledge, 2016); Nigel Rapport, "Knowing the Uniqueness of Ego and the Mystery of Otherness," *Current Anthropology* 58, no. 2 (forthcoming); Peter Benson, "Facing Risk: Levinas, Ethnography, and Ethics," *Anthropology of Consciousness* 18, no. 2 (2007): 29–55; **Area Studies**: Linda Bolton, *Facing the Other: Ethical Disruption and the American Mind* (Baton Rouge: Louisiana State University Press, 2010); Elias K. Bongmba, "Fabian and Levinas on Time and the Other: Ethical Implications," *Philosophia Africana* 4, no. 1 (March 2001): 7–26; Leah Kalmanson, "Levinas in Japan: The Ethics of Alertly and the Philosophy of No-Self," *Continental Philosophy Review* 43, no. 2 (2010): 193–206; Wu Xiaoming, "Mengzi and Levinas: The Heart and Sensibility," *Journal of Chinese Philosophy* 35, no. 4 (2008): 571–77; **Art Theory and Criticism**: Hanoch Ben-Pazi, "Emmanuel Levinas: Hermeneutics, Ethics, and Art," *Journal of Literature and Art Studies* 5, no. 8 (2015): 588–600; Sam B. Girgus, *Levinas and the Cinema of Redemption: Time, Ethics, and the Feminine* (New York: Columbia University Press, 2010); Akos Krassoy, "The Ethics of the Face in Art: On the Margins of Levinas's Theory of Ethical Signification in Art," *Estetika* 53, no. 1 (2016): 42–73; Alain P. Toumayan, *Encountering the Other: The Artwork and the Problem of Difference in Blanchot and Levinas* (Pittsburgh: Duquesne University Press, 2004); **Comparative Literature**: Ann Astell and J. A. Jackson, *Levinas and Medieval Literature* (Pittsburgh: Duquesne University Press, 2009); Peter Fifield, *Late Modernist Style in Samuel Beckett and Emmanuel Levinas* (New York: Palgrave Macmillan, 2013); Jill Robbins, *Altered Reading: Levinas and Literature* (Chicago: University of Chicago Press, 1999); Donald R. Wehrs and David P. Haney, eds., *Levinas and Nineteenth-Century Literature: Ethics and Otherness from Romanticism Through Realism* (Newark: University of Delaware Press, 2009); **Cultural Studies**:

Adital Ben-Ari and Roni Strier, "Rethinking Cultural Competence: What Can We Learn from Levinas?," *British Journal of Sociology* 40, no. 7 (October 2010): 2155–67; Steven Shankman, *Other Others: Levinas, Literature, Transcultural Studies* (Albany: State University of New York Press, 2011); Joanna Zylinska, *The Ethics of Cultural Studies* (London: Continuum, 2005); **Education**: Donald S. Blumenfeld-Jones, *Ethics, Aesthetics, and Education: A Levinasian Approach* (New York: Palgrave Pivot, 2016); Denise Egtakkuehna, *Levinas and Education: At the Intersection of Faith and Reason* (London: Routledge, 2011); Anna Strhan, *Levinas, Subjectivity, Education: Towards an Ethics of Radical Responsibility* (New York: Wiley-Blackwell, 2012); Sharon Todd, *Learning from the Other: Levinas, Psychoanalysis, and Ethical Possibilities in Education* (Albany: State University of New York Press, 2012); **Intellectual History**: Michael L. Morgan, *Discovering Levinas* (Cambridge: Cambridge University Press, 2008); Samuel Moyn, *Origins of the Other: Emmanuel Levinas between Revelation and Ethics* (Ithaca, NY: Cornell University Press, 2006); Benjamin A. Wurgaft, *Thinking in Public: Strauss, Levinas, Arendt* (Philadelphia: University of Pennsylvania Press, 2015); **Jewish Studies**: Richard A. Cohen. *Levinasian Meditations: Ethics, Philosophy, Religion* (Pittsburgh: Duquesne University Press, 2010); Claire Elise Katz, *Levinas, Judaism, and the Feminine: The Silent Footsteps of Rebecca* (Bloomington: Indiana University Press, 2003); Hillary Putnam, *Jewish Philosophy as a Guide to Life: Rosenzweig, Buber, Levinas, Wittgenstein* (Bloomington: Indiana University Press, 2008); Kenneth Seeskin, *Thinking about the Torah: A Philosopher Reads the Bible* (Philadelphia: Jewish Publication Society, 2016); **Legal Theory**: Marinos Diamantides, ed., *Levinas, Law, Politics* (New York: Routledge, 2007); Desmond Manderson, *Proximity, Levinas, and the Soul of Law* (Montreal: McGill-Queen's University Press, 2006); Matthew Stone, *Levinas, Ethics, Law* (Edinburgh: Edinburgh University Press, 2016); **Nursing**: B. H. Kong, "Levinas' Ethics of Caring: Implications and Limits in Nursing," *Asian Nursing Research* 2, no. 4 (2008): 208–13; A. Clancy and T. Svensson, "'Faced' with Responsibility: Levinasian Ethics and the Challenges of Responsibility in Norwegian Public Health Nursing," *Nursing Philosophy* 8, no. 3 (2007): 158–66; Maria J. F. Gonçalves, "The Ethics of Levinas: The Fundamental and Essential in Nursing Care," *Journal of Nursing UFPE* 5, no. 6 (August 2011); **Political Theory**: Howard Caygill, *Levinas and the Political* (London: Routledge, 2002); Michael L. Morgan, *Levinas's Ethical Politics* (Bloomington: Indiana University Press, 2016); Gavin Rae, *The Problem of Political Foundations in Carl Schmitt and Emmanuel Levinas* (New York: Palgrave Macmillan, 2016); Ernst Wolff, *Political Responsibility for a Globalised World: After Levinas' Humanism* (Bielefeld: Transcript Verlag, 2011); **Post-Colonial Studies**: Oona Eisenstadt, "Eurocentrism and *Colorblindness*," *Levinas Studies* 7 (2012): 43–62; John E. Drabinski, *Levinas and the Postcolonial: Race, Nation, Other* (Edinburgh: Edinburgh University Press, 2011); Santiago Slabodsky, *Decolonial Judaism: Triumphal Failures of Barbaric Thinking* (New York: Palgrave Macmillan, 2014); **Psychology**: David M. Goodman, *The Demanded Self: Levinasian Ethics and Identity in Psychology* (Pittsburgh: Duquesne University Press, 2012); Sarah

Harasym, *Levinas and Lacan: The Missed Encounter* (Albany: State University of New York Press, 1998); Kevin C. Krycka et al., eds., *Psychotherapy for the Other: Levinas and the Face-to-Face Relationship* (Pittsburgh: Duquesne University Press, 2015); Paul Marcus, *In Search of the Good Life: Emmanuel Levinas, Psychoanalysis and the Art of Living* (London: Karnac Books, 2010); **Religious Studies**: Tamara C. Eskenazi and Gary A. Phillips, *Levinas and Biblical Studies* (Atlanta: Society of Biblical Literature, 2003); Sarah Hammerschlag, *Broken Tablets: Levinas, Derrida, and the Literary Afterlife of Religion* (New York: Columbia University Press, 2016); Alain Mayama, *Emmanuel Levinas' Conceptual Affinities with Liberation Theology* (New York: Peter Lang Publishing, 2011); J. Aaron Simmons and David Wood, eds., *Kierkegaard and Levinas: Ethics, Politics, and Religion* (Bloomington: Indiana University Press, 2008); **Sociology**: Btihaj Ajana, "In Defense of Poststructural Ethics in Sociological Praxis," *Enquire* 1, no. 1 (2008): 23–31; Zygmunt Bauman, "Towards a Sociological Theory of Morality," in *Modernity and the Holocaust* (Cambridge: Polity, 1989); Stan J. Knapp, "Weber and Levinas on Modernity and the Problem of Suffering: Reconstructing Social Theory as Ethically Framed Rather than Epistemologically Framed," in Harry F. Dahms et al., eds., *Reconstructing Social Theory, History and Practice* (Bingly: Emerald Group Publishing Limited, 2016), 145–70; **Even Economics and Organizational Management**: Dag G. Aasland, *Ethics and Economy: After Levinas* (London: Mayfly Ephemera, 2009); Jacob D. Rendtorff, *French Philosophy and Social Theory: A Perspective for Ethics and Philosophy of Management* (New York: Springer, 2014); Naud van der Ven, *The Shame of Reason in Organizational Change: A Levinasian Perspective* (Dordrecht, Springer, 2010).

2. Peter Atterton and Matthew Calarco, "Editor's Introduction," in *Radicalizing Levinas* (Albany: State University of New York Press, 2010), ix.

3. I must single out Judith Butler and Annabel Herzog for special thanks here. Their relevant work planted the seeds that became this book.

4. Florian Rotzer. "Interview with Emmanuel Levinas," in *Conversations with French Philosophers*, trans. G. E. Aylesworth (New Jersey: Humanities Press, 1995), 63.

5. Emmanuel Levinas, *Unforeseen History*, trans. Nidra Poller (Champaign: University of Illinois Press, 2003), 108.

6. John E. Drabinski. *Levinas and the Post-Colonial: Race, Nation, Other* (Edinburg: Edinburg University Press, 2011), xi.

7. For an excellent review of work on Levinas in critical race theory, see Kris Sealey, "Levinas and the Critical Philosophy of Race," in *Oxford Handbook of Levinas, ed.* Michael L. Morgan (Oxford: Oxford University Press, 2018), doi: 10.1093/oxfordhb/9780190455934.013.41. I endorse Sealey's critical reading strategy: "coming to Levinas . . . [such that] we encounter a Levinas that is both himself and other than himself," but I'm not competent enough in the relevant literature to fairly assess her proposals.

8. Robert Bernasconi, "Who Is My Neighbor? Who Is the Other? Question 'the Generosity of Western Thought,' " in *Beyond Levinas: Critical Assessments of*

Leading Philosophers, Vol. 4., ed. Claire Katz and Lara Trout (London: Routledge, 2005), 27.

9. Simon Critchley, "Five Problems in Levinas' View of Politics and the Sketch of a Solution to Them," *Political Theory* 32, no. 2 (April 2004): 176.

10. Sonia Sikka, "How Not to Read the Other 'All the Rest Can Be Translated,'" *Philosophy Today* 43, no. 2 (Summer 1999): 195.

11. Lin Ma, "All the Rest Must Be Translated: Levinas' Notion of Sense," *Journal of Chinese Philosophy* 35, no. 4 (2008): 599. See also Andrew McGettigan, "The Philosopher's Fear of Alterity: Levinas, Europe and Humanities 'without Sacred History,'" *Radical Philosophy* 140 (2006): 15–25.

12. Xianglong Zhang, "The Philosophical Features of Confucianism in Inter-Cultural Dialogue: Universalism or Non-Universalism?," *Frontiers of Philosophy in China* 4, no. 4 (2009): 483.

13. Thanks to Oona Eisenstadt for providing me with a copy of her essay. I am also partially indebted to her for my categorization of the scholarship on this question. Oona Eisenstadt, "Eurocentrism and Colorblindness," *Levinas Studies* 7 (2012): 43–62. To my knowledge, Cohen has not written or published on this topic. He expressed this view in a post-paper discussion at Translating The World conference, Institute of Jewish Thought and Heritage, SUNY Buffalo, May 2, 2011. Cohen gestures to this approach in print in an interview with Chung-Hsiung Lai. See Richard A. Cohen, *Levinasian Meditations: Ethics, Philosophy, Religion* (Pittsburgh: Duquesne University Press, 2010), 169–98.

14. Sikka, "How Not to Read the Other," 195–206; Rudi Visker, "Is Ethics Fundamental?," *Continental Philosophy Review* 36, no. 3 (2003): 263–302.

15. Bernasconi, "Who Is My Neighbor?," 5–27; Enrique Dussel, *Ética de la Liberación en la Edad de la Globalización y de la Exclusión* (Madrid: Trotta, 1989). See also Dennis Beach, "History and the Other: Dussel's Challenge to Levinas," *Philosophy and Social Criticism* 30, no. 3 (2004): 315–30.

16. I am highly indebted to the work of Steven Crowell in my background research for this text, especially his *Husserl, Heidegger, and the Space of Meaning: Paths Toward Transcendental Phenomenology* (Evanston: Northwestern University Press, 2001) and *Normativity and Phenomenology in Husserl and Heidegger* (Cambridge: Cambridge University Press, 2013).

17. I follow Finlayson, who nicely captures what I attempt to practice here: ". . . like Horkheimer and Adorno before him, Habermas employs the method of *immanent criticism*. One can also call it internal, as opposed to external criticism. The critical theorists think this approach derives from Hegel and Marx. In some respects it is closer to the Socratic mode of argumentation, which assumes the position of the interlocutor, for the sake of argument, without actually endorsing it, in order to point out its [potential] incoherence . . . Whatever its origins, the critical theorists aim to criticize an object—a conception of society or a work of philosophy—on its own terms, and not on the basis of values or standards that transcend it, in order

to bring its [potential problems] to light." James Gordon Finlayson, *Habermas: A Very Short Introduction* (Oxford: Oxford University Press, 2005), 9.

18. Robert Bernasconi. "What Is the Question to Which 'Substitution' Is the Answer?," in *The Cambridge Companion to Levinas*, ed. S. Critchley et al (Cambridge: Cambridge University Press, 2002), 234–51.

Chapter 1

1. Emmanuel Levinas. *Totality and Infinity*, trans. A. Lingis (Pittsburgh: Duquesne University Press, 1961), 203, 172.

2. Nam-In Lee, "The Phenomenology of Sensible Life in Husserl and Levinas," *Graduate Faculty Philosophy Journal* 34, no. 2 (2013): 317–37.

3. See Robert Bernasconi, "Re-Reading Totality and Infinity," in *The Question of the Other*, ed. Arleen B. Dallery and Charles E. Scott (Albany: State University of New York Press, 1989), 23–34; Jacques Derrida, "Violence and Metaphysics," in *Writing and Difference*, trans. A. Bass (Chicago: University of Chicago Press, 1980), 97–192 [hereafter *VM*]; Nam-In Lee, 2013, 317–37; John Sallis, "Levinas and the Elemental," *Research in Phenomenology* 28, no. 1 (1998): 152–59; John Wild, "Introduction," *Totality and Infinity*, trans. A. Lingis (Pittsburgh: Duquesne University Press, 1961), 19; and David Wood, "Some Questions for My Levinasian Friends," in *Addressing Levinas*, ed. E. S. Nelson et al. (Evanston: Northwestern University Press, 2005), 152–69.

4. Lee, 2013, 317. For examples of this tradition, see Anthony Beavers, *Levinas beyond the Horizons of Cartesianism* (New York: Peter Lang, 1995), 81–86; Richard Cohen, *Ethics, Exegesis, and Philosophy* (Cambridge: Cambridge University Press, 2007), 153–55; Adriaan Peperzak, "Phenomenology—Ontology—Metaphysics: Levinas' Perspective on Husserl and Heidegger," *Man and World* 16, no. 2 (1983): 113–27; Edith Wyschogrod, *Emmanuel Levinas: The Problem of Ethical Metaphysics* (New York: Fordham University Press, 2001), 67–71.

5. Levinas, *TI*, 28–29. I here set aside the question of what "transcendental deduction" might mean for a method that claims to be a phenomenology.

6. Levinas, *TI*, 28–29.

7. See Dominique Janicaud et al., eds., *Phenomenology and the Theological Turn: The French Debate*, trans. B. G. Prusak (New York: Fordham University Press, 2000).

8. Richard Cohen, *Levinasian Meditations: Ethics, Philosophy, and Religion* (Pittsburgh: Duquesne University Press, 2010), 30.

9. Levinas, *TI*, 109.

10. Ibid., 28.

11. Ibid., 114.

12. Ibid., 110.

13. Ibid., 111.

14. Ibid., 114.
15. Ibid., 113.
16. Ibid., 115.
17. Ibid., 114, 119.
18. Ibid., 115.
19. Ibid., 118.
20. Ibid., 119.
21. Ibid., 113.
22. Ibid., 111.
23. Ibid., 119.
24. Ibid.
25. Ibid., 113–14.
26. Adriaan Peperzak, *To the Other: An Introduction to the Philosophy of Emmanuel Levinas* (West Lafayette: Purdue University Press, 1993), 152.
27. Levinas, *TI*, 55–56.
28. Ibid., 127.
29. Ibid., 118.
30. Ibid., 111–12.
31. Ibid., 131.
32. Ibid., 131.
33. Ibid.
34. Ibid., 132.
35. Ibid., 131.
36. Ibid., 132, 137, 161.
37. Ibid., 132.
38. Ibid. What can it mean to say "interiority is not convertible into exteriority" in an "*inside-out world*" (132) (my emphasis)?
39. Ibid., 131.
40. Ibid., 132.
41. Ibid., 137–38.
42. Ibid., 135.
43. Ibid., 138.
44. Ibid., 138, 140, 137.
45. Ibid., 144, 150.
46. Ibid., 140–41.
47. Ibid., 141.
48. Ibid., 143.
49. Ibid., 142.
50. Ibid.
51. Levinas emphasizes this because he will come to distinguish the *apeironic* "in-finity" of the elements from the Infinite proper that occurs with the face. Hence it appears that the sensible ego already *knows* where it's heading in this description.
52. See especially Levinas, *TI*, 135–36.

53. Emmanuel Levinas, *Existence and Existents*, trans. A. Lingis (Pittsburgh: Duquesne University Press, 1998).
54. Levinas, *TI*, 127.
55. Ibid., 39, 55, 58–59, 115, 132.
56. Ibid., 153.
57. Ibid., 154.
58. Ibid.
59. Ibid.
60. Ibid., 153–54 (*my emphasis*).
61. That is, the first introduction in the context of Levinas's actual phenomenological analyses. The entirety of the book is interspersed with references to and anticipations of the Other treated in section III, as Levinas seeks to distinguish what he is getting at from the accounts offered by other philosophers. I have sought to systematically ignore these references and anticipations, except when they are deemed necessary to reconstruct Levinas's meaning (as in my discussion of the ego's *stand* above).
62. Levinas, *TI*, 155.
63. I set aside for now the many questions this must raise, and follow Levinas in his description. For good treatments of Levinas's take on the feminine, see Tina Chanter, "Conditions: The Politics of Ontology and the Temporality of the Feminine," and Diane Perpich, "Sensible Subjects: Levinas and Irigaray on Incarnation and Ethics," in *Addressing Levinas*, ed. E. S. Nelson et al (Evanston: Northwestern University Press, 2005), 296–338.
64. Levinas, *TI*, 155.
65. Ibid., 155–56.
66. Ibid., my emphasis. It must be noted: Levinas seems to be presenting here a Janus-faced picture of God. The feminine is being obliquely construed as the feminine side of divinity, as his "primordial phenomenon of gentleness" makes plain. This move reflects rabbinic teaching that male and female jointly reflect the divine image. Yet, unlike rabbinic teaching, and when taken with his "the light of the face is necessary for separation" (150), this presents an essentially arbitrary picture of God. Levinas's God both *constitutes* and *totally contests* the ego's happy contentment, both *produces* and *judges*, simultaneously *gives* and *chastises* the ego for the very happiness S/He makes possible. As such, Levinas's God seems no less arbitrary than the "pagan gods," by virtue of the meanings he himself attributes to it. See Pinchas Kahn. "The Duality of Man: A Study in Talmudic Allegorical Interpretations," *Jewish Bible Quarterly* 36, no. 2 (2008): 102–8.
67. This claim that the character of *being intended* accounts for the alterity of the feminine is my own hypothesis, because Levinas never explicitly claims this. But this is what he assumes or performs. If the feminine were simply the pure experience of welcome, she could not be affectively distinguishable from, say, a pleasant landscape.
68. Levinas, *TI*, 155.

69. Ibid., 156.
70. Ibid.
71. Ibid.
72. I first penned these lines in January 2012, before subsequent tragic developments in Egypt and Syria. I retain this reference unaltered in solidarity with the noble struggle of the Egyptian and Syrian *demoi*.
73. Ibid., 156–57.
74. Ibid., 157.
75. Ibid., 158.
76. Ibid., 157.
77. Ibid., 157–58, 161–62.
78. Ibid., 157. I'll set aside for now the paradox in play in these two determinations. Labor as Levinas describes it *is* a process of change. And is it true that possessed objects lose their "independence"? Wood doesn't cease to be what it is when it becomes paper, frames, etc. This is why his attempt to exclude form from nature ultimately fails. He seems to be relying on an implicit analogy to human relations.
79. Ibid., 159, 160.
80. Ibid., 159.
81. Ibid., 161.
82. Ibid., 160.
83. Ibid., 169.
84. Ibid., 168.
85. Ibid., 169.
86. This move immediately mires him in vicious contradiction or infinite regress. Given how Levinas tries to situate affective life with respect to theory, we aren't licensed to choose between these poisons. Either way, however, fatality ensues.
87. Ibid., 169, 128.
88. Ibid., 127.
89. Ibid., 169.
90. Ibid., 168.
91. Ibid., 169.
92. Ibid., 55–56.
93. Ibid., 170.
94. Ibid., 299. This is straightforwardly equivocal. He presents theory in Kantian terms, yet talk of "possessing . . . its origin" in the ontology he's performing suggests some kind of realism. Is the origin *transcendental*, that is, the determin*ing* free activity of thinking? Or is it *real*, that is, the determin*ative* "discoveries" of inquiry? If it's somehow *both*, some form of conceptual or categorial mediation is necessarily in play.
95. Ibid., 170. This suggests that the ego's identity is *not only* its immediate enjoyings, but rather issues in whatever sense the pre-worldly "anterior" holds.

96. Ibid., 159, 161.
97. Ibid., 161.
98. Ibid., 160.
99. Ibid., 166.
100. While Heidegger's overall story in *Being and Time* warrants criticism, it must be said that Levinas does an injustice to Heidegger. Levinas interprets being-in-the-world in something like a quasi-Darwinian way, and this is ultimately unjustified on a fair reading of Heidegger's text. The same must be said of his critique of Husserl. Levinas forces Husserl into a procrustean metaphysical idealism and presents constitution in a way that the mature Husserl would, and did, reject.
101. Ibid., 158.
102. Ibid., 161. I note that Levinas seems to be equivocating between Aristotle's primary and secondary substances, that is, the empirical presence of "real" individuals and the *form* to which they belong.
103. Ibid., 136, 137, 160 (my emphasis).
104. Ibid., 163.
105. Ibid., 112.
106. Ibid., 144. What phenomenological justification do we have for prioritizing happiness or rendering it more original than suffering? Moreover, the categorial status assigned to enjoyment in its teleological function *idealizes* it, that is, transforms it from "pure immediacy" to a *memory* and event the ego can strive to *repeat* when it is in fact *not* enjoying. When it functions as a *telos*, immediacy is lost, and therefore the ego is *not* merely its immediate enjoyments.
107. Ibid., 113.
108. Ibid., 140.
109. Ibid., 113.
110. Ibid., 55–56.
111. Ibid., 158.
112. Ibid., 161.
113. Ibid., 161.
114. Ibid.
115. Ibid., 160, 169.
116. Ibid., 156.
117. Ibid., 161.
118. "The need for food does not have existence is its goal, but food. In enjoyment I am absolutely for myself. Egoist . . . outside of all communication and all refusal to communicate—without ears, like a hungry stomach. The world as a set of instruments forming a system . . . bears witness to a particular organization of labor in which 'foods' take on the signification of fuel in the economic machinery" (134). Given his nod to Marx here, it's perhaps fair to note: construing the ego as primitively sated "bears witness" to a specific social location in the system alluded to.
119. Ibid., 136, 160–61.

120. Ibid., 160, 161.
121. Ibid., 124.
122. Ibid., 155 (my emphasis).
123. Ibid., 157.
124. Ibid., 159.
125. Ibid., 161.
126. Ibid., 161, 154 (my emphasis).
127. Ibid., 165 (my emphasis).
128. Ibid., 166 (my emphasis).
129. Ibid., 165, 157.
130. Ibid., 165 (my emphasis). The givenness of the face must somehow empower a coherent account of the ego's self-relation and a functional treatment of nature.
131. Ibid., 161.
132. Ibid., 155.
133. Ibid., 155, 157.
134. Ibid., 165, 157. "The home that founds possession is not a possession in the same sense as the movable goods it can collect and keep. It is possessed because it already and henceforth is hospitable for its proprietor [thanks to the feminine]" (157). It is questionable whether there are really two different senses of "possession" in play here, because Levinas elsewhere refers to "sojourn in a dwelling" (157). The dwelling *moves* or is "transportable." Why is motility a freedom for dwelling and "violence" for the face? More saliently for my analysis here, the "hospitable" dimension of dwelling only emerges after suspending the full transcendence of the feminine, and in just this way presupposes the *grasp*.
135. Ibid., 162.
136. Ibid., 127.
137. Ibid., 128.
138. Ibid., 132.
139. Ibid., 161.
140. Ibid., 165.
141. Cf. Dennis Keenan, *Death and Responsibility: The "Work" of Levinas* (Albany: State University of New York Press, 1999), 33–45. I endorse Keenan's thesis that "lived body and physical body, the psychic and the physical" (45) is a site of ambiguity, and that it is bound up in the question of death. I might even endorse what he terms the "double origin" (35) implied by the ambiguity, if a cogent and coherent account of it could be mounted. But the ambiguity in question cannot function as Levinas suggests, Keenan's sensitive and generous attempt notwithstanding. The "*as though*" (34) as Levinas poses it is incoherent, and methodologically this means: we can derive literally anything from it, insofar as anything can follow from a contradiction. At best, the statement "anterior to the

world to which it is posterior" (36) can only mean something like "exists or holds throughout its worldly sojourn and our experiences of it," which does not exploit, as Levinas does, the epistemic or conditional logic the terms "anterior/posterior" possess. Acknowledging the ambiguity of the body does not necessarily commit one to Levinas's own equivocations.

142. Ibid., 113.
143. Ibid., 165.
144. Ibid.
145. Ibid., 204–5.
146. Ibid., 173.
147. Ibid., 170 (my emphasis).
148. Ibid., 54, 118.
149. Ibid., 169.
150. Ibid., 112.
151. Ibid., 157. "The ancient thesis puts representation at the basis of every practical behavior . . . is too hastily discredited" (94). Here, Levinas wants to both (i) contrast his position to Heidegger, and (ii) nevertheless rely on Heidegger for the priority he posits for sensibility to practice to theory. His critique of the concept and of the priority of action depends on a Heideggerian argument for the derived nature of theory. To critique ontology requires nevertheless granting priority to theory over practice. *TI* as a whole spins in this circle, as I conclusively demonstrate in the next two chapters.
152. 1) "Substantiality does not reside in the sensible nature of things" (161). 2) Labor "does not put into practice an antecedent 'knowledge,' it has immediately a hold on matter" (160). 3) "Labor grapples with the fallacious resistance of nameless matter, . . . [with] the resistance of nothingness" (160) Therefore, 4) labor depends on a "miraculous grasp of a thing in the night" (163).
153. Ibid., 109.
154. Ibid., 117.
155. Ibid., 118.
156. Ibid.
157. Ibid., 120 (his emphasis).
158. Ibid., 134.
159. Ibid., 147, 132.
160. Ibid., 118, 132. It should be noted, on his own very descriptions, that Levinas's ego analysis fails to specify what distinguishes the human from other mammals, because other sentient creatures also experience happiness and differentially respond to their environment for the sake of their own flourishing. The communicative, and not merely sentient, dimension is actually presupposed here to distinguish the human qua human.
161. Ibid., 118–19.

162. Ibid.

163. Derrida, *VM*, 110–11, 152–53. Derrida makes just this point in response to Levinas's tendentious treatment of Kierkegaard.

164. Ibid., 134, 75, 163. I dedicate this chapter to John Wild, the first English-language reader to "wonder why the original state of enjoyment is called purely subjective and even solipsistic when this separated self is clearly encompassed by the elements, and existing . . . with others in the world. He may seek more light on what [Levinas] calls 'inner life' and on its specific differences from the preceding subjective condition." John Wild, "Introduction," in *Totality and Infinity*, trans. A. Lingis (Pittsburgh: Duquesne University Press, 1961), 1.

Chapter 2

1. Levinas, *TI*, 127, 160–61.
2. Ibid., 136.
3. Ibid., 195.
4. Ibid., 198.
5. Ibid., 279, 295; 110, 215. It must be noted: given Levinas's affective understanding of the ego, to "be in a relationship while absolving oneself from this relation is to speak" (215) actually entails that egos are ultimately *indifferent* to *what* they say, that is, the content of communication doesn't *matter* to them. Clearly, Levinas can't know this a priori in particular cases. He is falling prey to his own attempt to recruit immediacy into the *logic* of his descriptive method.
6. Ibid., 195. To perhaps overstretch his metaphor: "overflowing" inherently implies "entering into" or passing through.
7. I examine closely what Levinas precisely means by "overflowing," "surplus," and "exceed" in the next chapter. For now, I simply try to present his case in its best light.
8. *TI*, 197. Note: he here describes the face-to-face in terms of sociality. He later uses sociality to refer to fraternal relations by contrast to the face-to-face (cf. 213).
9. Ibid., 195.
10. Ibid.
11. Ibid., 197, 199.
12. Ibid., 198.
13. Ibid., 199.
14. Ibid.
15. Ibid.
16. Ibid.
17. Ibid., 201.
18. Ibid., 199.

19. Ibid., 78.
20. Ibid., 199.
21. Ibid.
22. Ibid., 51.
23. Ibid., 199.
24. Ibid., 195.
25. Ibid., 262.
26. Ibid., 50–51.
27. Ibid., 204.
28. I borrow this felicitous phrase from Steven Galt Crowell and his fine book *Husserl, Heidegger, and the Space of Meaning: Paths Toward Transcendental Phenomenology* (Evanston: Northwestern University Press, 2001).
29. Ibid., 199.
30. Ibid., 197.
31. Ibid., 245.
32. Ibid., 201.
33. Ibid., 213.
34. Ibid.
35. Ibid., 201.
36. Ibid., 214.
37. Ibid., 137, 150, 130.
38. Ibid., 213–14.
39. Ibid. (my emphasis).
40. Emmanuel Levinas, "The Paradox of Morality: An Interview with Emmanuel Levinas," in *The Provocation of Levinas: Rethinking the Other*, ed. Robert Bernasconi and David Wood (London: Routledge, 1988), 168–80 (my emphasis).
41. To assert that the face is non-substitutable is not only to beg the question, but it's an abuse of language. Levinas *performs* the substitutability of the ego in the necessary generality performed in his descriptive analysis, and does so *before* the explicit generalization he performs in his account of the third party. My analysis demonstrates that the *force* he conjures in his descriptive rhetoric, a force that renders his claims for "asymmetry" and "infinite" responsibility plausible, doesn't issue from immediate faces, but internally depends on non-moral worldly descriptions. He simply fails to present a *purely* self-referring entity or meaning.
42. All of Levinas's talk of radical alterity and exhortations to refrain from "doing violence" to the other seem premised in an attempt to *a priori exclude* all genuinely competing accounts of what this meaning involves.
43. Ibid., 201.
44. Levinas appeals to the alleged "violence" of concepts against tradition while simultaneously utilizing them both before and subsequent to the face's appearance.
45. Ibid., 113.
46. Ibid., 42 (my emphasis).

47. Ibid., 66 (my emphasis).
48. Ibid., 61, 201 (my emphasis).
49. Ibid., 66. Is form a problem *as form*, or only because it might "congeal" into a "plastic" form? What determines whether a form is "real" or merely "plastic"? Moreover, what can it mean to say "alienate the exteriority of the other"? To *other* the *otherness* of the other, that is, alter its "content." Or to establish the idea of otherness purely *as* an idea, purely "internal," that is, without reference to a *reality* outside the mind? Such questions are pressing given Levinas's failure to discuss the phenomenological reduction.
50. Ibid., 61, 201.
51. Ibid., 150 (my emphasis).
52. Bernasconi, 1989, 32.
53. Levinas, *TI*, 181 (my emphasis).
54. Ibid., 53.
55. Cf. *TI*, 78, 293.
56. Ibid., 42.
57. Ibid., 150.
58. Ibid., 299, 201.
59. Ibid., 247.
60. Ibid., 269.
61. Ibid., 269, 254.
62. Ibid., 264.
63. Ibid., 255. Again, if even the face can be enjoyed, then it appears "absolute" alterity is meaningless talk on Levinas's own terms.
64. Ibid., 264.
65. Ibid., 264.
66. Ibid., 267.
67. Ibid., 284.
68. Ibid., 279.
69. Ibid., 247.
70. Given the central role ascribed to paternity, it is significant to note that Levinas does not devote an independent section to it. In section IV of the text, he clearly and thematically marks his subject matter as follows: A. The Ambiguity of Love, B. Phenomenology of Eros, C. Fecundity, D. Subjectivity in Eros, E. Transcendence in Fecundity, F. Filiality and Fraternity, G. The Infinity of Time. Because paternity is the key term around which the whole section is centered, why is it left dispersed and in the background?
71. Ibid., 267.
72. If we have more than one child, or more than one intimate friend, we experience an inner resistance to prioritizing them. Dan, Matt, Mike, and Bob are my best friends. I feel unable to pick one over the other as "the closest." Rather, each is chosen by me as uniquely "best," each in his own way. They are the *same*—

my best *friends*—and *other*, each of them *uniquely "best,"* and both simultaneously. Levinas seeks to generalize this paradox to humanity as such, that is, to *generalize* what is essentially *singular*. Clearly, however: my friends *instantiate* some form of experientially determinate and perfectly general notion of friendship. The singularity of my friendship with Dan, Mike, Matt, and Bob doesn't annul this generality, but in some sense depends on it: their singularity consists of realizing friendship for me *like no others*. And among them, their singularity doesn't sheerly issue in the fact that they are passively *there*, but in their positive and active commitment to me, that is, that they have *chosen* to be there *repeatedly*: they have laughed-, enjoyed-, fought-, made up-, and enduringly dwelled-with-me, *like no others*. Indeed, they at times "asymmetrically" aided me, that is, loved me unconditionally, and I them, more enduringly than all others. The immediacy and abiding force of our friendship involves a plenitude that is lost in this description and that resists total communication (e.g., to get my meaning, you must do more than comprehend my words, but must have actually experienced a like form of intimacy with others to whom you apply the term "best friend"), but this description in no way denigrates or annuls my friendship with these others. Indeed, it honors them by naming them as the unique ones who in fact have enriched my life: Daniel Chichester, Michael Dunstan, Matthew Heaney, and Robert Hoffman.

73. Ibid., 279.
74. Ibid., 269.
75. Ibid., 278.
76. Ibid., 280 (my emphasis).
77. This fits precisely with Levinas's early description: the Other "greets me in the primordial phenomenon of gentleness" is *not* a *human* feminine Other, but the divine other. Levinas is nodding to the Rabbis by painting an oblique picture of woman and man as jointly constituting the image of God. See Kahn, 2008.
78. Ibid., 213.
79. Ibid., 268.
80. Ibid., 214.
81. Ibid., 268.
82. Ibid., 278.
83. To assert that humanity and divine "effectuation" are not merely concepts, but "real" ontological events or structures, is to beg the question, for example, for a non-theist.
84. Ibid., 280, 201.
85. Ibid., 213, 247.
86. Bergo notes just this: "Yet even annihilating [the other] does not do away with the nudity of his face and the expression of his gaze, *which we understand*, Levinas will say (see note TI 174, 199–200). . . . Levinas is dangerously close, here, to losing separation of the two orders entirely. How do we understand anything, ethically?" Bettina Bergo. *For a Beauty That Adorns the Earth: Levinas between Ethics*

and Politics (Dordrecht: Kluwer, 1999), 94. It must be said, Levinas doesn't "lose" separation, he has simple failed to achieve it.

87. Lanei M. Rodemeyer, *Intersubjective Temporality: It's About Time* (Dordrecht: Springer, 2006).

88. Levinas, *TI*, 203, 150.

89. Levinas's equivocal method prevents us from concluding that the Other "creates" human *bodies*, because he illicitly refers to the face, and *assumes* an unthematized identity between moral command and divine creation. Divine creation, and the fraternity it "effectuates," is posited as the "condition for both the goodness and transcendence of the face" (247), hence prohibiting him from referring to the face in the creation of "infinite time" (ibid.) and "infinite being" (148, 284).

90. This is just to say that *TI*'s failures don't necessarily belong to Maimonides or pseudo-Dionysus. For those inclined to theology, my critique of Levinas does not decide more general questions in religious hermeneutics or theological semantics.

91. Levinas, *TI*, 279.

Chapter 3

1. Martin Kavka, "Humanizing Philosophy of Religion: On Language in Levinas and Sellars," *Journal for Culture and Religious Theory* 14, no. 2 (Spring 2015): 230. I thank Martin Kavka for supplying me an advance copy of his essay. Robert Bernasconi, "Levinas and the Struggle for Existence," in *Addressing Levinas*, ed. E. S. Nelson et al. (Evanston: Northwestern University Press, 2005), 180; Emmanuel Levinas, *Of God Who Comes to Mind*, trans. B. Bergo (Stanford: Stanford University Press, 1998), 89.

2. Michael Morgan, *Cambridge Introduction to Emmanuel Levinas* (Cambridge: Cambridge University Press, 2011), 130, 43 n23. For Morgan's own treatment, see his excellent book: *Discovering Levinas* (Cambridge, Cambridge University Press, 2007), 39–56.

3. Morgan, 2011, 53. I'm fully indebted to Atterton here. Peter Atterton, review of *Cambridge Introduction to Emmanuel Levinas*, by M. Morgan, *Notre Dame Philosophical Reviews*, July 18, 2011, https://ndpr.nd.edu/news/24763-the-cambridge-introduction-to-emmanuel-levinas/ (my emphasis).

4. See John Wild, "Introduction," in *Totality and Infinity*, by Emmanuel Levinas, trans. A. Lingis (Pittsburgh: Duquesne University Press, 1961), 19.

5. Jacques Derrida, "Violence and Metaphysics: An Essay on the Thought of Emmanuel Levinas," in *Writing and Difference*, trans. A. Bass (Chicago: University of Chicago Press, 1978) [hereafter *VM*]; Theodor de Boer, "An Ethical Transcendental Philosophy," in *Face to Face with Levinas*, ed. R. A. Cohen (Albany: State University of New York Press, 1988), 83–116; Robert Bernasconi, "Re-Reading Totality and Infinity," in *The Question of the Other*, ed. Dallery and Scott (Albany: State University of New York Press, 1989), 23–34.

6. For the purposes of this chapter, when I use the term "metaphysical," I mean it in the conventional sense. The special sense Levinas tries to attribute to the term suffers from precisely the incoherence I analyze here.

7. Levinas, *TI*, 25, 23, 67, 260.

8. Ibid., 195, 79, 64, 53.

9. I am deeply indebted to the long tradition of critical *TI* scholarship in my own proposed explanation. The "how" and "why" of my proposed explanation are my own contribution, because, next to Derrida's *VM*, I have been unable to find a single detailed and focused treatment of *TI's* explicit method. I am also partly indebted to both Steven Galt Crowell and Martin Kavka for my proposal herein. Without their superlative generosity in reading, commenting on, and debating my work through personal correspondence, this chapter would have likely taken different form. In my view, Crowell is one the most rigorous phenomenologist of our day. His Heideggerian-normative project is quite fascinating and original. He has had a transformative influence on my own thinking in ways I'm still sorting through. See Steven Galt Crowell, *Phenomenology and Normativity* (Cambridge: Cambridge University Press, 2013).

10. Moran notices precisely this: "[t]he sum total of these entirely unsupported, not to say downright contradictory, claims about the nature of this so-called non-disclosive encounter with the face is not going to add up to a coherent picture." Dermot Moran, *Introduction to Phenomenology* (London: Routledge, 2000), 351–52.

11. Beyond Derrida and Bernasconi, other critical treatments include Randy Friedman, "Alterity and Asymmetry in Levinas's Ethical Phenomenology," *Journal of Scriptural Reasoning* 13, no. 1 (2014), http://jsr.shanti.virginia.edu/vol-13-no-1-june-2014-phenomenology-and-scripture/alterity-and-asymmetry-in-levinass-ethical-phenomenology/; Martin Gak, "Heidegger's Ethics and Levinas's Ontology: Phenomenology of Prereflective Normativity," *Levinas Studies* 9 (2014): 145–81; Richard Kearney, "The Crisis of the Image: Levinas's Ethical Response," in *The Ethics of Postmodernity: Current Trends in Continental Thought*, ed. Madison and Fairbairn (Evanston: Northwestern University Press, 1999), 12–23; Moran, 2000, 351–52; Jean-Luc Marion, "From the Other to the Individual," *Levinas Studies: An Annual Review* 1 (2005): 99–118; Max Pensky, "The Limits of Solidarity. Habermas, Levinas, and the Moral Point of View," in *A Matter of Discourse: Community and Communication in Contemporary Philosophies*, ed. A. Nascimento (Avebury Press, 1998), 129–50; Paul Ricoeur, "What Ontology in View?," in *Oneself as Another*, trans. Blarney (Chicago: Chicago University Press, 1992), 329–56; David Wood, "Some Questions for My Levinasian Friends," in *Addressing Levinas*, ed. E. S. Nelson et al. (Evanston: Northwestern University Press, 2005), 152–69; and Wild, 1961, 11–20.

12. De Boer, 1988, 83–116; John Drabinski, "Difference and Sense: The Problem of Relation in the Work of Emmanuel Levinas" (PhD diss., University of Memphis, 1996). As Bernasconi already diagnosed, de Boer repeats Levinas's equivocal use of the term "transcendental." De Boer's interpretation ultimately turns on reading Levinas to perform something like the "ontological argument" (De Boer,

1988, 94). De Boer hence performs something like a theistic (onto-) *logic*, pointing to a "real," as opposed to the mere idea of, the infinite. Drabinski's reading also turns on positing various *logics* to shore up Levinas's account: a "logic of sensibility" (112), "logic of sense" (123), "logic of exteriority" (115), and a "general logic of materiality" (128–29). Drabinski attributes a *kath'auto* character to *both* natural entities *and* the face, such that they become two species of a more general "otherness." Correlatively, Drabinski also posits "a general logic of Desire" (111) where need is cast as an alternate mode of desire. In *TI*, desire and enjoyment are not presented as signifying two modes of a general logic of sense, these motivations are not presented as correlating to two different instantiations of a general otherness (natural entities, the face), and these alterities are not presented as sharing a single mode of disclosure (expression *kath'auto*). Such would render the face *derivative*, in fact, an *expression of a more general logic*, and no longer of solely itself. While Drabinski succeeds in suggesting a way in which "sense-bestowal from the outside" might coherently be construed, his treatment of *TI* is ultimately creative, that is, not what Levinas actually seeks to do. In the final analysis, the logics Drabinski posits are held to relate singularities "unmediated by form" (92). Of what can logics without form consist? Purely *formal* relations between abstract marks? Or "real" relations between "real" singular bodies? If the latter: *what*, precisely, is being related, and *how*? De Boer and Drabinski both perform an empirico-metaphysical coherence strategy, but in contrasting theistic and quasi-materialist forms. Either way, empirico-metaphysical strategies necessarily *fail* on the *TI*'s own descriptive terms.

13. Kavka, 2014; Martin Kavka, review of *Addressing Levinas*, ed. E. S. Nelson et al., *Notre Dame Philosophical Reviews*, November 14, 2005, https://ndpr.nd.edu/news/24904-addressing-levinas/ [hereafter *RAL*]. I risk doing Kavka an injustice, here. He is quite of aware of the fraught character of *TI*'s account of the face, and explicitly presents his readings as hypotheses intended to propose the text's best case. He further admits that on "[f]urther examination," his own interpretive strategy might "fall into insurmountable problems" (Kavka, *RAL*). Kavka seeks to rebut both Wood's Heideggerian critique of the alleged priority of the face and Gallagher's empirical realist skepticism of the face as "transcendent experience." In both cases, Kavka appeals to the essendi/cogniscendi distinction Kant utilizes in the in the 2nd *Critique* to provide reciprocal justification of freedom and the moral law. Setting aside the well-known internal problems Kant's own account must contend with, however we might interpret Kant, Kavka's strategy cannot work for *TI*. Kant is fundamentally dealing in *cognitive performances*, and clearly does *not* hold that we "receive" ideas from *pure* sensible qualities, *pure* experiences, *pure* human bodies, or *pure* divine "effectuators." As such, some form of tokening must be performed in relation to human faces. Kavka is certainly right that "as soon as one turns to science to defend Levinasian ethics, one must turn away from Levinas's specific arguments" (Kavka, 2015, 227). But is it *also* true that Gallagher "has gone wrong" for his claim that Levinas's ethics "'is based on an experience of

transcendence encountered in the other's face' "? (ibid., 226). It *also* seems true that "as soon as one turns to [Kant] to defend Levinasian ethics, one must turn away from Levinas's specific arguments." Kavka is well aware that *TI* is beset by problems, and acknowledges that these problems may be "insurmountable" (Kavka, *RAL*). He seems to recognize that the criticism performed by Wood and others, while formally sound, perhaps suffer from a certain generality. To acquire sufficient force, "Wood's critique of Levinas must be extended to the sphere of Levinas's method" (ibid.). I perform precisely this extension herein. In the last analysis, Kantian transcendental strategies must necessarily *fail* on *TI*'s own descriptive terms.

14. Steven Galt Crowell, "Why Is Ethics First Philosophy?," *European Journal of Philosophy*, doi: 10.1111/j.1468-0378.2012.00550.x (2012). I risk doing an injustice to Crowell, here, because his analysis in this paper alone is ultimately ambiguous. His central claim is that Levinas's ethics contributes to a description "[of] the conditions necessary for the possession of intentional content" (1). Yet Crowell's positive reading only works by reference to "our experience of the other subject *as* another subject" (ibid.). As *other subject*, not "pure other," Crowell must suppose either analogy-perception in the constitution of the alter ego and the transcendental life this ultimately involves, or existential-categorial *Mitsein*. Either way, "experience" is no longer construed in a *purely* empirical way. Given his "takes place in the recognition of the normative force of a command" (1), Crowell is unhinging obligation from its alleged *pure origination* in the face. Moreover, he explicitly rejects "the way Levinas begins the systematic part of [*TI*] with an analysis of 'separation as life'" (7). Crowell must assume either Husserl's *transzendentale Leben* or Heidegger's *Sein* for his own defense of Levinas. The "face," here, becomes either a modification of *being-with*, but nevertheless subject to the *same Seinsfrage* that confronts *all* Daseins, or an *alter ego* subject to the *same* phenomenological-teleological reason that orients *all* transcendental subjects. On either view, claims for "absolute" alterity, "absolute" singularity, and the alleged "violence" of participatory "totality" are simply abandoned. In just this way, Crowell indirectly exemplifies what I call the Husserlian transcendental coherence strategy for reading *TI*. Crowell is ultimately reading Levinas quite generously, and from the perspective of his own philosophical project. In the last analysis, Husserlian transcendental strategies necessarily *fail* on *TI*'s own descriptive terms.

15. Emmanuel Levinas, *Is It Righteous to Be*, ed. J. Robbins (Stanford: Stanford University Press, 2001), 105, 106 (my emphasis).

16. Ibid., 135 (my emphasis).

17. Levinas, *TI*, 27, 28. 25.

18. Ibid., 67, 187, 136, 27.

19. For exceptions, see note 11 above.

20. Levinas, *TI*, 42. Friedman diagnoses precisely this problem, demonstrating how Levinas forces "the acceptance of a moral obligation to an Other predicated on the rejection of the very possibility of relation. For Levinas, *every* subject is

a solipsist standing in need of overcoming by moral command" (my emphasis). See Randy Friedman. "Alterity and Asymmetry in Levinas's Ethical Phenomenology," *Journal of Scriptural Reasoning* 13, no. 1 (2014), http://jsr.shanti.virginia.edu/vol-13-no-1-june-2014-phenomenology-and-scripture/alterity-and-asymmetry-in-levinass-ethical-phenomenology/.

21. Theodor De Boer, *The Development of Husserl's Thought*, trans. T. Plantinga (New York: Springer, 1978), 299–302.

22. There are numerous attempts in the scholarship to justify Levinas's approach through comparison to Husserl's work. For good examples, see Leslie MacAvoy's "The Other Side of Intentionality," in *Addressing Levinas*, ed. E. S. Nelson et al. (Evanston: Northwestern University Press, 2005); and Drabinski, 1996. As interesting as these attempts stand on their own merits, they necessarily *fail* to justify Levinas's approach, at least on *TI*'s own posited and explicit terms. This is just to say that if we uproot Husserl's ur-impression, primal association, passive synthesis, and so forth from their supportive role in active position taking and active constitution, we annul the phenomenological character of the passive dimension, concomitantly lurch into the natural attitude, and consequently give up the necessary status of phenomenological meaning. On Husserlian terms, if the face is going to phenomenologically signify, it must necessarily pass through "the apriori form-system" or transcendental consciousness. Given Levinas's own claim that constitution functions at a temporal remove from sensible experience (*TI*, 127, 169), the temporal gap in play can only be bridged by probabilistic empirical reconstructions or necessary ontological determinations. Levinas's appeal to "actual perception" (127) and "life in reality" (169) over-against constitution clearly demarcates the problem. If we instead opt for the Heideggerian comparison, if the face is going to phenomenologically signify, it must necessarily pass through the "the apriori form-system" Heidegger labels "existentials." Levinas's appeal to "as-sociation" (100) over-against projective disclosure clearly demarcates the problem. In both cases, he is summoning psychologistic, empirically realist terms to twist free from Husserl and Heidegger, while simultaneously laying claim to phenomenology couched in Kantian language. Levinas presents the ego as *pre-worlded* (156, 161) yet nevertheless in "contact" (135, 165) with all sorts of "exterior" things. The problem is clear. See Suzanne Bachelard, *Study of Husserl's Formal and Transcendental Logic* (Evanston: Northwestern University Press, 1990), 191; Derrida, 1978, 133, 141. For an interesting treatment of Husserl on passivity and position taking, see Alejandro Arango, "Husserl's Concept of Position-Taking and Second Nature," *Phenomenology and Mind* 6 (2014): 224–35.

23. Levinas, *TI*, 79.
24. Ibid., 204.
25. Ibid., 195.
26. Ibid., 64–65.
27. Ibid., 26, 86.
28. Ibid., 67, 260.

29. Ibid., 38.

30. Pensky captures the problem precisely: "suffering is always concrete, and thus incapable of being reduced to concepts. Referring to such suffering as the substrate of moral feeling as such cannot appeal to a concept of physical suffering, which could only serve to replicate the suffering itself by reducing particulars to a general case. Nor can phenomenological analysis help, since the description of the vulnerability of the other . . . can only thematize that other's suffering through the category of my sensibility. 'Alterity' thus appears as a fascinating dialectical sibling to the Heideggerian blind invocations of a salvific, generous Being" (Pensky, 1989, 142–43). While Levinas and Levinasians would precisely contest naming the other's vulnerability a "physical substrate," this is nevertheless how Levinas's justificatory appeals function when he is in apparent anti-concept mode. While Pensky goes out of his way to give serious consideration to "substantive" anti-concept claims ("but simply as the vulnerability of the other, period" [144]), he is perhaps too generous to Levinas, and to "nominalists" in general. The nominalist always and necessarily presupposes a *general classification of entities* in the ascription of meaning or non-meaning, and in at least some of its so-called "postmodern" forms, makes the further claim that such classifications are always "contingent." Setting aside the question of whether this last assertion is in each case *true* (or even generally intelligible), it's clearly the case that the recognizability of suffering *as suffering* is dependent on *always already* performed generalizations, and without such generalizations, injurability could not make a claim on any particular subject. An individual's biographical witness to her or his particular suffering can serve to expand, revise, clarify, or transform our generalizations, but generality is always and necessarily there. Perhaps there is a further therapeutic dimension to such biographical testimonials, and we stand under an obligation to hear them for the sake of a particular other's overall well-being. Even granting limit-cases—events of suffering of such a radically catastrophic nature—that resist secure or completely settled understanding, such cases necessarily come to serve as *exemplars*, or primary and quasi-definitive instances, to which we come to refer in our talk of suffering. Think of the Shoah or reports of torture. Such limit-cases express *both* a general meaning *and* its limits, and bear both *within themselves*. This is why hearers spontaneously *know* that the particular sufferer bears a kind of authority for having *actually undergone* the event, spontaneously *know* that the generality involved in communicating the experience only "translates" or communicates inadequately. In other words, such limit-cases can potentially (i) revise and reconstitute the *concept* of suffering in general, and (ii) in such a way that the gap between communicability and actual experience is recognized, maintained, and inherent to its very conceptuality. But clearly, limit-cases don't or can't *ruin* conceptuality as such and in general, because they in some sense depend on it. The larger philosophical question of whether the "generality" in question issues solely from our cognitive capacities, or whether it is somehow sown into the fabric of the world, will ultimately depend on one's particular metaphysics or semantics. What

seems clear, however, is that generality and conceptuality—all by themselves—in no way constitute a "violence" to particular experience *as* particular experiences, because testimony itself must and does rely on general classifications. Without them, there would be no such thing as either "normal" or "limit" experiences.

31. On Levinas's own strict methodological terms, we are not licensed to describe his method as a "hermeneutics of lived experience," as Bergo does, for example. Because Levinas describes sensibility as yielding both a singular "concept-less individual" and a singular "absolute alterity," and specifies their "relation" as a "relation without relation," he denies himself the right to a hermeneutic relationality and the mediation it inherently involves. This is why Levinas himself never claims title to hermeneutic phenomenology to describe his own method. See Bettina Bergo, "Emmanuel Levinas," *Stanford Encyclopedia of Philosophy*, August 3, 2006, http://plato.stanford.edu/entries/levinas/; Levinas, *TI*, 120, 96, 80.

32. Levinas, *TI*, 153, 49, 197, 204, 41.

33. Ibid., 129, 153, 80, 28.

34. Ibid., 133, 66.

35. Ibid., 101, 135, 161, 172.

36. Ibid., 135.

37. Ibid., 153. In response to questions on whether animals have a "face," Levinas responds: "The human face is completely different and only afterwards do we discover the face of an animal. . . . It is because we, as human, know what suffering is that we can have this obligation." When forced to deal with non-human alterity, the *epistemic function* or "knowing" dimension of his account of alterity becomes explicit. See Emmanuel Levinas, "The Paradox of Morality: An Interview with Emmanuel Levinas," in *The Provocation of Levinas: Rethinking the Other,* ed. Robert Bernasconi and David Wood (London: Routledge, 1988), 168–80. I'm gratefully indebted to Aaron Bell for aiding me in this insight. Aaron Bell, "The Animal Without a Face," Unpublished Manuscript, 13–14.

38. Since writing these lines in early 2015 (in Pudong), I've come to discover a similar equivocation in Heidegger's *BT*, though embedded in a more complicated set of methodological questions.

39. His account of the third fails precisely from the problems I analyze: "every social relation leads back to the" face, yet only because "the I is already effectuated in fraternity [can] the face . . . present itself as face" (*TI*, 213, 280). In the first context, the face is a *transcendental condition* of intelligibility, in the second context, a "revealed" or *real condition*. Theory is left indeterminate, as I show more thoroughly below.

40. "Content 'overflowing' concept" is an *inherently mediated construction*. Content is *never absent* from its concept, while "overflowing" serves to merely add *immediate sensible force*, or *individuate* particular concepts. He is switching between psycho-metaphysical and transcendental genesis as what does the semantic/validating work.

41. Levinas, *TI*, 80.

42. To say that obligation is "non-adequation" (27, 34) is just to say, tautologically, that it's something like a *norm*, and leaves completely untouched the *non-moral* presuppositions necessarily in play in the ascription of moral meaning in general.

43. See Friedman, 2014.

44. Levinas defines the face by coincidence of expressing and she who expresses, formally separating *talking to* and *talking about*. Hence, the alleged ethical meaning of the former licenses simply ignoring the latter. Because conceptual mediation cannot be avoided, Levinas wins all debates or defeats all philosophically competing positions a priori.

45. Levinas, *TI*, 128, 129, 153, 169; 50. Notice: the very notion of "deformalization" entails *starting with* pure concepts, and working back to their alleged (transcendental or "real"?) contexts of origination.

46. Ibid., 112, 137. These two statements show the problem. Levinas is deploying Aristotle's "primary substances" in his description of the ego's own affective constitution by "exterior" content, while positing "secondary substances" by "miraculous grasp" (163) of what he describes as an essentially *blind* ego.

47. Ibid., 188–89 (my emphasis).

48. Ibid., 169.

49. Ibid., 127, 207.

50. Ibid., 157.

51. Ibid., 135.

52. De Boer simply repeats Levinas's question begging by asserting, "It is not a condition operative behind our backs, like transcendental apperception in Kant or the clearing (*Lichtung*) of being in Heidegger," de Boer, 1988, 100. By contrast, Derrida holds that "Levinas's metaphysics . . . presupposes . . . the transcendental phenomenology it seeks to put in question," and "Just as he implicitly had to appeal to phenomenological self-evidence against phenomenology, Levinas must ceaselessly suppose and practice the thought and precomprehension of Being in his discourse, even when he directs it against 'ontology,'" Derrida, *VM*, 133, 141. If my own analysis is sound, it amounts to an internal demonstration of Derrida's point within Levinas's own methodological self-description.

53. Levinas, *TI*, 169.

54. Ibid., 42, 82 (my emphasis).

55. Derrida makes this same point, *VM*, 82–83.

56. Levinas, *TI*, 200.

57. Ibid., 152–54, 157, 139.

58. Ibid., 203, 27. Levinas is very clearly tracking Heidegger, here, but is working with a different account of time. Ego, Face, and Eros can perhaps be read as filling in different content and attributing different meaning to Heidegger's three-fold ecstases of unified temporality. But Levinas's use of pure empirical reality and purely accessible empirical bodies (i) renders his realist pole a theistic, rather than a

Heideggerian, ontology, and (ii) performs an attribution of original, un-modifiable wholeness to the ego inconsistent with Heidegger's approach. Moreover, despite his attempt to present the ego as a "contraction," (104) and the face as a resistance to projection, the ego can only "contract" by an *initial* totalizing affective *projection*, and it can only "comprehend" (200) the face through having already performed spontaneous and projective analogy-perception. To read *TI* in a phenomenological vein, Levinas must presuppose either Heidegger's historicity or what Rodemeyer calls primordial Husserlian "intersubjective temporality." See Lanei M. Rodemeyer, *Intersubjective Temporality: It's About Time* (Dordrecht: Springer, 2006).

59. Levinas, *TI*, 203, 150. Bernasconi first identified this particular circle. See Bernasconi, 1989, 32.

60. Ibid., 213, 280 (my emphasis).

61. Ibid., 247, 268, 213, 279.

62. Ibid., 173.

63. Ibid., 26.

64. Ibid., 28.

65. Ibid., 27, 28, 98. Despite his reference to creation *ex nihilo*, it is not certain that Levinas's ontological God fully creates human *bodies*, because he seems to be reoutfitting a non-materialist reading of biblical creation. In other words, his creative God doesn't necessarily create the material universe, but S/He does create *human consciousness*. Nevertheless, Levinas's own descriptions entail that this involves non-moral dimensions (reflected in human creative activity, for example), and does not occur as *only* sheer moral summons.

66. Ibid., 203.

67. Ibid., "comprehension of this destitution and this hunger constitutes the very proximity of the other, (200) and "What is essential to created existence is not the limited character of its being, and the concrete structure of the creature is not deducible from this finitude" (105).

68. I want to stress: *TI*'s failures do not necessarily belong to pseudo-Dionysus or Maimonides. For those inclined to theology, my critique of *TI* doesn't decide more general questions in religious hermeneutics, theological method, or theistic metaphysics.

69. Ibid., 109 (my emphasis).

70. Ibid., 48. It should be noted, the alleged "violence" in question is not merely that of *closed* "totalities," that is, of strictly deterministic ontology, but of *all totalities*, including those that involve the *horizonal openness* of "the idea in the Kantian sense." See De Boer, 1988, 90; Jacques Derrida, *The Problem of Genesis in Husserl's Philosophy*, trans. M. Hobson (Chicago: University of Chicago Press, 2003), 94–99.

71. Levinas, *TI*, 120, 118, 40, 198, 80.

72. Ibid., 61.

73. Ibid., 131, 132.

74. Ibid., 61, 188–89, 133, 112 (my emphasis).
75. Ibid., 27, 251, 247, 268, 213, 279.
76. Ibid., 36, 251, 67, 66, 48.
77. Ibid., 26, 73 (my emphasis).
78. Levinas, *OGM*, 89.
79. Levinas, *TI*, 173.

80. At the conclusion of this immanent critique, it should be noted that *TI* is at least as indebted to Hegel for its positive philosophical contributions as it is negatively indebted to him in its spirited critique of "totality." I admit, this troubles me. We will have to mount a different way into a critique of Hegel.

81. Ibid., 213.
82. Ibid., 200.
83. Ibid., 86–89, 104–5, 115, 279; compare 213 and 280.

84. Levinas's account of the face uses a novel deployment of Husserl's categorial intuition. All the problems in *TI* are rooted in Levinas's insistence that constitution occurs at temporal remove from sensible "contact" (127). See Edmund Husserl, *Logical Investigations*, trans. M. Farber (London: Routledge, 1973); Robert Sokolowski, "Husserl's Concept of Categorial Intuition," in *Phenomenology and the Human Sciences*, Supplement to *Philosophical Topics*, 12 (1981): 127–41; Richard Cobb-Stevens, "Being and Categorial Intuition," *Review of Metaphysics* 44, no. 1 (1990): 43–66; Panos Theodorou, "Husserl's Original Project for a Normative Phenomenology of Emotions and Values," in *Values: Readings and Sources on a Key Concept of the Globalized World*, ed. I. de Gennaro (Leiden: Brill, 2012), 265–90.

85. In other words: "*this*" individual body is perceptually given, though it does *not* yield or reflect categorial *form*. The given individual body is *empirically perceived*, but not categorially or eidetically *known*. As such, Levinas's own use of "substance," and his critique of tradition, is question begging.

86. Levinas, *TI*, 199–200. (i) "unforeseeableness of his reactions" (199) and (ii) "destitution" (199–200).

87. Expression *kath'auto* consists in the "coinciding of the expressed with him who expresses" (66), "coinciding of the revealer and the revealed in the face" (67), "coinciding with his position as other and as exterior," (101), and "essential coinciding of the existent and the signifier." (262) *This* other is the owner of her speech-acts. What is coinciding? A specific body and a formal universal meaning.

88. Whether the generalizing theoretical performance is construed as transcendental or empirical, theory is explicitly and positively operative in his positing of "pre-theoretical" meaning. If we seek to determine the *meaning* of *theory in general*, we necessarily must show how the proposed meaning orients theory and what theory proper consists in. Levinas precisely *fails* to do this. His indeterminate account of theory renders his own claims question begging.

89. On his own terms, Levinas can only achieve "pre-theoretical" meaning through epistemically positive empirico-metaphysical categoriality, and he can only

disclaim realism through purely theoretical conceptual determination. Either way, others are merely relative.

Chapter 4

1. Moses Maimonides. *The Guide of the Perplexed of Maimonides, Volume 3*, trans. Michael Friedländer (London: Trubner, 1885), 35; Paul Ricoeur, *Freud and Philosophy: An Essay on Interpretation* (New Haven: Yale University Press, 1970), 247; Theodor Adorno, *Against Epistemology: A Metacritique, Studies in Husserl and the Phenomenological Antinomies*, trans. Willis Domingo (Cambridge, MA: MIT Press, 1983), 146; Levinas, *Proper Names*, 70.

2. See Bernasconi, 2002, and "Skepticism in the Face of Philosophy," in Re-reading *Levinas*, ed. R. Bernasconi et al (Bloomington: Indiana University Press, 1991) 149–61; Lisa Guenther, "'Nameless Singularity': Levinas on Individuation and Ethical Singularity," *Epoche* 14, no. 1 (Fall 2009): 167–87; and Annabel Herzog, "Benny Levy verses Emmanuel Levinas on 'Being Jewish,'" *Modern Judaism* 26, no. 1 (2006): 15–30.

3. I am of course aware that Levinas is performing a self-conscious stylistic strategy in *OB*. If I were to read the text in this vein, I would have to pose questions in a different style. I have instead chosen to read *OB* as a phenomenology in order to assess Levinas's Eurocentric statements by immanent critique. If Lyotard is to be believed, this is ultimately how Levinas himself wanted to be read: "It is not under the authority of the Bible that my thought is placed, but under the authority of phenomenology . . . You make of me a Jewish thinker." See Levinas, *Aurement que savoir* (Paris: Editions Osiris, 1988), 78–79; quoted in Kosky, 2001, 157.

4. Heidegger's account of *angst* is the best analogue for grasping what Levinas is up to. Proximity tears one away from mundane social or putatively "natural" life, with the Other, rather than intimations of death and the question of Being, occasioning this event. See Martin Heidegger, *Being and Time*, trans. John Macquarrie and Edward Robinson (Oxford: Basil Blackwell, 1962), 228–35.

5. Emmanuel Levinas, *Otherwise than Being or Beyond Essence*, trans. A. Lingis (Pittsburgh: Duquesne University Press, 1981), 14–19, 64, 89, 141; *In the Time of Nations*, trans. M. B. Smith (London: Continuum, 2007), 97.

6. Levinas, *OB*, 55, 121.

7. Ibid., 64, 103–6.

8. Emmanuel Levinas. *Is It Righteous to Be*, ed. Jill Robbins (Stanford: Stanford University Press, 2001), 89; quoted in Michael Morgan, *Discovering Levinas* (Cambridge: Cambridge University Press, 2007), 6. As Katz rightly notes: "Certainly we do not know what Grossman intended, nor do we know the real motivation of the woman." Claire Elise Katz, "Review of Discovering Levinas" *Notre Dame Philosoph-*

ical Reviews, January 12, 2008, http://ndpr.nd.edu/news/23305-discovering-levinas/.

9. Levinas, *OB*, 81, 137.

10. Ibid., 46, 67.

11. Ibid., 5. Emmanuel Levinas, *Difficult Freedom: Essays on Judaism*, trans. Sean Hand (Baltimore: Johns Hopkins University Press, 1990), 10, 101, 232.

12. In his middle work, Levinas suggests he is working in a tradition that includes 1) the primacy of pure practical reason in Kant, 2) Descartes's *Third Meditation*, and ultimately 3) Plato's *agathon*. Nevertheless, given his critique of "essence" in *OB*, and given his own determinations of what ontology is that structures this analysis, only Plato's *agathon* can be said to escape the "ontological tradition," and does so by virtue of how Levinas puts it to work in *OB*. I underline this here to preempt charges that I distort Levinas's take on Kant. Given Levinas's critique of essence and how he positively determines it to function (where he cedes too much to Heidegger, in my view), Kant and the idealist tradition in general fall under ontology as Levinas himself seems to determine it.

13. Heidegger's ontology provides Levinas with the paradigm for what ontology and self-interest ultimately are, and references to Spinoza, Hobbs, and Darwin all reflect Levinas's critical evaluation of Heidegger. See Robert Bernasconi, "Levinas and the Struggle for Existence," in *Addressing Levinas*, ed. Eric Sean Nelson et al. (Evanston: Northwestern University Press, 2005), 170–84.

14. Emmanuel Levinas, *Totality and Infinite*, trans. Alphonso Lingis (Pittsburgh: Duquesne University Press, 1969), 21.

15. Cf. Levinas, *OB*, 96–97.

16. See Edmund Husserl, *Crisis of the European Sciences and Transcendental Phenomenology*, trans. David Carr (Evanston: Northwestern University Press, 1970).

17. See Samuel Moyn, "Judaism versus Paganism: Emmanuel Levinas' Response to Heidegger and Nazism in the 1930s," *History and Memory* 10, no. 1 (Spring 1998): 25–58. For a good critical treatment of prevailing interpretations of Levinas's relation to Heidegger, see Martin Gak, "Heidegger's Ethics and Levinas's Ontology: Phenomenology of Prereflective Normativity," *Levinas Studies* 9 (2014): 145–81.

18. Levinas, *OB*, 157.

19. I owe this formulation of the questions of justice to Ernst Wolff, *Political Responsibility for a Globalized World* (Bielefeld: transcript-Verlag, 2011) [hereafter *PRGW*].

20. Levinas, *OB*, 76, 81.

21. Ibid., 56–57.

22. Ibid., 15, 136, 121, 101.

23. Ibid., 99–121.

24. Ibid., 126.

25. Ibid., 157.

26. Ibid., 157, 161.

27. Ibid., 159. Compare this "for empirical reasons" with roughly three paragraphs prior: "It is not that the entry of the other would be an empirical fact" (157).

28. Levinas, *OB*, 15.

29. Ibid., 112.

30. Ibid., 104, 114, 180.

31. Ibid., 126.

32. Levinas, *TI*, 207. See Adriaan Peperzak, *To the Other: An Introduction to the Philosophy of Emmanuel Levinas* (West Lafayette: Purdue University Press, 1993), 21.

33. See Joseph Lelyveld, *Great Soul: Mahatma Gandhi and his Struggle with India* (Vintage, 2012). Lelyveld's book is valuable precisely because he resists hagiography. He gives Gandhi in flesh and blood, but in such a way that detracts nothing from the moral grandeur of his accomplishments.

34. My point here is *not* to positively demonstrate the *necessity* of self-interest in moral action, but merely its *possibility*. Levinas's whole argument turns on casting moral motivation as an *immediate* urge toward good "action" as inherently *self-justifying*, and utilizes this to pose a "transcendental" argument for the priority of the good for the event of meaning in general. By showing the *possibility* of self-interest in the very structure he constructs to contrast the ethical (good, giving) and the ontological (self-interest), I undermine these claims to immediacy and structural priority, because the issue performatively requires *reflective* consideration of the relevant moral problems (for example, chauvinism or sanctimony) that implicate a wider cluster of concepts (and of course also: the will). This demonstrates that the pure immediacy Levinas claims for the urge is specious, and that he is actually presupposing a set of distinctions not derivable from the urge itself, but rather from what he himself designates as "ontology," that is, from the will and the concept (or reflective "thought" in general). If the immediate urge to give *can* originate from a self-oriented motive (as my "moral glory" analysis suggests), then it manifestly is *not* immediately self-justifying, and one must necessarily appeal to wider considerations to justify particular moral actions. That wider appeal undermines his central claims for the moral subject in *OB*. I thank an anonymous reviewer at SUNY Press for inviting me to clarify this matter.

35. Levinas, *OB*, 183, see also 120–21.

36. Ibid., 13–14, 127 (my emphasis).

37. Ibid., 157.

38. Because of his unique interpretation of Levinas and our email discussion regarding it, I am partially indebted to Ernst Wolff for orienting my questions on this point. See Wolff, *PRGW*, 183.

39. Levinas, *OB*, 157.

40. Ibid., 159.

41. Ibid., 157–58.

42. Ibid., 159.

43. Sarah Horton, "The Joy of Desire: Understanding Levinas's Desire of the Other as Gift," *Continental Philosophy Review* 51 (2018): 193. Though I do not endorse every turn in her analysis, Horton beautifully situates the cluster of senses at issue for the treatment of the relation between joy and responsibility, and above all: their relation to festival and celebration. She is right that Levinas contributes much to these considerations, just not on the exact terms he lays out (in *OB* especially).

44. Quoted in Horton, 2018, 196, 197. See Richard Kearney. *The God Who May Be: A Hermeneutics of Religion* (Bloomington: Indiana University Press, 2001), 69; and Merold Westphal, "The Many Faces of Levinas as a Reader of Kierkegaard," *Revista Portuguesa de Filosofia* 64 (2008): 1149.

45. Levinas's account of the ethical self claims that it "*is*" responsibility, that is, responsibility is not a predicate or attribute of a subject, but rather the very being of the ethical one. Hence, speaking of "infinite responsibility" suggests that "growing responsibility" amounts to *becoming* "infinite," or playfully: "getting bigger." He implicitly treats responsibility as a kind of "thing," such that his account exploits an equivocation between traditional philosophical determination (predicate/attribute) and phenomenological determination (presence, performance of the relation itself).

46. The description depends on either (i) a position outside of proximity in the manner just described, or (ii) treating "limitless responsibility" as a *general norm* the proximate other fails to embody. Whether construed as a transcendental performance of analogical ascription wherein the ego deals back to the proximate other the responsibility s/he initially invested, or as a general norm coextensive with some context of "real" relation, the mediation of thought and a larger context of relations is necessarily at play in his description. If there were no such larger relational context (whether in a realist or idealist sense), the ethical self could not attribute even limited responsibility to the other, and limited responsibility could not be judged a deficient form of responsibility.

47. Levinas, *OB*, 115.

48. Ibid., 104, 183, 189, and so forth.

49. Ibid., 116.

50. I first wrote this in 2015. Since then I've discovered that Heidegger actually does engage in significant equivocations in *Being and Time*, though in ways that are not wholly identical to Levinas.

51. The mechanics of Heidegger's ontic/ontological distinction is beyond the scope of this chapter. It's enough to note that the anthropology of the Dasein Analytic, and Heidegger's general method in *Being and Time*, eschews the purity Husserl is after in phenomenology as universal science. Nearly the whole of Levinas's coherence problems are rooted in his attempt to keep Husserlian purity within a structurally Heideggerian form of description.

52. Paul Ricoeur, "Otherwise: A Reading of Emmanuel Levinas's *Otherwise than Being or Beyond Essence*," *Yale French Studies* 104 (2004): 84.

53. Levinas, *OB*, 95.
54. Ibid., 113, 166.
55. Ibid., 128, 158, 160.
56. Ibid., 158, 159.
57. Ibid., 53.
58. Ibid., 196.
59. Ibid., 167, 19.
60. Ibid., 86, 54.
61. Ibid., 132.
62. Ibid., 104, 190.
63. Ibid., 86.
64. Ibid., 196, n. 21.
65. I'm grateful to Prof. Anna Gotlib for aiding me in parsing these statements.
66. Ibid., 162.
67. Ibid., 182, 74, 116, 120 (my emphasis).
68. Ibid., 52.
69. Lisa Guenther, "'Nameless Singularity': Levinas on Individuation and Ethical Singularity," *Epoche* 14, no. 1 (Fall 2009): 179, 187 n. 36; Levinas, *OB*, 52.
70. Levinas, *OB*, 192 n. 18, 14, 116.
71. Ibid., 6, 198, 123.
72. Ibid., 192 n. 27, 85.
73. Ibid., 74.
74. Ibid., 114, 115.
75. Ibid., 160 (my emphasis).
76. Ibid., 159, 158.
77. Ibid., 116.
78. Ibid., 4, 8.
79. Ibid., 4.
80. Ibid., 128.
81. Ibid., 128, 112, 118 (my emphasis).
82. Ibid., 128.
83. Ibid., 154.
84. Ibid., 16.
85. Ibid., 56.
86. Philosophy "abuses" language by treating Saying as a Said, though, as Levinas ceaselessly admits: this abuse is "necessary" (43). Ethics abuses language in giving the elected self a name—"me" or "I"—which partakes of the generality of the pronominal form. It is not clear who he can be indicting because both forms of abuse are said to be "necessary."
87. Ibid., 193.

88. Ibid., 57.
89. Ibid., 197.
90. Ibid., 43.
91. Ibid., 123.
92. Ibid., 15.
93. Ibid., 43.
94. Ibid., 159 (my emphasis).
95. Ibid., 116.
96. Ibid., 100, 52, 159.
97. Ibid., 82, 104.
98. Ibid., 197 n. 26, 52. "But in creation, what is called to being answers to a call that could not have reached it since, brought out of nothingness, it obeyed before hearing the order" (113). Here, Levinas makes explicit the point I analyzed above.
99. Ibid., 42, 133, 140.
100. Ibid., 125, 120, 115, 116.
101. Ibid., 143, 9–10.
102. Social media and bad policy in media markets that have driven the rise in eisogenic echo chambers involved in the emergence of global neo-nativism are themselves grounded in the issues at stake. I treat these issues in chapter 7. Levinas is not the only person in contemporary European philosophy to engage in esoteric practices, and given his personal plight as a Shoah survivor: that he did so is understandable, and I haven't treated the matter in detail here. By contrast, is Heidegger's esotericism at all justified? This question certainly doesn't endanger free speech, individual conscience, open questions, etc., but rather takes Levinas seriously by asking us to take responsibility for them.
103. It must be stressed that in OB Levinas is critically responding to Nietzsche and Heidegger (and Foucault and Derrida). Are critical problems in OB comprehensible absent those larger philosophical conversations?
104. Tomohiro Inukai, "The Status of Saying: Witness against Rhetoric in Levinas's Philosophy," *Religions* 9, no. 410 (2018): 2; see Catherine Chalier. "Témoignage et théologie," *Pardès* 42 (2007): 17–30.
105. Ibid., 128.
106. Ibid., 115, 44.
107. Gavin Rae, "The Politics of Justice: Levinas, Violence, and the Ethical–Political Relation," *Contemporary Political Theory* 17, no. 1 (2018): 50. Rae did not consult my dissertation (SUNY Binghamton, 2016) for his piece, but arrives at the same conclusions.
108. On the differences between *TI* and *OB*, see Guenther, 2009 and Annabel Herzog, 2006.
109. Levinas, *OB*, 192 n. 18, 14, 116.
110. Ibid., 142, 105, 102, 55, 18, 88.

Chapter 5

1. Emmanuel Levinas, *Difficult Freedom: Essays on Judaism*, trans. Sean Hand (Baltimore: Johns Hopkins University Press, 1990), 160; Florian Rotzer, "Interview with Emmanuel Levinas," in *Conversations with French Philosophers*, trans. G. E. Aylesworth (Atlantic Highlands, NJ: Humanities Press, 1995) 63; Emmanuel Levinas, *Unforeseen History*, trans. Nidra Poller (Champaign: University of Illinois Press: 2003), 108. My original treatment of sections of this chapter failed to distinguish between Levinas's articulated position and his own person, and hence haplessly lurched into a psychologizing, ad hominem argument. I'm sorry for that, and substantively correct the false impression I gave in the next chapter. See Jack Marsh, "Levinas, Chauvinism, Disinterest," *Philosophy Today* 59, no. 3 (Summer 2015): 451–73.

2. Levinas, *OB*, 157–58.

3. "The discourse then recuperates its meaning by repression or mediation, by just violences, on the verge of the possible injustice where repressive justice is exercised. It is through the State that reason and knowledge are force and efficacity." Levinas, *OB*, 170.

4. Gavin Rae, "The Politics of Justice: Levinas, Violence, and the Ethical–Political Relation," *Contemporary Political Theory* 17, no. 1 (2018), 50; Wolff, 2014, 202. Rae did not consult my dissertation (SUNY Binghamton, 2016) for his own piece, but he independently reaches the same conclusions. Again, I'm indebted to Wolff for orienting my focus on the relevant problems.

5. One might note, all Levinasian claims to "necessary tension," undecidability, or the moral value of "bad conscience," necessarily occur within an *already performed choice* held in and with relatively *untensive* or *good conscience*. In this case, the choice is for republican state form over-against the naive dreams of bourgeois libertarians. My point is that appeals to the "tensive" and the value of bad conscience are necessarily conservative, insofar as they are grounded in a prior decision, or settled acceptance of a field of contest in its currently constituted form. Because the slogans of contemporary anarchism fail to enlighten us on how global capital is to be brought to heel absent the rule of law and local/international democratic institutions, I remain happily conservative in my defense of the republican state at the level of form, while lending my critical and creative attention to improving and more thoroughly realizing the dreams of republicanism. I dream the normative dreams of anarchists. We can't seem to approximate those dreams in the world we've inherited without a state of some kind.

6. Steve Larocco, "The Other, Shame, and Politics: Levinas, Justice, and Feeling Responsible," *Religions* 9, no. 381 (2018): 14, doi:10.3390/rel9120381. Larocco performs a nuanced analysis of the potential for shame to motivate positive sorts of social change and solidarity. His classification of types of shame and description of their function remains, however, problematic.

7. I call Ophir's view "Gnostic" because, based on Larocco's treatment alone, it necessarily terminates in a judgment that finite, embodied, social, and terrestrial life—as such—is "evil." Burdens and harms are not necessarily identical, and how a polity distributes burden and collectively assume the tragic is precisely how we assess, measure, and distinguish between better and worse polities, by necessary reference to principles or exemplifications of the right or the good. Both Levinas and Heidegger are instructive here: if responsibility is what we are, then burden by itself cannot coherently be construed an "evil" without pronouncing a pox on human life as such.

8. Nathan Bell, "'In the Face, a Right Is There': Arendt, Levinas and the Phenomenology of the Rights of Man, *Journal of the British Society for Phenomenology* 49, no. 4 (2018): 305. Though I endorse Bell's reading on a conventional understanding of Levinas, it must be said that the theological move involved—the "extra-political principle" (302)—at its basis is theoretically controversial for political theory today. The reason why a liberal-statist interpretation of Levinas's politics entails a rejection of conventionally understood "disruption" talk is that protest in such a context is not a call for a whole other order, but rather a call to the institutions in question—and the policy they enact—to proceed in accord with the very sense said to issue in the face. Structurally, responsibility refers to the *presence* of a *measure* by which citizens can recognize their own institutions' *failure* to live up to.

9. Jason Caro, "Levinas and the Palestinians," *Philosophy and Social Criticism* 35, no. 6 (July 2009): 671–84.

10. Oona Eisenstadt and Claire Elise Katz, "The Faceless Palestinian: A History of an Error," *Telos* 174 (Spring 2016): 9–32. I thank Jeffrey Bernstein for alerting me to this essay.

11. Butler, *PW*, 23.

12. See the relevant discussion in Eisenstadt and Katz, 2016, 25–28.

13. Ibid., 25. See Emmanuel Levinas, "Ethics and Politics," in *The Levinas Reader*, ed. Sean Hand (London: Blackwell, 1989), 297.

14. Levinas, "Ethics and Politics," 294.

15. Emmanuel Levinas, "Zionisms," in *The Levinas Reader*, ed. Sean Hand (London: Blackwell, 1989), 282. Quoted in Caro, 673–74.

16. Ibid., 278.

17. See Caro, 679.

18. Ibid., 681.

19. In this light, Netanyahu is the Ahab of our time, and his Faustian bargain with the right-wing fascism he has helped nurture and institutionalize is a more significant threat to Israel's future and long-term peace than Hamas's brutal incompetence. I stand in firm solidarity with Palestinian struggle, but it must be said that Hamas's own fascism—and its standing tactics, which include ongoing, explicit, and premeditated targeting of Israeli civilians—itself amounts to *cynically*

Zionist in its actual effects. What I mean here should be obvious, but to avoid misunderstanding I explicate the point: insofar as Israel wields more power and exerts effective control in the situation, it bears primary responsibility for it. We are hence justified in holding the Israeli state to relevant account with honed and context-sensitive precision. But insofar as Hamas's terror tactics signal to Israeli citizens that *relevant* Palestinian leadership can't be trusted to honor, protect, and defend their lives and security, they give Israeli citizens good reason to vote for those who really will protect them. Meanwhile, Netanyahu, and the fascists he has helped empower, conduct their own cynical game—annexations, settlement expansion, demographic manipulation, collective punishment, Pyrrhic "deterrence," that is, punitive and terroristic military and police tactics, and so forth—at the expense of Palestinian civilians. Hamas in turn exploits these injustices to justify blowing up buses and shooting rockets at schoolchildren, even as it heaves its own internal Palestinian critics off the top of apartment buildings. So indeed: Netanyahu is an Ahab, and recent Israeli policy must be soberly judged for what it is. As should Hamas and the worst quarters of Palestinian leadership for continually playing the Israeli Right's useful idiots, not to mention its own ideological fascism that no mere change in the formal language of its Charter succeeds at concealing. A sustained, long-term change in both its *tactics* and principles *would* alter this tragic and criminal dynamic, but Hamas clearly cares as little for Palestinian lives and futures as Netanyahu. This of course can change, and if Hamas would relevantly reform itself—and live that reform out when it matters most—*in the face of threats to its own survival*—it would have no greater fan than I. The best in the Islamic political tradition cedes the right to rule to the *competent*, and specifically: to those who materially consult and formally empower the Ummah's own *self-governance*, with its neighbors, with all People's of the Book, and above all: to all peoples of good will. The best hope for resolution to the conflict is for both Israelis and Palestinians to either *collaboratively* self-reform in service to a just collective future, or oust the snakes in their own respective houses that keep this criminal dynamic alive; in an embrace of a common future of peace and prosperity for all inhabitants of the land. This sentiment is of course somewhat naive. I pray that Israeli and Palestinian youth direct their noble courage to embrace and enact just this sort of naiveté, with all the intelligence, strength, and passion they clearly have.

    20. Annabel Herzog. "Benny Levy verses Emmanuel Levinas on 'Being Jewish,'" *Modern Judaism* 26, no. 1 (2006): 16.

    21. Levinas, *ITN*, 72; *DF*, 225.

    22. Levinas, *DF*, 174. For the ambiguity of "proselytizing" in Levinas, see Sarah Hammerschlag, *The Figural Jew: Politics and Identity in Post-War French Thought* (Chicago: University of Chicago Press, 2010), 146–48.

    23. "For we assume the permanence and continuation of Israel and the unity of its self-consciousness throughout the ages" and the "unity of the consciousness of mankind, claiming to be fraternal and one through space and time." Emmanuel

Levinas, *Nine Talmudic Readings*, trans. Annette Aronowicz (Bloomington: Indiana University Press, 1990), 6. "Revelation . . . makes itself heard now, but can also pass down through the ages to announce the *same truth in different times*" (my emphasis). "Revelation in Jewish Tradition," in *The Levinas Reader*, ed. Sean Hand (Oxford: Basil Blackwell, 1989), 195. Cf. Emmanuel Levinas, "Contempt for Torah as Idolatry," in *In the Time of Nations*, ed. and trans. M. B. Smith (London: Continuum, 2007), 43–64.

24. Levinas, *DF*, 18.
25. Ibid., 176.
26. Levinas, *ITN*, 129. For his hesitation, see *DF*, 224.
27. Cf. Levinas, *DF*, 18; *ITN*, 97.
28. Putnam notices this problem when he writes: "But [Levinas] never attempts to tell gentiles what their equivalent to 'ritual and the heart-felt generosity' of traditional Judaism, their equivalent to 'the particular type of intellectual life known as study of the Torah,' might be." Hillary Putnam, "Levinas and Judaism," in *Cambridge Companion to Levinas*, ed. Simon Critchley et al. (Cambridge: Cambridge University Press, 2002), 52–53. Putnam claims this fact as a virtue, rather than a problem, for Levinas. He fails to note that Levinas can admit no structural equivalence between Judaism and other traditions in particular religious practices. Levinas must necessarily construe *all* other traditions as *idolatrous*, or at least the burden of proof lies with them to vindicate their "ethical" credentials. This is the full consequence of the way Levinas constructs his basic categories.
29. Levinas, *TI*, 48.
30. Levinas, *ITN*, 85.
31. Ibid., 7.
32. Levinas, *OB*, 182.
33. Ibid., 57.
34. Ibid., 43.
35. Levinas, *DF*, 9.
36. Emmanuel Levinas, *Beyond the Verse*, trans. Gary Mole (London: Continuum, 1994), 192.
37. Levinas, *DF*, 10.
38. Levinas, *DF*, 19.
39. Ibid., 121.
40. Levinas, *ITN*, 129. Also: "These essays . . . lay sufficient stress upon the remarkable role that devolves upon Israel, in its exception, as a formation and expression of the universal." Levinas, *ITN*, 96.
41. Ibid., 45.
42. Levinas, *DF*, 177.
43. Levinas, *ITN*, 97.
44. Judith Butler, *Giving an Account of Oneself* (New York: Fordham University Press, 2005), 93–94. Butler's point here planted one of the seeds that became this book.

45. Levinas, *OB*, 43–45; *ITN*, 43–64.
46. Levinas, *OB*, 77; *DF*, 14.
47. Cf. Levinas, *OB*, 19.
48. Levinas, *UH*, 108.
49. Levinas, *DF*, 18.

50. In response to questions on whether animals have a "face," Levinas responds: "The human face is completely different and only afterwards do we discover the face of an animal. . . . It is because we, as human, know what suffering is that we can have this obligation." When forced to deal with non-human alterity, the *epistemic function* or "knowing" dimension of his account of alterity becomes explicit! In fact, Levinas counts human alterity as the most radical (well, after divine alterity, which the human is said to open). This is strange, and in the same way his reference to a "lunar, Martian past" is strange. When his position is forced to deal with non-human alterity or non-Jewish ontology, the epistemic dimension of his account is forced into the open. See Emmanuel Levinas, "The Paradox of Morality: An Interview with Emmanuel Levinas," in *The Provocation of Levinas: Rethinking the Other*, ed. Robert Bernasconi and David Wood (London: Routledge, 1988), 168–80. I'm gratefully indebted to Aaron Bell for opening this insight to me. Aaron Bell, "The Animal Without a Face," Unpublished Manuscript, 13–14.

51. Levinas, *ITN*, 97.
52. Ibid., xvii (my emphasis).
53. Emmanuel Levinas, "Emmanuel Levinas," in Raoul Martley, *French Philosophers in Conversation* (London: Routledge, 1991), 18: cited in Bernasconi, "Who Is My Neighbor?," 26.

54. This is an important point to make. Every single tradition that populates human culture tells an arch-teleological story of some kind—where we come from, where we are going, how we got where we are, and how to live a good life throughout the journey: learning from and rectifying past mistakes, preserving what is worthy, and creatively confronting the problems of our time by inventing better ways to concretely coexist together. There is no justification for singling out Judaism for doing nothing other than this, or to resent its historical role in the development, with Amenhotep and Plato, of monotheism. Unlike Amenhotep and Plato, the relevant notion of *election* has played a relatively singular role in the evolution of democratic political thought, a fact that deserves closer study. Discourses that rely—as one of its more complex expressions—on Derrida's own implicit arch-teleological story, constructed in dialogue with Kojève, Hyppolite, and Bataille, are not exempt here; nor any other fashionable variety of scientism or nihilism we might imagine.

55. This is especially true for positions that claim to *have done* with stories altogether, a position often claimed by those telling an *apparently* new story, that is, those seeking to found a new tradition. For interesting reading on the relation of narrative, law, and ethics, see Naftali Cohen, *The Memory of the Temple and the Making of the Rabbis* (Philadelphia: University of Pennsylvania Press, 2012);

Moshe Simon-Shoshan, *Stories of the Law: Narrative Discourse and the Construction of Authority in the Mishnah* (Oxford: Oxford University Press, 2013); Jeffery Stout, *Ethics After Babel: The Language of Morals and their Discontents* (Princeton: Princeton University Press, 2001); J. K. A. Smith, "A Little Story About Metanarratives: Lyotard, Religion, and Postmodernism Revisited," *Faith and Philosophy* 18 (2001): 261–76.

56. Annabel Herzog, "Levinas and the Unnamed Balaam of Ontology and Idolatry," *The Journal of Jewish Thought and Philosophy* 19, no. 2 (2011): 144. Herzog's point here planted one of the seeds that became this book.

Chapter 6

1. Putnam, 2002, 33.
2. See Jeff Malpas and Ingo Farin, eds. *Reading Heidegger's Black Notebooks 1931–1941* (Cambridge: MIT Press, 2016).
3. Levinas, *DF*, 291 (my emphasis).
4. Unless otherwise indicated, I rely on Bernasconi and Critchley, 2002, xv–xxx, and Peperzak, 1997 for the biographical details that follow. I must say that I deeply admire Critchley's quite sensitive and well-formed chronicle.
5. Bernasconi and Critchley, 2002, xv–xvi.
6. Charles Blondel was a widely influential psychologist of the day, and a close personal friend of Marcel Mauss. A staunch critic of Freud, he helped pioneer social psychology in France as a discipline distinct from systematic sociology. He was also active in French public life as a Social Catholic and organizer in the Christian Democratic movement (see Chappel, 2018, 206; Fournier, 2015, 223; Misiak and Staudt, 1954, 220; Rauch, 1974, 209, 246–47). Maurice Halbwachs was a socialist, an internationally known Durkheimian sociologist of religion, and the founder of contemporary memory studies. The Gestapo arrested him after he formally protested the arrest of his Jewish father-in-law. He died in Buchenwald (see Novick, 1999, 3). Maurice Pradines was an interesting and original French philosopher, psychologist, and theist. He developed Bergson in unique ways, and was Levinas's thesis advisor. As Critchley notes, Pradines "made a very strong impression on the young Levinas [by] the way . . . [he] used the example of the Dreyfus affair to illuminate the primacy of ethics over politics" (see Brown, 1995, 633; Bernasconi and Critchley, 2002, xvi). Henri Carteron was a Catholic professor of ancient philosophy, to whom Levinas dedicated his first book on Husserl (see de Vries, 2005, 361).
7. Peperzak, 1997, 412.
8. Salomon Malka. *Emmanuel Levinas: His Life and Legacy* (Pittsburgh: Duquesne University Press, 2002), 37–38.
9. Bernasconi and Critchley, 2002, xvi–xvii.
10. See Wolin, 2015, 190, 271; Dostal, 2010, 249; Sánchez and Sánchez, 2016, 393–97; and http://www.husserlpage.com/hus_bio.html.

11. Ethan Kleinberg. *Generation Existential: Heidegger's Philosophy In France, 1927–1961* (Ithaca: Cornell University Press, 2005) 39.

12. Bernasconi and Critchley, 2002, xvii.

13. Colin Davis, *Levinas: An Introduction* (Notre Dame: University of Notre Dame Press, 1990), chapter 1.

14. Ibid.

15. Dupont, 2015, 139–45.

16. Ibid., 140.

17. Peperzak, 1997, 412–513; Bernasconi and Critchley, 2002, xvi–xviii; Dupont, 2015, 139–45.

18. Bernasconi and Critchley, 2002, xviii.

19. Bergo's biographical timeline in her *SEP* entry conflicts with both Peperzak's and Critchley's chronicles in a few minor details. I follow Bergo here because her piece is the most recent and she would not have published updated information without sufficient justification. See Bettina Bergo, "Emmanuel Levinas," *Stanford Encyclopedia of Philosophy*, August 3, 2011, http://plato.stanford.edu/entries/levinas/.

20. Levinas described *Esprit* as "a journal representing a progressive, avant-garde Catholicism." See Levinas, *RPH*, 63; and https://www.cairn-int.info/about-the-journal-esprit.htm.

21. Kleinberg, 2005, 66. As my analysis of *Totality and Infinity* appears to corroborate, Kojéve's Hegel seems to have deeply influenced Levinas philosophically, no doubt mediated by Sartre.

22. See Bergo, 2011. Bergo also translated Stanford University Press's 2003 English edition of the piece.

23. Bernasconi and Critchley, 2002, xviii.

24. "In 1983 Levinas was awarded the Karl Jasper prize by Heidelberg University. He sent his son [Michael] to receive the prize on his behalf," it seems in order to keep his vow. See Tal Sessler, *Levinas and Camus: Humanism for the Twenty-First Century* (London: Continuum, 2008), 90, note 111.

25. Critchley writes, "As a former student of the ENIO points out in a memoir of Levinas as a teacher, the school was neither normal, nor truly Israeli, nor completely oriental. The ENIO was located at 59 rue d'Auteuil and later on the rue Michel-Ange in the 16th arrondissement." Bernasconi and Critchley, 2002, xx–xxi.

26. Levinas's choice to go on as a Jewish school administrator deeply moves me, for reasons I'm still sorting through. Years ago I read a well-known philosopher quip, "I write for no community." I get his point, but it always bugged me somehow. Just at the time that I myself embraced the personae of a would-be avant-gardest (in late adolescence, as it happens), my pastor said something I never forgot. As was my custom in those days, I once more found myself at center of some banal sort of social mischief. As gracious as ever, John Groblewski responded to my ingeniously improvised, ex post facto justification with a loving giggle, and he said with a hint of jest: "Remember: the best thinkers are nearly always also *pastors*, or at least *care*

about the communities they inhabit. Whatever new or surprising gifts history always holds in store, they at least in part are meant for the well-being of the people who will receive them; however they might chose to reckon it. Let your mischievous creativity and *joie de vivre* be a blessing to all, and not only to yourself." Perhaps more greatly than any other twentieth-century philosopher, Levinas lived this bit of truth and mentory wisdom for me.

27. Bernasconi and Critchley, 2002, xxi.

28. Bergo, 2011. As Critchley notes, in contrast to the intellectual fashion of the time, dominated as it was "by the existentialism of Sartre and Camus, the book was published with a red banner around it with the words 'où il ne s'agit pas d'angoisse' ('where it is not a question of anxiety')." Bernasconi and Critchley, 2002, xxii.

29. As Sánchez and Sánchez recount, "Wahl became Professor at the Sorbonne in 1936, where he remained until World War II, when he was interned in the Drancy deportation camp. He managed to escape to the United States, where he established with Jacques Maritain and Gustave Cohen, the École libre des Hautes Etudes in New York with the support of the Rockefeller Foundation—a university for exiled French academics. The staff of the university included names such as anthropologist Claude Lévi-Strauss and linguist Roman Jakobson. He also held a position in Mount Holyoke, an art school for women in South Hadley, Massachusetts. Due to the initiative of a French professor, Helle Patch, Wahl organized the *Dècades de Mount Holyoke* from 1942 to 1944 (also known as *Pontigny-en-Amèrique*), which consisted of important gatherings of exiled French artists and intellectuals eager to discuss American and English culture. After the war, Wahl returned to France, where he founded the Collège philosophique in 1946, and the review *Deucalion*. He also took the position of director of the *Revue de métaphysique et de morale* in 1950 and became president of the *Société française de philosophie*. At that time he wrote poetry concerning his captivity during the war; these poetic works were compiled in the book, *Poèmes de circonstance*. From this time until his death on June 19, 1974 he intensively continued his work as researcher, but also as a teacher and author. He died at the age of 88 at the Faculty of Philosophy at the Sorbonne." See Sánchez and Sánchez, 2016, 393–97.

30. Richard Kearney, "Emmanuel Levinas," in *Debates in Continental Philosophy: Conversations with Contemporary Thinkers* (New York: Fordham University Press, 2004), 68.

31. Bergo, 2011. According to Malka (2002, 190–91), these lectures were the first time Levinas and Ricoeur met.

32. Bernasconi and Critchley, 2002, xxi–xxii; Bergo, 2011.

33. Martin Kavka, "Is Critique Jewish?," *Jewish Quarterly Review* 108, no. 2 (2018): 262. The journal was named after Charlie Chaplin's film, and it quickly became the pathbreaking center of Parisian intellectual life, with a founding editorial board that included Sartre, de Beauvoir, Raymond Aron, Michel Leiris, Maurice

Merleau-Ponty, and others. See http://www.gallimard.fr/Catalogue/GALLIMARD/Revue-Les-Temps-Modernes.

34. Shmuel Wygoda, "A Phenomenological Outlook at the Talmud: Levinas as Reader of the Talmud," published on Georges Hansel's personal website, http://ghansel.free.fr/wygoda.html.

35. Ibid.

36. Bernasconi and Critchley, 2002.

37. Bergo, 2011; Thomas Gale, "Les Colloques des Intellectuels Juifs de Langue Française," *Encyclopedia.com*, https://www.encyclopedia.com/religion/encyclopedias-almanacs-transcripts-and-maps/les-colloques-des-intellectuels-juifs-de-langue-francaise.

38. Bergo, 2011.

39. The story of Levinas's relationship with Father Van Breda has never been told, to my knowledge. Given the warmth evident in his piece on Van Breda in *Proper Names*, this seems worth pursuing.

40. Herman Leo Van Breda was a Franciscan monk, philosopher, and the founder of the Husserl Archives at Catholic University of Leuven. He studied in Freiburg in 1938 with Fink and others, after Husserl's death and as the *Anschluss*, Munich, and *Kristallnacht* unfolded around him. He had the presence of mind to see and act decisively to rescue Husserl's literary legacy from Nazi destruction. See https://www.onserfdeel.be/nl/blogs/detail/how-a-flemish-franciscan-rescued-philosopher-edmund-husserl%E2%80%99s-archive-from-nazi-germany.

41. Quentin Lauer, "Totalité et infini. Par Emmanuel Lévinas," *Dialogue: Canadian Philosophical Association* 9, no. 1 (1962): 207–10; Anna-Teresa Tymieniecka, "Review of Totalité et infini," *Philosophy and Phenomenological Research* 23, no. 2 (December 1962): 298–300; Raymond Vancourt, "Emmanuel Levinas. Totalité et Infini," *Critique [Paris]* 194 (1963): 663. Vancourt's review is brief, but noteworthy still insofar as he is recognized by Yad Vashem for sheltering Jews during the war. See http://db.yadvashem.org/righteous/family.html?language=en&itemId=4042961.

42. Bernasconi and Critchley, 2002, xxiv.

43. I'm deeply grateful to Roger Burggraeve and Jeffrey Bloechl for allowing me to interview them and for supplying information on the Flemish and Dutch reception of Levinas's work.

44. Rudolph Gerber, "Totality and Infinity: Hebraism and Hellenism: The Experiential Ontology of Emmanuel Levinas," *Review of Existential Psychology & Psychiatry* 7, no. 3 (1961): 177; Albert Dondeyne, "Inleiding tot het denken van E. Levinas (on *Totalité et Infini*)," *Tijdschrift voor Filosofie* 25, no. 3 (September 1963): 555–84.

45. Malka, 2002, 205–6.

46. Bernasconi and Critchley, 2002, xxv.

47. Bernasconi and Critchley, 2002, xxv–xxvi.

48. Malka, 2002, 208.

49. Bernasconi and Critchley, 2002, xxv–xxvi.

50. Bernasconi and Critchley, 2002, xxv–xxvii.

51. Bernasconi and Critchley, 2002, xxvi.

52. Roger Burggraeve, *Proximity with the Other. A Multidimensional Ethic of Responsibility in Levinas* (Bangalore, India: Dharmaram Publications, 2009), 125–46.

53. Ibid.

54. Disclosure: I first met Richard in 2002 as an undergraduate student at UNC Charlotte. He generously agreed to supervise an independent study with me on *Totality and Infinity* in spring 2003. This same semester I did another independent study on *Being and Time* with my friend Christopher Raymond Stapor and under the direction of Bill Gay (and took a Narrative Philosophy course with my first philosophical mentor, Laura Duhan Kaplan, who introduced me to phenomenology and supervised my senior thesis on Husserl). Though I entered this semester already under the sway of the sheer power of Heidegger's magnum opus, by June—and thanks to the vivacity of my and Richard's meetings—I became a full-fledged and pugnacious partisan for the author of *Totality and Infinity*. I remained one until my initially tentative critical turn in November 2010. Richard is a long-time philosophical mentor and a lifelong friend. Thanks, Richard, for agreeing to be interviewed for this chapter.

55. Richard A. Cohen, *Elevations: The Height of the Good in Levinas and Rosenzweig* (Chicago: University of Chicago Press, 1994), xi.

56. Cohen wasn't able to follow through with Ricoeur on the thesis, though the two kept in collegial correspondence over the years. Cohen coedited a volume on Ricoeur's work with James L. Marsh, *Ricoeur as Another: The Ethics of Subjectivity* (Albany: State University of New York Press, 2002). As it happens, Cohen was attending Levinas's seminars at the time of my birth, in April 1975.

57. See Malka, 2002.

58. Roger Burggraeve, *Proximity with the Other. A Multidimensional Ethic of Responsibility in Levinas* (Bangalore, India: Dharmaram Publications, 2009), 125–46.

59. Ibid.

60. Derrida, 1999, 16.

61. Bernasconi and Critchley, 2002, xxviii.

62. Malka, 2002, 209.

63. Bernasconi and Critchley, 2002, xxvii.

64. Malka, 2002, 192.

65. Malka, 2002, 203–4.

66. Bernasconi and Critchley, 2002, xviii.

67. Robert Bernasconi deserves special mention here. He began exploring the relationship between Levinas and Derrida's thought nearly a decade prior to when it became fashionable in the scholarship: "The Trace of Levinas in Derrida," in *Derrida and Différance*, ed. Bernasconi and Wood (Evanston: Northwestern University Press, 1985), 13–30; "The Ethics of Suspicion," *Research in Phenomenology* 20 (1990): 3–18; "Skepticism in the Face of Philosophy," in *Re-Reading Levinas*, ed. Bernasconi and Critchley (Bloomington: Indiana University Press, 1991), 149–61. The de Man affair and the English publication of *De l'esprit* roused considerable controversy and gave

the impression that Derrida was soft on fascism; or at the very least, on his friends and influences who flirted with it. This in the context of Lacoue-Labarthe's admirably frank nihilistic interpretation of the politics of deconstruction. Lacoue-Labarthe & Co.'s admirably frank nihilistic interpretations of the politics of deconstruction, well treated by Critchely (2002) and Fraser (1984), the latter well-before Derrida's subsequent, quite prudent explosion of normative rhetoric. Right in the midst of this controversy, Derrida authored and presented the text that some consider to mark or inaugurate his so-called "ethical turn" (*Force of Law*). Bernasconi not only anticipates Derrida's explicit turn to ethics, but himself does so in a way that does not merely absorb Levinas into the systemic casino of "*différance*."

68. Though there are some problems with the piece, for my own rough account of the history of English-language Levinas studies, see Jack Marsh, "Lévinas en Amérique du Nord aujourd'hui. Trois vagues et deux écoles," *Cahiers d'etudes Lévinassiennes* 11 (2012): 192–211.

69. Malka, 2002, 191.

70. Burggraeve, 2009, 125–46.

71. For a good introduction to the critical theological discussion surrounding Levinas's contributions, see Bettina Bergo, "Is There a 'Correlation' between Rosenzweig and Levinas?," *The Jewish Quarterly Review* 96, no. 3 (Summer 2006): 404–12; Aryeh Botwinick, *Emmanuel Levinas and the Limits to Ethics* (London: Routledge, 2016); Maurice Friedman, "Martin Buber and Emmanuel Levinas: An Ethical Query," in *Buber and Levinas: Dialogue and Difference*, ed. Atterton, Calarco, and Friedman (Pittsburgh: Duquesne University Press, 2004), 116–32; Martin Kavka, "Is There a Warrant for Levinas's Talmudic Readings?," *Journal of Jewish Thought and Philosophy* 14, no. 1/2 (2006): 153–73.

72. Levinas: "You know, one often speaks of ethics to describe what I do, but what really interests me in the end is not ethics, not ethics alone, but the holy, the holiness of the holy." Quoted in Derrida, 1999, 4.

73. Throughout the entirety of *OB*, Levinas rivets writing to ontology.

74. It goes without saying that Derrida and Foucault have each irreplaceably contributed critical tools and strategies to normatively oriented social theory, aesthetics, the theory of history, and much else. At the end of the day, however: if humanity exists 500 years from now, Derrida and Foucault will be considered minor footnotes to Heidegger. Beyond phenomenology, Horkheimer, Adorno, and Habermas will fare better historically for very substantive reasons, and Habermas's *The Philosophical Discourse of Modernity* will be as relevantly fair and valid then as it stands to this day on a various of questions.

75. A sample: Christina Hack, *Groter dan ons hart: De verhouding van God en mens bij Karl Barth en Emmanuel Levinas, met het oog op het nieuwe tijds denken* (Zoetermeer: Universiteit van Amsterdam, 1993); Kevin Jung, *Ethical Theory and Responsibility Ethics: A Metaethical Study of Niebuhr and Levinas* (New York: Peter Lang, 2011); John Patrick Koyles, *The Trace of the Face in the Politics of Jesus: Exper-*

imental Comparisons Between the Work of John Howard Yoder and Emmanuel Levinas (Eugene: Pickwick, 2013); Alain Mayama, *Emmanuel Levinas' Conceptual Affinities with Liberation Theology* (New York: Peter Lang, 2009); Glenn Morrison, *A Theology of Alterity: Levinas, von Balthasar, and Trinitarian Praxis* (Pittsburgh: Duquesne University Press, 2013); Michael Purcell, *Levinas and Theology* (Cambridge: Cambridge University Press, 2006) and *Mystery and Method: The Other in Rahner and Levinas* (Milwaukee: Marquette University Press, 1998); Michele Saracino, *On Being Human: A Conversation With Lonergan and Levinas* (Milwaukee: Marquette University Press, 2003); Stephen G. Smith, *Argument to the Other: Reason Beyond Reason in the Thought of Karl Barth and Emmanuel Levinas* (Chico: Scholars, 1983); Dorothee Tippelskirch, *Liebe von fremd zu fremd . . . Menschlichkeit des Menschen und Göttlichkeit Gottes bei Emmanuel Levinas und Karl Barth* (Freiburg: Alber-Reihe Thesen 22, 2002); J. Aaron Simmons and Kevin Carnahan, "When Liberalism Is Not Enough: Political Theology after Reinhold Niebuhr and Emmanuel Levinas," *Religions* 10, no. 439 (2019): doi: 10.3390/rel10070439.

76. Levinas, 1981, 190. Outside of pre-modern contexts and non-liberal states, esotericism is infantile. Though Levinas perhaps succeeds at occluding various historical content, the undecidability between God and the *il y a* is not merely plain, but *alive* in the text (by contrast with other quite distinct rhetorics of "undecidability" popular in bourgeois "theory"). I've not yet been able to track down the specific interview, but somewhere Levinas refers to God as *"probably* not an activity." Anyone actually familiar with his methodology and the structure of his descriptions in both major works knows that this "probably" was not merely a nod to the hoi polloi. Moreover, any sufficiently attentive reading of *TI*'s ironic treatment of "atheism" should put to rest any doubts on Levinas's stand on that question. Levinas—with admirable chutzpah—wrote this moreover in the wake of Kojève and at the height of Sartre's fame.

77. I argue this same point, though in this case against a quite different critical posture; see Jack Marsh, "Athens *or* Jerusalem? Puntel on Levinas," *Journal for Continental Philosophy of Religion* 2 (2020): 108–16.

78. For what it's worth, my library database returned the following results on a chronological search of "postmodernism": 1980: 29 hits, 1990: 810 hits, 1995: 2,512 hits, 2000: 4,394 hits.

79. Malka, 2002, 210–11.

80. Ibid., 158.

81. Levinas, 1985, 37.

82. Malka, 2002, 192–93.

83. Derrida, 1999, 12.

84. I thank Richard Kearney for allowing me to interview him for this chapter.

85. "Litvak" names a specific Jewish theological and hermeneutic tradition, centered on Levinas's native Lithuania and elsewhere in Eastern Europe, gathered around thinkers like Vilna Gaon and Chaim of Volozhin. This tradition took a

famously staunch critical view against Chassidism and other iterations of the Jewish mystical tradition. See Malka, 2002, 212–13.

86. Dussel, 1999, 126.

87. Malka, 2002, 199.

88. Bernasconi and Critchley, 2002, 2.

89. Simon Critchley, "Emmanuel Levinas, 1906–1995," *Radical Philosophy* 078 (July/August 1996): 53–56.

90. Derrida, 1999, 70–71.

91. Derrida, 1999, 122.

Chapter 7

1. Quoted in Manohla Dargis, "A Godard Odyssey in Dante's Land," *The New York Times*, October 2, 2004, https://www.nytimes.com/2004/10/02/movies/a-godard-odyssey-in-dantes-land.html. I'm indebted to Chris at Goddard Montage for this citation: http://godardmontage.blogspot.com/2010/11/godard-levinas-violence.htm.

2. Levinas, 1997, 70.

3. See note 1 of my introduction.

4. Peter Atterton and Matthew Calarco, "Editor's Introduction," in *Radicalizing Levinas* (Albany: State University of New York Press, 2010), ix.

5. If my institutional database is any indicator, a general search on "Emmanuel Levinas," filtered chronologically, returned the following results (books, dissertations, articles, reviews, etc.): 1920–1980: *281 hits*, 1980–1990: *402 hits*, 1990–2000: *2,033 hits*, 2000–2010: *5,440 hits*. The growth seems to have stabilized throughout our current decade, with Levinas on pace to receive roughly *5,720* treatments.

6. Rubens Ricupero, "Address by Mr. Rubens Ricupero, Secretary-General of UNCTAD," *United Nations Conference on Trade and Development Records*, Bangkok, Thailand, February 12, 2000, https://unctad.org/en/Docs/u9l353.en.pdf.

7. For what its worth, my library database returned the following results on a chronological search of "postmodernism": 1980: 29 hits, 1990: 810 hits, 1995: 2,512 hits, 2000: 4,394 hits.

8. The UN Millennium Project, www.unmillenniumproject.org/.

9. The UN Conference, Meeting, and Events: "The Millennium Summit," www.un.org/en/events/pastevents/millennium_summit.shtml.

10. Rubens, 2000.

11. Francis Fukuyama, "Against Identity Politics," *The Andrea Mitchell Center for the Study of Democracy Blog*, https://www.sas.upenn.edu/andrea-mitchell-center/francis-fukuyama-against-identity-politics; Matt McManus, "Right Wing Critiques of Identity Politics and Post-Modern Culture," *PoliticalCritique.org*, http://political-critique.org/opinion/2018/right-wing-critiques-of-identity-politics-and-post-modern-

culture/; David Remnick, "A Conversation with Mark Lilla on His Critique of Identity Politics," *The New Yorker*, https://www.newyorker.com; Tamar Abrams, "A Conversation with Laura Kipnis," *Conscience*, https://consciencemag.org/2017/04/19/a-conversation-with-laura-kipnis/; Melissa Naschek, "The Identity Mistake," *Jacobin*, www.jacobinmag.com/2018/08/. Slavoj Žižek, "Troubles with Identity," *Los Angeles Review of Books*, https://thephilosophicalsalon.com/troubles-with-identity/.

12. Staff, "Jews and the Civil Rights Movement," *Religious Action Center of Reform Judaism*, https://rac.org/jews-and-civil-rights-movement.

13. David Kenneth, "The Role of the Catholic Church During the Civil Rights Movement," *The Classroom*, https://www.theclassroom.com/the-role-of-the-catholic-church-during-the-civil-rights-movement-12087099.html.

14. Imam Khalid Griggs, "African American Muslims and the Social Justice Movement," *Why Islam? (Blog)*, https://www.whyislam.org/social-issues/african-american-muslims-and-the-social-justice-movement/.

15. Jamillah Karim, "Our Legacy, Too: Muslim Women and the Civil Rights Movement," *From The Square: NYU Press Blog*, https://www.fromthesquare.org/our-legacy-too-muslim-women-and-the-civil-rights-movement/#.XWK7unuQwd0; Ajamu Baraka, *Pambazuka News*, February 23, 2017, "Malcolm X and Human Rights in the Time of Trumpism: Transcending the Master's Tools," https://www.pambazuka.org/pan-africanism/malcolm-x-and-human-rights-time-trumpism-transcending-master%E2%80%99s-tools.

16. See Johanna Bockman, *Markets in the Name of Socialism: The Left-Wing Origins of Neoliberalism* (Stanford: Stanford University Press, 2011).

17. Quoted in Jack Marsh, "The Concept of Socialist Law, An Interview With Christine Sypnowich," *Rebel News*, https://newrevolutionary.com/jackmarsh/the-concept-of-socialist-law-an-interview-with-christine-sypnowich/.

18. Ibid.

19. See Bockman, 2011. Socialist economists actually contributed to neoliberal, neo-classical economic theory subsequently utilized by post-1989 planners.

20. At his clownish worst, the "postmodern Christian" imagines himself a "radical," in a vague and theatrical pseudo-Nietzschean sense. Radicality, here, amounts to craft beer connoisseurship, reading *Atlas Shrugged* or *Discipline and Punish*, periodic vegetarianism, mustering a vote for Gary Johnson or Jill Stein, socializing with queers at least once a year, daring to do yoga, and so forth.

21. Matthew Linder, "Music Matters: In Search of 90's CCM That Doesn't Suck," *Christ and Pop Culture Blog*, April 16, 2013, https://www.patheos.com/blogs/christandpopculture/2013/04/music-matters-in-search-of-90s-ccm-that-doesnt-suck/.

22. I'm proud to say that my own U2 story is relatively boring, thanks in part to my parent's working-class Pentecostalism, which unfolded as a jarring parallax of oscillating periods of secular austerity and secular festival, owing to my father's peculiar psychology. One must be willing to assume extreme measures in the cause

of the God of Abraham, but on the other hand, why fear the more ridiculous gestures of snobs rich enough to bid the Almighty *adieu*? Thanks to my cousin, Jennifer Knecht, I supplied my dad with a *Joshua Tree* CD. Having already been caught numerous times—oh, the rebellion!—secreting radio, the Violent Femmes, Def Leopard, the Beastie Boys, Guns-N-Roses, NWA, and Metallica: not two months later, I arrived home from school to an irregular gift: U2's *Rattle and Hum*, handed me with a hug by my father; thanks in large part to my mom's Aronic intercession (she despised my father's periodic aesthetico-religious austerity nearly as much my sister Liz and foster brother, Cody, did; my father was a singular market force for the sheer number of televisions bought and sold throughout the 1980s). Thankfully, our little sister, Sarah, grew up under a quite different aesthetic regime. My father taught me to distrust all-too-easy injunctions to just "enjoy!," but it was he and no one else who introduced me to Led Zeppelin and Black Sabbath. Such was the at times inscrutable tumult of my childhood in general.

23. The "liberal" in "theological liberal," here, is epistemological rather than political. As Protestants at the time saw it, there must be a "third way" between the mindless Biblicism of the aggressive fundamentalism of the day, and the uncritical surrender of the relative autonomy of theological reflection to the unilateral authority of scientism (as theological liberals were read to do). Evangelicalism positioned itself as a centrist ecclesial movement that tried to embody both the existential seriousness of fundamentalist religious commitment, wedded to an open, community-engaged, and intellectually serious spiritual culture. As Trump discloses, the ruthless fundamentalism it twisted free from in the mid-twentieth century ultimately pulled it back into the ghetto.

24. Ed Stetzer, "Pro-Choice Evangelicals?," *Christianity Today*, November 5, 2012, https://www.christianitytoday.com/edstetzer/2012/november/morning-roundup-11512-pro-choice-evangelicals-president.html.

25. My classification is theological, not historical. The genealogy of Methodism is distinct from Anabaptism, though they are proximate in their respective critiques of Calvinism. The Anabaptist tradition was born as a dissident movement, and like all such movements: it's much less organized and much more internally differentiated than Calvinist and Lutheran traditions.

26. Stanley Grenz, "Concerns of a Pietist with a Ph.D." *An Address at the American Academy of Religion*, Toronto, November 23, 2002, www.stanleygrenz.com/articles/pietist.html.

27. This story is a simplification of much more complicated situation. Evangelicalism as a whole is a grassroots ecclesial movement. There are in fact working-class Reformed churches and middle-class Anabaptist churches. But as a general description of broad historical trends, this accurately renders goings-on. Historically, the poorer the church, the more fundamentalist, insular, and tribalistic it tends to be; and the more susceptible to things like "prosperity gospel" charlatanism.

28. My wife and I met Maxwell on a transport bus that ferries folks from the plane to the airport terminal, at the Barcelona airport I believe. He's a very nice man.

29. Anonymous, "BET," *Wikipedia*, https://en.wikipedia.org/wiki/BET.

30. As my analysis in this chapter suggests, we cannot do without Marxist analysis. But we are still caught in the very contradictions that 1989 inaugurated, namely: how to integrate class analysis in a way that no longer implicitly rests on the idea of merely nationalizing economies. Any actual revolutionary who is politically serious and morally responsible knows: today's revolutionaries are by necessity reformists, because that is what our material actuality and normative commitments require. Above all, today's revolutionaries must populate and gather around experimental economists, organizational systems theorists, legal philosophers, international relations theory, psychologists in both behavioral economics and object-relations psychoanalysis, moral philosophers, and normatively oriented sociologists, political theorists, cultural theorists, religious theorists, and so forth. Let's invent something better, and get busy experimenting! Until we do, hybrid economies and constitutional democracies are what we have, and critical performances and strategic proposals that don't justify themselves in this light will increasingly be ignored. Those who attack comrades engaged in the socio-scientifically grounded and normatively oriented Gramscian task of the day do *not* signal purity and radicality, but rather ignorance and lack of political seriousness.

31. Vladimir Tismaneanu, "The Revolutions of 1989: Causes, Meanings, Consequences," *Contemporary European History* 18, no. 3 (August 2009): 271–88.

32. Naomi Klein, *The Shock Doctrine: The Rise of Disaster Capitalism* (New York: Picador, 2008).

33. Anonymous, "Woodstock '99," *Wikipedia*, https://en.wikipedia.org/wiki/Woodstock_%2799#Controversy.

34. Bradley S. Reichek, *Rake Sentimentalism, or the Libertine Re-Formed: Re-Evaluating Late Eighteenth-Century Libertinage, 1770–1812* (PhD diss., Northwestern University, 2008).

35. Anonymous, "Libertine Novel," *Wikipedia*, https://en.wikipedia.org/wiki/Libertine_novel.

36. Angela Rene Nacol, *Visions of Disorder: Sex and the French Revolution in a Suit of Erotic Drawings by Claude-Louis Desrais* (Senior thesis, University of Texas, 2006), 40.

37. Nacol, 2006, 22.

38. Lynn Hunt, "Pornography and the French Revolution," in *The Invention of Pornography, 1500–1800*, ed. L. Hunt (Brooklyn: Zone Books, 1996), 301–40.

39. Hunt, 1996, 312.

40. Quoted in Taylor Stoltz, *Aristocrats, Republicans, and Cannibals: American Reactions to French Women in Violence* (MA thesis, Virginia Polytechnic Institute and State University, 2015), 32.

41. Anonymous, *La Discipline Patriotique, from Révolutions de France et de Brabant*, 1791, Bibliothèque Nationale, Paris; in Nacol, 2006, 76.

42. Nacol, 2006, 77.

43. Nacol, 2006, 21–23.

44. Nacol, 2006, 21.

45. Nacol, 2006, 16, 19.

46. Theodor Adorno and Max Horkheimer, *Dialectic of Enlightenment: Philosophical Fragments*, trans. E. Jephcott (Stanford: Stanford University Press, 2002), 68–69.

47. Nacol, 2006, 23.

48. Andrea Dworkin, *Pornography: Men Possessing Women* (New York: G.P. Putnam's Sons, 1981).

49. Adorno and Horkheimer, 2002, 78.

50. Nacol, 2006, 41.

51. Quoted in Sabina Becker, "Why the Marquis de Sade is Nobody's Hero," *News of the Restless Blog*, December 27, 2014, https://www.sabinabecker.com/2014/12/why-the-marquis-de-sade-is-nobodys-hero.html.

52. Quoted in Hunt, 1996, 306.

53. Quoted in Sabina Becker, "Why the Marquis de Sade is Nobody's Hero," *News of the Restless Blog*, https://www.sabinabecker.com/2014/12/why-the-marquis-de-sade-is-nobodys-hero.html.

54. Lisa Tessman, *Burdened Virtues: Virtue Ethics for Liberatory Struggles* (Oxford: Oxford University Press, 2005).

55. Quoted in Nacol, 2006, 17; Adorno and Horkheimer, 2002, 80.

56. Quoted in Becker, 2014; Linda Martin Alcoff, "Dangerous Pleasures: Foucault and the Politics of Pedophilia," in Susan Hekman, ed., *Re-Reading the Canon: Feminist Interpretations of Michel Foucault* (University Park, PA: Pennsylvania State Press, 1996), 127–18.

57. Eduardo Mendieta and Jürgen Habermas, "A Post-Secular World Society? On the Philosophical Significance of Postsecular Consciousness and the Multicultural World Society," trans. Matthias Fritsch, *The Immanent Frame*, February 3, 2010, https://tif.ssrc.org/2010/02/03/a-postsecular-world-society/.

58. Anonymous, "Hossein Nasr," *Wikipedia*, https://en.wikipedia.org/wiki/Hossein_Nasr#Awards_and_honors.

59. Anyone who actually cares about a democratic future should, with critical caveats, absolutely love al-Attas. I'm willing to bet money that few are placed to understand why. Prove me wrong! Mona Abaza, "Intellectuals, Power, and Islam in Malaysia: S.N. al-Attas or the Beacon on the Crest of a Hill," *Archipel* 58 (1999): 189–217, https://www.persee.fr/doc/arch_0044-8613_1999_num_58_3_3541.

60. Tom Heneghan, "Turkey Presents Prophet's Sayings for the 21st Century," *Reuters*, May 22, 2013, https://www.reuters.com/article/us-turkey-islam-hadiths/turkey-presents-prophets-sayings-for-the-21st-century-idUSBRE94L0OJ20130522.

61. Anonymous, "Fethullah Gülen," *Wikipedia*, https://en.wikipedia.org/wiki/Fethullah_G%C3%BClen.

62. Fethullah Gülen, "Turkey's Eroding Democracy," *New York Times*, February 3, 2015, https://www.nytimes.com/2015/02/04/opinion/fethullah-gulen-turkeys-eroding-democracy.html.

63. Fethullah Gülen, "Behind the Failure of Turkish Democracy Is the Betrayal of Islam," *Asia News*, March 1, 2019, http://www.asianews.it/news-en/Fetullah-G%C3%BClen:-Behind-the-failure-of-Turkish-democracy-is-the-betrayal-of-Islam-46383.html.

64. Anonymous, "Abdallah Bin Bayyah," *Wikipedia*, https://en.wikipedia.org/wiki/Abdallah_Bin_Bayyah.

65. Sam Jones, Kerin Hope, and Courtney Weaver, "Alarm Bells Ring Over Syriza's Russian Links Greek Energy Minister Speaks Out Against Further Sanctions on Moscow," *Financial Times*, January 28, 2015, https://www.ft.com/content/a87747de-a713-11e4-b6bd-00144feab7de; Christo Grozev, Sebastian Mondial, Steffen Dobbert, and Karsten Polke-Majewski, "Caught in the Web of the Russian Ideologues," *Zeit Online*, https://www.zeit.de/politik/ausland/2015-02/russia-greece-connection-alexander-dugin-konstantin-malofeev-panos-kammeno/seite-3.

66. Michael Millerman, "Alexander Dugin's Heideggerianism," *International Journal of Political Theory* 3, no. 1 (2018), https://www.geopolitica.ru/en/article/alexander-dugins-heideggerianism.

67. Helena Sheehan, *The Syriza Wave* (New York: Monthly Review Press, 2017), 185; quoted in Anonymous, "Syriza," *Wikipedia*, https://en.wikipedia.org/wiki/Syriza#2004_general_election.

68. Staff, "Greek Prime Minister Condemns Sanctions against Russia," *News Front*, May 28, 2016, https://en.news-front.info/2016/05/28/greek-prime-minister-condemns-sanctions-against-russia/.

69. Rachel Keanan, "No, They Are Not the Same," *ConservativeMomma*, July 7, 2016, https://conservativemomma.com/2016/07/07/no-they-are-not-the-same/.

70. Nick Pemberton, "From MLK To Nathan Phillips: Love Can Defeat Hate," *CounterPunch*, January 25, 2019, https://www.counterpunch.org/2019/01/25/from-mlk-to-nathan-phillips-love-can-defeat-hate/. Before domestic neo-fascism was even a bleep on our social media screens, and the global unfolding of neo-nativism landed on the shores of mainstream US politics, I myself debated Pemberton's point with a few colleagues. Before we were introduced to the likes of Richard Spencer, I argued that "white identity" is chimera, a dead dog belonging to zombies like David Duke, the KKK, and other demons on the margins of US political life. Informed by the unfolding situation in Europe and worrying developments among reactionary theologians, I argued that the critical logic deployed in popular styles of anti-racist critique were helping to spur its adoption by white working-class folk eager to defend themselves and their cultural legacies from too-indiscriminate criticism. Neither conservative identity-theologians nor colleagues in Black struggle shared my worry at the time.

71. Edward Erwin, "The New McCarthyism: Blacklisting in Academia," *Quillette*, August 17, 2018, https://quillette.com/2018/08/17/the-new-mccarthyism-blacklisting-in-academia/.

72. There was core and defiant opposition to the prominent Hillary-hate-fest that characterized the atmosphere of the left-academy across social media at the time.

I'd like to thank CUNY's Anna Gotlib, who exercised prominent leadership against it in my own social-media circle, and Judith Butler, who publicly spoke up against the tide of the day. See Staff, "Judith Butler in Cairo Review: 'I Would Vote For Hillary,'" *100 Years Blog, The American University of Cairo*, https://www.aucegypt.edu/media/media-releases/judith-butler-cairo-review-%25E2%2580%259Ci-would-vote-hillary%25E2%2580%259D.

73. Tara Golshan, "Did Jill Stein Voters Deliver Donald Trump the Presidency?," *Vox*, November 11, 2016, https:/www.vox.com/policy-and-politics/2016/11/11/13576798/jill-stein-third-party-donald-trump-win.

74. Terry Eagleton, "In the Gaudy Supermarket," *London Review of Books* 21, no. 10 (May 13, 1999): 3–6, https://www.lrb.co.uk/v21/n10/terry-eagleton/in-the-gaudy-supermarket.

75. Cornel West. "The Dilemma of the Black Intellectual," *Culture Critique* 1 (1985): 109–24.

76. Nancy Fraser, "The Force of Law: Metaphysical or Political?," *Cardozo Law Review* 13, no. 4 (December 1991): 1325–32.

77. Sypnowich, 1990, 55.

78. Bockman, 2011, 168, 12.

79. Tim Barker, "Spontaneous Order: Looking Back at Neoliberalism," *Dissent* 61, no. 1 (Winter 2014): 91–94 (93).

80. Bockman, 2011, 104, 163, 162, 192. See Jack Marsh, "Markets in the Name of Socialism. An Interview with Johanna Bockman," *Socialist Economist*, January 5, 2018, http://www.socialisteconomist.com/2018/01/markets-in-name-of-socialism-interview.html.

81. Vivek Chibber, *Locked in Place: State-Building and Late Industrialization in India* (Princeton: Princeton University Press, 2006); and "What Is Living and What Is Dead in the Marxist Theory of History," *Historical Materialism* 19, no. 2 (2011): 60–91.

82. Louis Proyect, "Final Thoughts on Vivek Chibber," *Louis Proyect: The Unrepentant Marxist*, May 12, 2013, https://louisproyect.org/2013/05/12/final-thoughts-on-vivek-chibber/.

83. Chibber manifestly does not play the "out-radical" game, as his texts and style clearly show. Proyect and others are projecting this on him, recycling well-worn responses to prior Marxist critics of post-colonial theory.

84. Chibber's "Our Road to Power"—in its totality—courageously demonstrates that he is both a serious Marxist and that he judges our current situation dire enough to no longer countenance the more clownish habits convention has handed down. In my view, he is the most important Marxist intellectual writing today. Whatever Marxism's future might be, it certainly will have traveled with Chibber. I wholly endorse Spivak's point that Gramscian work is more important than Chibber seems willing to acknowledge, but that's largely because of the methodological and stylistic

abuses done under Gramsci's authority. Vivek seems to be saying: let's tighten up our game social scientifically and politically. I endorse his call, admire his courage, and value the example he has set. See Vivek Chibber, "Our Road to Power," *Jacobin*, December 5, 2017, https://www.jacobinmag.com/2017/12/our-road-to-power.

85. G. A. Cohen, *Self-Ownership, Freedom, and Equality* (Cambridge: Cambridge University Press, 1995).

86. Vivek Chibber, "Our Road to Power," *Jacobin*, December 5, 2017, https://www.jacobinmag.com/2017/12/our-road-to-power.

87. Jan Rovný, "What Happened to Europe's Left?," *London School of Economic Blog*, February 20, 2018, https://blogs.lse.ac.uk/europpblog/2018/02/20/what-happened-to-europes-left/.

88. Patrick Gillespie, "America's Part-Time Worker Problem Is Permanent, San Francisco Fed Says," *CNN Money*, April 11, 2018, https://money.cnn.com/2018/04/11/news/economy/part-time-unemployment/index.html; Jim Edwards, "'Full Employment' May Be Increasing Economic Inequality," *Business Insider*, May 19, 2019, https://www.businessinsider.com/full-employment-underemployment-part-time-work-and-inequality-2019-5; Staff, "6.4 Million Americans Are Working Involuntarily Part Time: Employers Are Shifting Toward Part-Time Work as a 'New Normal,'" *Economic Policy Institute*, December 5, 2016, https://www.epi.org/press/6-4-million-americans-are-working-involuntarily-part-time-employers-are-shifting-toward-part-time-work-as-a-new-normal/.

89. Adele Lindenmeyr, "The First Soviet Political Trial: Countess Sofia Panina before the Petrograd Revolutionary Tribunal," *The Russian Review* 60 (October 2001): 505–25.

90. John Simkin, "Father Georgi Gapon," *Spartacus Educational*, https://spartacus-educational.com/RUSgapon.htm.

91. Orlando Figes, "The Women's Protest That Sparked the Russian Revolution," *The Guardian*, March 8, 2017, https://www.theguardian.com/world/2017/mar/08/womens-protest-sparked-russian-revolution-international-womens-day.

92. Quoted in W. E. Mosse, "Interlude: The Russian Provisional Government 1917," *Soviet Studies* 15, no. 4 (April 1964): 408–19.

93. Harold Meyerson, "My Man Martov," *The American Prospect*, July 7, 2017, https://prospect.org/article/my-man-martov.

94. Anonymous, "Julius Martov," *Wikipedia*, https://en.wikipedia.org/wiki/Julius_Martov.

95. Harold Meyerson, "My Man Martov," *The American Prospect*, July 7, 2017, https://prospect.org/article/my-man-martov.

96. Lori Gruen and Alison Wylie, "Feminist Legacies/Feminist Futures: 25th Anniversary Special Issue—Editors' Introduction," *Hypatia* 25, no. 4 (Fall 2010): 725–32.

97. Gruen and Wylie, 2010, 725–26.

98. Rosemarie Tong and Nancy Williams, "Feminist Ethics," *Stanford Encyclopedia of Philosophy*; quoted in Anonymous, "Alison Jaggar," *Wikipedia*, https://en.wikipedia.org/wiki/Alison_Jaggar.

99. Rabbi Louis Jacobs, "Haskalah, the Jewish Enlightenment," *My Jewish Learning*, https://www.myjewishlearning.com/article/haskalah/.

100. David Assaf, "Hasidism: Historical Overview," *The Yivo Encyclopedia of Jews in Eastern Europe*, https://yivoencyclopedia.org/article.aspx/hasidism/historical_overview.

101. Tzvi Freeman, "Eighteen Joyous Quotations of the Baal Shem Tov," *Chabad.org*, https://www.chabad.org/library/article_cdo/aid/1391822/jewish/18-Joyous-Teachings.htm.

102. Freeman, 2019.

103. Immanuel Etkes, "Eliyahu ben Shelomoh Zalman," *The Yivo Encyclopedia of Jews in Eastern Europe*, https://yivoencyclopedia.org/article.aspx/Eliyahu_ben_Shelomoh_Zalman.

104. Eli Rubi, "In the Shadow of the Maggid (1765–1782)," https://www.chabad.org/library/article_cdo/aid/2084158/jewish/In-the-Shadow-of-the-Maggid-1765-1782.htm.

105. According to Etkes, movement veteran Rabbi Menahem Mendel evinces a desire for reconciliation, and singles out Gaon for stout criticism: "This has been my way from the start, before arriving in the Land of Israel I also yearned and desired for unity and unanimity. But what can I do? For between us was an orator who "testified lies" [Proverbs 14:5] and spoke falsehoods against us and "plotted evil plots" [Psalms 141:4] . . . and "were they wise, they would think on this" [Deuteronomy 31:32], that they had borne false witness against us. . . . For what can they do? Since one may judge only what one's eyes see and what one's ears hear, and the onus is on the witnesses" (Etkes, 2002, 97–98).

106. Immanuel Etkes, *The Gaon of Vilna: The Man and His Image*, trans. J. M. Green (Berkeley: University of California Press, 2002), 96.

107. Eli Rubin, "Persecution, Arrests & Liberations (1797–1801)," *Chabad.org*, September 14, 2019, https://www.chabad.org/library/article_cdo/aid/2084213/jewish/Persecution-Arrests-Liberations-1797-1801.htm.

108. Tzvi Freeman and Menachem Posner, "17 Facts Everyone Should Know About Hasidic Jews," *Chabad.org*, https://www.chabad.org/library/article_cdo/aid/4079238/jewish/17-Facts-Everyone-Should-Know-About-Hasidic-Jews.htm.

109. Immanuel Etkes, "Eliyahu ben Shelomoh Zalman," *The Yivo Encyclopedia of Jews in Eastern Europe*, https://yivoencyclopedia.org/article.aspx/Eliyahu_ben_Shelomoh_Zalman.

110. Gaon's role in Hassidic persecution straightforwardly contests efforts to present him as a *Haskalic* figure. Though Gaon's scholarly genius as an expert in Jewish law cannot be contested, Etkes conclusively demonstrates that assertions of his endorsement of secular learning are overstated: "As opposed to the *maskilim*, he

assigned no independent value to such study." See Etkes, 2002. Ḥayim of Volozhin holds the honor of carrying Haskalah forward in the Mitnagdim tradition.

111. Scott Edgar, "Hermann Cohen," *Stanford Encyclopedia of Philosophy*, 2015, https://plato.stanford.edu/entries/cohen/#LifWor.

112. Quoted in Steven S. Schwarzschild, "The Democratic Socialism of Hermann Cohen," *Hebrew Union College Annual* 27 (1956): 417–38.

113. Edgar, 2015.

114. Michael Zank and Zachary Braiterman, "Martin Buber," *Stanford Encyclopedia of Philosophy*, December 4, 2014, https://plato.stanford.edu/entries/buber/.

115. Rachel White, "Recovering the Past, Renewing the Present: The Buber-Scholem Controversy over Hasidism," *Jewish Studies Quarterly* 14, no. 4 (2007): 364–92.

116. Judith Buber Agassi, "Buber's Critique of Marx," in *New Perspectives on Martin Buber*, ed. M. Zank (Tübingen: Mohr Siebeck, 2006), 231–32.

117. See Sam Berrin Shonkoff, "Sacramental Existence and Embodied Theology in Buber's Representation of Hasidism," in *Martin Buber: His Intellectual and Scholarly Legacy*, ed. S. B. Shonkoff (Boston: Brill, 2018), 273–302.

118. Paul Mendes-Flohr, "Martin Buber's 'Greater Realism': Palestine and the Politics of Dialogue," *ABC Religion & Ethics*, September 16, 2019, https://www.abc.net.au/religion/martin-buber-on-zionism-palestine-and-the-politics-of-dialogue/10723326.

119. Hillel Goldberg, "The Early Buber and Jewish Law," *Tradition: A Journal of Orthodox Jewish Thought* 21, no. 1 (Spring 1983): 66–74.

120. Maurice S. Friedman, "Martin Buber: The Life of Dialogue," *Religion Online*, https://www.religion-online.org/book-chapter/chapter-26-buber-and-judaism/.

121. Ibid.

122. Hillel Goldberg, "The Early Buber and Jewish Law," *Tradition: A Journal of Orthodox Jewish Thought* 21, no. 1 (Spring 1983): 66–74.

123. Goldberg, 1983, 72.

124. My gloss on Cassirer relies on Michael Friedman, "Ernst Cassirer," *Stanford Encyclopedia of Philosophy*, March 18, 2016, https://plato.stanford.edu/entries/cassirer/.

125. Karl Korsch, "The Passing of Marxian Orthodoxy: Bernstein-Kautsky-Luxemburg-Lenin (1937)," *Marxist.org*, https://www.marxists.org/archive/korsch/1937/marxian-orthodoxy.htm.

126. Hermann Heller, *Sovereignty: A Contribution to the Theory of Public and International Law*, trans. D. Dyzenhaus (Oxford: Oxford University Press, 2019).

127. Anonymous, "Book Launch: Hermann Heller's Sovereignty," *NYU Law (Blog)*, April 4, 2019, https://www.iilj.org/events/book-launch-hermann-hellers-sovereignty/.

128. Nancy Fraser, *Scales of Justice: Reimagining Political Space in a Globalizing World* (New York: Columbia University Press, 2010), 2–3.

129. Axel Honneth, "The Other of Justice: Habermas and the Ethical Challenge of Postmodernism," in *Cambridge Companion to Habermas*, ed. S. K. White (Cambridge: Cambridge University Press, 1995), 291.

130. Christine Lafont, "Human Rights and Sovereignty," in *Critical Theory in Critical Times: Transforming the Global Political and Economic Order*, ed. Penelope Deutscher and Cristina Lafont (New York: Columbia University Press, 2017), 47–73.

131. Kenneth Baynes, "Discourse Ethics and the Political Conception of Human Rights," *Ethics and Global Politics* 2, no. 1 (2009): 18–19.

132. Seyla Benhabib, "Below the Asphalt Lies the Beach: Reflections on the Legacy of the Frankfurt School," *Boston Review*, http://bostonreview.net/philosophy-religion/seyla-benhabib-below-asphalt-lies-beach.

133. Max Pensky, *The Ends of Solidarity: Discourse Theory in Ethics and Politics* (Albany: State University of New York Press, 2008), 148.

134. Pensky, 2008, 149.

135. Pensky, 2008, 151.

136. Pensky, 2008, 152.

137. Benhabib, 2019.

138. Benhabib, 2019.

139. Benhabib, 2019.

140. Eduardo Mendieta, "On Left Kantianism: From Transcendental Critique to the Critical Ontology of the Present," *Foucault Studies*, no. 18 (October 2014): 245–52.

141. Stephen K. White, "Reason, Modernity, and Democracy," in *Cambridge Companion to Habermas*, ed. S. K. White (Cambridge: Cambridge University Press, 1995), 7.

142. Gerald W. Schlabach, "Excerpts from *Contra Celsus* by Origen*,*" *Bluffton University Blog*, August 8, 1997: https://www.bluffton.edu/courses/humanities/1/celsus.htm.

143. Catherine Kroeger, "The Neglected History of Women in the Early Church," *Church History Institute*, https://christianhistoryinstitute.org/magazine/article/women-in-the-early-church/.

144. Karl Kautsky, "Foundations of Christianity (1908)," Marxist.org, https://www.marxists.org/archive/kautsky/1908/christ/index.htm.

145. For example, Arete of Cyrene, Themistoclea, Aspasia, Hipparchia the Cynic, Leontion, Xenophon, Sappho, Korinna, Nossis of Locri, Claudia Severa, Perpetua the Martyr, Mary the Jewess, Perpetua of Carthage, Proba Betitia Faltonia, Egeria of Galicia, Hypatia, Eudocia, Syncletica of Alexandria, Faltonia Betitia Proba, Paula of Rome, Aelia Eudocia, Radegund, Mercian prayer books, Kassia, Dhuoda, Hrotsvitha of Gandersheim, Héloïse d'Argenteuil, Trotula of Salerno, Anna Comnena, Marie de France, Frau Ava, Elisabeth of Schönau, Herrad of Landsberg, Hildegard of Bingen, Anna Komnene, Gormonda de Monpeslier, Mechtild von Magdeburg, Hadewijch, Marguerite Porete, Catherine of Siena, Julian of Norwich, Margery Kempe, Christine de Pisan, Beatriz Galindo, Vittoria Colonna, Katharine Zell, Isotta Nogarola, Tullia d'Aragona, Catherine Parr, Louise Labe, Olympia Morata, Veronica Franco, Isabella Andreini, Elizabeth Jane Weston, Marie Le Jars de Gournay, Anne

Bradstreet, Katherine Philips, Aphra Behn, Hannah More, Olympe de Gouges, Phillis Wheatley, Madame Anne de Stael, Jane Austen, Mary Shelley, George Sand, Elizabeth Gaskell, Harriet Beecher Stowe, Charlotte Bronte, Emily Bronte, Louisa May Alcott, Mary Wollstonecraft, and who else?

146. Given the tragic history of post-Constantinian anti-Semitism, it is incumbent upon Christians to actively respect Judaism as a distinct though sibling religion, and to actively oppose racists everywhere, especially in our own communities. But it must also be said that the Judaism of the day did not take kindly to upstart Christian heretics. In the context of periodic religious repression, such as Caligula's mad plans, and in light of Rome's granting Jews an exception to the requirements of the emperor's cult, outing Christians as non-Jews had literally dire social consequences for early Christian communities. That doesn't excuse or justify subsequent history, but it does suggest that the New Testament—authored by Jews—doesn't merely reflect some ahistorical psychological defect, but rather active social realities early Christian communities had to face.

147. Arvind Sharma, "Ancient Hinduism as a Missionary Religion," *Numen* 39, no. 2 (December 1992): 175–92.

148. Hayim Goren Perelmutter, "Judaism's Missionary Tradition," *Sh'ma*, January 1994, 6.

149. Luke M. Herrington, "Globalization and Religion in Historical Perspective: A Paradoxical Relationship," *Religions* 4 (2013): 145–65.

150. See S. R. F. Price, *Rituals and Power: The Roman Imperial Cult in Asia Minor* (Cambridge: Cambridge University Press, 1984); N. T. Wright, "Paul and Caesar: A New Reading of Romans," in *A Royal Priesthood: The Use of the Bible Ethically and Politically*, ed. C. Bartholomew (Carlisle: Paternoster, 2002), 173–93, http://ntwrightpage.com/2016/07/12/paul-and-caesar-a-new-reading-of-romans/.

151. N. T. Wright, 2002, 173–93, http://ntwrightpage.com/2016/07/12/paul-and-caesar-a-new-reading-of-romans/.

152. Even among pre-contact Amerindians, from Peru up to the Arctic, among Maori and other Pacific Islanders, to Sub-Saharan Africa.

153. "[Popular enthusiasm] even led to the publication of a fake translation of the Cyrus Cylinder on the web (www.farsinet.com/cyrus/), in which mention is made of the Iranian god Auramazdā, Cyrus' announcement of freedom of religion, and the abolishment of slavery, none of which is present in the real Cyrus Cylinder." R. J. van der Spek, "Cyrus the Great, Exiles, and Foreign Gods: A Comparison of Assyrian and Persian Policies on Subject Nations," *Studies in Ancient Oriental Civilization* 68 (2014): 233–64.

154. Antoine Simonin, "The Cyrus Cylinder," *Ancient History Encyclopedia*, January 18, 2012, https://www.ancient.eu/article/166/the-cyrus-cylinder/.

155. Cristian Violatti, "Ashoka the Great," *Ancient History Encyclopedia*, April 11, 2018, https://www.ancient.eu/Ashoka_the_Great/. Violatti suggests that Ashoka's relation to Buddhism is unclear. If the Edicts are in fact attributable to

Ashoka himself, and for anyone who has read classical Hindu and Buddhist texts and their histories, the content of the Edicts are clearly and uncontroversially Buddhist.

156. Ven. S. Dhammika, trans., "The Edicts of King Asoka," *The Wheel Publication*, 386/387 (1994), https://www.cs.colostate.edu/~malaiya/ashoka.html.

157. Rekha Rani Sharma, "Slavery in the Mauryan Period (C. 300 B.C.-C. 200 B.C.)," *Journal of the Economic and Social History of the Orient* 21, no. 2 (May 1978): 185–94.

158. Michael Loewe and Edward L. Shaughnessy, eds., *Cambridge History of Ancient China* (Cambridge: Cambridge University Press, 1999), 486, 606.

159. E. G. Pulleyblank, "The Origins and Nature of Chattel Slavery in China," *Journal of the Economic and Social History of the Orient* 1, no. 2 (April 1958): 185–220.

160. Pullyblank, 1958, 201.

161. Anonymous, "Wang Mang," *Encyclopedia.com*, September 18, 2019, https://www.encyclopedia.com/history/encyclopedias-almanacs-transcripts-and-maps/wang-mang. Wang himself probably arranged this. According to Bielenstein, aspiring leaders often engaged in such tactics to win popular support. See Twitchett and Fairbanks, 2008, 223–51.

162. Denis Twitchett and John K. Fairbanks, eds., *The Cambridge History of China: The Ch'in and Han Empires, 221 B.C.–A.D. 220* (Cambridge: Cambridge University Press, 2008), 232.

163. Pullyblank, 1958, 214.

164. One reason Philo of Alexandria is such hugely important figure is that he is essentially a son of Pharisaical Judaism, resistant to the too-uncritical Sadducean tradition of reducing the content of religious practices and understandings to purely speculative philosophical rationalization. The Sadducees reproduced elite Greek and Roman attitudes that despised common Jews as merely superstitious peasants. By contrast, Philo engaged the best of both the theology and philosophy of his time—and with his own very Jewish mystical and communal sensibility: creatively innovated in a way that brought to life popular religious practice with a degree of theoretical rigor. The import of retaining an active link between theory and practice fundamentally connected to the common life of the people is one of ancient monotheism's enduring gifts to the European intellectual tradition. Given Philo's creative relation to Platonism and his influence on the church Mothers and Fathers, he stands—an Egyptian Jew—as one of the fathers of modern Europe.

165. Christianity really did innovate within this tradition. In the gospel of John, the author's emphasis on the *Logos* was not a dig aimed at Jewish law per se, or an endorsement of pagan philosophy over-against biblical tradition; but rather a creative theological intervention that implied political authority must be *justified by reasons*. John in a way symbolically codifies a recognition of the brutal realities of

unaccountable political practice for the historical life of commoners in the ancient world; a defiant and creative call that murderous injustice is neither the original intent for nor the ultimate destiny of human life. The aim of John's mysticism is not individual esoteric "deification," but a *communion* of flesh and spirit centered in the self-sacrificial love of the historical Jesus qua Messiah, realized both in the individual spiritual lives of the believer and in the *solidarity* of the ethico-liturgical life of the community of Jesus people; a living taste of the *anticipatory promise*, a repetition of Messiah come: the justice, peace, and restoration of *this world*, later symbolized by the "New Jerusalem" come to earth (Rev. 21). This is the substance of "dynamic agape," which connects divine creation and eschatological promise to the actual practices of individual and communal liturgical life of the Christian community. Rather than finite terrestrial life being a mere waystation en route to a disembodied *hinterwelt*, aboriginal Christianity envisioned the divine restoration of *this world*, God's redemptive work participated in and contributed to by the moral and vocational excellence of everyday Jesus people. For an interesting treatment of these issues, see Jeyaseelan Joseph Kanagaraj, *"Mysticism" in the Gospel of John: An Inquiry into the Background of John in Jewish Mysticism* (Doctoral Thesis, Durham University, 1995), http://etheses.dur.ac.uk/1032. Kanagaraj stresses the innovative dimensions introduced by John's author, but it is absolutely beyond doubt that oral and popular traditions of Jewish mysticism were a field of ongoing theological creativity.

166. What we know as the Apostle's Creed was already widely recognized and in use, based in an older version popular in the Italian church and mentioned in the second-century writings of Tertullian and Irenaeus.

167. R. A. Markus, *Saeculum: History and Society in the Theology of St Augustine* (Cambridge: Cambridge University Press, 1989).

168. John T. Bristow, *What Paul Really Said about Women* (New York: Harper One, 1991), 120, fn 2; quoted in Marg Mowczko, "The Early Church and Slavery," *Marg Mowczko Blog*, April 3, 2012, https://margmowczko.com/the-early-church-and-slavery/.

169. J. Kameron Carter, *Race: A Theological Account* (Oxford: Oxford University Press, 2008), 231.

170. Eric Denby, "The First Abolitionist? Gregory of Nyssa on Ancient Roman Slavery," *Unpublished Manuscript*, May 9, 2011, page 17, https://www.academia.edu/1485109/The_First_Abolitionist_Gregory_of_Nyssa_on_Ancient_Roman_Slavery.

171. Thomas V. Mirus, "St. John Chrysostom on Wealth Redistribution," *Catholic Culture.org*, December 31, 2014, https://www.catholicculture.org/commentary/st-john-chrysostom-on-wealth-redistribution/.

172. Noting some of its methodological problems, more attention should nevertheless be paid to Berger's descriptive work here. See Peter L. Berger, *The Sacred Canopy: Elements of a Sociological Theory of Religion* (New York: Anchor, 1990).

Chapter 8

1. Quoted in Nathaniel Popkin, "Václav Havel at Independence Hall," *hidden cityphilia.org*, 12/19/2011: https://hiddencityphila.org/2011/12/vaclav-havel-at-independence-hall/.

2. Malka, 2002, 199.

3. Anonymous, "The Kovno Garage Massacre: Lithuanian Nationalists Clubbing Jewish Lithuanians to Death, 1941," *Rare Historical Photos*, August 5, 2016, https://rarehistoricalphotos.com/kovno-garage-massacre-lithuania-1941/; Anonymous, "Description by a German Army Photographer of the Lithuanian Attacks on the Jews, July 1941," *Facing History.org*, https://www.facinghistory.org/holocaust-human-behavior/description-by-german-army-photographer.

4. Anonymous, "The Kovno Garage Massacre: Lithuanian Nationalists Clubbing Jewish Lithuanians to Death, 1941," *Rare Historical Photos*, August 5, 2016, https://rarehistoricalphotos.com/kovno-garage-massacre-lithuania-1941/; Anonymous, "Description by a German Army Photographer of the Lithuanian Attacks on the Jews, July 1941," *Facing History.org*, https://www.facinghistory.org/holocaust-human-behavior/description-by-german-army-photographer.

5. Anonymous, "Kaunas pogrom," *Wikipedia*, https://en.wikipedia.org/wiki/Kaunas_pogrom#cite_note-Oshry-5, quoting Ephraim Oshry, *Annihilation of Lithuanian Jewry* (New York: Judaica Press, 1995), 3.

6. Andrew McGettigan, "The Philosopher's Fear of Alterity Levinas, Europe and Humanities 'Without Sacred History,'" *Radical Philosophy* 140 (November/December 2006), https://www.radicalphilosophy.com/article/the-philosophers-fear-of-alterity.

7. McGettigan, 2006.

8. McGettigan, 2006.

9. Martha Nussbaum, *Cultivating Humanity: A Classical Defense of Reform in Liberal Education* (Cambridge: Harvard University Press, 1997), 131.

10. Nathan Bell, "'In the Face, a Right Is There': Arendt, Levinas and the Phenomenology of the Rights of Man, *Journal of the British Society for Phenomenology* 49, no. 4 (2018): 305. Though I endorse Bell's reading on a conventional understanding of Levinas, it must be said that the theological move involved—the "extra-political principle" (302)—at its basis is theoretically controversial for political theory today. The reason that a liberal-statist interpretation of Levinas's politics entails a rejection of conventionally understood "disruption" talk is because protest in such a context is not a call for a whole other order, but rather a call to the institutions in question—and the policy it enacts—to proceed in accord with the very sense said to issue in the face. Structurally, responsibility refers to the *presence* of a *measure* by which citizens can recognize its own institutions *failure* to live up to.

11. Honneth, 1995, 313.

12. Honneth, 1995, 313.

13. Marc A. Thiessen, "The Rise of anti-Semitism on the Left," *The Washington Post*, August 13, 2019, https://www.washingtonpost.com/opinions/2019/08/13/rise-anti-semitism-left/.

14. Staff, "Incidents of Anti-Semitism Continue to Mark Occupy Movement," *Anti-Defamation League (Blog)*, April 20, 2012, https://www.adl.org/blog/incidents-of-anti-semitism-continue-to-mark-occupy-movement; Leah McSweeney and Jacob Siegel, "Is the Women's March Melting Down?," *Tablet*, December 10, 2018, https://www.tabletmag.com/jewish-news-and-politics/276694/is-the-womens-march-melting-down; Staff, "Black Lives Matter Has an Israel Problem," *Mosaic*, June 1, 2018, https://mosaicmagazine.com/picks/israel-zionism/2018/06/black-lives-matter-has-an-israel-problem/.

15. See, for example, Jimmy Carter, *Palestine: Peace Not Apartheid* (New York: Simon & Schuster, 2007).

16. Salman Masalha, "The Israelification of Israeli Arabs," *Haaretz*, June 28, 2019, https://www.haaretz.com/opinion/premium-the-israelification-of-israeli-arabs-1.7580002.

17. Ibid.

18. See Yossi Klein Halevi, *Letters to My Palestinian Neighbor* (New York: Harper, 2018).

Bibliography

Abaza, Mona. "Intellectuals, Power, and Islam in Malaysia: S.N. al-Attas or the Beacon on the Crest of a Hill," *Archipel* 58 (1999): 189–217, https://www.persee.fr/doc/arch_0044-8613_1999_num_58_3_3541.

Adorno, Theodor. *Against Epistemology: A Metacritique, Studies in Husserl and the Phenomenological Antinomies*. Translated by Willis Domingo. Cambridge: MIT Press, 1983.

Adorno, Theodor, and Max Horkheimer. *Dialectic of Enlightenment: Philosophical Fragments*. Translated by E. Jephcott. Stanford: Stanford University Press, 2002.

Agassi, Judith Buber. "Buber's Critique of Marx." In *New Perspectives on Martin Buber*, edited by M. Zank, 231–32. Tübingen: Mohr Siebeck, 2006.

Alcoff, Linda Martín. "Dangerous Pleasures: Foucault and the Politics of Pedophilia." In *Re-Reading the Canon: Feminist Interpretations of Michel Foucault*, edited by Susan Hekman, 127–28. University Park, PA: Pennsylvania State University Press, 1996.

Arango, Alejandro. "Husserl's Concept of Position-Taking and Second Nature," *Phenomenology and Mind* 6 (2014): 224–35.

Atterton, Peter. "The Proximity between Levinas and Kant: the Primacy of Pure Practical Reason," *The Eighteenth Century* 40, no. 3 (1999): 244–60.

Bachelard, Suzanne. *Study of Husserl's Formal and Transcendental Logic*. Evanston: Northwestern University Press, 1990.

Bar On, Bat-Ami. *The Subject of Violence: Arendtean Exercises in Understanding*. London: Rowman & Littlefield, 2002.

Bar On, Bat-Ami, and Ann Ferguson, eds. *Daring to Be Good: Essays in Feminist Ethico-Politics*. London: Routledge, 1998.

Barker, Tim. "Spontaneous Order: Looking Back at Neoliberalism." *Dissent* 61, no. 1 (Winter 2014): 91–94.

Baynes, Kenneth. "Discourse Ethics and the Political Conception of Human rights." *Ethics and Global Politics* 2, no. 1 (2009): 18–19.

Beach, Dennis. "History and the Other: Dussel's Challenge to Levinas." *Philosophy and Social Criticism* 30, no. 3 (2004): 315–30.

Beavers, Anthony. *Levinas beyond the Horizons of Cartesianism.* New York: Peter Lang, 1995.
Bell, Nathan. " 'In the Face, a Right Is There': Arendt, Levinas and the Phenomenology of the Rights of Man. *Journal of the British Society for Phenomenology* 49, no. 4 (2018): 291–307.
Benson, Bruce Ellis. *The Improvisation of Musical Dialogue: A Phenomenology of Music.* Cambridge: Cambridge University Press, 2003.
Benhabib, Seyla. "Below the Asphalt Lies the Beach: Reflections on the Legacy of the Frankfurt School." *Boston Review*, http://bostonreview.net/philosophy-religion/seyla-benhabib-below-asphalt-lies-beach.
Berger, Peter L. *The Sacred Canopy: Elements of a Sociological Theory of Religion.* New York: Anchor, 1990.
Bergo, Bettina. *For A Beauty That Adorns the Earth: Levinas between Ethics and Politics.* Dordrecht: Kluwer, 1999.
———. "Emmanuel Levinas." *Stanford Encyclopedia of Philosophy.* August 3, 2011, http://plato.stanford.edu/entries/levinas/.
———. "Is There a 'Correlation' between Rosenzweig and Levinas?" *The Jewish Quarterly Review* 96, no. 3 (Summer 2006): 404–12.
Bernasconi, Robert, et al., eds. *The Cambridge Companion to Levinas.* Cambridge: Cambridge University Press, 2002.
———, et al., eds. *The Provocation of Levinas: Rethinking the Other.* London: Routledge, 1988.
———. "Levinas and the Struggle for Existence." In *Addressing Levinas*, edited by Nelson et al., 170–84. Evanston: Northwestern University Press, 2005.
———. "No Exit: Levinas' Aporetic Account of Transcendence." *Research in Phenomenology* 35 (2005): 101–17.
———. "Re-Reading Totality and Infinity." In *The Question of the Other*, edited by Dallery and Scott, 23–34. Albany: State University of New York Press, 1989.
———. "Skepticism in the Face of Philosophy." In *Re-Reading Levinas*, edited by R. Bernasconi et al., 149–61. Bloomington: Indiana University Press, 1991.
———. "What Is the Question to Which 'Substitution' Is the Answer?" In *The Cambridge Companion to Levinas*, edited by S. Critchley et al., 234–51. Cambridge: Cambridge University Press, 2002.
———. "Who Is My Neighbor? Who Is the Other? Question 'the Generosity of Western Thought.' " In *Beyond Levinas: Critical Assessments of Leading Philosophers, Vol. 4*, edited by Katz and Trout. London: Routledge, 2005.
Bockman, Johanna. *Markets in the Name of Socialism: The Left-Wing Origins of Neoliberalism.* Stanford: Stanford University Press, 2011.
Botwinick, Aryeh. *Emmanuel Levinas and the Limits to Ethics.* London: Routledge, 2016.
Brennan, Daniel. "Vaclav Havel's Levinas: Timely Remarks on Humanism." *Ethics & Bioethics* 6, no. 3–4 (2016): 119–33, doi: 10.1515/ebce-2016-0012.

Bristow, John T. *What Paul Really Said about Women*. New York: HarperOne, 1991.
Brown, Stuart, et al., eds. *Biographical Dictionary of Twentieth-Century Philosophers*. London: Routledge, 1995.
Burggraeve, Roger. *Proximity with the Other. A Multidimensional Ethic of Responsibility in Levinas*. Bangalore, India: Dharmaram Publications, 2009.
———. *The Wisdom of Love in the Service of Love*. Milwaukee: Marquette University Press, 2002.
Butler, Judith. *Giving an Account of Oneself*. New York: Fordham University Press, 2005.
———. *Parting Ways: Jewishness and the Critique of Zionism*. New York: Columbia University Press, 2013.
Canning, Gregory. "The "Madman" and Nietzsche: Searching, Creation, and Finding." *Jahrbuch für Religionsphilosophie* 11 (2012): 72–97.
Card, Claudia. *Unnatural Lottery: Character and Moral Luck*. Philadelphia: Temple University Press, 1996.
Caro, Jason. "Levinas and the Palestinians." *Philosophy and Social Criticism* 35, no. 6 (July 2009): 671–84.
Carter, Jimmy. *Palestine: Peace Not Apartheid*. New York: Simon & Schuster, 2007.
Carter, J. Kameron. *Race: A Theological Account*. Oxford: Oxford University Press, 2008.
Caygill, Howard. *Levinas and the Political*. London: Routledge, 2002.
Chanter, Tina. "Conditions: The Politics of Ontology and the Temporality of the Feminine." In *Addressing Levinas*, edited by E. S. Nelson et al., 296–338. Evanston: Northwestern University Press, 2005.
Chappel, James. *Catholic Modern: The Challenge of Totalitarianism and the Remaking of the Church*. Cambridge: Harvard University Press, 2018.
Chibber, Vivek. *Locked in Place: State-Building and Late Industrialization in India*. Princeton: Princeton University Press, 2006.
———. "Our Road to Power." *Jacobin*, December 5, 2017, https://www.jacobinmag.com/2017/12/our-road-to-power.
———. *Postcolonial Theory and the Specter of Capital*. London: Verso, 2013.
———. "What Is Living and What Is Dead in the Marxist Theory of History." *Historical Materialism* 19, no. 2 (2011): 60–91.
Cobb-Stevens, Richard. "Being and Categorial Intuition." *Review of Metaphysics* 44, no. 1 (1990): 43–66.
Cohen, G. A. *Self-Ownership, Freedom, and Equality*. Cambridge: Cambridge University Press, 1995.
Cohen, Naftali. *The Memory of the Temple and the Making of the Rabbis*. Philadelphia: University of Pennsylvania Press, 2012.
Cohen, Richard A. *Elevations: The Height of the Good in Rosenzweig and Levinas*. Chicago: University of Chicago Press, 1994.
———. *Ethics, Exegesis and Philosophy: Interpretation after Levinas*. Cambridge: Cambridge University Press, 2001.

———, ed. *Face to Face with Levinas*. Albany: State University of New York Press, 1986.

———. *Levinasian Meditations: Ethics, Philosophy and Religion*. Pittsburgh: Duquesne University Press, 2010.

Cohen, Richard A., and James L. Marsh. *Ricoeur as Another: The Ethics of Subjectivity*. Albany: State University of New York Press, 2002.

Coleman, Kari Gwen. "Computing and Moral Responsibility." *Stanford Encyclopedia of Philosophy*, February 16, 2018, https://plato.stanford.edu/entries/computing-responsibility/.

Critchley, Simon, et al., eds. *The Cambridge Companion to Levinas*. Cambridge: Cambridge University Press, 2002.

———. "Emmanuel Levinas, 1906–1995." *Radical Philosophy* 78 (July/August 1996): 53–56.

———. *The Ethics of Deconstruction: Levinas and Derrida*. London: Blackwell, 1992.

———. "Five Problems with Levinas's View of Politics and a Sketch of a Solution to Them." In *Radicalizing Levinas*, edited by Atterton and Calarco, 41–56. Albany: State University of New York Press, 2010.

Crowell, Steven Galt. *Husserl, Heidegger, and the Space of Meaning: Paths Toward Transcendental Phenomenology*. Evanston: Northwestern University Press, 2001.

———. *Normativity and Phenomenology in Husserl and Heidegger*. Cambridge: Cambridge University Press, 2013.

———. "Why Is Ethics First Philosophy?" *European Journal of Philosophy*, doi: 10.1111/j.1468-0378.2012.00550.x (2012).

Croy, Marvin. "Teaching the Practical Relevance of Propositional Logic." *Teaching Philosophy* 33, no. 3 (2010): 253–70.

Dargis, Manohla. "A Godard Odyssey in Dante's Land." *The New York Times*, October 2, 2004, https://www.nytimes.com/2004/10/02/movies/a-godard-odyssey-in-dantes-land.html.

Davis, Colin. *Levinas: An Introduction*. Notre Dame: University of Notre Dame Press, 1990.

De Boer, Theodor. "An Ethical Transcendental Philosophy." In *Face to Face with Levinas*, edited by R. A. Cohen, 83–116. Albany: State University of New York Press, 1988.

———. *The Development of Husserl's Thought*. Translated by T. Plantinga. New York: Springer, 1978.

Denby, Eric. "The First Abolitionist? Gregory of Nyssa on Ancient Roman Slavery." Unpublished Manuscript. May 9, 2011, https://www.academia.edu/1485109/The_First_Abolitionist_Gregory_of_Nyssa_on_Ancient_Roman_Slavery.

DeRoo, Neal. *Futurity in Phenomenology: Promise and Method in Husserl, Levinas and Derrida*. New York: Fordham University Press, 2013.

Derrida, Jacques. *Adieu to Emmanuel Levinas*. Translated by Brault and Naas. Stanford: Stanford University Press, 1999.

———. "At This Very Moment in This Work Here I Am." In *Psyche: Inventions of the Other*. Vol. 1, edited by Kamuf and Rottenberg, 143–90. Stanford: Stanford University Press, 2007.

———. *The Problem of Genesis in Husserl's Philosophy*. Translated by M. Hobson. Chicago: University of Chicago Press, 2003.

———. "Violence and Metaphysics: An Essay on the Thought of Emmanuel Levinas." In *Writing and Difference*, translated by A. Bass, 79–153. Chicago: University of Chicago Press, 1978.

Dhammika, Ven. S., trans. "The Edicts of King Asoka." *The Wheel Publication* 386/387 (1994), https://www.cs.colostate.edu/~malaiya/ashoka.html.

Drabinski, John. "Difference and Sense: The Problem of Relation in the Work of Emmanuel Levinas." PhD diss., University of Memphis, 1996.

———. *Levinas and the Postcolonial: Race, Nation, Other*. Edinburgh: Edinburgh University Press, 2011.

Dondeyne, Albert. "Inleiding tot het denken van E. Levinas (on Totalité et Infini)." *Tijdschrift voor Filosofie* 25/3 (September 1963): 555–84.

Dostal, Robert J. "Gadamer's Relation to Heidegger and Phenomenology." In *The Cambridge Companion to Gadamer*, edited by R. J. Dostal. Cambridge: Cambridge University Press, 2010.

Dudiak, Jeffery. "A Levinasian Reading of Caputo Reading Levinas." In *Knowing Other-wise*, edited by J. Olthius, 172–213. New York: Fordham University Press, 1997.

———. *The Intrigue of Ethics*. New York: Fordham University Press, 2001.

Dupont, Christian Y. "Jean Héring and the Introduction of Husserl's Phenomenology to France." *Studia Pheanomenologica* 15 (2015): 129–53.

Dussel, Enrique. *Ética de la Liberación en la Edad de la Globalización y de la Exclusión*. Madrid: Trotta, 1989.

———. "Sensibility and 'Otherness' in Emmanuel Levinas." *Philosophy Today* 43 (1999): 126–34.

Dworkin, Andrea. *Pornography: Men Possessing Women*. New York: G.P. Putnam's Sons, 1981.

Eagleton, Terry. "In the Gaudy Supermarket." *London Review of Books* 21, no. 10 (May 13, 1999): 3–6, https://www.lrb.co.uk/v21/n10/terry-eagleton/in-the-gaudy-supermarket.

Edgar, Scott. "Hermann Cohen." *Stanford Encyclopedia of Philosophy*, 2015, https://plato.stanford.edu/entries/cohen/#LifWor.

Eisen, Arnold. "The Fence and the Neighbor: Emmanuel Levinas, Yeshayahu Leibowitz, and Israel Among the Nations." *Modern Judaism* 22, no. 3 (2002): 281–84.

Eisenstadt, Oona. "Eurocentrism and Colorblindness." *Levinas Studies* 7 (2012): 43–62.

Eisenstadt, Oona, and Claire Elise Katz. "The Faceless Palestinian: A History of an Error." *Telos* 174 (Spring 2016): 9–32.

Eldridge, Michael. *Transforming Experience: John Dewey's Cultural Instrumentalism*. Nashville: Vanderbilt University Press, 1998.

Etkes, Immanuel. "Eliyahu ben Shelomoh Zalman." *The Yivo Encyclopedia of Jews in Eastern Europe*, https://yivoencyclopedia.org/article.aspx/Eliyahu_ben_Shelomoh_Zalman.

———. *The Gaon of Vilna: The Man and His Image*. Translated by J. M. Green. Berkeley: University of California Press, 2002.

Fagenblat, Michael. *A Covenant of Creatures: Levinas's Philosophy of Judaism*. Stanford: Stanford University Press, 2009.

Finlayson, James Gordon. *Habermas: A Very Short Introduction*. Oxford: Oxford University Press, 2005.

Fishman, Stephen, and Lucille McCarthy. *John Dewey and the Philosophy and Practice of Hope*. Champaign: University of Illinois Press, 2007.

Fournier, Marcel. *Marcel Mauss: A Biography*. Princeton: Princeton University Press, 2015.

Franck, Didier. *L'un-pour-l'autre: Levinas et la singification*. Paris: Presses Universitaires de France, 2008.

Fraser, Nancy. "The Force of Law: Metaphysical or Political?" *Cardozo Law Review* 13, no. 4 (December 1991): 1325–32.

———. "The French Derrideans: Politicizing Deconstruction or Deconstructing the Political?," *New German Critique*, No. 33 (Autumn, 1984): 127–54.

———. *Scales of Justice: Reimagining Political Space in a Globalizing World*. New York: Columbia University Press, 2010.

Friedman, Maurice. "Martin Buber and Emmanuel Levinas: An Ethical Query." In *Buber and Levinas: Dialogue and Difference*, edited by Atterton, Calarco, and Friedman, 116–32. Pittsburgh: Duquesne University Press, 2004.

———. "Martin Buber: The Life of Dialogue," *Religion Online*, https://www.religion-online.org/book-chapter/chapter-26-buber-and-judaism/.

Friedman, Randy. "Alterity and Asymmetry in Levinas's Ethical Phenomenology." *Journal of Scriptural Reasoning* 13, no. 1 (2014), http://jsr.shanti.virginia.edu/vol-13-no-1-june-2014-phenomenology-and-scripture/alterity-and-asymmetry-in-levinass-ethical-phenomenology/.

———. Review of *A Covenant of Creatures*, by M. Fagenblat, *H-Judaic, H-Net Reviews*, January 2013, https://networks.hnet.org/node/28655/reviews/30816/friedman-fagenblat-covenant-creatures-levinass-philosophy-judaism.

Gak, Martin. "Heidegger's Ethics and Levinas's Ontology: Phenomenology of Pre-reflective Normativity." *Levinas Studies* 9 (2014): 145–81.

Gale, Thomas. "Les Colloques des Intellectuels Juifs de Langue Française." *Encyclopedia.com*, https://www.encyclopedia.com/religion/encyclopedias-almanacs-transcripts-and-maps/les-colloques-des-intellectuels-juifs-de-langue-francaise.

Gallagher, Shaun. "In Your Face: Transcendence in Embodied Interaction." *Frontiers in Human Neuroscience* 8 (article 495): 1–6.

Gay, William. "Justification of Legal Authority: Phenomenology vs. Critical Theory." *Journal of Social Philosophy* 11, no. 2 (May 1980): 1–10.
Goldberg, Hillel. "The Early Buber and Jewish Law." *Tradition: A Journal of Orthodox Jewish Thought* 21, no. 1 (Spring 1983): 66–74.
Golshan, Tara. "Did Jill Stein Voters Deliver Donald Trump the Presidency?" *Vox*, November 11, 2016, https://www.vox.com/policy-and-politics/2016/11/11/13576798/jill-stein-third-party-donald-trump-win.
Gotlib, Anna. "Girl, Pixelated—Narrative Identity, Virtual Embodiment, and Second Life." *Humana Mente Journal of Philosophical Studies* 26 (2014): 153–78.
———. ed. *Moral Psychology of Sadness*. London: Rowman & Littlefield, 2017.
Greisch, Jean. "Ethics and Ontology: Some Hypocritical Considerations." *Graduate Faculty Journal* 20/21, no. 1/2 (1998): 41–69.
Grenz, Stanley. "Concerns of a Pietist with a Ph.D." *An Address at the American Academy of Religion*, Toronto, November 23, 2002, www.stanleygrenz.com/articles/pietist.html.
Gruen, Lori, and Alison Wylie. "Feminist Legacies/Feminist Futures: 25th Anniversary Special Issue–Editors' Introduction." *Hypatia* 25, no. 4 (Fall 2010): 725–32.
Guenther, Lisa. *The Gift of the Other: Levinas And the Politics of Reproduction*. Albany: State University of New York Press, 2006.
———. "'Nameless Singularity': Levinas on Individuation and Ethical Singularity." *Epoché* 14, no. 1 (Fall 2009): 167–87.
Gülen, Fethullah. "Turkey's Eroding Democracy." *New York Times*, February 3, 2015, https://www.nytimes.com/2015/02/04/opinion/fethullah-gulen-turkeys-eroding-democracy.html.
Habermas, Jürgen. *The Philosophical Discourse of Modernity: Twelve Lectures*. Translated by F. G. Lawrence. Cambridge: MIT Press, 1990.
Habermas, Jürgen, and Eduardo Mendieta. "A Post-Secular World Society? On the Philosophical Significance of Postsecular Consciousness and the Multicultural World Society," translated by Matthias Fritsch, *The Immanent Frame*, February 3, 2010, https://tif.ssrc.org/2010/02/03/a-postsecular-world-society/.
Hack, Christina. *Groter dan ons hart: De verhouding van God en mens bij Karl Barth en Emmanuel Levinas, met het oog op het nieuwe tijds denken*. Zoetermeer: Universiteit van Amsterdam, 1993.
Halabi, Selman. "A Useful Anachronism: John Locke, the Corpuscular Philosophy, and Inference to the Best Explanation." *Studies in History and Philosophy of Science Part A* 36, no. 2 (2005): 241–59.
Halevi, Yossi Klein. *Letters to My Palestinian Neighbor*. New York: Harper, 2018.
Hand, Sean, ed. *The Levinas Reader*. London: Blackwell, 1989.
Hammerschlag, Sarah. *The Figural Jew: Politics and Identity in Post-War French Thought*. Chicago: University of Chicago Press, 2010.
Hatley, James. "Skeptical Poetics and Discursive Universality: An Etiquette of Legacy in the Time of Shoah" *Levinas Studies* 6 (2011): 89–111.

Havel, Vaclav. *Letters to Olga.* Translated by P. Wilson. New York: Henry Holt and Company, 1989.

Heidegger, Martin. *Being and Time.* Translated by Macquarrie and Robinson. Oxford: Basil Blackwell, 1962.

Heller, Hermann. *Sovereignty A Contribution to the Theory of Public and International Law.* Translated by D. Dyzenhaus. Oxford: Oxford University Press, 2019.

Herman, Judith. *Trauma and Recovery: The Aftermath of Violence—from Domestic Abuse to Political Terror.* New York: Basic Books, 1992.

Herrington, Luke M. "Globalization and Religion in Historical Perspective: A Paradoxical Relationship." *Religions* 4 (2013): 145–65.

Herzog, Annabel. "Benny Levy verses Emmanuel Levinas on 'Being Jewish.'" *Modern Judaism* 26, no. 1 (2006): 15–30.

———. "Levinas and the Unnamed Balaam of Ontology and Idolatry." *The Journal of Jewish Thought and Philosophy* 19, no. 2 (2011): 144.

Hodge, Joanna. "Ethics and Time: Levinas Between Kant and Husserl." *Diacritics*, 32, no. 3–4 (2005): 107–34.

Hollenbach, David. *The Common Good and Christian Ethics.* Cambridge: Cambridge University Press, 2002.

Honneth, Axel. "The Other of Justice: Habermas and the Ethical Challenge of Postmodernism." In *Cambridge Companion to Habermas*, edited by S. K. White, 289–323. Cambridge: Cambridge University Press, 1995.

hooks, bell. *All About Love: New Visions.* New York: William Morrow, 1999.

———. *Salvation: Black People and Love.* New York: Harper, 2001.

Horton, Sarah. "The Joy of Desire: Understanding Levinas's Desire of the Other as Gift." *Continental Philosophy Review* 51 (2018): 193–210.

Husserl, Edmund. *Analysis Concerning Passive and Active Synthesis.* Translated by A. J. Steinbock. Dordrecht: Kluwer, 2001.

———. *Crisis of the European Sciences and Transcendental Phenomenology.* Translated by David Carr. Evanston: Northwestern University Press, 1970.

———. *Logical Investigations.* Translated by M. Farber. London: Routledge, 1973.

Hunt, Lynn. "Pornography and the French Revolution." In *The Invention of Pornography, 1500–1800*, edited by L. Hunt, 301–40. Brooklyn: Zone Books, 1996.

Janicaud, Dominique, ed. *Phenomenology and the "Theological Turn": The French Debate.* New York: Fordham University Press, 2000.

Johnston, Sean D. "Conceptions of the Good and the Ubiquity of Power: John Stuart Mill Responding to John Rawls." *Social Philosophy Today* 26 (2010): 83–90.

Jung, Kevin. *Ethical Theory and Responsibility Ethics: A Metaethical Study of Niebuhr and Levinas.* New York: Peter Lang, 2011.

Kahn, Pinchas. "The Duality of Man: A Study in Talmudic Allegorical Interpretations." *Jewish Bible Quarterly* 36, no. 2 (2008): 102–8.

Kanagaraj, Joseph. *"Mysticism" in the Gospel of John: An Inquiry into the Background of John in Jewish Mysticism.* Doctoral Thesis, Durham University, 1995, http://etheses.dur.ac.uk/1032.

Kaplan, Laura Duhan. "Eros and the Future: Levinas's Philosophy of Family." *Philosophy in the Contemporary World* 6, no. 2 (1999): 9–13.
Katz, Claire Elise, and Oona Eisenstadt. "The Faceless Palestinian: A History of an Error." *Telos* 174 (Spring 2016): 9–32.
———. *Levinas and the Crisis of Humanism*. Bloomington: Indiana University Press, 2013.
———. *Levinas, Judaism, and the Feminine: The Silent Footsteps of Rebecca*. Bloomington: Indiana University Press, 2003.
———. Review of *Discovering Levinas*, by M. Morgan. *Notre Dame Philosophical Reviews*, January 12, 2008, https://ndpr.nd.edu/news/23305-discovering-levinas/.
Kautsky, Karl. "Foundations of Christianity (1908)," *Marxist.org*, https://www.marxists.org/archive/kautsky/1908/christ/index.htm.
Kavka, Martin. "Humanizing Philosophy of Religion: On Language in Levinas and Sellars." *Journal for Culture and Religious Theory* 14, no. 2 (Spring 2015): 225–40.
———. "Is Critique Jewish?" *Jewish Quarterly Review* 108, no. 2 (2018): 253–67.
———. "Is There a Warrant for Levinas's Talmudic Readings?" *Journal of Jewish Thought and Philosophy* 14, no. 1/2 (2006): 153–73.
———. *Jewish Messianism and the History of Philosophy*. Cambridge: Cambridge University Press, 2004.
———. Review of *Addressing Levinas*. Edited by E. S. Nelson, et al. *Notre Dame Philosophical Reviews*, November 14, 2005, https://ndpr.nd.edu/news/24904-addressing-levinas/.
Kearney, Richard. *The God Who May Be: A Hermeneutics of Religion*. Bloomington: Indiana University Press, 2001.
———. "Levinas and the Ethics of Imagining." In *Between Ethics and Aesthetics: Crossing the Boundaries*, edited by Dorota, 85–96. Albany: State University of New York Press, 2002.
Keenan, Dennis. *Death and Responsibility: The "Work" of Levinas*. Albany: State University of New York Press, 1999.
Klein, Naomi. *The Shock Doctrine: The Rise of Disaster Capitalism*. New York: Picador, 2008.
Kleinberg, Ethan. *Generation Existential: Heidegger's Philosophy In France, 1927–1961*. Ithaca: Cornell University Press, 2005.
Korsch, Karl. "The Passing of Marxian Orthodoxy: Bernstein-Kautsky-Luxemburg-Lenin (1937)." *Marxist.org*, https://www.marxists.org/archive/korsch/1937/marxian-orthodoxy.htm.
Kosky, Jeffrey. *Levinas and the Philosophy of Religion*. Bloomington: Indiana University Press, 2001.
Koyles, John Patrick. *The Trace of the Face in the Politics of Jesus: Experimental Comparisons Between the Work of John Howard Yoder and Emmanuel Levinas*. Eugene: Pickwick, 2013.

Kroeger, Catherine. "The Neglected History of Women in the Early Church." *Church History Institute*, https://christianhistoryinstitute.org/magazine/article/women-in-the-early-church/.

Kyle, Jessica. "Protecting the World: Military Humanitarian Intervention and the Ethics of Care." *Hypatia* 28, no. 2 (Spring 2013): 257–73.

Lafont, Christine. "Human Rights and Sovereignty." In *Critical Theory in Critical Times: Transforming the Global Political and Economic Order*, edited by Penelope Deutscher and Cristina Lafont, 47–73. New York: Columbia University Press, 2017.

Lauer, Quentin. "Totalité et infini. Par Emmanuel Lévinas." *Dialogue: Canadian Philosophical Association* 9, no. 1 (1962): 207–10.

Lee, Nam-In. "The Phenomenology of Sensible Life in Husserl and Levinas." *Graduate Faculty Philosophy Journal* 34, no. 2 (2013): 317–37.

Lelyveld, Joseph. *Great Soul: Mahatma Gandhi and His Struggle with India*. Vintage, 2012.

Levinas, Emmanuel. *Beyond the Verse*. Translated by G. Mole. London: Continuum, 1994.

———. *Difficult Freedom*. Translated by S. Hand. Baltimore: Johns Hopkins University Press, 1990.

———. *Ethics and Infinity*. Translated by R. A. Cohen. Pittsburgh: Duquesne University Press, 1985.

———. *Existence and Existents*. Translated by A. Lingis. Dordrecht: Kluwer, 1988.

———. *Humanism of the Other*. Translated by N. Pollar. Chicago: University of Illinois Press, 2006.

———. *In the Time of Nations*. Translated by M. B. Smith. London: Continuum, 2007.

———. *Is It Righteous to Be*. Edited by J. Robbins. Stanford: Stanford University Press, 2001.

———. *Nine Talmudic Readings*. Translated by Annette Aronowicz. Bloomington: Indiana University Press, 1990.

———. *Of God Who Comes to Mind*. Translated by B. Bergo. Stanford: Stanford University Press, 1998.

———. *On Escape*. Translated by B. Bergo. Stanford: Stanford University Press, 2003.

———. *Otherwise than Being or Beyond Essence*. Translated by A. Lingis. Pittsburgh: Duquesne University Press, 1998.

———. "Reflections on the Philosophy of Hitlerism." *Critical Inquiry* 17, no. 1 (Autumn 1990): 62–71.

———. "Revelation in Jewish Tradition." In *The Levinas Reader*, edited by Sean Hand, 195. Oxford: Basil Blackwell, 1989.

———. *Totality and Infinity*. Translated by A. Lingis. Pittsburgh: Duquesne University Press, 1961.

———. *Unforeseen History*. Translated by N. Pollar. Chicago: University of Illinois Press, 2004.
Levy, Benny. *Etre juif: Etude levinassienne*. Paris: Verdier, 2003.
Lindenmeyr, Adele. "The First Soviet Political Trial: Countess Sofia Panina before the Petrograd Revolutionary Tribunal." *The Russian Review* 60 (October 2001): 505–25.
Ma, Lin. "All the Rest Must be Translated: Levinas' Notion of Sense." *Journal of Chinese Philosophy* 35, no. 4 (2008): 599.
Macavoy, Leslie. "Thinking through Singularity and Universality in Levinas." *Philosophy Today* 47, no. 5 (2003): 147–53.
———. "Levinas and the Possibility of History." *Philosophy Today* 49 (2005): 68–73.
Maier-Katkin, Birgit, and Daniel Maier-Katkin. "Hannah Arendt and Martin Heidegger: Calumny and the Politics of Reconciliation." *Human Rights Quarterly* 28, no. 1 (2006): 86–119.
Maimonides, Moses. *The Guide of the Perplexed of Maimonides, Volume 3*. Translated by Michael Friedländer. London: Trubner, 1885.
Malka, Salomon. *Emmanuel Levinas: His Life and Legacy*. Pittsburgh: Duquesne University Press, 2002.
Malpas, Jeff, and Ingo Farin, eds. *Reading Heidegger's Black Notebooks 1931–1941*. Cambridge: MIT Press, 2016.
Marion, Jean-Luc. "The Care of the Other and Substitution." In *The Exorbitant: Emmanuel Levinas Between Jews and Christians*, edited by Hart and Singer, 201–10. New York: Fordham University Press, 2010.
———. "A Note Concerning the Ontological Difference." *Graduate Faculty Journal* 20/21, no. 1/2 (1998): 25–40.
———. "From the Other to the Individual." *Levinas Studies: An Annual Review* 1 (2005): 99–118.
Markus, R. A. *Saeculum: History and Society in the Theology of St Augustine*. Cambridge: Cambridge University Press, 1989.
Marsh, Jack. "Athens *or* Jerusalem? Puntel on Levinas." *Journal for Continental Philosophy of Religion* 2 (2020): 108–16.
———. "'Difficult Questions': Singularity and Particularity in Cohen and Levinas." *Continental Philosophy Review* 45, no. 1 (2012): 143–51.
———. "Lévinas en Amérique du Nord aujourd'hui. Trois vagues et deux écoles." *Cahiers d'etudes Lévinassiennes* 11 (2012): 192–211.
———. "Of Violence: The Force & Significance of Violence in the Early Derrida." *Philosophy and Social Criticism* 35, no. 3 (March 2009): 269–86.
Martley, Raoul. *French Philosophers in Conversation*. London: Routledge, 1991.
Mayama, Alain. *Emmanuel Levinas' Conceptual Affinities with Liberation Theology*. New York: Peter Lang, 2009.

McGettigan, Andrew. "The Philosopher's Fear of Alterity: Levinas, Europe and Humanities 'Without Sacred History.'" *Radical Philosophy* 140 (2006): 15–25.

McGuirk, James N. "Responsibility and Crisis: Levinas and Husserl on What Calls for Thinking." In *Transcendentalism Overturned*, edited by A. Tymienieckan, 193–212. New York: Springer, 2011.

Mendieta, Eduardo. "On Left Kantianism: From Transcendental Critique to the Critical Ontology of the Present." *Foucault Studies* 18 (October 2014): 245–52.

Millerman, Michael. "Alexander Dugin's Heideggerianism." *International Journal of Political Theory* 3, no. 1 (2018), https://www.geopolitica.ru/en/article/alexander-dugins-heideggerianism.

Moran, Dermot. *Introduction to Phenomenology*. London: Routledge, 2000.

Morgan, Michael. *Cambridge Introduction to Emmanuel Levinas*. Cambridge: Cambridge University Press, 2011.

———. *Discovering Levinas*. Cambridge: Cambridge University Press, 2007.

Morrison, Glenn. *A Theology of Alterity: Levinas, von Balthasar, and Trinitarian Praxis*. Pittsburgh: Duquesne University Press, 2013.

Mosse, W. E. "Interlude: The Russian Provisional Government 1917." *Soviet Studies* 15, no. 4 (April 1964): 408–19.

Moyn, Samuel. "Judaism against Paganism. Emmanuel Levinas's Response to Heidegger and Nazism in the 1930s." *History and Memory* 10 (1998): 25–58.

Misiak, Henryk, and Virginia M. Staudt. *Catholics in Psychology: A Historical Survey*. New York: McGraw-Hill, 1954.

Nacol, Angela Rene. *Visions of Disorder: Sex and the French Revolution in a Suit of Erotic Drawings by Claude-Louis Desrais*. Senior Thesis, University of Texas, 2006.

Novick, Peter. *The Holocaust in American Life*. New York: Mariner Books, 1999.

Nussbaum, Martha. *Cultivating Humanity: A Classical Defense of Reform in Liberal Education*. Cambridge: Harvard University Press, 1997.

Okrant, Mark. "Intentionality, Teleology, and Normativity." In *Appropriating Heidegger*, edited by J. Faulconer et al., 191–206. Cambridge: Cambridge University Press, 2000.

Oliver, Kelly. "Fatherhood and the Promise of Ethics." *Diacritics* 27, no. 1 (Spring 1997): 45–57.

Payson, Jessica B. "The Meta-Level of Integrity: Integrity in the Context of Structural Injustice." *Hypatia* 32, no. 2 (2017): 363–79.

Pemberton, Nick. "From MLK To Nathan Phillips: Love Can Defeat Hate." *Counter Punch*, January 25, 2019, https://www.counterpunch.org/2019/01/25/from-mlk-to-nathan-phillips-love-can-defeat-hate/.

Pensky, Max. *The Ends of Solidarity: Discourse Theory in Ethics and Politics*. Albany: State University of New York Press, 2008.

———. "The Limits of Solidarity. Habermas, Levinas, and the Moral Point of View." In *A Matter of Discourse: Community and Communication in Contemporary Philosophies*, edited by A. Nascimento, 129–50. Avebury Press, 1998.

Peperzak, Adriaan. "Emmanuel Levinas." In *Encyclopedia of Phenomenology*, edited by Lester Embree, 412–15. New York: Springer, 1997.

———. "Phenomenology–Ontology–Metaphysics: Levinas' Perspective on Husserl and Heidegger." *Man and World* 16, no. 2 (1983): 113–27.

———. *To The Other. An Introduction to the Philosophy of Emmanuel Levinas*. West Lafayette: Purdue University Press, 1993.

Perpich, Diane. "Figurative Language and the 'Face' in Levinas's Philosophy." *Philosophy and Rhetoric* 38, no. 2 (2005): 103–21.

———. "Sensible Subjects: Levinas and Irigaray on Incarnation and Ethics." In *Addressing Levinas*, edited by E. S. Nelson et al., 296–338. Evanston: Northwestern University Press, 2005.

Price, S. R. F. *Rituals and Power: The Roman Imperial Cult in Asia Minor*. Cambridge: Cambridge University Press, 1984.

Pulleyblank, E. G. "The Origins and Nature of Chattel Slavery in China." *Journal of the Economic and Social History of the Orient* 1, no. 2 (April 1958): 185–220.

Purcell, Michael. *Levinas and Theology*. Cambridge: Cambridge University Press, 2006.

———. *Mystery and Method: The Other in Rahner and Levinas*. Milwaukee: Marquette University Press, 1998.

Putnam, Hilary. "Levinas and Judaism." In *Cambridge Companion to Levinas*, edited by Bernasconi and Critchley, 33–62. Cambridge: Cambridge University Press, 2002.

Rae, Gavin. "The Politics of Justice: Levinas, Violence, and the Ethical–Political Relation." *Contemporary Political Theory* 17, no. 1 (2018): 49–68.

Rancher, Shoni. "Suffering Tragedy: Hegel, Kierkegaard and Butler on the Tragedy of Antigone." *Mosaic* 40, no. 3 (September 2008): 63–79.

Rasmussen, David M., ed. *The Handbook of Critical Theory*. Hoboken: Wiley-Blackwell, 1999.

Rauch, William R. *Politics and Belief in Contemporary France: Emmanuel Mounier and Christian Democracy*. New York: Springer, 1972.

Raymer, Reginald. "Sound of Silence." *International Journal of Applied Ethics* 16, no. 2 (2002): 181–83.

Reichek, Bradley S. *Rake Sentimentalism, or the Libertine Re-Formed: Re-Evaluating Late Eighteenth-Century Libertinage, 1770–1812*. PhD Dissertation, Northwestern University, 2008.

Ricoeur, Paul. *Freud and Philosophy: An Essay on Interpretation*. New Haven: Yale University Press, 1970.

———. "Otherwise: A Reading of Emmanuel Levinas's Otherwise than Being or Beyond Essence." *Yale French Studies* 104 (2004): 82–99.

———. "What Ontology in View?" In *Oneself as Another*, translated by Blarney, 329–56. Chicago: University of Chicago Press, 1992.

Ricupero, Rubens. "Address by Mr. Rubens Ricupero, Secretary-General of UNCTAD." *United Nations Conference on Trade and Development Records*. Bangkok, Thailand, February 12, 2000, https://unctad.org/en/Docs/u9l353.en.pdf.

Rodemeyer, Lanei M. *Intersubjective Temporality: It's About Time*. Dordrecht: Springer, 2006.

Rovný, Jan. "What Happened to Europe's Left?" *London School of Economic Blog*, February 20, 2018, https://blogs.lse.ac.uk/europpblog/2018/02/20/what-happened-to-europes-left/.

Rubenstein, Jason. "The Importance of What We Believe." *Mechon Hadar*, http://www.mechonhadar.org/torah-resource/importance-what-we-believe.

Rule, Regan. *O My Friend, There Is No Friend: A Non-Ideal, Feminist Theory of Aristotelian Friendship and Eudaimonia*. PhD Dissertation, SUNY Binghamton, 2016.

Sallis, John. "Levinas and the Elemental." *Research in Phenomenology* 28 (1998): 152–59.

Sánchez, Alejandro C., and P. Sánchez Azucena. "Jean Wahl: Philosophies of Existence and the Introduction of Kierkegaard in the non-Germanic World." In *Kierkegaard and Existentialism*, edited by Jon Stewart, 393–414. London, Routledge, 2011.

Saracino, Michele. *On Being Human: A Conversation With Lonergan and Levinas*. Milwaukee: Marquette University Press, 2003.

Sealy, Kris. "Levinas and the Critical Philosophy of Race." In *Oxford Handbook of Levinas*, edited by Michael L. Morgan. Oxford: Oxford University Press, 2018, doi: 10.1093/oxfordhb/9780190455934.013.41.

Sessler, Tal. *Levinas and Camus: Humanism for the Twenty-First Century*. London: Continuum, 2008.

Sharma, Arvind. "Ancient Hinduism as a Missionary Religion." *Numen* 39, no. 2 (December 1992): 175–92.

Sharma, Rekha Rani. "Slavery in the Mauryan Period (C. 300 B.C.-C. 200 B.C.)." *Journal of the Economic and Social History of the Orient* 21, no. 2 (May 1978): 185–94.

Shonkoff, Sam Berrin. "Sacramental Existence and Embodied Theology in Buber's Representation of Hasidism." In *Martin Buber: His Intellectual and Scholarly Legacy*, edited by S. B. Shonkoff, 273–302. Boston: Brill, 2018.

Sikka, Sonia. "How Not to Read the Other: All the Rest Can Be Translated." *Philosophy Today* 43, no. 2 (Summer 1999): 195–206.

Simmons, J. Aaron. *God and the Other: Ethics and Politics after the Theological Turn*. Bloomington: Indiana University Press, 2011.

Simmons, J. Aaron, and Kevin Carnahan. "When Liberalism Is Not Enough: Political Theology after Reinhold Niebuhr and Emmanuel Levinas." *Religions* 10, no. 439 (2019), doi: 10.3390/rel10070439.

Simon-Shoshan, Moshe. *Stories of the Law: Narrative Discourse and the Construction of Authority in the Mishnah*. Oxford: Oxford University Press, 2013.

Smith, J. K. A. "A Little Story About Metanarratives: Lyotard, Religion, and Postmodernism Revisited." *Faith and Philosophy* 18 (2001): 261–76.

Smith, Michael B. "Recurrence in Levinas." *Journal of Jewish Thought and Practice* 14, no. 1–2 (2006): 1–15.

Smith, Stephen G. *Argument to the Other: Reason Beyond Reason in the Thought of Karl Barth and Emmanuel Levinas*. Chico: Scholars, 1983.

Sokolowski, Robert. "Husserl's Concept of Categorial Intuition." In *Phenomenology and the Human Sciences*, Supplement to *Philosophical Topics* 12 (1981): 127–41.

Stoltz, Taylor. *Aristocrats, Republicans, and Cannibals: American Reactions to French Women in Violence*. MA Thesis, Virginia Polytechnic Institute and State University, 2015.

Stout, Jeffery. *Ethics After Babel: The Language of Morals and their Discontents*. Princeton: Princeton University Press, 2001.

Strhan, Anna. *Levinas, Subjectivity, Education: Towards an Ethics of Radical Responsibility*. Hoboken: Wiley-Blackwell, 2012.

Stroup, Caleb. "International Deal Experience and Cross-Border Acquisitions." *Economic Inquiry* 55 (2012): 73–97.

Sypnowich, Christine. *The Concept of Socialist Law*. Clarendon, 1990.

Taminiaux, Jacques. *The Metamorphoses of Phenomenological Reduction*. Milwaukee: Marquette University Press, 2004.

———. "The Presence of *Being and Time* in *Totality and Infinity*." *Amsterdam Studies in Jewish Thought* 14 (2009): 3–22.

Tepper, Rowan. "After God: The Revolutionary Absolute." In *The Immanence of Myth*, edited by James Curcio et al. Guildford: Weaponized, 2011.

Tessman, Lisa. *Burdened Virtues: Virtue Ethics for Liberatory for Liberatory Struggles*. Oxford University Press, 2005.

Theodorou, Panos. "Husserl's Original Project for a Normative Phenomenology of Emotions and Values." In *Values: Readings and Sources on a Key Concept of the Globalized World*, edited by I. de Gennaro, 265–90. Leiden: Brill, 2012.

Tismaneanu, Vladimir. "The Revolutions of 1989: Causes, Meanings, Consequences." *Contemporary European History* 18, no. 3 (August 2009): 271–88.

Thomas-Fogiel, Isabelle. "Fichte and Levinas. The Theory of Meaning and the Advent of the Infinite." In *Fichte and the Phenomenological Tradition*, edited by V. Waibel et al., 327–40. Berlin: de Gruyter, 2010.

Tippelskirch, Dorothee. *Liebe von fremd zu fremd . . . Menschlichkeit des Menschen und Göttlichkeit Gottes bei Emmanuel Levinas und Karl Barth*. Freiburg: Alber-Reihe Thesen 22, 2002.

Truth, Sojourner. *Narrative of Sojourner Truth*. Oxford: Oxford University Press, 1991.

Twitchett, Denis, and John K. Fairbanks, eds. *The Cambridge History of China: The Ch'in and Han Empires, 221 B.C.–A.D. 220*. Cambridge: Cambridge University Press, 2008.

Tymieniecka, Anna-Teresa. "Review of Totalité et infini." *Philosophy and Phenomenological Research* 23, no. 2 (December 1962): 298–300.
Vancourt, Raymond. "Emmanuel Levinas. Totalité et Infini." *Critique [Paris]* 194 (1963): 663.
van der Spek, R. J. "Cyrus the Great, Exiles, and Foreign Gods: A Comparison of Assyrian and Persian Policies on Subject Nations." *Studies in Ancient Oriental Civilization* 68 (2014): 233–64.
Visker, Rudy. "Is Ethics Fundamental?" *Continental Philosophy Review* 36, no. 3 (2003): 263–302.
de Vries, Hent. *Minimal Theologies: Critiques of Secular Reason in Adorno and Levinas*. Translated by Geoffrey Hale. Baltimore: The Johns Hopkins University Press, 2005.
Walker, Margaret Urban. *Moral Repair: Reconstructing Moral Relations After Wrongdoing*. Cambridge: Cambridge University Press, 2006.
———. *Moral Understandings: A Feminist Study in Ethics*. Oxford: Oxford University Press, 1998.
West, Cornel. "The Dilemma of the Black Intellectual." *Culture Critique* 1 (1985): 109–24.
Westphal, Merold. *Levinas and Kierkegaard in Dialogue*. Bloomington: Indiana University Press, 2008.
———. "The Many Faces of Levinas as a Reader of Kierkegaard." *Revista Portuguesa de Filosofia* 64 (2008): 1141–62.
White, Rachel. "Recovering the Past, Renewing the Present: The Buber-Scholem Controversy over Hasidism." *Jewish Studies Quarterly* 14, no. 4 (2007): 364–92.
White, Stephen K. "Reason, Modernity, and Democracy." In *Cambridge Companion to Habermas,* edited by S. K. White. Cambridge: Cambridge University Press, 1995.
Wild, John. "Introduction." In *Totality and Infinity*, by Emmanuel Levinas, translated by A. Lingis, 11–20. Pittsburgh: Duquesne University Press, 1961.
Wolfe, Judith. *Heidegger and Theology*. London: Bloomsbury, 2014.
Wolff, Ernst. *Political Responsibility for a Globalized World*. Bielefeld: transcript-Verlag, 2011.
Wolin, Richard. *Heidegger's Children: Hannah Arendt, Karl Löwith, Hans Jonas, and Herbert Marcuse*. Princeton: Princeton University Press, 2015.
Wood, David et al., eds. *The Provocation of Levinas: Rethinking the Other*. London: Routledge, 1988.
———. "Some Questions for My Levinasian Friends." In *Addressing Levinas*, edited by E. S. Nelson et al., 152–69. Evanston: Northwestern University Press, 2005.
Wright, N. T. "Paul and Caesar: A New Reading of Romans." In *A Royal Priesthood: The Use of the Bible Ethically and Politically,* edited by C. Bartholemew, 173–93. Carlisle: Paternoster, 2002, http://ntwrightpage.com/2016/07/12/paul-and-caesar-a-new-reading-of-romans/.

Wygoda, Shmuel. "A Phenomenological Outlook at the Talmud: Levinas as Reader of the Talmud." Georges Hansel's personal website, http://ghansel.free.fr/wygoda.html.

Wyschogrod, Edith. *Emmanuel Levinas: The Problem of Ethical Metaphysics*. New York: Fordham University Press, 2001.

Zank, Michael, and Zachary Braiterman. "Martin Buber." *Stanford Encyclopedia of Philosophy*, December 4, 2014, https://plato.stanford.edu/entries/buber/.

Zhang, Xianglong. "The Philosophical Features of Confucianism in Inter-Cultural Dialogue: Universalism or Non-Universalism?" *Frontiers of Philosophy in China* 4, no. 4 (2009): 483–92.

Name Index

Adorno, Theodor, 99, 199–200, 202, 224, 239, 245, 290, 312, 328
Ahmad, Aijaz, 212
Al-Attas, Syed Muhammad Naquib, 206, 334
Al-Haqqani, Nazim, 206
Al-Hibri, Azizah, 205, 230, 232
Al-Jifri, Ali, 205
Al-Yaqoubi, Muhammad, 205
Alcoff, Linda Martin, 230, 232
Allen, Richard, 189
Angelou, Maya, 180, 285
Anzaldúa, Gloria E., 230
Arendt, Hannah, 152, 154, 161, 173, 182, 224
Aristotle, 26, 39, 57, 83, 85, 93, 254, 295, 309
Arminius, Jacob, 268–269
Aron, Raymond, 153, 325
Ashoka, 257, 259
Atterton, Peter, 1, 70, 175, 302
Augustine, 264–266
Aurelius, Marcus, 257

Ba'al Shem Tov, 234–235
Baker, Ella, 180
Baliber, Étienne, 133
Bar On, Bat-Ami, 230–231
Barth, Karl, 189
Bartky, Sandra, 230

Bataille, Georges, 154, 322
Baudrillard, Jean, 161
de Beauvoir, Simone, 153, 157, 180, 325
Bebel, August, 244
Benhabib, Seyla, 231, 247, 249–251
Benjamin, Jessica, 231
Benjamin, Walter, 239
de Boer, Theodore, 70–71, 303–304, 309
Bergo, Bettina, 133, 159, 167, 301, 308, 324
Bergson, Henri, 152, 171–173, 323
Bernasconi, Robert, 2–3, 6, 60, 69–70, 72, 91, 166–167, 275, 303, 310, 327
Bernstein, Eduard, 239
Berrigan, Daniel, 181
Bhutto, Benazir, 204
Bin Bayyah, Abdallah, 208
Blanchot. Maurice, 152, 155, 160, 164–166
Bloechl, Jeffrey, 167, 326
Blondel, Charles, 152, 323
Bockman, Johanna, 213–214, 216, 218–219, 244–245
Bolsonaro, Jair, 220
Bouckaert, Luc, 160
Bréhier, Émile, 154
Brezhnev, Leonid, 182

Brown, H. Rap, 182
Brown, Wendy, 231
Brunschvicg, Léon, 153
Buber, Martin, 160, 172, 239–243, 245
Burggraeve, Roger, 160, 162–164, 166–167, 326
Bush, George W., 177, 193
Butler, Judith, 134, 145, 230, 289, 321, 336

Calarco, Matthew, 1, 175
Card, Claudia, 231
Carnap, Rudolf, 153
Caro, Jason, 134–136
Carteron, Henri, 152, 323
Cassin, René, 155, 284
Cassirer, Ernst, 153, 243, 245
Castellio, Sebastian, 234
Castro, Fidel, 193
Cavaillès, Jean, 153
Chagall, Marc, 25
Chalier, Catherine, 125, 165, 167, 232
Chanter, Tina, 167, 293
Chaouat, Bruno, 135
Chatterjee, Partha, 215
Chavez, Cesar, 180
Chavez, Hugo, 193
Chibber, Vivek, 212, 214–216, 218–219, 244–245, 336–337
Chizuko, Ueno, 212
Chomsky, Noam, 180
Chouchani, 156–159
Clinton, Hillary, 210–212
Clinton, William J., 184, 187, 193, 195
Cohen, G. A., 183, 218, 245
Cohen, Hermann, 213, 238, 243, 245
Cohen, Richard, 3, 11, 163–165
Corbyn, Jeremy, 281
Crenshaw, Kimberlé, 230–231

Crescas, Hasdai, 233
Critchley, Simon, 2, 154–155, 157–161, 165, 167, 173
Crowell, Steven, 71, 290, 299, 303, 305
Cudd, Ann, 231
Cyprian of Carthage, 253
Cyrus, 258

Daley, Mary, 180
Day, Dorothy, 181
Derrida, Jacques, 4–5, 68, 70, 91, 100, 118, 165, 167–168, 171, 173–174, 194, 213
Descartes, Renee, 27, 159, 176, 313
Dhawan, Nikita, 213
Dolezal, Rachel, 211
Dondeyne, Albert, 160, 166
Dooyeweerd, Herman, 189
Drabinski, John, 2, 71, 167, 304, 306
Dufrenne, Mikel, 161
Dugin Alexander, 209
Dupont, Christian, 154
Dupuy, Bernard, 170–171
Dussel, Enrique, 3, 167, 172, 276

Eagleton, Terry, 212
Earnest, John Timothy, 280–281
Eisenstadt, Oona, 3, 134–135, 290
Erasmus of Rotterdam, 234, 268
Erdoğan, Recep Tayyip, 207, 220
Esack, Farid, 205
Etkes, Immanuel, 235–236, 338

Falwell, Jerry, 189–190
Fanon, Frantz, 154, 179
Ferguson, Ann, 232
Farrakhan, Louis, 281
Fincher, Leta Hong, 233
Fink, Eugene, 152, 160, 326
Fiorenza, Elisabeth Schussler, 233

NAME INDEX 367

Foley, Albert, 181
Foucault, Michel, 163–164, 168
Fraser, Nancy, 183, 213–214, 231–232, 246–247, 327
Friedan, Betty, 180
Frye, Marilyn, 231
Fukiyama, Francis, 177

Gallagher, Sharon, 180
Gadamer, Hans Georg, 88, 94, 152
Gandhi, Mahatma, 110–111, 179, 237
de Gandillac, Maurice, 153
Gaon, Saadi, 233
Gaon, Vilna, 235–237, 329, 338
Gapon, Georg, 226–227
Gentili, Alberico, 268
Gerber, Rudolf, 160
Gibbs, Robert, 167
Gingrich, Newt, 187
Godard, Jean-Luc, 1, 175
Gogol, Nikolai, 152, 224
Goldberg, Hillel, 242
Golshan, Tara, 211
Gore, Al, 177
Gotlib, Anna, 232, 336
Greisch, Jean, 166
Grenz, Stanely, 188
Gross, Rita, 232
Grotius, Hugo, 268–269
Guenther, Lisa, 121
Guevara, Che, 179
Gülen, Fethullah, 207–208

Habermas, Jürgen, 204, 224, 246, 250–252, 290, 329
Haden, Casey, 180
Hafiz, Umar bin, 206
Haider, Asad, 212
Halbwachs, Maurice, 152, 323
Halpérin, Jean, 159
Harding, Sandra, 230

Harvey, David, 213
Havel, Vaclav, 1, 175, 273
Hegel, G. W. F., 18, 26, 44, 145, 154, 164, 171, 243, 290, 311, 324
Heidegger, Martin, 4, 10, 17, 19, 26, 31, 34, 37, 42, 67, 73–74, 77–78, 85, 88–89, 93–94, 100, 103–105, 116–118, 126, 151–154, 157, 161, 165, 168–169, 171, 177, 209, 224, 243, 279, 295, 297, 306, 308–310, 312–313, 315
Heinämaa Sara, 232
Held, Virginia, 231
Heller, Hermann, 244–245
Heraclitus, 14
Héring, Jean, 152–154
Herman, Judith, 231
Herodotus, 259
Hertzog, Annabel, 149
Heschel, Abraham Joshua, 181
Hippolyte, Jean, 154
Hirsch, Emmanuel, 71
Hirsch, Samson Raphael, 238
Hitler, Adolf, 154, 241
Hobbes, Thomas, 133
hooks, bell, 230, 232
Honneth, Axel, 246, 277–278
Horkheimer, Max, 199–200, 204, 224, 245, 250–251, 291, 328
Horton, Sarah, 114
Huerta, Dolores, 180
Husserl, Edmund, 4, 9–10, 17, 26–28, 37, 42, 73–74, 77, 83, 85, 88, 89, 92–94, 100, 104–105, 116–117, 126, 152–154, 157, 160, 165, 168, 177, 224, 238, 243, 275, 279, 295, 305–306, 310–311, 315, 323, 326–327

Idhe, Don, 163
Ingarden, Roman, 152, 160, 165

Iqbal, Muhammad, 205
Irigaray, Luce, 166, 230

Jackson, Jesse, 181, 191
Jaggar, Alison, 229–231
Jankélévitch, Vladimir, 159
James, CLR, 178
Jameson, Fredric, 212
Jay, Martin, 183
Jelloun, Tahar Ben, 205
Jesus Christ, 187, 253–256, 260–262, 264–266, 343
Jinping, Xi, 193, 210
John Paul II, Pope, 1, 165–166, 171, 175
Johnson, Boris, 220, 252

Kabbani, Hisham, 206
Kant, Immanuel, 26, 71, 77–78, 83, 85, 89, 93, 103, 111, 171, 233–234, 238–239, 243, 275, 304–306, 309, 313
Kaplan, Kivi, 181
Kaplan, Laura Duhan, 232
Kathrada, Ahmed, 205
Katz, Claire-Elise, 167, 232, 312
Kautsky, Karl, 244, 253
Kavka, Martin, 69, 71, 157, 302–305
Kearney, Richard, 114, 156, 172–173
Kerensky, Alexander, 227
Khan, Abdul Ghaffar, 179
Khan, Syed Ahmad, 205
King Jr., Martin Luther, 179–180, 181–182
King, Mary, 180
King, Steve, 281
Kipnis, Laura, 210
Klein, Naomi, 193
Kleinberg, Ethan, 153
Kojève, Alexandre, 154, 322, 324, 329
Korsgaard, Christine, 232
Koyré, Alexander, 152, 154

Kripke, Saul, 183
Kropotkin, Peter, 226
Krym, Solomon, 225

Lacan, Jacques, 154
Lafont, Christine, 247
Larocco, Steve, 133, 318–319
Lauer, Quentin, 160
Le Pen, Marine, 209, 220
Lee, Na-Min, 9–10, 160
Lefebvre, Henri, 161
Leib, Aryeh Yehudah, 236
Leibniz, Gottfried Wilhelm, 233
Lenin, Vladimir, 225–226, 228–229, 244
Lessing, Gotthold Ephraim, 233
Lewis, John, 181
Lincoln, Abraham, 204
Lindemann, Hilde, 231
Lingis, Alphonso, 161, 163, 165, 167
Llewelyn, John, 167
Longino, Helen, 230–231
Lorde, Audre, 180
Lowery, Joseph, 181
Löwith, Karl, 152
Lugones, Maria, 231
Luxemburg, Rosa, 244
Lyotard, Jean-François, 161, 165–166, 312
Luzzatto, Samuel David, 238

Ma, Lin, 2
MacAvoy, Leslie, 232
Maimonides, Moses, 99, 233, 310
Malcolm X, 179, 182
Malka, Salomon, 135, 166, 170, 172
Mandela, Nelson, 179, 192
Mang, Wang, 260
Manji, Irshad, 204
Marcel, Gabriel, 154, 159–160
Marcuse, Herbert, 152, 180
Marion, Jean-Luc, 173

Maritain, Jacques, 154, 325
Martov, Julius, 228–229
Marx, Karl, 238–242, 244–245, 290, 295
Mattson, Ingrid, 204, 232
Maurin, Peter, 181
McGettigan, Andrew, 2, 275
Mélenchon, Jean-Luc, 209
Mendelssohn, Moses, 144, 233–234, 236, 238, 245
Meyers, Diane, 230
Mercier, Louis-Sébastien, 198
Merleau-Ponty, Maurice, 153–154, 156, 159, 179, 276
Modi, Narendra, 220
Mohammed, Warith Deen, 205
Mohanty, J. N., 160
Moller Okin, Susan, 230
Morales, Aurora Levins, 230
Morgan, Michael, 69–70
Mouff, Chantel, 231
Mounier, Emmanuel, 154
Muhammad, Clara, 182

Nabuco, Joaquim, 268
Nasr, Seyyed Hossein, 205–206
Neher, André, 159, 171
Nerson, Henri, 156–158
Netanyahu, Benjamin, 137, 220, 281–282, 319–320
Nussbaum, Martha, 148, 230, 276
Noddings, Nel, 230–231
Nyssan, Gregory, 265–266

Obama, Barack, 195, 209–210
Okamura, Tomio, 220
Ophir, Adi, 133, 319
Oshry, Ephraim, 274
Osovsky, Zalman, 275

Paquda, Bahya ibn, 234
Parry, Benita, 213

Patočka, Jan, 160
St. Paul, 187, 202, 254–258, 260–263, 266
Pedersen, Bettina Tate, 233
Pensky, Max, 249–250, 268, 307
Peperzak, Adriaan, 13, 21
Perpich, Diane, 167, 293
Pfeiffer, Gabrielle, 152, 154
Piketty, Thomas, 220
Plato, 26, 171, 176, 187, 255, 313, 322
Plaskow, Judith, 233
Plekhanov, Georgy, 227, 244
Pradines, Maurice, 152, 323
Pushkin, Alaxander, 152, 225
Putin, Vladimir, 55–56, 67, 193, 209–210, 212, 220, 230
Putnam, Hillary, 151, 321

Rachi, 156, 170
Rasmussen, David, 183
Rauschenbusch, Walter, 189
Rawls, John, 183, 216, 219, 232
Reagan, Ronald, 182, 192
Richardson, William, 160
Ricoeur, Paul, 88, 94, 99, 117, 153–154, 159, 161, 163, 165–167, 171, 173, 177, 273, 326, 327
Ricupero, Rubens, 271
Rokeya, Begum, 205, 233
Rolland, Jacques, 166
Romero, Oscar, 180
Roosevelt, Eleanor, 283–284
Rorty, Richard, 184
Rötzer, Florian, 71
Rouhani, Hassan, 220
Rovný, Jan, 221–224
Rosenzweig, Franz, 177, 239–240
Ruether, Rosemary Radford, 233
Rummel, Joseph, 181

Sanders, Bernie, 210, 224

Sartre, Jean-Paul, 153–154, 157, 177, 179, 324–325, 329
Scalise, Steve, 281
Scanzoni, Letha Dawson, 232
Schmidt, Carl, 244, 277
Scholem, Gershom, 170–172, 239–240
Schutz, Alfred, 160
Senghor, Leopold Sedar, 154, 179
Sheehan, Helena, 209
Shestov, Lev, 153–154
Shuttlesworth, Fred, 181
Sider, Ron, 180
Sikka, Sonia, 2–3
Sofia Panina, 225–226
Solzhenitsyn, Aleksander, 182, 224
Spartacus, 254
Spinoza, Baruch, 103, 233–234, 313
Spivak, Gayatri, 212, 215, 336
Stalin, Joseph, 188, 228–229
Stanford, Max, 182
Steinem, Gloria, 180
Sypnowich, Christine, 183, 213–214, 216, 244–245

Taminiaux, Jacques, 160
Taylor, Keeanga-Yamahtta, 212
Tessman, Lisa, 203, 231
Tolstoy, Leo, 152, 224–226, 237
Tong, Rosemarie, 231
Toure, Askia Muhammad, 182
Touraine, Alain, 161
Trebilcot, Joyce, 230
Trible, Phyllis, 232
Tronto, Joan, 231
Trump, Donald, 196, 204, 210, 212, 220, 252, 267
Truth, Sojourner, 189, 267
Tsipras, Alexis, 208–209

Turgenev, Ivan, 152, 224
Tutu, Desmond, 179
Tymieniecka, Anna-Teresa, 160

Van Breda, Herman, 160, 326
Vancourt, Raymond, 160, 326
Vandeputte, Robert, 166

Wadud, Amina, 205, 232
Wahl, Jean, 152, 156, 159, 325
Walker, Alice, 281
Walker, Margaret Urban, 231
Walker, Rebecca, 231
Walker, Wyatt T., 181
Wallis, Jim, 180
Warren, Elizabeth, 224
Wenig, Margaret, 232
Wesley, John, 189
Wessely, Naphtali Hirz, 238
West, Cornel, 211–213
Westphal, Merold, 114, 167
Wiesel, Eli, 157
Wright, N. T., 258, 260
Wygoda, Shmuel, 157–158
Wyschogrod, Edith, 162, 167

Xenophon, 259
Xiaoping, Deng, 182

Yacob, Halimah, 204
Young, Andrew, 181
Young, Iris Marion, 231
Yousafzai, Malala, 204, 232

Zahavi, Dan, 160
Zalman, Schneur, 236–237
Zedong, Mao, 193
Žižek, Slavoj, 212, 331
Zwelithini, Goodwill, 220

www.ingramcontent.com/pod-product-compliance
Ingram Content Group UK Ltd.
Pitfield, Milton Keynes, MK11 3LW, UK
UKHW041915140426
5217IPUK00013B/162